FIFTY YEARS OF HANCOCK'S HALF HOUR

1954 marked the beginning of a radio series that was to change British comedy for ever. Only two years later the first of 63 television scripts had been screened and *Hancock's Half Hour* became the yardstick against which all subsequent British sitcoms have since been measured.

Tony Hancock's genius along with outstanding scripts penned by the writers Galton and Simpson made for a remarkable combination and, more than 30 years after Hancock's death, the shows continue to enjoy enormous widespread appeal.

This book tells the story of how the idea for the show was originally conceived; with behind-the-scenes stories from Hancock's fellow cast and crew members and the reasons behind why the show came to an end in 1961. With a foreword by Ray Galton and Alan Simpson and including previously unheard scripts, along with numerous photographs, *Fifty Years of Hancock's Half Hour* is the definitive companion to Britain's best-loved comedy classic.

PB
7/6

FIFTY YEARS OF HANCOCK'S HALF HOUR

Richard Webber

BBC
LARGE
PRINT

First published 2004
by
Century
This Large Print edition published 2005
by
BBC Audiobooks Ltd
by arrangement with
The Random House Group Limited

ISBN 0 7540 9449 9

British Library Cataloguing in Publication Data available

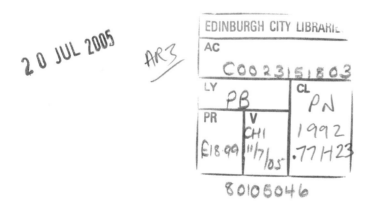
Printed and bound in Great Britain by
Antony Rowe Ltd., Chippenham, Wiltshire

To Gale Pedrick, without whose eye for talent none of this would have happened

Contents

Acknowledgements

So many people have helped in a myriad of ways during the writing of this book. First and foremost, I'd like to thank Ray Galton and Alan Simpson for authorising the project, giving up so much of their time to answer hundreds of questions and for allowing me to reproduce not only script extracts but two complete scripts, both unheard by the public. Tessa Le Bars, their agent, has also been a great help throughout this project.

A special mention must be made of everyone involved with the Tony Hancock Appreciation Society who have been extremely generous with their time, answering questions, providing materials during the research period and helping in a host of other ways. In particular, I'd like to thank Dan Peat, Malcolm Chapman, Jeff Hammonds (I enjoyed our numerous chats on the phone, Jeff), Keith Mason, Mick Dawson and Lesley Hidden. For further information on the Tony Hancock Appreciation Society, write to Dan Peat (enclosing a s.a.e.) at 426 Romford Road, Forest Gate, London E7 8DF.

I'd also like to thank everyone who agreed to interviews, committed their thoughts and memories to paper or provided photos. Sincerest thanks to you all, including Bill Kerr, Moira Lister, Andrée Melly, Freddie Hancock, Harold Snoad, Peter Goodwright, Anne Marryott, Graham Stark, Alec Bregonzi, June Whitfield, Hugh Lloyd, Dennis Chinnery, Warren Mitchell, William G. Stewart,

Valerie James, Terence Alexander, Stewart Marshall, Beryl Vertue, Gerry Mill, John Eden-Eadon, Norman Taylor, Angela Morley, Nancy Boyle and Barbara Evans.

Other people I'd like to thank include Roger Hancock, my agent Jeffrey Simmons, Lindsay Davies, everyone at Random House (especially Hannah Black), Paul James, Gill Kenyon, Carolyn Bartholomew, Simon Hall, the staff at the BBC's Written Archive Centre, the BFI, Don Smith, who took the majority of the photos used in this book, Ian Abraham for lending material and conducting some research and, once again, Hilary Johnson.

Richard Webber
Minehead, 2004

Foreword

There are many advantages to writing a foreword to a book about your own work. First of all, it's much easier than writing the work itself, and, secondly, one can write about how brilliant it all is without being accused of rampant arrogance and delusions of grandeur and the risk of finishing up with ego all over your face.

This is a remarkable *tour de force* by Richard Webber, particularly in his unearthing of a veritable cornucopia of memoranda, facts, trivia and astounding historical treasures while sifting through the BBC archives at Caversham which must rate alongside the achievements of Howard Carter in the Valley of the Kings at Thebes when he smashed through the breeze-blocks of the burial chamber and discovered the tomb of Two-Tun-Khamun and his wife Tessie. Dear, oh dear, we're still coming out with them.

Some of this historical data goes back fifty years and for the most part will be a revelation for you as it was to us—and we were there! For instance, the disappearance of Tony Hancock and his replacement by Harry Secombe at the beginning of the second series. Hancock's whereabouts on the Continent was a complete mystery to us, as we thought it was to the BBC. But no, they knew exactly where he was and what had happened but didn't deign to tell us. Mind you, we were only eleven at the time and you know what kids are, it would have been the talk of the playground by milk break.

We cannot recommend this book highly enough, and not just because of the royalties. It is a fascinating study of the evolution of a comedy series and should take pride of place in your library. If you haven't got a library, put it on your bookshelf. And if you haven't got a bookshelf, leave it nonchalantly on your coffee table and let the world see you're a person of exquisite taste and refinement. If you haven't got a coffee table, where do you put your feet when the missus is doing the hoovering? Blimey, even the Steptoes had a coffee table.

Finally, if you are reading this in the confines of your home we assume you've already bought a copy, but if you are reading it in a bookshop, hesitate no more. Close the book quietly, and clasping it in your right hand stuff it deep into your overcoat pocket and walk purposefully out of the . . . no, no, no, rather, walk up to the cash desk and say, hopefully, 'How much discount on six copies?'

Ray Galton and Alan Simpson
April 2004

Introduction

It's a memorable scene: a doctor's surgery in the South London General Hospital, full of commendable citizens waiting to donate blood. In walks a naïve individual, hat and raincoat having seen better days, prepared to do his bit for the community. A bespectacled doctor, sitting behind a wooden desk, stethoscope hanging round his neck, pierces the man's finger, thus collecting a sample of his blood. Job done, or so the donor thinks: a huge sense of relief rushes through his veins like a tidal wave as he stands up, bids the doctor farewell and heads for his tea and biscuits.

The doctor, though, has bad news for the donor: that was just a smear and he wants some more. Stunned, the donor enquires further:

DONOR: A sample, how much do you want then?
DOCTOR: Well, a pint of course.
DONOR: A pint! Have you gone raving mad? You must be joking.
DOCTOR: A pint is a perfectly normal quantity to take.
DONOR: You don't seriously expect me to believe that. I mean, I came in here in all good faith to help my country; I don't mind giving a reasonable amount, but a pint, that's very nearly an armful!

The donor, of course, was none other than Anthony Aloysius St John Hancock, a comic creation from the pens of British scriptwriters Ray

1

Galton and Alan Simpson, and the prodigious acting talent of Tony Hancock, who in that single line, 'A pint, that's very nearly an armful!', summed up the character from East Cheam beautifully: a green, ineffectual, doleful individual relentlessly battered and bruised by the trials of life, he cuts a forlorn figure in a world passing him by.

Ask anyone to recall a memorable scene from Galton and Simpson's sitcom, a show that was in the vanguard of a new style of comedy in the UK, and you can bet your bottom dollar that most will pick this moment from the penultimate episode, 'The Blood Donor'. There are countless risible moments in the programme but this particular scene certainly induced more than its fair share of laughs over the years, and will undoubtedly continue to do so, so it's a mark of the programme's quality that, for many, it doesn't even represent the best piece of work from the vast array of scripts penned during the show's lifetime. Although such judgements are always subjective, it's pretty clear that Hancock, understandably, wasn't at his best. A recent car accident, which left him badly shaken and carrying two black eyes, meant he had insufficient time to learn his lines, forcing the producer, Duncan Wood, to utilise Teleprompters to help him through the recording. At the time of transmission, viewers were oblivious to Hancock's discomfort, and it's only since these facts have been made public that people have scrutinised the episode and begun to notice that Hancock's stare veers away from the eyeline of the character with whom he's conversing in order to read his lines on the Autocue, which was conveniently sited just below the cameras.

Hancock's Half Hour serves, even after all these years, as a paradigm of classic comedy. If we could dissect this venerated sitcom and peer inside to discover what makes it tick, what would we find? Comedy gleaned from the situation, for starters, which adds a degree of realism and means the show relies less on gags and quips for laughs. When Galton and Simpson settled down to create this comedy vehicle for Tony Hancock, they were keen to write a show which broke the mould of how comedy shows were structured; banishing the old format, whereby a series of sketches was interspersed with musical interludes, they wanted to concentrate on a running storyline rooted in realism. Although it took a while for them to sever their ties with funny voices and fantastical ideas, they eventually achieved their goal with great success.

Unlike Galton and Simpson's other big hit, *Steptoe and Son*, *Hancock's Half Hour* couldn't be regarded as a social document exploiting and exploring the conditions of society through dialogue. The humour was obtained, especially in the early days, from the central character getting caught up in some madcap scheme, usually the brainchild of the incorrigible Sid James. In 'The Insurance Policy', for example, which was broadcast on radio in 1958, Hancock is duped into taking out an insurance policy which is so expensive that he ends up working all hours just to pay the premiums. Most of the fantastic plots were, however, found in the radio episodes, and when the series transferred to the small screen, in 1956, the scripts became increasingly steeped in realism.

Once *Hancock's Half Hour* had ensconced itself

in the public's psyche it wasn't prepared to give up its lofty position as a leading light in the genre of British comedy. What helped the show become such a firm favourite was the viewing public's familiarity with and understanding of the central character, an angst-ridden individual who feels he's carrying the world's entire problems on his shoulders. At times, you could wring Hancock's neck for being so inane, getting coerced into yet another of Sid's silly schemes; occasionally you can empathise with the man: like the time he returns home from an extended holiday to find Sid has left every electrical appliance invented plugged in, gobbling electricity, a doorstep full of milk bottles and a mountain of newspapers, resulting in a hefty bill which Hancock can't afford to pay; he's left with no alternative but to go on an economy drive. Other times, you can feel anger towards him for showing pomposity or his selfish streak. Being able to arouse such emotions in millions of people says everything for the quality of characterisation. As producer Dennis Main Wilson once commented, 'The character encompassed all known vices to man: he was a coward, he was an arrogant snob, pretentious, he was against authority, delusions of grandeur, pompous, conceited, insecure.'[1] Actor Bill Kerr added: 'Tony was part of us all. He was part of every man and every woman watching. He was the personification of the human condition in comedy. You only had to listen to Tony Hancock for about five minutes and you knew he was talking about you.'[2]

Quality scripts and a fine cast are interdependent, of course. The finest dialogue in the world won't work if uttered by a miscast actor, but under the experienced leadership of Dennis Main Wilson, for radio, and Duncan Wood, for television, actors of a high calibre were always recruited to support the eponymous character, even down to the level of walk-ons occupying background scenes, as in the library during 'The Missing Page' or the launderette in 'The Big Night'.

Tony Hancock was an enigma, a complex character, but someone whose adroitness in comedy technique and timing made him, given the right material, a sure-fire winner in the genre of situation comedy. But while the majority of the British public were in no doubt about his talents, the man himself was full of indecision and uncertainty. Throughout the period he worked for the BBC on *Hancock's Half Hour*, he remained wary and noncommittal regarding pledging his future to further radio or television shows, always striving to achieve his ultimate goal: to become an international star in the film world. Despite helping to pioneer a new dawn in comedic values, sadly, the man never fully realised just how deep-rooted his talents were. But while Hancock was the undisputed star of the show, one can't forget the contributions made by Sid James, Bill Kerr, Hattie Jacques, Kenneth Williams, Moira Lister, Andrée Melly and all the other artists hired for single performances or those whose faces became familiar as they earned one of the coveted places in what became known affectionately as Duncan Wood's Repertory Company. Without them, the show couldn't have succeeded.

Nowadays, writers of situation comedy are frequently strafed by critics, while audiences express their feelings by swiftly flicking the off switch on the remote control. The genre is notoriously tough to master and few shows go on to be regarded as classic examples of their genre; such golden nuggets of televisual history can almost be counted on one hand, but when we analyse such programmes, from *Dad's Army* and *Steptoe* to *Fawlty Towers* and *Porridge*, we find that the components forming their structure are identical: quality scripts, top-notch personnel (in front and behind the camera) and a focused leader at the helm. *Hancock's Half Hour* was the forerunner, the doyen of sitcoms, against which subsequent productions have always been measured. The inanities of less durable sitcoms are accentuated by comparison with such a gem. With its half hour plotline and injection of realism, the arrival of the show was a day of portent for the genre of situation comedy.

Hancock's Half Hour—which was retitled *Hancock* for the final series—ran from 1954 to 1961: beginning life on radio in 1954, it extended to six series by the time it came off air in 1959; at that point, it was already established on the small screen thanks to the first of seven series being screened in 1956. During its seven-year life, 103 radio episodes (107 if you include the four specially re-recorded for sales overseas) and 63 television shows were broadcast—83 hours of comedy. Regrettably, many of the instalments no longer exist in the BBC archives, wiped like so many other gems from the world of television and radio, all part of the Beeb's recycling policy of yesteryear. Those that do exist are occasionally dusted off and given an airing, helping to preserve the memory of *Hancock's Half*

Hour and affording younger generations the chance to enjoy this fine example of British comedy. This book's publication coincides with the 50th anniversary of the first episode, 'The First Night Party', which was aired on the BBC's Light Programme, in 1954.

One thing needs clarifying from the beginning: this is not another Tony Hancock biography. The tragic life story of one of the nation's finest comedy actors has already been meticulously detailed by other authors, and I have no intention of adding to that volume of work. Although elements of his life are inevitably entwined in every instalment of Galton and Simpson's situation comedy, I have steered clear of this wherever possible because this book is a biography of a radio and television series, a celebration of a show which, even now, fifty years later, provides pleasure to the millions who continue to listen to or watch *Hancock's Half Hour*. Such is the show's popularity, it seems that fans' thirst for anything associated with the programme will never be assuaged. For them, and for new generations being introduced to the man in the homburg hat, their idea of nirvana is settling down to wallow in the delights of Galton and Simpson's finely tuned scripts brought to life by Tony Hancock, Sid James, Hattie Jacques, Bill Kerr et al.

Chapter 1

Writing partnerships are born in a whole manner of ways: Dick Clement and Ian La Frenais, whose small-screen output includes *The Likely Lads* and *Porridge*, met at the Uxbridge Arms, a pub in London's Notting Hill, back in 1961, three years before 'Entente Cordiale', the first instalment in the life of Terry Collier and Bob Ferris, hit our screens. Bob Larbey and John Esmonde, responsible for, among others, *The Good Life* and *Ever Decreasing Circles*, became friends while on a school trip in Switzerland. Although Bob was three years ahead of John at Clapham's Henry Thornton Grammar School, they discovered they were 'both loonies . . . who had lots in common, including a crass schoolboy humour.'[1] Other friendships evolve from working together. A year after Jimmy Perry was cast in a cameo role for a 1966 episode of *Hugh and I*, a sitcom directed by David Croft, he was offered the chance to play Reg Varney's uncouth brother in *Beggar My Neighbour*; while taking a break during rehearsals, Perry approached Croft with a script he'd written titled 'The Fighting Tigers' and asked him if he'd read it. Within months *Dad's Army* was born.

None, however, can match the unusual circumstances in which Ray Galton and Alan Simpson's partnership came into being during the late 1940s: both were patients at Milford Sanatorium, a TB hospital, set amid the Surrey countryside.

When a 16-year-old Ray Galton was admitted to Milford in January 1947, his chance of survival was so low that at one point he was given no more than two weeks to live. He was working in the head office of the Transport and General Workers' Union, in London's Smith Square, when he was rushed to the sanatorium. 'I had all the symptoms of TB without actually haemorrhaging or coughing up blood, including tiredness, a bad cough and loss of weight—I was only nine stone,' recalls Ray. 'My older brother, who was in the Merchant Navy, came home on leave, took one look at me and said: "You have got to go for an X-ray as soon as possible." ' Ray followed his brother's advice and, to his horror, learnt he was suffering from advanced tuberculosis of the lungs. There was a two-year waiting list for beds in sanatoriums in those days, but Ray was admitted within ten days.

Fortunately, he was strong enough eventually to beat the infectious disease but spent his first year resting, unable to get out of bed. Aged 20 when he walked out of the doors at Milford for the final time, he'd endured three and a half years at the hospital—it had felt like a life sentence. 'Funnily enough, I did have some good times but it was horrible in other ways. Sometimes I got very depressed and would turn my face to the wall, not wanting to speak to anyone. I even thought there was a conspiracy among the doctors to keep me in there; it might sound silly, but that is what you start to believe.'

Ray had been at Milford just over a year when an 18-year-old Alan Simpson arrived after enduring thirteen months at a holding base while he waited for a bed at the sanatorium. He'd been working as a shipping clerk in the centre of London when one fine morning in 1947, while travelling to the office by bus, he cleared his throat and discovered blood in his mouth. Upon reporting for work, he was rushed to St George's Hospital, near London Bridge, for examination. An X-ray revealed tuberculosis. 'I was given strict instructions: go home, don't run, don't make any sudden movements and go straight to bed. They gave me a letter and told me to make sure my mother took it to our doctor, which she did. The doctor came round and that night I suffered a full-blown haemorrhage in bed. I was put on the list to get into a local staging place prior to entering a sanatorium. Everywhere was full up, though, and I ended up lying at home for thirteen weeks.' It had been a tragic week for the Simpson household. Alan was taken ill on the Wednesday, and his father, stricken with leukaemia, died the following day. 'In one swoop, my mother lost her husband, and her son was given the last rites.'

When at last he was transferred to Milford Sanatorium, Alan spent a further two years there. Reflecting on his time in hospital, he describes it as like 'being in a very amenable prison'. 'You were confined, for your own benefit, to bed. Initially this meant absolute bed rest, you weren't allowed out. Then you were able to get out two times a day to use the toilet, then three times, and gradually you spent more and more time up and about, including a walk around the sanatorium. It was very institutionalised, but you got used to it. When you came out, it seemed a very strange world. Once I was given a weekend away from Milford and couldn't wait to get back in; everything seemed so claustrophobic: I felt like I was crushed at home, where the rooms seemed so small compared to the sanatorium.'

TB was a rampant disease during this period; a four-year stay at sanatoriums wasn't unusual and the mortality rate was high. Almost everybody would have known someone who had been whisked away from home to a sanatorium, often miles from their family.

Now, nearly sixty years later, Ray still remembers clearly the day Alan arrived. 'Up until that time, the place was full of mainly ex-servicemen. I was the youngest in the place, so when Alan arrived, together with a load of other young guys, the atmosphere changed immediately. It was good for me because, at last, there were people of my own age to speak to.'

Only a matter of months separated the births of Ray Galton and Alan Simpson. Ray was born in Paddington in July 1930, and his family moved to Morden, Surrey, when he was just six months old. His father was a regular in the navy for most of his working life, serving in both world wars. He returned to civvy street for a short period during the 1930s and worked as a bus conductor but remained a naval reserve; he was called up again when the fleet was mobilised during the Munich Crisis of 1938. He remained in the forces until 1946, by which time he'd split from his wife. Ray says: 'It was a traumatic time for me. I was kept in the dark about their separation for some time—I used to wonder where he was. In those days, it was such a disgrace to even contemplate divorce or splitting up. I used to pray every night that the war wouldn't end so that the kids wouldn't ask me where my father was. It had a terrible effect on me.'

After leaving school at the age of 14, Ray started work as a plasterer's apprentice in a building firm. When the work became tedious, he turned his attention to labouring and was hired to repair bomb-damaged sites in Wimbledon. Before long, he was working behind a desk at the Transport and General Workers' Union in London, where he stayed until finding himself bed-bound at Milford.

Alan was born in November 1929, in Brixton, the son of a draughtsman. His father worked at Vickers just after the war, before becoming a milkman with United Dairies.

When Alan was four, the family moved to the 'posher suburb' of Streatham. 'My parents bought a house for £425 and had to save two years just to put down a deposit of £25!' recalls Alan. 'I lived most of my life in Streatham until I married.' Reflecting on his childhood days, he regards them as 'very happy'. 'I don't have many memories of Brixton, except the day my father looked after me one evening, as well as the boy next door. We were playing table tennis in the basement and this other kid started crying his eyes out—he must have been missing his mother or something. My father, normally a very patient man, was getting more and more frustrated, and I remember me, at the age of three, being a very smarmy boy, a right little crawler, saying things like: "Look at me, Daddy, I'm not crying." Being an only child meant I was very spoilt.'

Soon after the outbreak of war, Alan, who was attending Mitcham County Grammar School, was evacuated with the rest of the school to Weston-

13

super-Mare for ten months: he hated every minute of the experience, feeling a deep sense of loneliness. During his first night in the Somerset seaside town, the docks at Cardiff, just across the Bristol Channel, took a pounding from German bombers. 'On their way home, the bombers jettisoned some bombs over Weston—it was a frightening time. Of course, I'd been evacuated to, supposedly, keep me away from such dangers.'

When his father was called up in 1940, Alan's mother allowed him to return home. 'I used to write such pathetic letters,' he recalls, smiling. 'When she died a few years ago, I found she'd kept all these letters I'd written as a ten-year-old, saying things like: "Mummy, I love you, please bring me home. I'll do everything you want, including going shopping with you without complaining . . ."'

Before the cessation of hostilities, Alan's father was invalided out of the army after contracting Hodgkin's disease. Within months he was dead, aged just 43. 'He was such a gentle man. One of my great regrets is that he never lived to see my success. I owe him so much, including introducing me to show business because every Monday evening he'd take me to the pictures.'

Alan completed his education in disappointing circumstances. 'I was brilliant as a kid up until the age of 11—I was top of the class; it was downhill from then onwards, though. By the time I reached 16, I was quite thick, educationally. I took my matriculation but failed, ending up with a dodgy School Certificate. A meeting was set with the headmaster, who asked what I wanted to do with my life; when I told him I hoped to be a sports journalist he laughed his head off.' There was an ulterior motive behind Alan's desire to follow a journalistic path: being a keen sportsman himself, he thought the job would provide him with complimentary tickets to various sporting events.

In the end, Alan's first job was at a firm of shipping agents in Leadenhall Street, London. He remembers his interview well. 'I was considered for a position in the postal department by this very old man, one of the original partners, who must have been in his eighties. He said: "We can start you off at £81 a year, with annual increments of· five shillings." All I could think of was £81—I'd never heard of so much money in one go. It wasn't until I got on the bus home that I started realising that, of course, you had to divide it by 52, which worked out at something like one pound, ten shillings a week; after I'd deducted my lunch and fares into town each day, plus my board and keep, there wouldn't be much left.'

But the onset of the disease brought his life to a standstill as he spent what seemed like an eternity trapped inside hospital, trying to recuperate from this deadly illness.

Before long, Alan and Ray were moved into the same ward and it soon became apparent that they had much in common. 'When we got talking we found we had identical likes in terms of entertainment,' explains Alan. 'We were both comedy fans. We were also film fans and had the same taste in music—in fact, it's amazing how close our thoughts are regarding politics, culture, wine, food. More importantly, though, our sense of humour was almost identical, which meant that as soon as we started working together we became almost telepathic. We could finish off each other's

15

sentences.'

The seeds of their working partnership were sown at Milford. The hospital possessed its own radio system, installed by the Friends of the Sanatorium, a charitable organisation who tried its utmost to make the patients' lives just a little more bearable. Eventually additional money was provided for a dedicated internal network system, and Ray played a part in the creation of Radio Milford. 'These two guys—Tony Wallis and another patient called Saunders—installed the radio line throughout the entire sanatorium,' he recalls, 'and although I wasn't allowed out of bed, I spent ages drilling wooden blocks for the wall in which the sockets were inserted.

'Between them, they not only developed the idea but also equipped the sanatorium with this additional network. In their pyjamas and dressing gowns they ran around the entire place, including the administration and the girls' block, fixing up the new channel.

'The sanatorium blocks were all one storey, divided into two- and four-bedders,' recalls Ray. 'At the time I shared a room with Tony Wallis. He was a mad engineering geek whose father owned an engineering firm. The walls and the floor were covered with engineering and radio equipment—there was hardly enough room for me and my bed to be in there.

'He had a lovely RAF radio called a 1155 which had come out of a Lancaster, I think. This radio allowed us to listen to American Forces Network AFM Munich-Stuttgart at night-time, and also in the afternoon if the reception was good. If he approved of some of the people in other cubicles he'd run the wire to them and let them listen to it as well, and we'd be up half the night.'

Initially, Radio Milford broadcast for an hour a day, playing record requests from a converted linen cupboard acting as a studio. Lots of romances blossomed at the hospital, with patients meeting each other at film shows or card evenings in the utility hall, and records would be requested for partners. As the station's popularity grew, a radio committee was established to evaluate new programme ideas; it wasn't long before Ray and Alan were identified as fervent supporters of the station and invited to join the committee. 'The station had become more ambitious; we'd extended the broadcasting hours to two a day, and started introducing new aspects rather than just playing records,' explains Alan. 'We tried our own version of BBC panel games, like *Twenty Questions*, and a show called *A Seat in the Circle*, where once a week, the presenter would go to a cinema and record a half hour programme; if you were listening at home it was like being at the pictures. We thought that was a good idea, so at our film show every Wednesday evening we made our own version of *A Seat in the Circle*.'

'Alan and I happened to mention one day that we weren't doing any drama or comedy shows, so *they* [members of the radio committee] asked us to come up with an idea,' adds Ray. 'We decided on a comedy series titled *Have You Ever Wondered?* and agreed to write six 15-minute instalments—trouble was, we ran out of ideas after four! But that was the start of our partnership. The show contained extended sketches, and in 1949 we received our first fan letter, which was published in the *Milford*

17

Bulletin, the hospital newspaper.'

Galton and Simpson enjoyed the process of writing comedy sketches so much that they realised they wanted to pursue the art further. Although still far from being fully fit, their stay at Milford was coming to an end and they would soon be returning to civvy street. Neither had any idea how to nurture their interest into, perhaps, a future career, so sought advice from two of their heroes, Frank Muir and Denis Norden. Muir began writing for the Forces radio while serving with the Royal Air Force in Iceland during the Second World War. After demob he acquired an agent and subsequently met Norden. They had just begun writing their hit show, *Take It From Here*, when a letter from Galton and Simpson dropped through their office letterbox, asking how they could become scriptwriters. The would-be writers offered their services as tea boys in their office, hoping to observe how Muir and Norden went about their job. Keen to advise, Muir and Norden replied, suggesting they send a sample of their work to Gale Pedrick, who was employed as script editor at the BBC. It was another year before Alan and Ray had scripted a piece of work they regarded fit for scrutiny by the Beeb. In the meantime, they continued on their recovery programme and looked forward to the day when they could wave farewell to the many friends they had made during their enforced stay at Milford.

Alan left hospital six months before Ray, reasonably fit and able to resume work, albeit part-time, at the London shipping office. Ray wasn't so fortunate: he wasn't allowed to work, was ordered not to smoke or undertake anything strenuous, and had to ensure he had early nights.

He didn't take too kindly to the doctor's suggestion that he adopt a more sedentary lifestyle and spent the first night of freedom tapping away to the music at Ronnie Scott's Jazz Club in London.

From the age of 14, Alan Simpson had been a member of his local church concert party, occasionally contributing to their performances with a stand-up routine or a mime act based on the antics of comedian Red Skelton. As soon as news of Simpson's release from Milford reached members of the concert party, they got in touch asking if he'd return to the fold. He declined the chance to perform with the group, but agreed, instead, to think up ideas for sketches. Alan immediately made contact with Ray and they resumed their budding partnership. Their writing sessions were limited mainly to evenings and weekends, when Alan wasn't trying to earn a living as a shipping clerk, and took place at Alan's mother's house at 6 Church Walk, Streatham Vale, London. One evening they were intending to generate a few ideas for the concert party but before long had devised their own version of the popular soap opera, *Mrs Dale's Diary*, titled 'Mrs Low Place Between Two Hills Diary'; when it was eventually performed on stage, the show received a healthy reaction from the audiences who had crammed into the tiny church hall to watch the local production.

Suitably enthused by this, Ray and Alan settled down for some serious discussion about where their future lay. Although becoming professional scriptwriters was a mere dream, they remembered the advice of Muir and Norden, a year before, and decided it was time they prepared some material

19

for Gale Pedrick at the BBC. 'We didn't know if we had the ability or not, but knew there was only one way to find out,' explains Alan. 'We'd started writing together again and knew it was time to take the plunge.' Shutting themselves away each evening in Mrs Simpson's front room, they scribbled ideas on sheets of paper until they had formulated a synopsis strong enough, in their view, to warrant a stab at a full-blown script.

Ray says: 'By this time, Muir and Norden's *Take It From Here* was a big show. It contained three main sketches; one of these was often an eight- or nine-minute pastiche, taking the mickey out of a current film or something, so we wrote a piece about Captain Henry Morgan, the pirate, sent it in and crossed our fingers.'

Pedrick was so impressed with the sketch, and the quality of Galton and Simpson's writing that he invited them to the BBC for an informal interview. When the invitation arrived at Alan's house, he was ecstatic. 'I remember running down the street to Ray's house, waving the letter above my head—we were over the moon with excitement. On the strength of the letter, we went out and celebrated with friends by getting drunk. We must have taken the view that even if nothing happened, we had a letter from the BBC stating they were "highly amused" with a sketch we'd actually written. We couldn't believe it.'

In the subsequent meeting, script editor Gale Pedrick agreed to gauge the reaction of various producers in Light Entertainment. One copy landed on Roy Speer's desk. At the time, Speer was producing *Happy-Go-Lucky*, a comedy vehicle for Derek Roy, which was rapidly running out of steam. In his accompanying memo, Pedrick said: '... if you are really up against it for some material, you might do worse than give a chance to Alan Simpson and Ray Galton. They are new to the game but I know they would be anxious to have a shot at anything on spec—and no harm done to anybody if nothing came of it.' In Pedrick's opinion, for inexperienced writers, their script showed promise: 'they seem to me to have a good wit and a really good grasp of situation,' he added. 'But everybody has their own opinion and if you think their material stinks, don't feel that there is the slightest obligation to do anything but say so!'[2]

It wasn't Speer who responded to the memo, but Derek Roy himself. While he was in the producer's office one morning, he picked up the script and started reading. He liked what he saw and asked who had penned the material. Upon hearing it was two young writers trying to break into the business, Roy arranged for Galton and Simpson to contact him direct. Alan called Derek Roy's home and a meeting was convened for 8.30 that evening at Roy's house in Bryanston Street, just behind Marble Arch. It was a meeting that would launch their careers as professional writers.

The rain had begun to fall as Galton and Simpson turned into Bryanston Street. After welcoming the writers, Ray's secretary Johnny Vyvyan ushered them through the opulent flat to Roy's study, where they awaited his presence. 'I remember the meeting so clearly,' explains Alan, 'partly because there was Ray and myself, both over six foot, being met initially by little Johnny Vyvyan, who was under five foot tall, saying: "You are the boys we are trying to help, aren't you?"

When Derek Roy finally joined us, he said: "I read the script, lads, and think there is potential. Tell you what, you go away and write me some one-liners and I'll pay you five shillings for every one I accept."' Being offered the chance of writing for one of the nation's top comedians was too good an opportunity to miss, so Galton and Simpson rushed back to Mrs Simpson's house and began compiling an array of one-line gags which spread over three pages of paper.

'We tried hard to make it our own material and not to be influenced by the radio or joke books,' recalls Ray. 'When we had enough we arranged a further meeting. Derek looked through the list, saying, "Yes, no, yes, yes, no" and so on, and the seven one-liners he liked he bought for five shillings each. Thirty-five shillings—seventeen and sixpence each. We were professionals!' Their writing careers had begun.

Chapter 2

Attempting to establish your name in the world of entertainment is an uphill struggle and when the show you're working on is doomed to failure, it makes your job even more arduous. On 2 August 1951, the first of 14 episodes of a Derek Roy-fronted sketch show, *Happy-Go-Lucky*, was broadcast; it struggled from day one and by Christmas was assigned to history, yet it proved to be an important milestone in the careers of Galton and Simpson.

Until this juncture, their writing careers had involved penning one-line gags for Roy, some of which were used in *Happy-Go-Lucky*, but by the time the final instalment was broadcast on 10 December, Galton and Simpson had written their first full-length scripts for the radio show. Through their association with the programme, they would also meet the two individuals who would play crucial roles in shaping their future careers: Dennis Main Wilson and Tony Hancock.

Broadcast on the BBC's Light Programme, *Happy-Go-Lucky* starred Derek Roy along with Doreen Harris, Peggy Cochrane and Harry Noble. The show's format consisted of a series of sketches, often including special guests, ranging from Terry-Thomas and Dick Emery to Beryl Reid and Charlie Chester. Also present in the show was a self-contained script, 'The Eager Beavers', with Peter Butterworth, Graham Stark and Bill Kerr cast as Boy Scouts, and Tony Hancock as Mr Ponsonby, their scoutmaster. Although they never wrote directly for Hancock in the show, it marked the beginning of their relationship, as Ray Galton explains. 'One day, just after something we'd written had been rehearsed at the Paris Cinema, we were sitting in the stalls when Tony Hancock walked past and asked, "Did you write that?" We told him we had, to which he replied, "Very funny", before moving on. These were the first words we ever spoke to each other, and as soon as the show finished, he asked if we'd write a single for him.'

Unfortunately, their first meeting with Dennis Main Wilson happened under less happy circumstances. The incumbent producer of *Happy-Go-Lucky*, Roy Speer, found the strain of the programme too much and during the recording of the eleventh episode he collapsed. With only three shows remaining, the then Head of Light Entertainment, Jim Davidson, asked Main Wilson to step in and salvage what he could from the floundering show. 'It was a dreadful programme,' admits Alan Simpson. 'A lot of the sketches were influenced by American shows; Derek Roy's wife, Rona Ricardo, had an enormous collection of American scripts and a lot of the material used in *Happy-Go-Lucky* was based on them. A couple of Scottish journalists wrote other pieces, while the "Eager Beaver" sketches were written by two Australian writers, who'd had some success with them back home; all they did was anglicise them. Ray and I were in the background, contributing five-shilling jokes which Derek Roy was using.'

But they were propelled into the foreground when Speer's departure triggered an urgent meeting to discuss the programme's future. Jim

Davidson assembled the cast and launched into an emotional pep talk. 'It was just like a speech out of an American musical—tears were rolling down people's faces. Then we were introduced to the new producer, Dennis Main Wilson, who later asked if we were writers. With sweaty palms, we said yes, and he replied: "What about writing the last three shows?" We had to accept his offer, partly because we thought we could do better.'

'We agreed and worried about it afterwards,' smiles Alan. 'After all, we couldn't tell the truth and say we'd only just started writing.'

On the strength of the three-episode commission, for which they each received 21 guineas, Alan Simpson tendered his resignation at the shipping office. 'It was an astronomical fee for us in those days, much more than the eight guineas per show Derek Roy was paying us for his stand-up slots. But my mother was worried about me giving up the job. Out of my £6 weekly wage, I was giving her 30 shillings for food and upkeep, and she made a bargain with me: if after four weeks I couldn't afford to pay her 30 shillings, I'd return to work.' Fortunately Alan never looked back.

By now, *Happy-Go-Lucky* was alternating in the schedules with *Variety Bandbox*, a long-running variety show in which Derek Roy was also a regular, together with the likes of Max Wall, Reg Dixon and Arthur English. Fortnightly episodes afforded Galton and Simpson more time to complete their scripts, which were still being written at Alan's mother's house—it would be another four years before they rented their own offices. Early each morning, Ray would make his way to the Simpsons' house at Church Walk, and wouldn't return home until the last bus at night. In the lounge, they worked all day on their scripts, initially writing them in longhand. But as soon as their first cheque arrived, they headed to a nearby John Lewis department store and purchased a typewriter. Alan, with his experience of working in the shipping office, picked up responsibility for typing the scripts. 'We worked all hours, sometimes to two or three in the morning,' he says. 'If the doctors at the sanatorium had known they would have gone berserk. Of course, we didn't know how to write a full script, so blindly we moved forward. Dennis Main Wilson was a great help, often coming around at one in the morning, feeding us fish and chips, cheering us along.'

Having to produce one script a fortnight, although very challenging for two green scriptwriters, was a blessing in disguise, as Alan explains. 'If it had been one a week I'm sure it would have been too much for us, but we scrambled through with one every two weeks. One thing in our favour was that the previous eleven had been so bad that no matter how poor ours were, they couldn't be any worse—we couldn't lose, really. If our scripts weren't any good, people would simply say: "It's not their fault, they didn't have a chance and were on a hiding to nothing."' As it turned out, Main Wilson was impressed with their work.

Soon after the demise of *Happy-Go-Lucky*, Galton and Simpson's working relationship with Tony Hancock began in earnest when he contacted the writers asking them to pen a five-minute piece for his appearance on *Workers' Playtime*. He agreed to pay them half his fee, which meant a 25-guinea pay cheque, substantially more than they were receiving from Derek Roy.

By now, Galton and Simpson's names were known by the BBC hierarchy in the Light Entertainment team, and within a few months they were asked to take over the scriptwriting for the last six instalments of *Calling All Forces*, an hour-long sketch show, which by June 1952 was being co-compered by Tony Hancock and Charlie Chester, a job previously occupied by Ted Ray. After more than eighty weeks, the resident writers, Bob Monkhouse and Denis Goodwin, had moved on and Galton and Simpson wrote the final six scripts.

When the final episode was heard on 28 July 1952, the basic structure of the show was retained and broadcast under a new title, *Forces All-Star Bill*, followed by *All-Star Bill*, eight weeks later, with Galton and Simpson writing all 13 episodes. Further evolution saw the show retitled *Star Bill* with Galton and Simpson engaged as resident scriptwriters, while the regular cast consisted of Tony Hancock, Graham Stark and Geraldine McEwan for the first series broadcast between June and October 1953. When the second season began the following February, Moira Lister had replaced McEwan. It was a rewarding period: 'We were writing for virtually every comedian in the country,' says Alan. 'Each show had guest comics, guest actors and singers, and we had to adapt our writing for their different styles. This is how we learnt our craft, it was an invaluable apprenticeship.'

During this period, Galton and Simpson were asked to write for Frankie Howerd's new radio show. 'Frank was happy for us to contribute, provided Eric Sykes oversaw our work,' recalls Alan. 'Eric wasn't really interested but agreed to look at our scripts, topping and tailing them. All he ever did was change the "ands" and "buts". It was another sketch show, though, with guest comedians and actors, so we were writing for the likes of Richard Burton, Claire Bloom and Richard Attenborough. It was incredible experience.'

Despite hearing their lines uttered by top-ranking performers in some of the country's best-loved shows, Galton and Simpson were still scribbling away in Alan's mother's house, although by now they had acquired a telephone, thanks to Jacques Brown, the producer of *Calling All Forces*. Alan explains: 'Whenever the BBC wanted to get in touch with us they had to send a telegram, saying something like: "Please call Mayfair 8411 re. urgent script appointment". I'd then rush round to the public phone box and call in. Eventually Jacques said: "We can't work like this, you'll have to get a phone." When I told him there was a two-year waiting list, he replied: "Don't worry, leave it to me. I'll write you a letter complaining about the fact that we cannot get in touch with you." We sent the letter to the GPO and within two days had a phone installed at my mother's house.'

Before long they had swapped Mrs Simpson's lounge for their own office, in keeping with the image of up-and-coming comedy writers, even if the location, sited above a fruit and veg shop in Uxbridge Road, Shepherd's Bush, wasn't the most salubrious setting in London. The move was prompted by a phone call from fellow writer Spike Milligan, who shared the offices with Eric Sykes.

Ray Galton recalls the conversation. 'He asked if we had an agent, which at that time we didn't. He said: "There are two agencies in town, the Kavanagh Agency and Monkhouse Goodwin Agency, and they're trying to sign us. We don't want to know, so we're trying to get all the writers who haven't got agents together. Why don't you come and discuss it with us?" So we did.' Reaching the fruit and veg shop, they entered a side door and climbed a rickety staircase to be greeted by Milligan and Sykes, who presented their idea. They wanted to form their own writers' agency, whereby everyone would contribute 10 per cent of their earnings into a central fund to cover the cost of hiring a secretary and renting the office, which was owned by Frankie Howerd.

Galton and Simpson agreed to join Milligan and Sykes in a co-operative, which they christened Associated London Scripts. 'It didn't take us long to decide,' says Alan. 'We had a good deal because 10 per cent of our earnings was far less than Spike and Eric's share. After all, we'd only been in the business three years whereas they were established stars.'

When it came to hiring a secretary, Galton and Simpson knew just the person. In their pre-typewriter days, their work was written in longhand, spoken into a Dictaphone and passed to an old schoolfriend of Alan's, from his days at Surrey's Mitcham County School, who typed them in her spare time. The friend was Beryl Vertue, who now runs her own company, Hartswood Films, and has become a leading producer in her own right: her list of credits include television series *Men Behaving Badly* and *Coupling* and films *The*

Plank, *Up the Chastity Belt* and *Steptoe and Son Ride Again*. 'I suggested Beryl for the job,' says Alan, 'because I'd known her since we were ten, and her husband was my best friend at school.' In time, Beryl would become an agent and represent all the writers working within the co-operative.

All four writers were waiting for Beryl, who was 20, as she arrived for her interview. It was a day she'll never forget. 'Alan sat on the floor throughout, and no one asked the questions you'd normally expect at interviews regarding my shorthand and typing skills. They were more interested in knowing about what made me laugh— I had a wonderful time! All of a sudden Spike shouted: "I think she'll be fine!" He looked at the others, who all nodded, and suddenly I had this job.'

As the years passed, more writers joined Associated London Scripts and the company grew into one of the largest writing agencies around. Before long, Beryl's role of secretary-cum-assistant-cum-dogsbody had transformed into that of agent, negotiating contracts and fees for everyone at the company; fortunately she possessed a natural flair for such tasks, which was just as well considering her lack of experience in either finance or business affairs. 'Luckily, I became quite good at the job without really knowing what an agent did. In fact, I'd been organising all the contracts for some months when someone asked me how long I'd been an agent. I hadn't realised that is what I was, I thought of myself as simply a secretary who did a lot.' Working for Messrs Galton, Simpson, Milligan and Sykes was an enjoyable, if hectic, period in Vertue's career. 'We were very busy. The phone didn't stop ringing, and, of course, in the early days I was switchboard operator as well, but it was an exhilarating time.'

For Galton and Simpson, honing their style of writing was a continual process. 'Neither of us had ever written before,' says Alan, 'so we developed our style together. Ray and I met, of course, before we were writers whereas others meet through the profession. Frank Muir and Denis Norden are prime examples: Muir used to write everything Jimmy Edwards did and Norden wrote for Dick Bentley, so when the BBC wanted to do a show with Edwards and Bentley, they hired Frank and Denis.'

Still using the trusty old typewriter, which they had bought with their first wage cheque from *Happy-Go-Lucky*, Alan and Ray established a working practice that would serve them well throughout their careers. While Alan typed up the scripts, Ray sat next to him. Nothing was committed to paper until they both agreed it warranted inclusion. Once they were satisfied with a line, Alan's two-finger typing recorded it and they moved on to the next line. Sitting in their Shepherd's Bush office, they beavered away each day, turning out scripts and sketches for many of the nation's top comics. But soon they would be writing their own series for Tony Hancock, placing them firmly on the map as leading scriptwriters.

Chapter 3

Writers are always looking ahead to the next script, the next series, the next project, and Galton and Simpson were no exception. While they were turning out scripts for the second season of *Forces All-Star Bill*, in 1953, their minds were already beginning to focus on the future; it would be a year and a half before *Hancock's Half Hour* was aired by which time they would have written two series of *Star Bill*. They had decided Tony Hancock would be the fulcrum of their plans, and although the show would involve familiar facets, including many faces they had worked with previously, there was one significant difference from anything they had written before.

For years, whenever the British public wanted a little light relief from the mundanities of life, they tuned in to the radio and were entertained by the traditional variety show, where sketches were punctuated with musical turns; Galton and Simpson, however, marked a course which would see them venturing beyond the rigidity of variety-style shows into relatively uncharted waters: instead of a series of sketches, they wanted to place their characters within a half hour uninterrupted storyline, a situation comedy. They wanted the humour to emanate from the character or the storyline rather than relying on funny voices and jokes. It was a gradual process, especially as the recruitment of Kenneth Williams to the cast afforded the writers the golden opportunity to exploit his predilection for humorous voices—just the kind of thing they had set out to avoid.

During a meeting with Dennis Main Wilson in his Bond Street office, Galton and Simpson discussed their idea. Main Wilson felt Hancock was worthy of his own show after the success of *Educating Archie*, *Star Bill* and its various permutations; and the writers were equally impressed with him. 'His performance and our writing gelled so well, so we were keen to work with him some more,' explains Ray Galton. 'He was an instinctive comedian and out of that comes timing. You never had to worry about Tony timing a laugh—it's not every comedian who can do that.'

'We rarely had to explain anything to him regarding the script—except, perhaps, the odd cockney phrase,' adds Simpson. 'We never had to explain what a joke meant—it's amazing how many comedians don't get the joke and it has to be explained. We tried writing more and more character lines, attitude lines, and getting more laughs out of the situation, and Tony was a master of that.'

Main Wilson had spotted the understanding that was developing between the artist and the writers and was enthusiastic about Galton and Simpson's new idea. When Main Wilson asked Galton and Simpson to devise a format he could present to his bosses, they developed an idea for a programme centred around Tony, a friend, a girlfriend and a character who was continuously involved in shady schemes in which Hancock was invariably implicated.

The one-page outline was handed to Dennis Main Wilson, who was excited about Galton and

Simpson's proposals. 'By the time the Americans came into the war they were light years ahead of us in radio comedy—they were much more mature,' admitted Main Wilson. 'As the war finished, the Muirs and Nordens of this world started producing polished comedy like *Take It From Here*, which was of a very high order, but it was still all jokes. Galton and Simpson wanted none of this, they wanted to do a real truth storyline. They saw Tony as a true character.'[1]

They weren't the only ones who had explored the idea of a comedy vehicle for Hancock: his close friend, writer Larry Stephens, who would later be involved in the first two episodes of Hancock's ill-fated 1956 ITV series, *The Tony Hancock Show*, idled away many hours discussing programme ideas that could be developed for him; most fell by the wayside but one, in particular, was detailed sufficiently for an outline to be presented to Peter Eton, a producer at the BBC, in the summer of 1952. The BBC were receptive to the idea, especially as Hancock, himself, was 'genuinely enthusiastic'[2], and in a memo to the then Head of Variety, dated 8th July 1952, Eton wanted to tell Michael Standing about the proposal, despite it being at a preliminary stage. The detailed outline stated:

Tony Hancock plays the part of an estate-agent-cum-bachelor-town-councillor, who lives with his old aunt in one of those frightful semi-detached villas in a small South Coast town. Our hero is an unimaginative, unenterprising, charming idiot who has a lot of trouble with his eccentric aunt because of her ambition for him

34

to marry into the County 'set'. Tony, on the other hand, prefers the local girls and is, of course, considered an eligible and reliable bachelor by their mothers. The villain of the piece is a local garage proprietor, a loud-mouthed, witless, back-slapping oaf, always ready with a clumsy, unfunny leg-pull and a raucous laugh.[3]

Eton added: 'Apart from the fact that each of the six or more half-hour programmes would consist of a complete story about Tony's pompous, yet likeable, blundering, there would be no set formula.[4] Their plans were for a show with no audience, orchestra or singers, relying on recorded music for the opening and closing theme, as well as the scene links. Eton asked whether he should encourage Stephens and Hancock to develop the idea further; within a week, Standing had replied, in the affirmative, offering 15 guineas for a script treatment. Stephens penned a pilot script, titled *Welcome to Whelkham*, but the project was shelved; yet it provides evidence that the BBC were keen to secure a comedy project for Tony Hancock.

On 1 May 1953, after conferring with Hancock and with Galton and Simpson, Main Wilson sent a memo to his boss explaining that he wanted Hancock to have his own half hour series 'based on reality and truth rather than jokes, merry quips, wheezes, breaks for crooners who have no reason to be on the show anyway.'[5] He wanted to leave behind the rigidity of what he termed 'the old mould of first sketch, singer, second sketch, band number, last sketch.'[6]

Although discussions regarding Hancock's new

35

show had begun early in 1953, it wasn't until November that arrangements began in earnest, by which time Hancock had completed the first series of *Star Bill* and made his début on the big screen, playing bandmaster Lieutenant Cartroad in *Orders Are Orders*. The BBC's Light Programme scheduled 13 programmes for Hancock's show, with an option of a further 13 and suggested that Main Wilson secure Hancock's signature on the contract at the earliest date. By the end of November Marjory Lipscomb, working in the BBC's Variety Booking Section, had contacted Hancock's new agent, Jack Adams, to discuss the forthcoming series. Although Adams confirmed Hancock's willingness to go ahead with the show, timing was to prove more difficult. The BBC's hope that the show could start on 17 October 1954 was dashed. Lipscomb explained: 'As his plans are at the moment he is to go into a summer season which will not end until the middle of October and after that, for reasons of health, he would want to go for a holiday, presumably about four weeks, which would mean that a more realistic starting date for this series would be the end of November to possibly the beginning of December.'[7] Adams also informed Lipscomb that if Hancock happened to be working in London during the period of the radio series, he would want to pre-record on a weekday. Lipscomb stated in her memo that 'it is impossible for him, again owing to health reasons, to work during the week and pre-record on Sunday.'[8]

Adams' references to 'health reasons' were indicative of how Tony Hancock felt during any long-running theatre show. As Alan Simpson explains: 'He used to get mentally exhausted after a stage show; he hated the twice-nightly format in theatre, as well as the repetition, and used to feel that the walls were crowding in on him. He didn't like performing on stage but had to do it because in those days playing music halls and the like was the way you made your name. He always knew that after three months or so in a summer season he'd be exhausted and need to get away.'

Jack Adams informed the BBC that he wouldn't be able to confirm the actual date Hancock could begin his new series until the end of January 1954. With no alternative but to wait, plans for Hancock's show were put on hold until the New Year. His contract was finally dispatched from the BBC on 6 January. After giving Hancock sufficient time to digest the terms on offer, Dennis Main Wilson contacted Tony and invited him to his home on Sunday, 14 February 1954, hoping to secure the artist's signature. Main Wilson had already discussed the programme extensively with the writers, Galton and Simpson, and Hancock, but decided it was time he provided his bosses with a more in-depth overview of the show's structure. In a memo to the Assistant Head of Variety, dated 12 February 1954, Main Wilson explained:

This show would not be tied down to any set number of comedy spots each week—indeed, the construction of the show will have as loose a formula as possible—some weeks three different spots on three different subjects—some weeks a complete half hour storyline—occasionally running a serial story over into the next week if the situation presents itself. The comedy style will be purely situation in which we shall try to build Tony as a real life character in real life surroundings. There will be no 'goon' or contrived comedy approaches at all. We shall be experimenting with a 'semi-domestic Hancock' in the new series of 'Star Bill' which will give you some idea of the eventual approach we shall make.[9]

Adams returned the contract, duly signed, on 16 February. Hancock was to be paid 50 guineas per show and recording would start on the Saturday, 30 October. It was imperative that Hancock left the studio every Saturday in time to be at the Adelphi Theatre, where he'd be appearing in a revue, *The Talk of the Town*.

The first recording of *Hancock's Half Hour* was still more than eight months away. In the interim, Tony Hancock was busy on stage and radio, including the second series of *Star Bill*, which Galton and Simpson wrote and Main Wilson produced. Galton and Simpson had struck up a good relationship with Main Wilson, and were looking forward to working with him on their new series. 'He was a remarkable character, very supportive and extremely talented,' enthuses Ray.

'He was very manic,' adds Alan. 'For a 100 per cent result he put in 120 per cent effort. Sometimes he would overwork, become over-enthusiastic, but that's better than being under-enthusiastic. Whatever you wanted from Dennis in terms of the programme, you got; when he directed *Till Death Us Do Part* he insisted on hiring a helicopter to film the opening credits. He must have spent the entire budget of the series on that one opening shot!'

By the time Main Wilson settled down to produce the final 10 instalments of *Star Bill*, he was already ruminating about Hancock's new situation comedy and the performers he wanted to cast alongside the star name. Galton and Simpson, meanwhile, envisaged four characters in the regular team.

Talk of Hancock's new show had filtered down to the rest of the tight-knit team in *Star Bill*, with some people expecting the same team to transfer to the situation comedy ready for its autumn launch. Unlike the USA's *Phil Harris and Alice Faye Show* with its husband–wife relationship, Galton and Simpson opted for a boyfriend and girlfriend scenario, and Moira Lister, who had been working with Hancock in the second series of *Star Bill*, was deemed suitable for the part. One of the characters the writers wanted to include, as a side kick for Hancock, was based on a breezy friend of Harris', played by Remley, in *The Phil Harris Show*. Galton and Simpson knew exactly the actor they wanted to play this bright, jaunty chum: Bill Kerr, whom they had met at the Buxton Club in London's West End. Frequented by thespians, the club was run by Gerald Campion, who'd made his name playing Billy Bunter in the BBC television series. Campion would later find himself hired for the opening instalment of *Hancock's Half Hour*. One advantage was that Kerr had previously worked with Hancock. The fact that Bill had grown up in Australia, after moving from South Africa, wasn't a requisite in the selection process, but it would later provide the writers with an extra avenue to explore in terms of comedy.

With Hancock, Kerr and Lister's names already in the frame, and Main Wilson wanting to

39

introduce some new blood to complete the foursome for the new show, no room was left for the only other regular member of the *Star Bill* team—Graham Stark. An actor of great experience, Stark's association with Hancock extended way beyond *Happy-Go-Lucky*, *Forces All-Star Bill*, *All-Star Bill* and *Star Bill* to their days touring together in the RAF Gang Shows. Stark was called to the Aeolian Hall office of Dennis Main Wilson, who was placed in the invidious position of breaking the bad news that he wouldn't be needed for Hancock's new show. The actor was told, 'We are making some changes', a decision which upset Stark. 'I remember asking Dennis, "Am I not in it, then?" He just went red in the face and, apologising, said: "It's just that we . . ." I interrupted at that point and enquired just who he meant by "we". It turned out he meant Tony, so I asked: "Is Tony producing the show, then?" In other words, Tony had decided what he wanted. After that, my relationship with Tony was very formal. He always had in his mind he would do his own show—I don't blame him for that. Although it was disappointing at the time, I hold no grudges now.'

Securing the services of Kerr and Lister was an important step forward. As a boy in Australia, Kerr had played vaudeville in Melbourne, worked on radio for ABC and performed with various touring shows, including a national tour where he was billed as Wee Willie Kerr, dressed in white tie, top hat and tails. At the outbreak of the Second World War he enlisted for the Air Force Reserve, working as a comic entertaining the troops in the South Pacific and returning to vaudeville after demob;

40

before long, he'd acquired a passage to England on a cattle steamer and, thanks to a friend, secured an audition for a play. His big break came in *Variety Bandbox*, and by the time he was offered a part in Hancock's new show, he was already an experienced radio and film actor, with big-screen credits including *Harmony Row*, *Appointment in London* and *The Dam Busters*.

Bill believes it was while he was sharing a few drinks one evening with Tony Hancock, Ray Galton, Alan Simpson and Graham Stark that the writers decided to use him in the show. 'We'd been somewhere in London, Berkeley Square I think, and I was regaling the boys with a couple of yarns about Australia. They were laughing, and I think it gave Ray and Alan a little dig to think they might use me.' It was Kerr's ebullience more than his ability to make them laugh which convinced the writers.

Recruiting Moira Lister introduced a degree of stability, as she had worked with Hancock, the writers and the producer. Despite just turning 30, Lister was a fine actress, oozing experience in all mediums. Like Kerr and Sid James, she was born in South Africa and had been performing since childhood. Various stage productions in her homeland followed before she headed for England to further her career on stage, screen and radio, where she often played genteel characters.

On the big screen, her credits prior to *Hancock's Half Hour* included *The Shipbuilders*, *Wanted for Murder*, *So Evil My Love*, *Love Story*, *Once a Jolly Swagman*, *Pool of London* and *Trouble in Store*, while on the stage she was seen in *Present Laughter*, *French Without Tears*, *The Love of Four Colonels*

41

and *Birthday Honours*. After several radio shows, such as the popular series *Simon and Laura* and *Life of Bliss*, her voice was also familiar to the public, making her an ideal choice to play Hancock's girlfriend. In the emerging genre of situation comedy it was becoming a tradition to have a girlfriend as love interest for the leading character: although she materialised into nothing more than a close friend, the idea provided an extra strand of comedic possibilities. As it eventually turned out, the introduction of a girlfriend proved unsuccessful.

To complete the team of four, Galton and Simpson wanted someone to portray a hood. Although Dennis Main Wilson was ultimately responsible for casting the show, he always listened with interest to any suggestions the writers submitted; late one afternoon, while Galton and Simpson were sitting in his office, they told the director they knew the man they wanted for the remaining part in the team; they had spotted a rugged-faced actor in the classic Ealing comedy, *The Lavender Hill Mob*—the trouble was, they couldn't remember his name. Fortuitously, the film received a three-day airing at a fleapit in Putney the following week, so Galton and Simpson went along. By the time they reached the cinema and had settled down in their seats, the lights had dimmed and they had missed the credit titles, leaving them no alternative but to sit through the entire film and wait for the cast list; as soon as they saw the name Sid James, they rushed to the nearest phone box and called Main Wilson.

James arrived on British soil in 1946, determined to become a full-time actor; back home in

Johannesburg he'd trained as a hairdresser and had run his own salon. But he'd set his heart on becoming an actor and had gained vital experience turning out for the Johannesburg Repertory Players, an amateur company, before enlisting for the South African Defence Force. Shortly after the war he decided to head for England and within a fortnight of arriving had secured an agent and a small part in a film. By the time he arrived for a preliminary chat at the Garrick Theatre one Sunday evening, he was a recognised character actor with around thirty credits to his name, including *Once a Jolly Swagman*, *The Small Back Room*, *I Believe in You* and *The Gift Horse*. He was, however, relatively inexperienced in the medium of radio, a factor that worried him and would affect his performance in the opening shows.

In between the rehearsal and live broadcast of *Star Bill*, Sid James entered the Garrick and was met by the writers, who ushered him through to Hancock's dressing room, where the actor and Main Wilson were waiting to discuss the new series. Aware that James was nervous about accepting the role because of his lack of radio experience, the meeting had been arranged to try and alleviate any worries. The show was outlined to James, together with an overview of the character they wanted him to play, who started life as a rather perfidious individual whose philosophy was, 'Drink, be merry, tomorrow we snuff it. If you've got it, spend it, and if you ain't got it, get it.' As Alan Simpson explains, 'We told him all about our plans, but he still wasn't very keen, so Tony, Ray and I tried to persuade him, with Tony's point being that it was a piece of cake: it was written down and all he had to do was read it.'

Still undecided, Sid was persuaded to stay and watch the live *Star Bill* broadcast; afterwards he hesitantly told Main Wilson that he'd give the Hancock show a try. The BBC issued a contract on 14 October, confirming a fee of 25 guineas for each of the 13 episodes (the first series was later extended to 16 instalments) and that, depending on the success of the first season, the Corporation had the right to take an option on his services for up to a further 13 episodes.

With Hancock, Kerr, Lister and now James all committed to the show, Main Wilson had one more vacancy to fill, which he termed the odd job man: someone who would be used for cameos and additional characters outside the regular quartet. He wrote to every London agent pointing out he'd be happy to audition for the role any promising character comedy actors on their books, but his appeal generated little interest; then he received a phone call from agent Peter Eade, suggesting a visit to the Arts Theatre to watch a young thespian playing the Dauphin in a production of *St Joan*. The actor was Kenneth Williams. Main Wilson saw the show and was impressed with Williams' 'tremendously dramatic, but funny'[10] performance. As soon as the curtain came down, he took Williams around the corner for a drink; he congratulated him on a performance which had already earned him many plaudits from the critics, before eulogising the planned comedy he wanted Williams to be part of. Williams was sufficiently impressed for a formal interview to be arranged, on Tuesday, 19 October, just eleven days before the first episode was to be recorded.

44

Passing a copy of the opening script across his desk, Main Wilson offered Williams the part of Lord Bayswater, a monocle-wearing old gent who returns to his opulent flat to find Hancock using it for the launch party of his new radio series. In his diary entry for that day, Williams noted he was to play 'some old Lord in a minute spot.'[11] Despite the character's fleeting appearance at the end of the episode, he knew without doubt that he could inject humour into the lines written by Galton and Simpson, whose skills as scriptwriters he later acknowledged in his autobiography, stating, 'their facility for comic characters and amusing lines makes me smile to this day'[12]. The promise of other character roles in the coming series, for which he was paid eight guineas per show, Williams found appealing. His gift for comedy and ability to elicit laughter from the meanest of audiences via a range of humorous voices proved valuable to *Hancock's Half Hour*, and even though the writers' and Hancock's drive for realism in the plots eventually rendered the funny voices obsolete, he was still occasionally invited back to Railway Cuttings.

With all the key players signed up and ready to go, Main Wilson's attention turned to the remaining components needed before the show's launch. The working title, 'The Tony Hancock Show,' was replaced with *Hancock's Half Hour*, as confirmed at the BBC's Light Programme Variety Meeting of Wednesday, 22 September 1954, while the writers had already concentrated on the character's identity in terms of name and setting. 'Anthony Aloysius St John Hancock was an attempt at being pretentious, and suited the character down to the ground,' says Simpson.

As for placing him at 23 Railways Cuttings, East Cheam, as Ray Galton explains, his own childhood was an influence: 'I lived in Morden, Surrey, and used to help the milkman on his round at weekends. His depot was in Cheam, and we used to travel all around Cheam, Sutton and Belmont on his horse and cart. I always regarded Cheam as very posh—the Beverly Hills of South London. Hancock wouldn't have made Cheam proper, he was too tatty and not successful enough, so we made it East Cheam. As for Railway Cuttings, there was a tendency, particularly during Victorian times, to name streets after great engineering events, but for us, Railway Cuttings fitted the bill because it would have been the scruffiest part of East Cheam.'

An important factor for any programme, particularly on the radio, is the music: the theme tune, incidental music and any pieces used for scene links. Originally the respected composer Stanley Black, who scored nearly seventy films and numerous BBC shows during his lengthy career, was asked to compose the music, but when he had to cancel at the eleventh hour, Main Wilson turned to 30-year-old Wally Stott, who became Angela Morley in the early 1970s. Now based in Arizona, where her long career in music has involved work on myriad projects, including *Happy Go Lucky*, *When Eight Bells Toll*, *Watership Down* for the big screen, and *Dallas*, *Dynasty* and *Wonder Woman* for television, Angela had just taken over the music on *The Goon Show* when Dennis Main Wilson asked her to write for *Hancock's Half Hour*. 'I'd worked for Dennis on several projects, so he popped over to see me at my flat in Kensington Court, London. I'd never seen Tony or even heard him speak, so Dennis did his best to help by doing an impersonation to try and give me an idea of what sort of things to write; incidentally, some weeks into the show I visited the Paris Cinema where they had been recording an episode and I was introduced to Tony Hancock; I must say, I then realised Dennis' impersonation wasn't at all like the man himself and perhaps I'd been a little unkind!'

After Main Wilson had explained the premise of the show, Morley settled down to write the music. 'My first thoughts weren't directed so much to the melody, but to find the kind of instrument that would be appropriate for the character's personality. Dennis mentioned that Hancock was going to be pompous, which made me choose the tuba. I started playing around with different ideas on my piano at home; the whole theme only lasted about 40 seconds at the most, but the tuba at the beginning set the momentum, then the orchestra came in and, at the end, the voiceover. Once that was complete, I wrote a lot of comedy cues that could be used whenever necessary.' The music was recorded at the BBC's Piccadilly Studio on 29 October, just a day before the first episode was recorded: Harry Rabinowitz conducted the BBC Revue Orchestra, with the tuba, employed as the musical representation of Hancock, played by Jim Powell. The music was to become, arguably, the most recognisable theme tune on radio and, later, television during the 1950s, where one snatch of sound would fill the awaiting audience with excitement and anticipation.

With cast, scripts and theme music organised, *Hancock's Half Hour* was under way.

Chapter 4

On Saturday, 30 October 1954, a handful of actors dodged the autumn showers and made their way to London's Camden Theatre, ready for the 10 a.m. rehearsal for the opening episode of *Hancock's Half Hour*. Before the day was out, they had helped lay the foundation for a radio show that would become a British institution.

Two hours were assigned to rehearsals, beginning with a script read-through and a technical run, which allowed Dennis Main Wilson and his technicians a chance to test all the equipment needed for the recording. Once the producer was satisfied, everyone would break for lunch before reconvening for the recording, which for the first two episodes was scheduled between 12.30 and 1.15 p.m. to allow the ever-busy Sid James time to race back to the West End where he was appearing in the matinée performance of the musical *Guys and Dolls*.

It was a tense morning, as Bill Kerr recalls. 'It was like the first day of school, everyone was on edge. But there's always tension on the first read-through because you don't want to be the one to let the team down; you also become very aware of how the other cast members are playing their parts and begin questioning whether your own performance is up to scratch. It's called self-preservation.'

Kerr sensed an air of expectation as he sat sipping coffee with the rest of the cast who were awaiting the arrival of Dennis Main Wilson to get the morning under way. 'Always at the back of your mind is the feeling that you could be on to something really big here; every performer knows when you've got a dud script, but there was never the slightest doubt that the words supplied by those brilliant writers, Galton and Simpson, would be a joy to perform. Fortunately we all gelled from the first moment.'

Looking around him, Bill was impressed with the faces gathered there—some were even familiar. He'd first met Tony Hancock at the Grafton Arms, a pub just off Victoria Street in London's Westminster area, which was owned by scriptwriter Johnny Grafton and frequented by a host of aspiring comics. 'We were all young, just out of the services. We all wanted to be comics and there was great camaraderie. Everyone was eager to make their mark in the business and it was a joy to be with people who spoke your language. When they made Tony, they broke the mould because no one could be like him, he was unique.' Sid James was also a familiar face, having first met Kerr in 1934 while touring South Africa.

In *Hancock's Half Hour*, Bill's character started off as the principal foil for Hancock, but as the series progressed this mantle was inherited by Sid. This didn't worry Bill. 'Sid was marvellous. Once he'd settled into his character there was no stopping him. He became the main feed for Tony, while my character hung around the periphery.' Bill was equally impressed with Kenneth Williams. 'He brought his own special dimension to the show. He was very gifted with his brilliant voices; he could just pull them out of the air and was particularly good playing old men. At times, he

50

almost overshadowed Tony. The two of them worked well together and it was a joy to watch them, both like greyhounds in the slips after the rabbit. Both were vain with each other and, I feel, brought out the best in one another. If Kenneth got a laugh, Tony would top it. It was a smashing cast.'

Just like Bill Kerr, Moira Lister wasn't facing strangers when she arrived at the Camden Theatre. She'd worked with Sid James in South Africa as a child. 'It was lovely to find him in the show: we had much in common and had a lot of laughs together.' She found Sid easy to work with, but not Tony. 'He was very depressive. He was always concerned about the next episode being better than the last; he was very hard on himself and others. But he had a wonderful comedy sense; all his characters were so true, one got stuck into a real situation. His great triumph was that he could be funny but very real at the same time. As for the others, Bill and Kenneth were lovely. Ken was a laugh a minute, although he took himself very seriously sometimes. He was brilliant at repartee, very quick witted. Everything he did, he did sensationally.'

It wasn't just the actors who were feeling nervous. The writers were venturing into a new genre and anxious about how their scripts would be received by those responsible for bringing them alive on the radio. As Galton and Simpson took their seats on the very first morning, Dennis Main Wilson handed everyone a crisp, freshly typed copy. Unlike the medium of television, where actors receive scripts in advance of the recording, this was the first time anyone, other than Main Wilson, had cast their eyes over the script. 'We were always worried about what people would think,' admits Ray Galton. But their concerns were unfounded, as the writers soon discovered. 'Tony was excellent—an instinctive reader who hardly made any mistakes,' says Ray. 'His inflections were right at the first reading. He was also a good audience, as was Sid James. Bill Kerr and Kenneth Williams had enormously big laughs, too, so the read-throughs were often very funny. Tony would sometimes be rolling about on the floor laughing, kicking his heels.' Any nerves quickly dissipated as the writers realised it was actually good fun watching the team read their scripts for the first time.

After the read-through and the technical run, the audience were ushered into the theatre, keen to see Tony Hancock in his new show. Each programme was introduced by a BBC staff announcer. Adrian Waller was assigned the opening few episodes before others stepped in, such as Robin Boyle, who became the most regular announcer on the show. Recalling his time on the show he wrote:

By the time I arrived at the Playhouse Theatre, they were at the stage of final rehearsal, followed by the recording. This applied whether I had one line, or the more lengthy part on 'Friday the 13th'. Even on this final rehearsal, it was not uncommon for parts of the script to be revised or rewritten if any of the cast thought of a different way of doing something. Sometimes, it was Tony himself who suggested changing a line. Alan Simpson and Ray Galton were always in attendance, and, often prompted by Ray, would discuss a situation, then the paper would go into the typewriter, and a new page was clipped into the script. I think of those two as 'coarse and sandpaper'. Ray frequently had the inspiration, but it was Alan who smoothed it into the work with finesse.

The most constant factor in these rehearsals was laughter—in fact, the rehearsals were often even funnier than the show itself. Many times, I have made that opening announcement with my sides aching—it took all my self control not to break up. The thing that I most dreaded was one of Tony's straight stares as he waited to say 'H-H-Hancock's 'Alf Hour'—even without moving a muscle, he could start that laughter which threatened to engulf me.

Tony, put simply, was a genius. Listen to 'Sunday' ['Sunday Afternoon at Home'] and marvel that he could have an audience helpless without the aid of gags, or even words. In fact, there was a buzz of anticipation from people as they came into the theatre. There was not much 'warm-up' necessary, although sometimes, Tony could be persuaded to do his impression of a lighthouse before the show. For this, he closed his eyes, and slowly rotated, opening his eyes and mouth each time he turned to face the audience. Before he had completed three circles, we were all in hysterics, no matter how many times we had seen him perform this trick.[1]

As the actors gathered around the mikes, the murmuring out front gave way to silence. It was then that Sid James' nerves started to surface. 'He appeared with his trilby pulled right down over his eyes and the script covering the rest of his face from the stare of the audience,' recalls Ray Galton. 'He was shaking so much you could see the script move. Within a few weeks, though, he realised it was a doddle, so off came the cap, and he started playing to the audience, confidently throwing the pages of his script away as he finished with them.'

When the final line had been uttered, Wally Stott's theme tune signified the end of the first instalment in the life of Anthony Aloysius St John Hancock and his small coterie of friends. Everyone at the Camden Theatre was pleased with the results, with Kenneth Williams recording in his diary, 'went very well really, and I got through OK'.[2] Now, they awaited the verdict of the nation. The first broadcast took place the following Tuesday, 2 November, at 9.30 p.m. To help launch the show, a high profile personality was needed to record a special prologue before the inaugural episode. The actor Robert Donat was chosen and, in preparation, Galton and Simpson penned a few lines of dialogue, even though, as the following piece shows, the show's title and recording dates had yet to be agreed.

ANNOUNCER: We now present a short prologue to a new radio series . . . And here to read it is Mr Robert Donat.

ROBERT: Good evening, ladies and gentlemen. In a few moments you are about to hear the first broadcast of a new radio series—'The Tony Hancock Half Hour'. Yes at last, at long last, Tony Hancock has been given a radio series of his own . . . someone has blundered. However it is too late for tears—the damage has been done—the show will inevitably go on, scheduled to run until next

April—it's going to be a long, hard winter. But before this unfortunate series commences, it is my duty to present to you some of the players in this . . . tragedy. To find someone willing to play opposite Mr Hancock was an impossible task—to find someone to play in the *vicinity* of Mr Hancock was an impossible task. By August they had scraped the bottom of the barrel. It was there we found Mr William Kerr, the internationally famous vagrant. Although it is perfectly true that Mr Kerr is a native of Australia, we *would* like to point out one thing . . .

BILL: I am *not* an Albino Aborigine.

ROBERT: Just before he left Australia, however, we understand Mr Kerr was bitten by a deadly poisonous snake and received injuries from which the snake has since died. So we come to the feminine interest in the programme, provided by the charming Miss Moira Lister—who was of course, tricked into doing it.

MOIRA: That's right—they told me I was going to do a series with Errol Flynn.

ROBERT: Miss Lister has since discovered that the only thing Mr Flynn and Mr Hancock have in common is their sex—which brings us to the star of our show, Anthony Alouitious St John Hancock the Second—or to give him his full name—Fatty. What of the man himself? Mr Hancock has always led a very sheltered life—which is not surprising considering he *lives* in one. His main hobby, he tells me, is collecting valuable coins—in fact his cloth cap and his concertina are a common sight outside our busier tube stations. Yes—a very busy man, who when first approached to do this show said . . .

TONY: No I'm sorry—I can't possibly do it for another four months—right out of the question. I'm tied up until the end of October—terribly sorry.

VOICE: All right—time's up.

TONY: Coming, warder.

(*Effects: Clang of cell door*)

ROBERT: The other voice listeners heard in that short episode was that of Mr Sidney James, playing the role of a prison warder, a complete reversal of his private life.

ANNOUNCER: And here to summarise the epilogue is Mr Robert Donat.

ROBERT: These then are the people who each week for the next few months, will be coming into your home—if I were you I'd hide your silver. And so ladies and gentlemen, as the Players assemble and the curtain rises, it is with heavy heart that I leave you with—'The Tony Hancock Half Hour'.

(*Orchestra: into opening signature*)

Whether the prologue was ever recorded and used is uncertain: no contract for Donat exists in the BBC archives in respect of this work, but what it does show is the ambition and the commitment to *Hancock's Half Hour* by Dennis Main Wilson. Whenever he believed in a project he went about his duties with gusto, doing his utmost to ensure the show was given its chance to prosper.

'The First Night Party' set the tone for what was to come: a plot built around Hancock being persuaded, usually by Bill, to turn to Sid James for help in overcoming a problem, in this case finding plush accommodation in which to entertain and, hopefully, impress the top critics and BBC executives after the first night of his new radio show. Although Hancock's character changed cosmetically, inside he possessed the same foibles, weaknesses and personality traits throughout his radio and small-screen life. Hancock cut a sad, lonely figure, a man whose gullibility was his biggest undoing. Whenever he experienced a problem, he lacked the confidence and maturity to tackle it himself, and felt that his only route out of the mess was to turn to Kerr and James. Time and again, he'd be taken in by Bill's and, to a much greater extent, Sid's dubious schemes. From this opening instalment, Hancock sowed the seeds for the comedic success that followed. It was paradoxical that in Hancock, a character who could infuriate the listeners, there was also a man with whom people could identify and empathise.

The same traits remained with the character throughout his life at Railway Cuttings, but some of his mannerisms evolved with time. For example, although his voice retained a comic style associated with his variety days, his delivery was slower, the pitch generally higher and he uttered his lines in a clipped manner; Hancock himself was still getting acquainted with his newly created character, and it would be some time before he'd settle down and adopt a more natural tone. Ray Galton says: 'We had to start off with what he'd already created for himself. We couldn't say to him, "forget all that," we had to work on what he was already and build on that.'

'At this stage Hancock was still playing the seedy character, as he'd been doing with his Higgins role in *Star Bill*,' adds Alan Simpson. 'There were also elements of *Educating Archie*. We gradually got away from all of that, but this was right at the beginning of the series—we were all fumbling our way forward. The Hancock character was just carrying on from what we'd been doing for the previous two years or so.'

As for the fictitious Hancock, Ray adds: 'Not all the attributes we gave the screen character were those of Tony Hancock, the man—he was an intelligent, deep, thoughtful, serious man; we just took what we wanted from him and invented the rest, such as being very gullible and only half read, the sort of guy who reads all his information from the colour supplements.'

While considering the influences behind their central character, Alan Simpson admits he wasn't based on any specific person they knew. 'I suppose there was a bit of Ray and me in him, particularly as he was seeking to educate himself. Both of us were really self-educated, always trying to better ourselves, perhaps by reading philosophy. So we had Hancock doing things like that, but of course he was always unsuccessful at it. He had a desire to climb the social scale, believing he'd been born into the wrong circumstances and society. If he'd been born into royalty that would have been his true niche. He always felt it was a shame his dad was only a bus conductor—he was pompous, the original man with feet of clay. Tony played it perfectly: he sounded and looked right for the part.'

Sid is introduced to the show as a friend of Bill Kerr's, an unscrupulous estate agent whose help is summoned when Hancock needs a luxurious pad in which to impress his party guests.

MOIRA: All right, who's going to help us get a place for the party?

BILL: A guy I've known for years, the boys tell me he's just opened an estate agent's office and he's an honest, upright, respectable, law-abiding member of the community.

TONY: What's his name?

BILL: Smooth-talking Sidney. He's as honest as the day is long.

TONY: That's not much of a reference in November.

Sid, especially in the early years of the radio series, employed a bunch of cronies to assist him in his unlawful businesses. The writers admit they could have been influenced by the musical *Guys and Dolls*, where such names as Nicely Nicely Johnson, Rusty Charlie and Benny Southstreet were used. 'There were so many characters with weird names,' says Ray, 'all these hoods with esoteric names—we might have been trying to achieve something like that: our home-brew gangsters with exotic names.'

Sid James' character had a finger in every pie, usually illegally, and with each passing episode switched his criminal activities from one angle to the next. His suspect reputation is evident from this first episode, when he tells Hancock that he had to pack up his previous business because the Post Office complained that he had more mailbags than they did; he later announces he can't let Hancock use one of the properties on his books, which is above a bank, for the party because he's sent a couple of his men there to lift the floorboards.

Despite requiring time to settle down, and for the actors to find their feet with their radio characters,

59

it was evident from day one that Hancock, Kerr and James would intertwine successfully, complementing each other through the storylines. One role that jarred somewhat, and provided little mileage in terms of plot progression was that of Tony's girlfriend. The talented Moira Lister did her utmost, creating a strong, outspoken girl. There was never any indication of romantic links between Hancock and Lister's character, assuming a relationship enjoyed more between friends than lovers. More importantly for the future of the series, the female role, being strong and forceful, afforded few opportunities for Hancock to bounce off in comedic terms. The problem wasn't in the acting—Lister was an actress of some standing—but in Galton and Simpson's inability, at this stage of their careers, to write for women. This problem resurfaced when Andrée Melly replaced a pregnant Moira Lister as the love interest for the second series. Realising that the idea of a steady girlfriend jarred with the overall image of Hancock, Galton and Simpson decided to drop Hancock's girlfriend from the format. Although it's a subject we'll return to later in the book, it's worth noting here that for Galton and Simpson it was an area that worried them from the earliest days. 'It's something that originally started with Geraldine McEwan in *Star Bill*—Ray and I found it difficult writing for straight women: all they ended up doing was straight feeding. Moria was superb, there for the glamour and the sophisticated manner she injected into her character; the trouble was, we never gave her any acting roles, anything meaty she could get her teeth into. She might have got the odd character voice to do but she was much better than that.' The lack of success with their female characters, excepting Hattie Jacques' Miss Pugh, was partly due to compatibility between the supposed sweethearts. The fictional Hancock's personality, manner and general approach to life riddled with insecurity, gullibility and lack of direction made the idea of him attracting and keeping a girlfriend almost farcical.

Another voice heard in the opening episode was that of Alan Simpson. It would become a regular in the series. Notching up a total of 60 instalments, including 15 in the first series, Alan Simpson was called upon by Dennis Main Wilson to make cameo appearances; often he would utter no more than a solitary word, or, in the case of 'The First Night Party', strike up a conversation with Hancock at the dinner party. Usually heard speaking at a lower volume, Simpson was regularly given the inconsequential character parts, which made economic sense, considering the meagre production budget allocated to the show.

A smile spreads across Ray Galton's face as he turns to his writing partner and remembers those days. 'Alan was a complete ham anyway,' he laughs. 'He'd done a concert party. He liked the idea of performing. Whenever we did a warm-up before a recording, I'd come and go as quickly as possible, while Alan developed a routine and would be there ten or fifteen minutes. Although we were only usually in crowd scenes, the parts Alan played were usually bigger than mine, especially on something we did quite often with Tony where in the middle of a storyline someone would ask where Tony was, and we'd hear him having a conversation with an unknown character for a couple of minutes, after which we'd return to the plot.'

The first episode of a new series always poses a tough challenge for the writers, who have to introduce the characters to their audience without disrupting the storyline and creating a pedestrian script. Galton and Simpson acknowledge it wasn't the best show they ever wrote, a view echoed by members of the sample audience who offered opinions on the show. It was estimated that 12 per cent of the adult population listened to the show, below the average attracted by other recent programmes in this slot; meanwhile, the programme's appreciation index, which was based on a panel of viewers grading certain aspects of the programme, culminated in a rating of 52, well short of the average of 62 for variety shows at this time. In comparison, nine editions of Hancock's previous series, *Star Bill*, gained indices averaging 65. Many viewers were disappointed and directed criticism towards the script, claiming it fell away towards the end, with the ransacking of Lord Dockyard's palatial home classed as ' "poor stuff" for adult amusement'.[3] One person commented: 'Hancock is one of the funniest . . . but even the best must have good material'. Despite the negative response to the script, people were delighted to see Hancock given his own show and felt the team, as a whole, worked well together, regarding Hancock and Kerr as 'ideal partners-in-crime.' Listeners helped justify the decision to break away from the traditional variety programme's structure of singers and dance bands punctuating the show, feedback which particularly pleased Dennis Main Wilson, who'd persuaded his bosses to take a chance on this new-style format. Writing in 1963, Hancock looked back on the episode and remarked: 'That first show was received fairly poorly really but we survived.'[4] And survive they did. At the next Light Programme variety meeting, attended by the heads and assistant heads of the various strands of the Variety Department, on Wednesday, 3 November, it was noted that *Hancock's Half Hour* was 'off to a moderate start but promising',[5] and that the series was likely to be extended to 16 episodes, which was subsequently agreed.

The medium of radio, where rehearsals and recordings were completed on the same day, allowed the actors the chance to continue working in other fields, particularly the stage. This was understood and, so long as it didn't affect *Hancock's Half Hour*, duly supported by Dennis Main Wilson. Sid James was one of the busiest actors in the business, so when he was offered a role in a musical, *Wonderful Town*, it was agreed that as from Saturday, 18 December, the recording time would be shifted to the earlier time of midday to allow James the chance to appear. Galton and Simpson have nothing but happy memories of working with the actor. 'He was a consummate professional,' says Alan. 'He'd been in the business years and was never out of work. He'd be earning one of the highest daily rates for character actors—twice as much as others. He was known in the film industry as "One Take James" because he just got on with the job, and whereas others might need four or five takes to get a scene right, he needed just one attempt.'

The second episode, 'The Diamond Ring', attracted an increased audience when transmitted on 9 November. Nearly 400,000 more people (total audience estimated at 4.888 million) tuned in around the British Isles to find Hancock and Kerr on the streets begging 'a penny for the guy'. When they later find a diamond ring in their evening's takings, which attracts a generous reward for its safe return, Moira believes it's an engagement ring from Tony. Hancock is torn between claiming the reward and upsetting Moira so decides to get a copy made, turning—as expected—to Sid James. Once again providing a perfect counterpoint to Hancock's idealistic attitudes and unachievable aspirations, James' character (if we ignore his criminal tendencies) epitomises a hard-working, working-class approach to life. While Hancock has his head in the clouds, dreaming of reaching the higher echelons of the acting profession, or simply getting his feet on the first rung of the ladder, James, albeit often unsuccessfully, is seeking out employment opportunities all around him.

As the series progressed, the team settled into their individual roles, and although it would be some time before Hancock's voice adopted a more natural feel, he was beginning to lose the almost haughty manner with which he'd kicked off the programme. When the BBC commissioned an audience research report after the fourth episode, 'The Boxing Champion', had been broadcast, listeners made a point of praising the entire cast. Although many extolled Hancock's adroit timing and ability to make any script funny, a significant number complimented the others on their fine support and teamwork.

Occasionally during the show's run, Tony Hancock's portly appearance was spotlighted and used for comedic value, something which is evident from day one when Bill refers to Hancock as 'Tub'. As Alan Simpson explains: 'We used to make jokes about Hancock being a bit overweight. We even suggested that he had big, flat feet. I remember we wrote a line in one of the scripts in this series, I can't remember which, claiming that Hancock suffered from a condition called Flatus Feetus. We thought the line was funny, but Moira said: "You can't say that!" Sid agreed, so we decided to cut it.' In 'The Boxing Champion' it's Hancock's weight that causes him to adopt a fitness routine. When the doctor tells him to shed a few pounds or suffer the consequences, Hancock visits a gym, only to find the proprietor is none other than Sid James. The exchanges between Hancock and James were becoming more effective, paving the way for Sid James' eventual elevation to second spot on the bill, ahead of Bill Kerr. At this early stage, Sid's characterisation was granite-like; he later mellowed, revealing a little vulnerability of his own, and became more of a friend than someone who was hell bent on ripping off his punters.

In addition to Kenneth Williams, who was used regularly in the series, the script for 'The Boxing Champion' necessitated the casting of a guest artist—in this case Paul Carpenter—which placed considerable strain on the budget. Although it was anticipated that the ultimate cost of each episode would total approximately £350, this figure was finally reduced to £260, with Main Wilson given strict instructions not to exceed it. In a memo dated 2 December, he was informed that the Head of Variety didn't want to use guest stars, prompting him into a frank response highlighting the constraints in which he operated. Main Wilson pointed out that he was left with the meagre sum of £20 for any additional voices he required for an episode, and was perplexed as to why the Head of Variety had placed a ban on using guest stars. He added: 'Obviously, having spent three years suffering the normal run of guest stars in the conventional hackneyed manner, I am not going to be so foolish as to go back to an "old hat" production style, especially after having received a certain amount of kudos on the first Listener Research report for having *no* guest stars.'[6] However, he wanted to make it clear that, in his capacity as co-deviser and producer of the show, it was agreed long before the programme began that it should be as near to true life as possible, resulting in situations where 'if Hancock buys a race horse, it could only strengthen the show if he were rude to Gordon Richards about Gordon Richards' horsemanship—with motorcars, to Mike Hawthorn about his driving—Hancock the great actor being rude to Jack Hawkins about the latter's acting—Hancock the footballer to Stanley Matthews etc.'[7] Main Wilson closed his memo with a forthright opinion on the prohibitive budget he had at his disposal: 'Surely this arbitrary cutting down of budgets is going to be a danger to enthusiasm and enterprise of writing/production teams?'

Realising the value of casting such names for a given episode, C. F. Meehan, Assistant Head of Variety, put Main Wilson's mind at ease by confirming that specific guest stars, if required, could be used so long as prior notice was given. Main Wilson had to make judicious use of his limited budget and invested wisely in guest stars. A discerning producer, his decision to hire well-known personalities from time to time paid dividends, as can be seen from listeners' comments after the broadcast of 'The Monte Carlo Rally', number 12 in the series. To add authenticity to a show based around Hancock entering the world famous rally, even if the plot's credibility was somewhat weakened by the fact he was driving a late nineteenth-century vehicle supplied by Sid James, Main Wilson recruited the BBC's famous commentary team of Brian Johnston and Raymond Baxter, who pre-recorded their contributions to the show. Some people claimed their presence had prompted them to listen when they might not have done so, while others felt the voices 'added considerably to the fun'.[8]

Occasionally Galton and Simpson would pen a script which strayed away from the normal straight half hour show; the first of these was 'The Hancock Festival', consisting of three playlets performed by Hancock and his fellow actors and written in the style of Somerset Maugham by A. Somerset Hancock. Some fans of the programme saw this departure from the normal format as a refreshing break, while the writers themselves feel it happened, probably, through desperation. 'Already after four episodes we ran into problems with storylines,' says Alan Simpson. 'When we couldn't think of anything, we'd write a script based around a little repertory company. We did one based on the film *The Blackboard Jungle*; these were all little techniques that we fell back on. We did the East Cheam Repertory Company about three times. Ideas would last for half a script and then disappear—they didn't have the legs for a full plot.'

But nothing was ever wasted. Alan explains: 'We'd write all these half-ideas down and after a couple of years we'd have two or three sheets of paper full of half-ideas.' Before they ever started a new script, they'd glance through the list. 'Sometimes coming back to it you had the angle to extend it, or sometimes we'd take two and find out that together they'd make a whole show.'

When short of plots, turning to these parody-style shows was an easy option for Galton and Simpson, who'd cut their comedy writing teeth on a similar format: the sketch based on Henry Morgan, the pirate, which had been influenced by Frank Muir and Denis Norden's successful show *Take It From Here*. Another tool they used from time to time, which also helped them whenever a plot was flagging, was the dream sequence. A notable example was heard in the 1956 episode, 'The Diary', where Hancock, while flipping through his 1956 diary, imagines himself as a surgeon, lion-tamer and test pilot; it was during this sequence that one of the most famous sketches of the entire show, 'The Test Pilot', was heard.

Hancock is a test pilot, flying a newly designed aircraft. He receives a call from the control tower. The character Snide is played by Kenneth Williams.

AIR CONTROLLER: Control tower, control tower to Hancock. We're worried about possible sabotage: the mechanic who was working on your aircraft is missing—think you should come down. Land immediately. Repeat: LAND IMMEDIATELY.
HANCOCK: Nonsense, she's going beautifully. I

don't know a thing about a mechanic. Taking her up to 2400 miles an hour.

(Repeated knocks are heard on the cockpit)

HANCOCK: Hancock to control tower. Something strange is happening, there's a peculiar knocking sound on the windscreen.

(Repeated knock)

HANCOCK: Seems to be coming from outside the plane. Am slowing down to 1800 miles an hour. Will slide cockpit open to see what's wrong.

(Slides cockpit open)

SNIDE: Good evening. It ain't half cold out here, can I come in?

HANCOCK: What's that?

SNIDE: I say, it ain't half cold out here, can I come in?

HANCOCK: There's no room, get off.

SNIDE: Oh, don't be like that. Move over. I'll sit on your lap.

HANCOCK: Get your boot off my joystick—do you mind! Who are you?

SNIDE: Me? I'm a mechanic. I was still working on the tail when you took off. Honestly, frightened the life out of me. I mean, I wasn't expecting it. I was just sitting there singing happily to myself and then next minute, WHOOSH!, I was up here.

HANCOCK: Sit still, I can't control the plane with you jumping about.

SNIDE: Oh, I'm only trying to get comfortable. All these knobs and levers here, sticking in me. 'Ere, what's this one?

HANCOCK: Don't touch it!

(Bang)

SNIDE: Ooh, it's the ejector seat. Come back, where are you?

69

HANCOCK: *(off mike)* I'm out here, sitting on the tail.

SNIDE: Now, stop messin' about. Now come back in. It's no use sitting out there sulking. I can't drive the thing.

HANCOCK: *(off mike)* Well go into a dive so I can slide down.

SNIDE: All right. I'll try this lever.

(Bang)

SNIDE: Hello. You might have told me there was another ejector seat.

As the first series of *Hancock's Half Hour* progressed, it was steadily increasing in popularity: audience figures for the first five episodes averaged just under five million per instalment, while the final five in the series attracted nearly 6.3 million. Meanwhile, the BBC's Audience Research Department was the bearer of more good news: it had calculated that the show's appreciation index had now reached 69, with nine other broadcasts in the series averaging 64; this was reassuring to hear. Comments from the audience sample were encouraging for the longevity of the show. As a Methodist minister enthused: 'This has been the funniest thing on radio recently. All good fun and no crooners or jazz. No rowdiness.'[11]

By the time the curtain fell after the transmission of 'The End of the Series', a second series of *Hancock's Half Hour* had already been commissioned, to exploit the buoyant atmosphere surrounding this new-style comedy. No one could have foreseen the troubles which lay ahead.

Chapter 5

The success of the first radio series bode well for the new season. It was of paramount importance to cash in on the public's growing enthusiasm so the first recording of the next series of *Hancock's Half Hour* was scheduled for 17 April 1955, just two months after the end of series one. Another positive for the show's long-term development was the decision to transmit a repeat the following Sunday, five days after the original broadcast, which pleased producer Dennis Main Wilson who'd been fighting for this for some time.

All but one of the episodes were repeated the Sunday following the original Tuesday transmission. The only episode not to receive a second airing was 'The Three Sons', which was inspired by the French film, *The Sheep Has Five Legs*, starring Fernandel. In the episode, a dying Ebadiah Hancock wants to see his three sons before his death, so sends his butler to find them. One of his offspring has turned into an incompetent sailor who sailed his ship into a mine. On 16 June a naval disaster shocked the country: while taking part in a training exercise in Portland Harbour, a sizeable explosion tore apart the submarine HMS *Sidon*, killing thirteen people. After the episode's initial transmission on Tuesday, 21 June, the BBC switchboards lit up with listeners complaining that the transmission of such a storyline was in bad taste, considering recent events.

At this stage, everything was in place for the new series, or so it seemed. Before the first recording, though, the programme's entire future was placed in jeopardy when Tony Hancock, who had been appearing at London's Adelphi Theatre in *The Talk of the Town* since November 1954, slipped quietly into the cool April night and jetted off to Italy. The long theatre run had taken its toll: Hancock, a perfectionist, a performer who was always striving to better his last performance, had reached the end of his tether. Suffering physical and mental exhaustion, he saw little alternative but to escape the pressures of daily and, sometimes, twice-daily performances. He failed to discuss this major decision with Dennis Main Wilson, who only discovered Hancock was missing when he popped round to the theatre one evening to show him the first script of the new series.

'I wanted to show Tony how the boys had developed in the weeks since the end of the previous series,' Main Wilson explains. It was eight o'clock in the evening by the time he reached the stage door at the Adelphi:

Old Toothless Fred, the stage doorman, told me the boy [Tony Hancock] had gone. I said to him: 'He can't have gone, they haven't done the finale for the first house yet.' But Fred told me that he couldn't take any more so walked off stage and had gone, which meant they had to call Dickie Henderson Jnr [his understudy] to take over his spot for the second house. We had the audience booked, the studio booked and this was Friday—we were doing the first of the series on Sunday.[1]

Desperate to find out what had happened to his star performer, Main Wilson raced down to Jimmy Edwards' dressing room, but he didn't know where Hancock had gone. While the performers were called for the second house, Main Wilson scoured the local pubs—but still no sign of Hancock. Knowing he needed to search further afield, he waited for Jimmy Edwards to come off stage and then Main Wilson and Edwards visited every nightclub and pub the two used to frequent together. No one knew of the actor's whereabouts, not even Hancock's wife, Cicely, or his agent, Jack Adams.

By the time an exhausted Main Wilson returned home the clock had just struck four, but the stillness of the night was disturbed when the phone rang. It was his good friend, 'Ginger' Rose, the Chief Superintendent of Special Branch at Scotland Yard. Only a few days previously, Main Wilson had bumped into Rose outside Aeolian Hall in Bond Street. Main Wilson told Rose about the new Hancock series and offered him tickets to visit the studio and watch the first recording. Rose's question, in the early hours of the morning, stunned Main Wilson. 'What's the bloke we're going to see on Sunday doing catching the last plane to Rome? Do you want him followed?'

Later, the Italian police confirmed that Hancock had booked into a hotel in Rome before hiring a car and driving south to the picturesque village of Positano on the Neapolitan Riviera, where multicoloured villas cling to the side of a cliff, a town which, later, became known as a refuge for artists during the sixties.

Problems had surfaced between George Black Limited, with whom Hancock was under contract while appearing at the Adelphi in *The Talk of the Town*, and the BBC. On 4 April 1955, Laurence Hill, a representative of Black's, wrote to Hancock's agent, referring to a discussion they had held concerning Tony's 'indisposition', for which a certificate had been produced. They felt his recovery would be hampered by appearing on the radio in the new series, and that it wouldn't go down well with their customers if Hancock was deemed unfit to appear on stage when he was fit enough to perform on the radio. They asked Adams for confirmation that Hancock wouldn't complete any broadcasts without their prior consent. The BBC's view was that George Black Limited had rescinded the permission they had granted Hancock, which had originally enabled him to sign the contract with the Beeb. Patrick Newman of the BBC pointed out that there was still a faint possibility of Tony Hancock returning from abroad and being ready to complete the opening programme, which would presumably mean he would be sufficiently fit to have returned to the Adelphi Theatre. However, as Newman advised Adams:

Since there is a very considerable element of doubt here, you will appreciate that we cannot possibly wait until the last moment but must make other plans to cope with the eventuality that he may not in fact be available. You will realise that we have been put to considerable inconvenience over all this (and it may turn out that we shall also be put to additional expense) and though we are hoping to have Tony back with us fit and well as soon as possible, we are nevertheless putting alternative arrangements in hand.[2]

Newman followed up his letter with a phone call on 18 April, informing Jack Adams that the BBC must know by Wednesday, 20 April if Hancock would be available for programme three in the series, and by the 27th for the fourth show.

Whether the exact dates of when Hancock actually left the production will ever be confirmed, only time will tell, but while Hancock took refuge, Dennis Main Wilson faced one of the biggest dilemmas of his career. Too much expense had already been involved to justify cancelling the series until Hancock eventually returned from Italy, so there was no alternative but to find a replacement actor. When Main Wilson phoned Alan Simpson and Ray Galton, the writers weren't overly surprised to hear of Hancock's disappearance. Alan says: 'Tony had these problems working in the theatre. I don't know if he realised that the radio series was about to start, but he must have just had a minor nervous breakdown. He had missed performances before at the Adelphi under similar circumstances.'

After considering his options, Dennis Main Wilson decided he wanted Harry Secombe, who was working on *The Goon Show*, and approached the producer, Peter Eton. He had no objection to Secombe covering for the absent Hancock, and generously rearranged rehearsal times to enable him to record *Hancock's Half Hour*. Next, Main Wilson phoned Secombe's agent, Jimmy Grafton, who, although not entirely satisfied with the situation, gave permission for Main Wilson to approach Secombe direct with the request.

Secombe was at the Camden Theatre rehearsing *The Goon Show* when an overwrought Dennis Main Wilson called, asking him to step into Hancock's shoes for the opening episode of the new series. Secombe recalled the conversation in his autobiography. 'I knew Tony Hancock well, but I also knew that his timing and delivery were different to mine and before I read the Ray Galton and Alan Simpson script I was afraid it might not work as well with me in a role that had been tailor-made for Tony. As it turned out, the script was so beautifully written and the supporting cast of Sid James, Bill Kerr and Kenneth Williams was so strong in performance, that anyone could have done it.'[3]

With Secombe saving the day, the first episode, 'A Holiday in France', was recorded at the Camden Theatre on 17 April 1955 between 9.30 and 10.15 p.m. The story saw Harry and Bill taking a train journey to Southend-on-Sea but ending up in Paris. While attending a fancy-dress party, Harry meets a young lady who takes a shine to him; later, upon returning to British shores, Harry learns that he's inadvertently smuggled in the French girl within his luggage. The episode was used to introduce Andrée Melly, who'd replaced the pregnant Moira Lister.

Andrée—sister of the jazz legend, George Melly—was born in Liverpool in 1932; after being educated in the city and in Switzerland, she began her acting career in repertory theatre at Bromley, and had already made her big-screen début by the time she joined the cast of *Hancock's Half Hour*, at the age of 23. On stage, she was already a leading lady, having attracted much publicity for her role in *The Moon is Blue*. When offered the role in *Hancock's Half Hour*, she hadn't heard of Tony Hancock or the radio series.

> At that time in my career I wanted to do anything and everything, to feel I was in demand. When I received the first script, with the opening line of 'H-H-H-H-ancock's Half Hour', I thought: 'What the hell is this!' On the written page it didn't look right, it wasn't gagged, but as soon as I heard Hancock do it, it worked. Normally when you read a comedy script you can spot the laughs, but Galton and Simpson's scripts weren't like that, it was all about what Tony did with it. The writers knew what he needed in order to make the character work.

Andrée thinks she got the part because she had a French-sounding name. 'I played the character with a French accent, although not a very good one. The accent didn't really work, though, so it was dropped for my second series.'

The opening episode, broadcast on Tuesday, 19 April, was heard by 4.1 million people, the smallest audience to date. Thereafter, the remaining 10 episodes in the series averaged an audience of just over five million, although none was to eclipse 'The Marriage Bureau', the penultimate show in the first season, which was heard by 6.8 million listeners. Although from a professional viewpoint Dennis Main Wilson would have been concerned and, perhaps, disappointed that the audience figures had, on average, declined slightly, the anxiety and tension he was feeling as a result of Hancock's unauthorised trip abroad dissipated with every minute Harry Secombe spent uttering his lines into the microphone; he was relieved that, at the eleventh hour, he'd been able to find another performer capable, and willing, to step into a difficult situation. Although it had been too late to alter the script for the first episode to accommodate Secombe, it was necessary to at least explain Hancock's absence and Secombe's presence in the episode, so Galton and Simpson amended the introductory announcement read by Adrian Waller.

ADRIAN: This is the BBC Light Programme.
(*Opening signature*)
ADRIAN: We present Bill Kerr, Sidney James, Andrée Melly and Kenneth Williams in . . . *Hancock's Half Hour*.
(*Theme up*)
ADRIAN: And in place of Tony Hancock who is indisposed—meet Harry Secombe!
(*Theme up*)
ADRIAN: I personally was working on Easter Monday, but Bill Kerr? Oh no. At the end of the last series he left Tony Hancock in England and spent a holiday in Paris with . . . well he says it was with a great friend of his . . . Harry Secombe. But even these good things had to come to an end . . .
(*Theme up*)

When it came to episodes two and three, Galton and Simpson were able to pen scripts with

Secombe in mind. Secombe rose to the challenge. Reflecting on his performance, Dennis Main Wilson said: 'The first one was like a Goons show, the second one he got the hang of it and by the third one Harry showed, potentially, what a fabulous comedy actor he was; it's a shame he never developed it, but he didn't want to.'[4]

The BBC were lucky to secure Secombe for the first four episodes because, from the initial conversation Dennis Main Wilson had with Secombe's agent, Jimmy Grafton, and the performer himself, it was stressed that Secombe's agreement to join the cast of *Hancock's Half Hour* was purely for one episode. The day after the opening episode was aired, and with no sign of Hancock's return, Main Wilson approached Grafton again, hoping he could persuade Secombe to remain with the show; his request was not favourably received. The following morning at his office, Jimmy Grafton typed a letter to Jim Davidson, assistant head of variety, and hand delivered it to his BBC office at Aeolian Hall in Bond Street. He confirmed what Main Wilson had been told when he first requested the services of Secombe. Grafton explained to Davidson that he'd received a late and 'somewhat unhappily conducted'[5] phone call from Main Wilson the previous evening requesting Secombe did a further three episodes of *Hancock's Half Hour*. Grafton stressed: 'I have continually emphasized to him that Harry would only do one programme and I hoped that this decision would be passed on. I have not been in touch with Harry and he reiterates his decision.'[6] Knowing the BBC would be facing major problems if they couldn't persuade Secombe to change his mind, Davidson phoned Grafton on Thursday 21st April and after a protracted conversation finally managed to secure Secombe for another three episodes, by which time it was hoped Hancock would be fit enough to return to the series. On the bottom of Grafton's original letter, Davidson scribbled a record of his conversation, stating: 'We have promised him [Secombe] his own series in the 4th quarter 1955 or 1st quarter 1956 in which he will sing.'[7]

In his 1996 autobiography, Harry Secombe recalled the occasion when, after the transmission of the second episode, a delighted Dennis Main Wilson hinted that, perhaps, he could take over the remainder of the series. He said: 'It was a real pleasure to perform those three scripts . . . I admit I was tempted but Tony was an old friend and I had enough on my plate with the *Goon Show*, so that was that.'

Hancock returned to the show in the fourth episode, 'A Visit to Swansea', which was recorded on 8 May 1955. Just before his return, he spoke to journalist Anthony Carthew about the incident, the second in two years at the Adelphi Theatre. (Earlier, in 1953, he'd encountered problems in *London Laughs*, which he blamed on the strain of twice-nightly performances at a time when he didn't feel ready for the West End.) Hancock treated every performance as if it were the first night, generating a self-induced pressure and tension that would last as long as the show; if the run was lengthy, there was potential for the pressure to become so unbearable it culminated either in illness or in a situation from which Hancock had to escape. He told Carthew: 'I think I am fit enough to cope with a broadcast again, but I shall have to be very leisurely about it.'[8] Enduring such a gruelling schedule—he had been working almost non-stop since 1952, with BBC recordings occupying weekends, as well as long-running stage engagements—was inevitably going to take its toll.

Before recording the fourth of the series, Tony Hancock travelled to Shrewsbury, where Harry Secombe was appearing in theatre, to thank him for covering during his absence. Secombe didn't feel it was right to enquire as to his whereabouts during the previous weeks, and Hancock offered no explanation. Galton and Simpson's occasional reference to real-life issues was in evidence in this episode, with Andrée (to whom Hancock had taken an instant liking) and Bill continually probing Hancock about his absence, which he explains was due to a severe cold; then, after explaining that Harry, who has now returned to life in the coal mines, did such a good job in the show that he should thank him personally, they travel to Wales. Hancock assures Secombe that he'll never miss another show, but when his back seizes up after hours spent crawling around the mine shafts, Secombe is almost called upon to step in one final time.

Nearly a million more people listened to Hancock's return. When the BBC completed their research report, it was clear most listeners were pleased that Hancock was back. Many people felt the entire cast had worked well to help Hancock settle back into his role, with particular praise going to Kenneth Williams, whose character voices were increasingly appreciated by the audience. In some episodes, Williams, whose fee had risen from two guineas to 12 guineas for this series, was playing several characters. This deflected Simpson and Galton from their original objective: to write a comedy based on situation without relying on funny voices or jokes. 'He got such laughs, though, that we had to keep those funny character voices in,' admits Ray Galton.

Alan agrees. 'We set out to write storylines that would run through with no interruptions, trying to build on the characters, and to get the comedy out of the situation, the characterisations and the interrelationships between those characters, rather than wisecracks, which we thought would play on Hancock's strengths. That went by the board early on with the voices Kenneth brought to the series.' Eventually Kenneth's involvement in the show would diminish, but it was still some time before Galton and Simpson's desire for a reality-driven comedy would come into effect.

In Kenneth Williams, Galton and Simpson saw a complex man, but someone apparently in love with their work. It was only with the publication, in 1993, of the actor's private diaries, that they learnt there was another side to Williams. Alan explains:

Ray and I worked with Ken every week from 1954 to '59—my mother was even very friendly with his mother because they came from the same part of the world. Ken was always a loner, but one never dreamt that he was ever anything other than extremely happy—until thirty years later when we read his diaries. We found it unbelievable, it didn't seem like the same man. All day long he would have everyone in fits of laughter. Hancock would only have to look at him to fall about laughing. Then he'd go home and write about having to perform another dreadful script, but the following Sunday he'd be back laughing. It was like Dr Jekyll and Mr Hyde.

The sixth episode in the series, 'The Chef That Died of Shame', was recorded at the Playhouse Theatre on 23 May and marked a departure from the normal style of episode, with Hancock playing 'Iggins, a pie-stall owner who becomes a celebrity in the world of *haute cuisine* until drink causes his fall from grace. It was an episode Galton and Simpson enjoyed. 'It was very funny,' says Ray. 'In the films you saw great artists suffering from drink, but you don't associate a pie-stall cook with that fate.' Pie stalls were in vogue when the writers were growing up. 'The most famous one in my memory was at Chelsea Bridge, where you'd see people in evening dress, at one in the morning; the stalls would open all night and sell everything from steak and kidney pies to sausage or bacon sandwiches.'

Although this one-off episode, in which the cast left their regular characters behind for a week, was enjoyed by the writers and many of the sample audience, some people weren't entirely enamoured of the script. The Audience Research Department focused specifically on the listeners' comments concerning the new style of show. One listener questioned the change in format, asking: 'Why the new idea? The other type of scripts was far superior. Easily the poorest show yet.'[9] A bank official stated: 'A very poor change from the usual. It might have been a good idea but it didn't work out. The script was unfunny and tedious, the characters were colourless and unconvincing and the cast seemed uncertain and at sea.' But these views were marginally outweighed by favourable comments. One listener claimed: 'This was an outstanding script which made a refreshing and successful attempt to get away from the formula which most shows of this kind seem to have worked to over the last few years,' while another felt it was 'unusual but very acceptable'. However, he added, the only ingredient missing from this successful episode was the 'confidential chat' between Hancock and the 'unknown'. He didn't want to see this element of the show dropped. Unfortunately he would be disappointed, as would thousands of other listeners, because the nameless character who listened to Hancock's various monologues, with just the occasional utterance, did disappear from the scripts. Alan Simpson, who brought this anonymous man to life, says 'It was funny at the time, but it had reached its natural end.'

Another character who emerged as a regular during the second series, and who would eventually be dropped, despite being popular with the audience, was Snide. The character's origins date back to the fourth episode, 'A Visit to Swansea', where Williams is heard aggravating Hancock at the railway station's ticket office. But the character's name isn't seen in the scripts until 'Prime Minister Hancock', the seventh of the series, which denotes Snide's official début. Having decided to stand for Parliament, Hancock is out canvassing votes with Bill and Andrée, who's using her feminine charms as a form of persuasion, much to Hancock's disgust— at first.

TONY: Andrée, what did you do? What went on in there?

ANDRÉE: What does it matter, Tony? He's going to vote for us.

TONY: It's disgusting. I have no desire to get votes that way. It undermines the whole structure of the British electoral system. I'm very ashamed of you.

BILL: Well come on, let's try next door.

(*Knock on door. Door opens*)

KENNETH: (*Snide*) Yes?

TONY: Good evening. I'm Anthony Hancock, your local candidate. Can I count on your vote?

KENNETH: Er, no I don't think so. I'm very sorry . . .

TONY: Andrée, I'll go and have a cup of tea, you've got ten minutes.

(*Later*)

BILL: About time she came out of that house isn't it?

TONY: Give her a chance.

BILL: She's been in there three hours.

TONY: Perhaps she's having trouble persuading him.

In the next episode, 'The Rail Strike', Snide plays a more prominent role as a rail passenger who's foolish enough to use Sid and Hancock's train during the national rail strike.

BILL: Come back, you lazy lot of perishers. Now listen. There'll be a train coming in on platform four in just a few minutes. The 10.23 relief train calling at all stations to Brighton. So get those beds wrapped up, pull those tents down, and stamp these fires out. That's all. Roger and out.

85

KENNETH: (*Snide*) This is most unusual. They've never had a 10.23 to Brighton since *I've* been travelling on this line. Have you heard anything about it, Miss?

ANDRÉE: I'm afraid not, Monsieur. But I'm glad it's running, my friends in Brighton will be wondering what's happened to me.

KENNETH: Oh, so you're going to Brighton as well?

ANDRÉE: Yes, I am.

KENNETH: Well so am I, isn't that lucky.

ANDRÉE: (*Dubious*) Yes.

KENNETH: Here, you're French, aren't you?

ANDRÉE: Yes.

KENNETH: (*Sly laugh*) French, eh? Oh good, cos . . . cos my wife doesn't understand me, you know.

ANDRÉE: You should speak more plainly.

KENNETH: Oh don't be like that. Here, I'm a commercial traveller, you know.

ANDRÉE: Really?

KENNETH: Yes. I travel in suitcases.

ANDRÉE: Do you?

KENNETH: Yes, well it saves renting a room. Har har. It saves renting a room . . . cor dear. Cos we've got a lot of jokes like that, us travellers have you know. I bet you know some good jokes . . . being French and that, eh what? Eh? Cor (*Laughs*)

ANDRÉE: (*Sour laugh*)

KENNETH: We're going to have a lot of fun travelling down to Brighton together, aren't we? I think you'll enjoy my company, cos I'm a bit of a ladies' man as I expect you've noticed.

ANDRÉE: No.

KENNETH: Oh, I am cor, I'm a bit of a devil when I get going. Many a time the communication cord's

86

been pulled out when I'm on board, I tell you. Here wait a minute—can you hear something?

ANDRÉE: Yes, I think the train's coming, thank goodness.

KENNETH: You're right, it's just coming round the bend.

(*Effects: rocking, chugging along, approaching hiss of steam, etc.*)

KENNETH: Blimey, what's this? I don't believe it. I'm going potty. I'm seeing things, tell me I'm seeing things. What is it?

ANDRÉE: It's a train . . . isn't it?

BILL: The thing now arriving on platform four is definitely a train, whatever you may think. It's the 10.23 special calling at all stations to Haywards Heath. The front two bathtubs for Brighton . . . the pram and the wheelchair for Worthing. Get your tickets off the little fat guy on the train.

(*Effects: Train stops with hiss of steam*)

Kenneth Williams' character portrayals always went down well with the listening audience, but one particular voice elicited an even greater response. As a result, Galton and Simpson wrote him into the scripts on a regular basis. Fans of the programme began to view Snide as an integral part of the show, eagerly awaiting his entrance each week. 'Tony worked with him beautifully,' says Alan Simpson. 'He was such an irritating character and we used him for ages.'

Later reflecting on the role he was asked to play, Williams said: 'Galton and Simpson said they wanted someone who creeps up on you, and it went awfully well. It was always an eleventh-hour advent: they'd have me come in just before the programme came to its conclusion—they thought it gave it a lift, but Hancock didn't much like the character and in the end he wanted it out.'[10]

The use of such comic-cut characters meant that the writers were far from achieving their original aim; instead, they were exploiting every tool possible in pursuit of laughs. Another factor also shackling their drive towards realism was the frequent use of incredible storylines, such as those in 'Prime Minister Hancock' and, in particular, 'The Rail Strike'. Such improbable tales would remain throughout the life of the radio programme, albeit less regularly as the series progressed. They would occasionally be cloaked by the idea of Hancock living out such bizarre situations within a dream. In other radio episodes Hancock becomes a barrister, a surgeon or a bullfighter, even though he remains at the same time an actor, if a second-rate one. Worrying about such matters as continuity was less important to listeners in the days of *Hancock's Half Hour*; present day fans would be writing to production offices questioning such obvious changes. 'It never bothered us when we altered his profession,' admits Ray Galton. 'When you're writing all the time it's often a problem finding storylines, so when you think of one you want to use it. Over the years we dropped the more absurd and childish storylines, but before doing that, some weeks Hancock would have money, others he wouldn't; some weeks he was a star, others he wasn't; some weeks he was a lawyer, others an actor; some weeks he lived in a flat, others in a house—no one, on radio or television, ever thought it was strange, but you couldn't do it now. Back then, the public didn't question the more outlandish episodes.'

The final episode of series two was transmitted on Tuesday, 5 July 1955, by which time a third season had already been commissioned. What had started off as a fraught, worrying series for those involved in the show, due to Hancock's unexplained absence, had turned out to everyone's satisfaction. However, average audience figures of 4.86 million per episode were lower than those for the first series and would be easily capped by the instalments in the third season, where some episodes topped the seven million mark for the first time.

Chapter 6

By the time the opening instalment of series three was recorded at the Fortune Theatre on 16 October 1955, Galton and Simpson were nearly halfway through the exclusive three-year BBC contract signed the previous July. They agreed to supply the Beeb with thirty 30-minute sound or television shows; remuneration started at 75 guineas per episode, rising to 85 by the end of the contract. Their earnings, however, could be significantly boosted. An initial repeat broadcast attracted an additional full fee, with a subsequent full payment being made whenever instalments were accepted by the BBC's Transcription Services, a branch of the Beeb which offered apposite episodes to overseas radio stations for an agreed period.

The third season of *Hancock's Half Hour* was the first of three, comprising 20 episodes and placing, one would imagine, inordinate amounts of pressure on Galton and Simpson; despite admitting to enjoying flexible working hours, they beavered away in their office each day turning out a succession of scripts which needed minimal amounts of editing. Normally arriving at their Shepherd's Bush offices by 11 a.m., they would work until 7 p.m. 'Most of the work was completed during the afternoon,' recalls Alan Simpson, 'while the morning—what was left of it—would be taken up with discussion—anything rather than getting it down on paper, I suppose.' They sat around a large desk, with Alan in charge of the typewriter, and the sound of keys wasn't heard until both were satisfied with the lines. 'In our heyday we were writing forty shows a year and taking a month's holiday. Eventually when the television series came along, we'd alternate between the two media, as well as slipping a Bernard Braden series in between. Nowadays people would say it was impossible, but no one told us that—we thought it was normal.'

Reflecting on their output, Ray Galton finds it hard to believe they turned out so many scripts, and doesn't recall feeling the strain. 'Stress didn't come into it; I don't think we'd heard of the word in those days. We'd go into the office and had hardly been in there five minutes when we'd break for lunch. We'd often eat, drink and be merry with Eric Sykes and Spike Milligan and then return to work. If I did that now, I'd fall asleep!'

Generating enough storylines to fill a 20-episode run was no mean feat. 'It was entirely down to us what we wrote, but it was always difficult, especially when you're doing such a long series,' says Alan Simpson. 'It was a godsend when you had a particular date to focus on, such as Christmas or Valentine's Day, because you didn't have to worry about the subject for that week.'

The ideas for their storylines came from every conceivable source; the writers even gained inspiration from a script they saw while visiting Derek Roy's house, and turned it into 'The Christmas Eve Party', which was broadcast during the first series. The plot revolved around Hancock's appearance in court for running a noisy party. While the prosecution explained what had happened, the listener eavesdropped on a raucous party with people destroying the house. Back at the court, Hancock gave his version of events, describing the evening as a discreet affair. 'We saw the script when we first met Derek Roy and just remembered it. Of course it doesn't matter where the plot comes from, it's what you do with it that matters,' states Ray Galton, who also recalls times when it seemed an idea would never come.

'Some days would be easy, others hard. I remember when we were writing scripts for the *Comedy Playhouse*. Come Friday night, when we should have delivered the script to the BBC because it was being recorded on the Sunday, we hadn't even started. Then, the girl on the switchboard contacted us to say the actor Graham Stark was downstairs and wanted to see us. People often popped in to see us but we'd told everyone not to let anyone up to see us because we were up against it. By then, though, we said, "Oh, sod it, let him come up." We had a chat and then he told us about this funny story he'd read in the paper the previous day. He got this little cutting out of his pocket, it was just three or four lines about two cars that met in a narrow lane in Cornwall and neither driver would back up. I remember we both said: "That's it! That's it!" We took him around the pub and came in on Saturday morning and wrote for four hours non-stop. In fact, the script, which was titled "Impasse", wrote itself.'

The same cast of Hancock, Sid James, Bill Kerr, Kenneth Williams, Andrée Melly (minus her French accent) and Alan Simpson, who was still providing occasional background voices, brought the series to life with 'The Pet Dog', 'The Jewel Robbery' and 'The Bequest'. In the third episode,

Hancock only discovers he had an Uncle Ebadiah when a solicitor's letter arrives announcing his death and that Hancock will be £40,000 richer if he finds a bride. The episode illuminates successfully many of the character's personality traits, including his belief that royal blood runs through his veins, his lack of self-confidence (particularly with the opposite sex), and his pompous attitude to life: in one scene Bill suggests to Hancock that they visit the local Palais to try and find a partner so he can claim his inheritance.

HANCOCK: The Palais? That's where they do all that modern dancing, isn't it?
BILL: Yeah!
HANCOCK: Well, I'm sorry, I'm having no part in those sort of goings-on. I do not hold with this modern dancing. I don't mind the lancers or an occasional gavotte, where you hold the young lady at a respectable distance, but I'm having none of this close-up work.

Storylines within the third series still contained a sprinkling of incredible scenarios and paid little attention to continuity. It would not be until the final series, in late 1959, by which time the television series was also in full swing, that Galton and Simpson's radio scripts would contain the degree of realism they had originally intended.

One episode which received an unusual amount of criticism when the Audience Research Department conducted their regular survey of listeners' opinions was 'The Red Planet'. The cause of the complaints wasn't the storyline or performance of the actors, both of which met with approval, but the hysterical laughter heard from members of the studio audience. One person felt the episode was spoilt by this 'high-pitched laughter'.[1] Dennis Main Wilson felt it necessary to write to the Head of Variety to express his concerns, pointing out that this series was the first he'd worked on where he deemed it necessary to ask the studio manager to restrain audience laughter. It hadn't been easy. He explained that 'with some of the mad hysterical fan audiences we have had this has often proved extremely difficult'.[2] Main Wilson took steps to prevent such occurrences: he relocated the audience microphone, asked studio supervisors to ensure that 'no hysterical-looking bobby-soxers get near to the front of the theatre'[3] and spoke directly to each audience, asking them to refrain from applause or hysteria after gags. Main Wilson warned his superior that the following episode, 'The New Year Resolutions', still contained a fair amount of applause for gags, but assured him that he'd try and eliminate most of the incidents during the editing process. He felt helpless, however, to prevent a recurrence of the problem, stating that 'short of barring these hysterical guardians of Britain's future from the studio, I don't see what else we can do'.[4]

Hancock's Half Hour reached its acme during the third series with three episodes—'How Hancock Won the War', 'The Greyhound Track' and 'The Conjurer'—attracting audiences of over seven million, while more than 50 per cent of the shows had viewing figures topping six million, including 'The Blackboard Jungle', a skit on the 1955 Glenn Ford movie of the same name, for which the BBC obtained permission to use the original theme tune (Bill Haley and the Comets' 'Rock Around the Clock') as incidental music.

It was rare for a member of the public to object to the content of a particular *Hancock's Half Hour* script, but the broadcasting of 'The Blackboard Jungle', spotlighting a young teacher trying to educate a school of juvenile delinquents, caused a handful of listeners to complain. When the letters were referred to Main Wilson, the producer was forthright in his assessment of the situation in his reply to the Assistant Head of Variety, claiming that much of the 'calligraphy is obviously neurotic'.[5] Main Wilson was keen to point out that the aim of Hancock was to be different, to present a 'satire on real life today.' He confirmed that *Hancock's Half Hour* must be controversial, which wouldn't satisfy everyone, but was far better than if it were to become just another run-of-the-mill radio series.

The dawning of 1956 was greeted with the aptly named episode 'The New Year Resolutions', with Hancock still suffering from extreme bouts of gullibility. This time, he agrees to run Sid's nightclub, The Tres Flamingoes Rouge, but ends up being arrested when the establishment is raided by police. If Hancock's character traits remained unchanged, the same couldn't be said about the show's development. The twelve months of 1956 marked a landmark period for *Hancock's Half Hour*, with a crucial juncture being reached which would shape the future. By the end of the year, Hancock would not only be recording the fourth radio series, but would have transferred his talents to the small screen, dividing his services between

Associated-Rediffusion, for ITV, and the BBC.

Before his move into television, the intervening period between radio series had been little more than two months, but to accommodate Hancock's burgeoning workload, nearly eight months elapsed between the closing episode of the third season, 'The Test Match', heard on 29 February, and the opening show in series four, 'Back from Holiday', broadcast on Sunday, 14 October.

Amidst all the activity, the year was blighted somewhat by wranglings involving Jack Hylton, under whom Hancock was still contracted for stage appearances, and the BBC. As well as wanting Hancock to commit to another radio series, the BBC had started formulating plans for the transfer to television, hoping to screen the new series before the end of the year. Hylton considered that his contract with Hancock extended beyond stage work to include other media as well, and wanted the artist for a series with the newly formed Independent Television Network. Discussions between Jack Hylton and Hancock's agent, Jack Adams, regarding the programme for commercial television had been proceeding since 1955. Hylton had launched his own television production company to make programmes for Associated-Rediffusion and wanted Hancock's first television series to be on the commercial channel; the principal sticking point was securing the services of Galton and Simpson to write the show. On 19 August 1955, after discussing scriptwriters with Hancock, Jack Adams told Hylton that it would be 'impossible for him [Hancock] to work with writers other than Galton and Simpson as these two writers have worked with him as a team to build up his radio show as one of the top comedy shows on the air, and they are part and parcel of his success.'[6] Adams reminded Hylton that when he accepted the terms of the commercial television project on behalf of Hancock, it was on the understanding that Galton and Simpson would be hired as writers.

Hancock visited his solicitor to establish where he stood legally in the contract he'd signed with Jack Hylton. On 30 September, Adams told Hylton that Hancock's concerns were largely as a result of his venture into a new medium (although Hancock had worked on television before, these were largely one-off appearances in variety shows), and that he didn't want to stop further negotiation; Adams confirmed that Hancock would consider working with other scriptwriters, if necessary, and asked who Hylton had in mind. Hylton was still keen to secure the services of Galton and Simpson and, in early 1956, phoned William Streeton, Head of Programme Contracts at the BBC, suggesting a compromise. Hylton, once again, confirmed his belief that he held a contract which secured Hancock's exclusive services in television and that would also prevent him signing a further sound broadcasting contract. In return for allowing Hancock to undertake the BBC sound and television series, Hylton wanted Galton and Simpson to be allowed to write six television programmes for the first ITV series, which he hoped would be transmitted during April. Streeton, who acknowledged the proposal's merit, communicated details of the call to controllers and heads of departments in a memo dated 3 February. Three days later, a reply from Ronald Waldman,

Head of Light Entertainment (Television), landed on Streeton's desk: confirming an earlier phone conversation, he said it was his belief, from conversations he'd had with Jack Adams, that Hylton's hold over Hancock wasn't as restrictive as he led them to believe. He asked to be kept informed because he wanted to transmit the first BBC television series fortnightly from the end of May. As it transpired, it was early July before the first episode was seen.

Galton and Simpson had undertaken not to write for commercial television, so when, during the summer of 1955, they asked about writing for Hancock in his proposed commercial television venture, it was no surprise when the Corporation declined their request. Upon hearing of Hylton's compromise, one head of department felt that on the surface it appeared a fair deal. However, she questioned the feasibility, considering the demands the BBC would be placing on the shoulders of Messrs Galton and Simpson. In reply to Streeton's memo of 3 February, she stated:

I cannot see how two writers can do thirty 30-minute sound variety programmes . . . plus 6 BBC television shows at fortnightly intervals plus 6 commercial television shows. It does not seem to me possible to get this amount of work out of two writers in the course of a year.[7]

If schedules had dictated the need to write the shows simultaneously, her views would have been justified, but although Galton and Simpson wrote scripts for both media successfully for three years, the sound and television series never overlapped. It was, however, something the BBC had considered, briefly, in 1957 but the writers' response halted the idea in its tracks. A handwritten, unsigned note dated 15 November in the BBC archives confirms the writers' views. They were quoted as saying:

> Absolutely impossible to write both programmes. Inevitably both series must suffer; it takes us a week to write the TV series and as you already know it took us a week to write the sound series. It would be absolutely impossible for us to undertake to write both.[8]

Although Galton and Simpson were clear about the impossibility of writing more than one script a week, they harboured no concerns about their increasingly busy work schedules and were confident that within the year they could produce scripts for not just their own radio and television series, and for a 12-part Bernard Braden show they had already agreed to do, but for Hylton's commercial series, too. Others didn't share their optimism, including the BBC's Head of Variety, Pat Hillyard, who was worried the writers would over-commit themselves. After the final episode of the third radio series had been aired on 29 February, Galton and Simpson felt they had sufficient time to write the scripts for Hylton; expecting to complete the work by the end of March, it would, in their view, leave sufficient time to begin work on the Braden radio show, which would begin transmission on Tuesday, 24 April. Aware that they would have to fit in the first television series of *Hancock's Half Hour* as well, Hillyard felt it was impossible: 'I must say that I am not entirely happy about all this, as although Galton and Simpson say that they can carry out these two assignments it often happens that what writers feel they can do and what they actually accomplish are two very different things.'9

As a result of the contractual issues, Tom Sloan, then Assistant Head of Light Entertainment, had to delay *Hancock's Half Hour*'s transfer to the small screen until 6 July. But by the end of March, the situation was clearer: Hancock's agent had reached a compromise with Hylton, whereby Hancock was able to commit to a six-part television series and a new sound series for the BBC, as well as 12 television programmes for Associated-Rediffusion, sandwiched either side of the Beeb's television series. To try and prevent such a complex state of affairs in future, William Streeton stressed the importance of securing Hancock exclusively for the Corporation, attempts which Hancock would always resist. By the end of April 1956, contracts were issued to Tony Hancock for the fourth radio season and the first BBC television series, earning him fees of 65 guineas and £500 per episode respectively.

The first series of Jack Hylton's television show with Associated-Rediffusion, *The Tony Hancock Show*, began transmission on 24 April 1956. Starring alongside Hancock in this sketch-based show were June Whitfield, John Vere and Clive Dunn. With Galton and Simpson still contracted to the BBC and so unable to write the scripts, Hylton pulled in Eric Sykes, who was in New York with Max Bygraves when he received a cable from the impresario. Sykes had already written for Hancock in the radio series, *Educating Archie*, and after

100

discussing the project in depth upon his return, agreed to write six instalments, with sketches broken up by a song from June Whitfield and a dance routine by resident hoofers, The Teenagers.

Meanwhile, preparations were under way for the BBC's first television series of *Hancock's Half Hour*. Ronnie Waldman, then Head of Light Entertainment, gave the responsibility for transferring the show to television to Duncan Wood. With his instinctive knowledge for whether an idea or script would work, as well as discerning eye when it came to casting a show, Wood became a leading television comedy producer. He'd started his BBC career in the regions, based in his home town of Bristol, before moving to London. The relationship he formed with Galton and Simpson extended beyond *Hancock's Half Hour* because he was also at the helm for their next series, *Steptoe and Son*. When they were first introduced to Wood to discuss the upcoming small-screen version of *Hancock's Half Hour*, it didn't take long for the writers to realise they were in safe hands. 'He was a very confident, decisive director,' enthuses Alan Simpson. 'Duncan did virtually everything we wrote for television, so we took his competence for granted. When we wrote our *Comedy Playhouse* series we worked with other directors and were amazed just how unorganised they were; sometimes they were so slow we didn't even get a chance for a dress rehearsal, whereas with Duncan we always did. He was so efficient we normally ended up with around an hour to spare before the show, which gave the cast plenty of time to relax. Everyone respected Duncan, and he was good for Tony, too.'

When the television series was in its infancy, editing was out of the question, so any fluffed lines became a major headache, as Ray recalls. 'First you had to debate whether it was bad enough or not; if it was unacceptable, we had to do a retake, so even if one line was wrong it meant doing the whole scene again, which could mean around ten minutes of the show.' When faced with such a decision, Wood demanded complete silence for a moment while he weighed up the options. 'Unlike other producers, he'd never panic,' says Ray. 'After a few seconds, he'd simply say: "OK, this is what we'll do." He was always in control of the situation.'

The success of the radio series, together with the continuing development of television as a medium, meant that the transfer of *Hancock's Half Hour* to the small screen was a natural progression. Television was blossoming: the launch of commercial television in the early 1950s provided welcome competition as far as viewers and those working in the industry were concerned. While Associated-Rediffusion supplied programmes during the week, ATV stepped in to cover weekend scheduling for viewers in London and the Home Counties. Five months later, ABC provided coverage in the Midland region, followed by Granada in the north. Although it wasn't until 1962 that the ITV network was complete, it nevertheless opened up an array of opportunities for actors, writers and those working behind the camera; the BBC lost a plethora of staff to the new independent channels, enticed by new opportunities and higher salaries. Having to fill the schedules meant more openings for writers and actors, with commercial television offering bigger fees to attract actors and writers of the highest calibre. It was some time before the new channel became a serious competitor to the nationwide coverage offered by the Beeb, but the competition was significant enough for the BBC to boost their programme budgets. The climate was changing rapidly, as Alan Simpson explains:

When we started on radio in 1954, nobody was doing television—certainly comedians weren't because they couldn't afford to as the money on offer was so poor. If you did television, of course, it meant you didn't have time to play the music halls, where the comedians mostly earned their money. The Tony Hancocks, Frankie Howerds and Jimmy Edwards of the entertainment world were on the halls all week making big money; then on a Sunday, their day off, they'd do a radio show. If they did television they'd be rehearsing all week and couldn't go out on the halls—people just couldn't afford it.

Galton and Simpson realised their future lay in television and were eager to begin writing for the medium, so when asked to bring *Hancock's Half Hour* to the screen they jumped at the chance. When they settled down to consider the show's format, they felt it would be foolhardy to alter a winning formula and were keen to retain the basic premise; however, they knew they wouldn't require such a large cast. 'We found that we couldn't put Bill Kerr, Kenneth Williams and Hattie Jacques [Jacques joined the fourth radio series as Hancock's secretary] into the television series on a regular basis—it would be too crowded,' says Ray Galton. As it transpired, Kerr never appeared in the small-screen version, while Jacques and Williams were both seen in just six episodes. 'On radio, of course, you don't see the artists,' adds Ray, 'so they used to sit at the side of the stage when they didn't have any lines and only came up to the microphone when it was their turn. I know one could argue that if they're outside the picture it's the same situation, but somehow it wasn't. To us, it seemed impossible to write a show to include them all, every week, on the screen. So we decided to simplify it.'

'We also realised you didn't need as much happening as on the radio,' says Alan Simpson, 'so we decided to go without Bill, Hattie and Kenneth as regular members of the cast.' As some form of continuity was required if they were to retain the general structure of the show, they decided Hancock's foil would be Sid James. As far as Alan is aware, although the rest were disappointed, no one was too upset about not being carried over to television. 'I think they all accepted it,' he says. 'Hattie had other things going on, and Bill—he was always filming or on stage—accepted the fact that life goes on.'

Rivalry existed between media, even within the BBC, with radio battling with this new, all-encompassing form of entertainment called television. The chiefs of the Light Programme were desperate to safeguard what they perceived as their crown jewels in the schedules, and one of those was certainly *Hancock's Half Hour*. Even if they had wanted to, it would have been impossible to prevent its transfer to television, but those working in radio didn't want to find themselves losing out in terms of audience share. Ultimately this happened, and although fans and critics alike regard many of Hancock's later radio episodes as among the best, the diminution of audience numbers was significant. While the third season averaged 6.28 million listeners per episode, the fourth—which began a month after the first television series had finished—lost over two million listeners, with each episode being heard by just 4.19 million people on average. For the fifth series the figures recovered marginally (average 4.4 million per instalment) but by the time the final radio episode ('The Impersonator' in series six, transmitted on 29 December 1959) was offered to the nation, only 3.44 million people decided to tune in.

On 7 June 1956, just a month before the first BBC television series kicked off, Tom Sloan informed Duncan Wood that the Controller of the Light Programme had permitted them to use the theme tune and programme title; in an attempt to ensure potential audiences were aware that the radio and television versions were separate entities, the controller wanted Sloan to stress in any publicity material that it was not a television version of the sound series. However, adopting not just the same title but the now familiar and well-liked theme tune meant it was inevitably linked with its sister show on radio.

When Galton and Simpson contemplated writing the television scripts they anticipated having to relearn the trade, but in reality the structure of their scripts changed very little. 'The television scripts ended up being around the same number of words,' says Alan. 'You would have thought they would have been shorter because of lots of visuals, but our writing remained dialogue orientated—lots of talking heads.'

'Eric Sykes used to say to us: "Now you're on television, you have to write visual, you can't just do what you've been doing on radio," ' recalls Ray. 'We weren't sure if he was right and, to be honest, we didn't really pay any attention: having said that, the first one we did we tried to take advantage of the fact it was a visual medium by doing a show in hospital.' There were, of course, visual gags, particularly in some of the early scripts. However, they soon realised that this resulted in characters rushing around to provide movement, thereby suppressing the comedic effect they were trying to achieve, and confusing the audience at the same time. In the writers' eyes, the visual jokes were the least productive elements of the show. Ray Galton once commented: 'We were finally confirmed in our opinion when we wrote a scene which consisted entirely of Tony Hancock and Sidney James sitting in chairs talking to each other, very simply presented in cross-cut close-ups. This ran nine full minutes by the watch, and no one noticed except to remark that it was the funniest part of the show.'[10] The writers did, however, acknowledge the technical limitations when writing the scripts, especially as the first series was transmitted live. Ray adds: 'We tried to avoid violent scene changes or big costume changes.'

This was a consideration when creating the televisual character of Hancock. On radio, Galton and Simpson may have created an image in their own minds of Hancock and the world in which he existed, but they didn't have to interpret this in the actual script; now they had to pay attention to such detail. The generously sized overcoat sporting an astrakhan collar, the homburg hat and cane that became Hancock's trademarks were chosen because the writers regarded such items as traditional gear of actor-managers and ideal for their character. There was also a practical reason why they chose them. With episodes initially recorded live, there was little time—especially for the main character—for costume changes. Once episodes were recorded, new scenes necessitating a change of clothes would result in a quick break in recording. In the pre-recording days, Hancock would often wear a second set of clothes under his overcoat to allow a speedy change.

Director Duncan Wood began to assemble his production team, the personnel who would oversee every aspect of the television series. When it came to bringing Hancock's world at 23 Railway Cuttings alive, as well as other scenes in East Cheam, production designer Stewart Marshall was given responsibility. In addition to consulting with the director and forming his own opinions, he would take note of the explicit descriptions that were often included in the script, something Galton, in particular, enjoyed providing. 'Ray was always keen on stipulating designs of wallpaper, types of furniture—it was almost a hobby of his. I would have been tempted to leave it to the designer,' says Alan with a smile.

The writers were instructed to keep the number of sets to a minimum due to limited space in the studio, so tried to use no more than two main sets and a couple of side sets. 'The sets were pretty grim,' admits Ray. 'They were like cardboard. As far as set design was concerned, it was very difficult to see any improvements on those used in early silent films. They were often painted; when we had scenes in the library there were painted bookshelves and painted doorways. They were nothing like you see today, where you'd think the programmes were filmed in someone's house.'

Unlike radio, television scripts had to be delivered well in advance to allow time for the construction of sets and the actors to learn their lines. Despite this change in working practice, the writers were confident and excited about transferring *Hancock's Half Hour* to the small screen. 'You had to be appearing on television—it was the future,' explains Ray. 'The number of people owning sets, and being able to receive a signal accelerated, especially around the time of the Queen's Coronation. Audiences were deserting radio in droves, while actors found they had to appear on television or you became a nobody. It wasn't an option to stick to radio, otherwise—and quite unfairly—performers were classified as second-rate comics.'

With the scripts complete, the sets ready, the first television series was ready to roll.

Chapter 7

Although from time to time, guest artists like Fenella Fielding and Dora Bryan were used in the radio show, the lion's share of episodes required nothing more than the principal characters of Hancock, Sid, Bill, Moira, Andrée or Hancock's secretary Miss Pugh. Additional parts were usually allocated to the man of a thousand voices, Kenneth Williams, who frequently played more than one part per episode. As well as Williams, Hattie Jacques and Bill Kerr were occasionally heard adopting other roles, and if there were any one-line cameos required, the likes of Alan Simpson (who made over sixty radio appearances) were called upon. From the very beginning, Main Wilson was concerned about the lack of funds in his programme budget for extra performers, but the nature of the medium meant there was less reliance on walk-ons, extras or guest stars. If, on radio, a scene was set in a library, it wasn't necessary to recruit extra actors to play non-speaking members of the public browsing the shelves; and if the script called for an interjection by a fellow reader, it was easy to ask Jacques, Williams or Simpson to utter the solitary line.

The visual world of television demanded a different approach: in the library scene, background figures strolling around, flicking through periodicals and enquiring at the information desk were needed to add a degree of realism, colour and depth to the scene. Eagle-eyed viewers watching a scene set, for example, inside an aeroplane, like the opening sequence in the 1957 episode, 'The Alpine Holiday', would expect to see other passengers making the journey, not just as a human sponge, soaking up Hancock's nervous chatter, or providing someone against whom he could react, but to make the scenario as realistic as possible.

During the five-year run of the television series, producer Duncan Wood gathered around him a group of character actors he would regularly call upon. Valuable elements of the programme's success, they were affectionately known as the Duncan Wood Repertory Company and were employed to bring alive myriad roles, from doctors and nurses to shop assistants and police officers. Often the roles didn't warrant any dialogue: they were just nameless characters who appeared in background scenes to react to Hancock's behaviour. This is beautifully illustrated by Peggy Ann Clifford's cameo in 'The Missing Page' from the sixth series, when Hancock is causing a disturbance in East Cheam Public Library with his constant chatter and gesticulating before reverting to an adroitly executed piece of miming to explain a storyline to Sid. Clifford portrays a frustrated reader, huffing and puffing, who's disturbed by the man's antics. Words are superfluous when you possess not only a highly expressive face but an extensive repertoire of mannerisms: a flick of the head, a shrug of the shoulders, a couple of deep sighs and the audience instantly empathises with the poor woman whose peaceful few moments in the library are shattered. In this particular scene, it isn't just Peggy Ann Clifford's talents on show; the library is full of Wood's trusted employees, from little Johnny Vyvyan and the ever-reliable Alec Bregonzi to the immaculately dressed Totti Truman Taylor and dependable Joanna Douglas.

Although the majority of these faces were usually cast in small roles on television, they were, nevertheless, experienced actors, many of whom had learnt their trade, just like the principals, treading the boards up and down the country in rep. Many never had more than a handful of words to utter in their entire *Hancock's Half Hour* career, but some were occasionally given more extensive roles. Hugh Lloyd, for example, made twenty-five appearances in the show, in a variety of roles, from Smudger Smith in 'The Reunion Party', and the helpful shop assistant in 'The Photographer' to, arguably, his most popular role, as the lift attendant in 'The Lift'.

Duncan Wood wasn't alone in creating his own pool of character actors: other producers, such as David Croft, employed a similar strategy. The pressures of turning out a weekly situation comedy were intense, with casting minor roles just one piece of the jigsaw; but the pressure was eased somewhat by knowing that one had a supply of actors—whom Galton and Simpson agree were worth their weight in gold—who could play small parts, and who could be trusted to bring these frequently speechless citizens of East Cheam alive. Hugh Lloyd recalls speaking to Wood one day about using the same troupe. 'Quite simply, he told me it was easier for him; he knew we could do the job and he didn't have to worry about it. That was his attitude.' Lloyd thought he had something to worry about, though, after completing the read-

111

through for his first episode. 'Duncan made a few observations, then finished early so that people could go away and learn their parts. He said: "Everyone home, except you." He was pointing at me. I wondered what I'd done. He told me to be back by two. I had a worrying lunch hour only to return to find that Tony, Sid and Duncan wanted a game of snooker and needed a fourth player!' Hugh enjoyed working with Duncan Wood. 'He had a good ear for what was funny, as well as anything that was out of context. Something can be very funny but not part of the context, which can detract from the storyline. Duncan was good at spotting that.'

As another regular, Alec Bregonzi, recalls, Duncan Wood 'enjoyed working with people he knew, and I remember him saying to me, "I always know I'm going to get the right reaction from you." That's why a few of us were asked back again and again. After all, most directors like to have their familiars around them, and Duncan was no exception. Also, I'm sure that it made things easier and more secure for Tony to have a known group to work with. Later on, I worked on many episodes of *The Two Ronnies* and it was interesting that Ronnie Barker knew a lot of the walk-ons by name. As there were several directors on the series over the years, Ronnie had obviously had a hand in choosing them, and for the same reasons.'

Alec enjoyed his days as part of the repertory company. 'Most of us were character actors and had worked in weekly rep where you had to be a quick learner and grasp your character almost immediately. Although we rehearsed for nearly a week, Duncan knew he didn't have to waste time

112

coping with the smaller parts and could concentrate on the main characters. Some faces were chosen because they immediately evoked the type of character wanted, such as Herbert Nelson, Arthur Mullard and Peggy Ann Clifford, and then there were the interesting faces that could play all sorts of roles, and that's presumably why I was in so many. That, I think, is what it was all about, plus reliability, security and being liked.' The members of the Company established friendships, helping to develop a sense of team spirit. Whereas guest stars and principals were contracted before the series was recorded, members of the rep company were, generally, booked on a week-to-week basis. 'If you were in one there was always the hope that on transmission day you would be asked if you were free for the next, and saddened if someone else was given a script and you weren't. You thought that was it, you'd never be asked back—fortunately you were.'

A small part, with few, if any, lines, doesn't guarantee a lack of butterflies in the stomach when the camera is just about to turn over. 'Playing small parts is a nerve-racking business because there's no time to get over your nerves—you're on, utter and flee!' admits Alec. 'You have to establish the character immediately. In those days the shows were live and filmed as they went out. They were never edited, to my knowledge, so if anything went wrong you ploughed on, regardless.'

Although most ambitious thespians aspire to long-running leading roles, the saying 'Variety is the spice of life' can be applied when analysing the work of some of the actors during their days on *Hancock's Half Hour*. Hugh Lloyd recalls: 'Overall,

I played the most extraordinary range of characters: Clerk of the Court, Last Man, First TV Repair Man, a Sergeant, Tree Inspector, First Old Man, Librarian (twice), a Disbeliever, the Usher, Railway Ticket Clerk, Ship's Steward, Launderette Attendant, Secretary, Turnstile Attendant, Smudger Smith, Bert, Photographer's Assistant, Second Councillor, Florist, Liftman and Blood Patient—of course, from the legendary "Blood Donor" sketch.'[1] From a line or two in 'The Adopted Family', back in November 1957, Lloyd graduated to more substantial roles, perhaps as a result of his growing friendship with Hancock, whom he performed with overseas while entertaining the troops in the Mediterranean. 'Immediately after the overseas tours, I started to get better parts in *Hancock* than the one-liners I had had before.' He adds: 'Of course, I have a lot to thank *Hancock's Half Hour* for. It made my face well known on the screen, and today I am still getting royalties from the sales of videos and cassettes. Not bad for a job I did more than 40 years ago!'[2]

Hugh Lloyd has one of the most recognisable faces in showbusiness. A character actor of vast experience, whose career spans more than five decades, he grew up in Chester with a dream of making people laugh. After training as a Merchant Navy radio operator, he joined ENSA and spent three and a half years with the George Thomas Globetrotters, touring Britain, the Faroe Islands and Iceland. After the war, he worked in repertory companies around the country and appeared in summer seasons, beginning in Ventnor on the Isle of Wight, but it was *Hancock's Half Hour* that established his face, if not his name, in the viewing public's psyche.

Clocking up twenty-two appearances was London-born Alec Bregonzi, whose professional acting career began, like so many of his contemporaries, in repertory theatre in the mid-1950s. In venues at Farnham, York, Bromley and Leatherhead he learnt the ropes of a profession he dearly loves. Before long, West End opportunities came his way, including parts in *Camino Real* and as understudy to Ronnie Barker.

While his theatre career progressed, offers to appear on television came his way and he made his *Hancock's Half Hour* début in the opening instalment of series three, in 1957: in 'The Continental Holiday', Alec was cast as the curiously named Crimson Alligator. It was the first of many cameos he'd be offered by Duncan Wood. 'I'd joined an agent who specialised in walk-on and small parts for television. I started doing walk-ons because I thought it was a way to be discovered. It wasn't! But at least he sent me to see Duncan because they needed some new people,' explains Alec, who remembers the interview well. 'I was very nervous. It was the first interview I'd done for a television director and it was awe-inspiring. I was booked for the shows as they came along, but it was always a cliffhanger—you rarely knew if you were wanted for the next one until the very last minute.'

Dennis Chinnery was another regular. The son of a draughtsman, Dennis was born in Ilford, Essex, in 1927. After completing his education at Woking Grammar School for Boys, he did his National Service in the navy before enrolling at RADA in 1949. Seen in ten episodes, he was introduced to the series via his next-door neighbour, who happened to be the sister of Duncan Wood's assistant, Valerie Willis. 'I was at the Old Vic at the time, doing a lot of classics. I'd spent years in weekly rep, learning my trade. When I was introduced to Duncan Wood we took a liking to each other and he gave me a few parts in the show. They were minor roles but interesting, nonetheless.' After rehearsing *Hancock* during the day, Dennis would return to the stage in the evening to play his serious roles in, among others, *Macbeth*. 'Tony was always very interested in what I was doing. He'd always ask how I'd got on the previous evening or enquire as to what I was playing at that moment—I always got the impression that he wanted to go there, to be invited to the Old Vic, or somewhere like that. Unfortunately he never achieved that.'

Whenever Duncan Wood wanted someone to play a capable young nurse, he often turned to Anne Marryott, whose husband, John Rickword, was a member of the production team throughout the show's life. Among her fifteen appearances in the show, the first being the second episode, 'The Artist' in 1956, she played no fewer than five nurses, including her last time on the show, in 'The Blood Donor', by which point she was pregnant and struggling to fasten her overall. At other times she was seen playing secretaries, a tea girl, policewoman, air hostess and a Tannoy announcer.

Anne thought it 'fascinating' work. 'I found Tony Hancock and Sid James very creative, and there was a good rapport between them, Duncan Wood and the scriptwriters.' Like all actors, she would have jumped at the chance to play more substantial characters, but appreciated what she was given. 'It was fun, you see, and that made all the difference. Everyone loved the scripts, too. We felt like a little team and it was great being in any of them.'

The screen lives of their characters may have been short, but this wasn't reflected in the degree of preparation and professionalism required by the artists, as Anne explains. 'You had to be absolutely alive in your scene, being aware of how you would react as a character, as well as keeping in character without overacting: you can react but not overact.' Having such trusted allies in the small parts, Duncan Wood was usually content to let the performer interpret their part, while he concentrated on other matters. There was only one occasion, 'The Blood Donor', when Anne's portrayal wasn't what Duncan was after. 'There were one or two things that Hancock said that I felt a nurse would react to, but because my part was small I had to simply play with the instruments in the background. In one scene, I just decided to look up and glance at him because he was talking such utter rubbish,' she laughs. 'Other reactions I suggested to Duncan he didn't want to use—not that I wanted to hog a scene, I couldn't have done that anyway, but as a character I feel she would have reacted more in that episode. But being young—I was only in my twenties—you don't push yourself forward.'

Anne Marryott, whose parents were copywriters, completed her education at a boarding-school in Salisbury, by which time she'd already gained acting experience in school productions. Visits to the local Arts Theatre to see Shakespeare and Shaw plays convinced Anne that her future lay in acting, and

117

after graduating from the London Academy of Music and Dramatic Art, where she met her future husband, in 1953, she gained valuable experience touring in revues, working with various repertory companies and via the occasional speaking part in films made at Elstree and Merton Park studios.

Anne still has clear memories of other members of the repertory company. 'John Vere was a sensitive, kindly, well-educated man who played rather uptight characters: vicars, solicitors, clerks, that sort of thing.

'I was always fascinated by Evelyn Lund's expressive face, with arched eyebrows and gaunt cheekbones. She used to wear a lovely tweed coat; there was a good cut to it and it was always worn with style. She must have been between 60 and 70 when I met her: she was always kind and rather intense, and had a good stage face and presence.'

This is a feature Alan Simpson also noticed in Lund, a grand actress very much of the old school. 'She always came up to us before the recording and wished us all the best with our play—it was as if we were all in the theatre just about to perform on the first night.'

'Johnny Vyvyan was lugubrious, sometimes chatty, sometimes sour, but he came over well with his rather brooding and mocking expression,' Anne recalls. 'He could tell a good story, and his timing and physique were perfect for the pugnacious characters he played. Then there was Mario Fabrizi, a wonderful character: kind, funny and perfectly cast, and, of course, Peggy Ann Clifford, a large actress who played determined, strong-minded parts and was a good foil for Tony. She could also play placid women, too. I remember she

118

had a very dry sense of humour.'

Born in Bournemouth, Peggy Ann Clifford worked in rep before establishing herself as a supporting actress, normally playing jolly characters, on film and television, but also appearing in many films, including *Kind Hearts and Coronets*, *Man of the Moment*, *Doctor at Large* and *Chance of a Lifetime*. Her television credits range from *Bless This House*, again with Sid James, to *Man About the House*, *Are You Being Served?*, *Hi-De-Hi!* and *Alas Smith and Jones*. Like most thespians, she had lean periods, so she sold a block of flats she owned in Fulham and bought a grocery shop in Chelsea, which she ran for three years. She was only 65 when she died in 1984.

London-born actor John Vere, meanwhile, notched up twenty-three television appearances, all within the first four series, and one radio. His début in the television production was as a rich man in an episode in the first series, 'The Chef That Died of Shame', but he went on to play a range of roles, including three vicars.

After training at RADA he joined the Coventry Repertory Company before spending the summer of 1936 at Regent's Park in a production of *Henry VIII*, playing the Marquis of Dorset and the Bishop. His career was temporarily halted when he served in the army during the war; when he was invalided out with pneumonia he worked for the Admiralty in Bath before being demobbed and returning to the stage in a Shakespeare season at the Westminster Theatre. By the time he joined the cast of *Hancock's Half Hour* he had gained good experience on stage, radio and screen, while the emergence of television brought a host of small parts and walk-on work in series like *Dixon of Dock Green*.

Tragically, Vere committed suicide in January 1961, at the age of just 46. His sister, Isabel Chidell, says: 'He'd had fallow periods as far as work was concerned, and he hadn't been in the best of health. During the war he suffered the trauma of being buried alive for a time, and he was only 17 when he lost his mother, so altogether he didn't have an easy life. He became depressed and took an overdose of sleeping pills—perhaps the pressures of life had got to him.'

Ray Galton became friends with Vere, and later asked the actor to become his son's godfather. 'He was a lovely man,' says Ray. 'We adored all those people, like John, Mario and Arthur Mullard. They were all essential to the success of the show.'

The smartly turned out Totti Truman Taylor was born in 1915 and after years in repertory and provincial theatre, made her screen début in the 1947 film *The Woman in the Hall*.

Alec Bregonzi remembers Totti well. 'She was a true eccentric and a delightful lady,' he says. 'She was always elegantly dressed.' She toured briefly with Hancock and Bregonzi in the 1958 show playing an old frump who rushes up to Tony, who is dressed in a zoot suit as the crooner, and starts tearing his lapels off. 'But at the final walk down she was so elegantly dressed that nobody knew who she was.'

Evelyn Lund also worked on both stage and screen, with appearances in *The Benny Hill Show*, *Citizen James*, *Maigret*, *Julius Caesar*, *The Charlie Drake Show*, *The Ted Ray Show* and *Strictly T-T*.

She was born in 1897 and spent much of her early

120

career in Ireland. During the Second World War she worked with ENSA in Northern Ireland entertaining the British and American troops. After the war, she moved to London and continued her theatre career, including an appearance at the Cambridge Theatre playing Miss Twelvetrees in *Trouble in the House*. She also clocked up several film credits. In the mid-1960s she developed cancer but continued to work until her death in 1968.

While most members of the repertory company had a background in acting, some were better known in other fields of the entertainment business. Ivor Raymonde, for example, was known for his musical skills: a composer, arranger, record producer and musical director, Raymonde was a close friend of Duncan Wood. Responsible for numerous hit records of the 1950s and '60s, he was musical director and arranger for the Springfields and, later, Dusty Springfield, directing all her records until her departure for the States. From the mid-1950s to the late 1970s, he worked with a host of artists, at home and abroad, including Roy Orbison, Paul Anka, Helen Shapiro and Julio Iglesias.

During the sixties, the music business dominated his career and among his achievements was the writing of his first song, 'I Only Want To Be With You', which was recorded by several artists and reached number 4 in the charts for Dusty Springfield.

One of the most familiar faces Wood hired was Mario Fabrizi, one of the select bunch who clocked up over twenty appearances. Born in London, of Italian parents, in 1925, he became a seaside photographer for a while before the opportunity to play small parts in films and television came his way, including the 1957 film, *The Naked Truth*, and 1960's *Two Way Stretch*. Other big-screen credits included *Operation Snatch*, *Village of Daughters*, *Postman's Knock*, *Carry On Cruising*, *On the Beat*, *The Wrong Arm of the Law* and both of Hancock's films, *The Rebel* and *The Punch and Judy Man*. Fabrizi became good friends with Tony Hancock and lived with him and Cicely for a while before he married.

Other supporting actors included Doncaster-born Patrick Milner, who was an electrician's mate for two years before moving to London in the early 1950s. While working in the same capacity, he earned extra cash after enrolling at a modelling agency. His assignments included being photographed for Kay's mail order catalogue. Television work soon came his way and he was regularly employed as a continuity policeman in *Z Cars*, as well as another BBC police series, *Juliet Bravo*. He retired from the business in 1986, his last job being an appearance in *EastEnders*.

Robert Dorning was adept at playing official characters and during his eighteen appearances in *Hancock's Half Hour* he played his fair share of managers, police inspectors and mayors. Born in St Helens in 1913, he trained as a ballet dancer before turning to musical comedy prior to the war. Following demob from the Royal Air Force, he resumed his career in musical comedies and moved into acting. He worked for three years with Arthur Lowe in Granada's *Pardon the Expression*, having previously appeared with him in *Coronation Street*. He made over twenty-five films, including *They Came by Night, The Secret Man, No Safety Ahead* and *Carry On Emmannuelle*.

Familiar faces from the screen world were also brought into the repertory company from time to time, including Patricia Hayes, who played Hancock's waspish landlady Mrs Cravatte; and burly actor Arthur Mullard, who continued to ply his trade as a heavy or policeman, with such roles as First Bruiser in 'The Two Murderers', Bruiser in 'The Wrong Man' and PC Trubshawe in 'The Lawyer: The Crown v. James, S.' Veteran film actor John Le Mesurier made eight appearances. In his autobiography, he recalled the time Tony asked him to appear in the show. 'Tony was looking to set up a new repertory of support actors. He had noticed me in one or two movies and also came to see me in a well-received play at a minute theatre in Wilton Crescent. He called round after the show and we went to the bar where he said, among other things, that he liked my work and wanted me to be in his programmes.'[3] His first appearance was as the judge in 'The Lawyer: The Crown v. James, S.' which he recalled as a 'delightfully confusing trial sketch'.

LEAGUE TABLE OF LEADING REPERTORY COMPANY APPEARANCES
(excluding radio appearances)

John Vyvyan—37
Hugh Lloyd—25
Manville Tarrant—24
John Vere—23
Alec Bregonzi—22
Mario Fabrizi—22
James Bulloch—21

Robert Dorning—18
Patrick Milner—17
Ivor Raymonde—16
Anne Marryott—15
Evelyn Lund—15
Herbert Nelson—15
Arthur Mullard—14
Con Courtney—13
Claude Bonser—13
George Crowther—12
Richard Statman—11
Laurie Webb—10
Dennis Chinnery—10
Philip Carr—9
Rose Howlett—8
John Le Mesurier—8
Frank Littlewood—8
Peggy Ann Clifford—8
Gordon Phillott—8
Patricia Hayes—7
Totti Truman Taylor—7
Harry Drew—7
Paddy Edwards—7
Cameron Hall—7
Charles Julian—7
Anthony Shirvell—7

Chapter 8

For the first two series of the television show, episodes were transmitted fortnightly. Before the initial television series began with the appropriately titled 'The First TV Show', which was shown live at 8.45 p.m. from Studio G at Lime Grove, on Friday, 6 July 1956, several days were scheduled for rehearsing at the Inns of Court Mission, in London's Drury Lane. During the show's lifetime, and before the construction of the BBC's own purpose-built rehearsal block, many cheerless venues, including church halls, drill halls and boys' clubs, were used for rehearsals.

Some of television's future directors/producers cut their production teeth on *Hancock's Half Hour*, including Gerry Mill—who went on to direct such shows as *London's Burning*, *A Kind of Loving*, *Second Chance* and *Heartbeat*; and Harold Snoad, who produced and directed such classic shows as *Don't Wait Up*, *Brush Strokes*, *Ever Decreasing Circles* and *Keeping Up Appearances*. Both began their association with *Hancock's Half Hour* in the junior position of call boy (a position now known as floor assistant, thanks to Snoad himself) during the second series, but while Snoad moved on to other projects, Mill remained with the show until series six.

The process of rehearsing involved marking sets out on the floor with different coloured tape and utilising various items of old, neglected furniture to simulate the pieces that would be used during the actual transmission. Harold Snoad recalls: 'Each episode generally had five days of rehearsals. By the end of the fourth day the director, Duncan Wood, had worked out his camera script and on the fifth the heads of the various elements of the technical team (Cameras, Sound and Lighting) as well as Costume and Make-up would attend to see the action and find out the director's plans for the recording day.'

Snoad has happy memories of working with the cast:

I got on very well with Sid. It's now fairly well known he had quite a severe gambling habit. At the time I was working with him he was trying to keep this fairly dark and I can remember him coming up to me on the recording day of the first episode of the series that I worked on and giving me the telephone number of his bookmaker. He explained that as he was so busy would I mind ringing the bookie and placing a bet for him on such and such a horse in the 2.30 at Kempton and another in the 3.30. Then he'd say: 'Ooh . . . and also this one in the four o'clock at Newmarket.' The stake was generally two pounds. Later he would ask me to ring up and check the results. This happened regularly on every recording day. What I didn't know at the time was that he had a code with his bookie and when I said two pounds it actually meant twenty which, of course, was quite a lot of money in those days.

The first time Snoad spent any time with Kenneth Williams was during the lunch break of

126

the first recording he worked on:

> As I made my way across the canteen at Riverside Studios with my meal on a tray I was about to pass a table where Kenneth was sitting on his own. He invited me to join him. I did so but then rather regretted it as he showed me a tear on his trousers and went on to complain in no small way that he had torn them in a scene we had rehearsed just before lunch which had involved him climbing over a prop wall. He moaned and moaned about the fact that he should never have been asked to rehearse the scene in his own trousers, saying that they should have waited until he was wearing the costume provided by the wardrobe department and paid for by the BBC. During the meal he must have referred to this and shown me the tear at least half a dozen times! It was a bit boring but also quite amusing, especially as it was done in his usual camp manner.

On Wednesday, 27 June, the first day of rehearsal, Galton and Simpson arrived at the venue in Drury Lane to see what everyone made of their opening script. They would always attend the initial read-through and stay with the cast for the entire day. Alan Simpson says: 'Then we'd go back to the office because we were normally working on some other script. I can't recall ever being asked to come in and write additional material—usually we overwrote—so we wouldn't normally attend again until the day of transmission, if it was live, or the day of recording. I liked going along, although Ray used to get very nervous about it all: he used to be convinced everything would be a disaster, so I'd have to reassure him.'

Ray admits he often needed reassuring, and not just on *Hancock's Half Hour*. 'I used to get terribly depressed, particularly on *Steptoe*, during the last day of rehearsal or the day of transmission. I used to think it was terrible; sometimes I'd be in a suicidal mood and Alan would say: "It's fine, don't worry about it."' Both writers, though, enjoyed going along to read-throughs when they were enamoured of a particular script. 'Then, I couldn't wait to hear them read it,' enthuses Ray. 'If we knew it was good, we knew everyone would be pleased with it.'

Read-throughs usually began at 10.30, by which time everyone had assembled, enjoyed a coffee and a chat. Completion of the first read provided the director with a timing, so he knew if the script was running short or over the alloted time in the schedules. Often this necessitated the editing of a couple of minutes of material, at which point the cast would move on to 'blocking', whereby the actors learn their positions for each particular scene. Duncan Wood would usually finish early on the first day, sending the actors home to learn their lines. The following day, they would be working largely without the script. As the week progressed and they became increasingly confident about their lines, they eventually discarded the script and concentrated on the minute detail of their performance.

Actors use different methods to learn their lines, but some find the entire process more arduous and taxing than others. Whereas the experience Sid James had picked up in the film world helped when it came to learning television scripts, Hancock struggled, as Ray Galton recalls. 'It didn't come naturally to Tony. I think it took quite a toll on him. A week's rehearsal is barely enough time for a main actor to learn the part—how to move, how to play it and so on. We would put the odd new line in during rehearsal time, but there came a point when Duncan would stop us unless it was something sensational.'

Tony Hancock's second wife and widow, Freddie, who ran her own public relations company for many years and has acted as consultant and adviser to a number of companies, used to watch her husband struggling to cram the lines into his head. 'He used a tape recorder. He'd pour in all the words of the other performers and leave blanks for his own lines. Then he'd go through it again and again until he knew everybody else's lines as well as his own. But he found it all very difficult, which is why it was such a relief for him when he had to read off cue cards, later on in the series.'

The opening episode, 'The First TV Show', saw Hancock hospitalised with a broken leg and a bandage skullcap covering his head, just as his television series is due to begin. Sid feels he's invested so much money in Hancock over the years that the show must go on. He arranges for the last ten minutes of the programme to be transmitted from the hospital, with Hancock's bed converted to represent HMS *Victory* and with Hancock playing Nelson. The reason for his hospitalisation is explained in the first scene:

ANNOUNCER: The next part of our programme,

Hancock's Half Hour, follows immediately.

(*Working class living room. There is a television set facing the camera. Four chairs are arranged round the set. The husband enters. He is in his shirt sleeves and is chewing.*)

HUSBAND: Come on, Edie, hurry up. Telly'll be on in a minute. You can leave the washing up till the morning.

WIFE: Coming, Bert.

(*She enters drying her hands with tea towel.*)

WIFE: What's on?

HUSBAND: What do you mean, what's on? You've never worried about that before. We just switch it on and sit there till bedtime. With a bit of luck we might enjoy it tonight.

WIFE: Well, I just wondered what's on, that's all.

HUSBAND: What does it matter? Something to do, isn't it? Saves going out, or reading, or talking, or looking at you.

(*While the husband has been talking she has picked up the* Radio Times *and has found the appropriate page.*)

WIFE: Oh here it is, Bert. Quarter to eight, weather forecast . . .

HUSBAND: We've missed that . . . that's you being late in from work. First programme I've missed in three years . . .

WIFE: Ah here we are . . . eight forty-five. *Hancock's Half Hour* starring Tony Hancock.

HUSBAND: Who's he?

WIFE: I'm not sure, Bert. I think he's one of them radio blokes.

HUSBAND: Radio?

WIFE: Yes, you know, one of those things people have in cars.

HUSBAND: Tony Hancock. Hmmm. He hasn't been on telly before, has he?

WIFE: No. It says this is his first time on BBC television, and tonight's the first programme in the series.

HUSBAND: Well all right then, we'll give him a chance. See what he's like. If we don't like him we can always . . . we can always . . . er . . .

WIFE: Always what?

HUSBAND: Well we can sit in front of the set. We don't have to watch him, do we? Go on switch it on, Edie, you never know, he might be all right.

(*She switches the TV set on. The announcer appears.*)

ANNOUNCER: Good evening.

BOTH: Good evening, Peter.

ANNOUNCER: Tonight we present the first programme in the new television series of *Hancock's Half Hour*. And here to introduce the programme is the star of the show—Tony Hancock.

(*Close-up of Tony in front of a curtain sitting at a desk. He is wearing a dinner jacket with Slim Jim tie.*)

TONY: Good evening, and I would like to welcome you to the first programme in my new series. This is of course my first appearance on BBC Television and I'm very thrilled at the chance of at last coming into your homes.

WIFE: I don't think I'm going to like him.

(*Tony reacts very slightly*)

TONY: This programme will be coming to you once a fortnight and I do hope that you will like what we have in store for you over the next few weeks.

WIFE: I don't like his face.

(*Tony reacts a bit more obviously*)

131

TONY: (*Intense and serious*) I do realise of course that this is an entirely new venture for me and I am well aware of the famous names of television that I will be following, and if I can entertain you as well as they have I shall be happy . . .

HUSBAND: He hasn't made me laugh yet, look at his face, a right misery.

(*Tony jollies himself up. A broad smile. Lots of teeth, gay bubbling laugh.*)

TONY: I hope you're going to like me and . . .

HUSBAND: Rotten teeth he's got. Don't fit very well, do they?

(*Tony closes his mouth and tries to talk without opening it.*)

TONY: I hope you're going to like me and . . .

WIFE: He ought to get something done about his hair as well.

(*Tony covers up his hair with his hand.*)

TONY: I hope you're going to like me and . . .

WIFE: He's much fatter than I expected.

(*Tony pulls in his cheeks.*)

TONY: I hope you're going to like me and . . .

HUSBAND: Well, I wish he'd get off and let somebody else have a go.

TONY: Now I'd like to introduce you to some of the cast. First, I have with me a man whose face you've seen many times on the films, a very fine actor and a close friend of mine . . . Sidney James.

(*Sidney moves into the picture, beaming.*)

WIFE: Oh yes, I like him. Much better looking, isn't he?

(*Tony signals to camera. Signals cut.*)

TONY: Ha, ha! So much for the cast. Now about the show.

HUSBAND: Cor it's him again! Let's switch over. He's a right wash-out, he is.

TONY: Well, let's get started.

WIFE: Got no life in him, has he?

(*Tony moves gaily about effervescently burbling with force.*)

HUSBAND: Not as good as Arthur, is he? He could learn a few things off Arthur, he could.

(*Tony puts on a pair of horn-rimmed spectacles*)

TONY: And so, playmates, I'd just like to finish by saying, I thank you.

(*Holds his nose and goes down out of screen like Arthur Askey does.*)

WIFE: I wish it was Norman Wisdom, he's much better.

(*Tony comes up again with a cloth cap on, laughing à la Wisdom. He goes to sit down. Misses chair and gets up laughing.*)

TONY: I fell over. But I'd just like to finish by . . .

HUSBAND: Terry-Thomas is the boy I like.

(*Tony puts a long cigarette holder in his mouth and starts sucking.*)

TONY: (*Terribly posh*) How do you do. Are you terribly well? Good show.

HUSBAND: Well I don't fancy his face looking at me for six weeks. Wish I could think of something else to do.

(*Tony is getting furious. The next dialogue he looks from one to the other.*)

WIFE: He's too old for my liking.

HUSBAND: Very brought down, I am. Not my cup of tea at all—we pay three guineas a year for that.

WIFE: I can't understand it. I heard he was all right on the radio.

HUSBAND: Well he should have stayed there. He's

133

not going to be any good on telly, I'll tell you that, and I've spotted 'em all. He's a wash-out.

WIFE: I wouldn't mind if he was better looking, but he's so ugly.

HUSBAND: I'd like to know how much he's getting for this. It's a disgrace. A waste of public money. Look, the dog's crawled under the table now, and he'll watch anything. I've never seen a bigger load of rubbish in my life.

(*This is the last straw for Tony who has gradually been getting more and more furious. He puts toy windmill on table. Moves the arms and spins.*)

TONY: Interlude.

(*He gets up and stalks out of camera, leaving an empty screen. The camera tracks back from the TV set showing the living room as before with the husband and wife sitting down looking at the set.*)

WIFE: Where's he gone now?

HUSBAND: I don't know, but this bit's an improvement. (*Knock at door*) Come in.

(*Door opens. Enter Tony in dinner jacket and plus fours. He walks straight up to the television set and puts his foot through the screen. He then advances on the husband.*)

TONY: Now . . . so you don't like the choppers, eh? I'm fat, am I? I see . . . etc . . .

(*Fade vision*)

Six million people switched on their sets to watch the opening episode on Friday, 6 July 1956. It was an anxious time for everyone involved in the new show. 'It was also the most rewarding,' says Ray Galton. 'Obviously there was plenty of tension, wondering how it would go with the audience, wondering how well the actors would perform.

There's nothing better than being there when the audience are laughing and enjoying themselves, while the actors are performing well because the script is good.'

It was also an apprehensive time for the actors. Alan Simpson recalls: 'Tony would be particularly nervous just before we went on. You wouldn't go near him for half an hour before the show started, and could hear him in his dressing room dry-heaving; but as soon as the show started he was fine. Hancock was very professional in those days and never had a drink until after the show. As soon as Duncan Wood confirmed the episode had finished he'd return to his dressing room and drink the night away; we all had a drink, though, partly because we were so relieved the show was out of the way.'

Throughout the period of *Hancock's Half Hour*, Tony would normally leave any drinking until after rehearsals or when the episode was complete. Harold Snoad recalls having occasionally to help a worse for wear Hancock into a taxi.

The episodes I worked on were recorded at Riverside Studios. There were two studios and we used the larger one, Riverside 1. Opposite the studios was a pub which had become known as Riverside 3. After the long hours given over to camera rehearsals followed, of course, by the recording of the episode in front of an audience, the cast and the production team used to go in there for a relaxing nightcap. Unfortunately Tony never really knew where to draw the line when it came to alcohol intake and I can remember several occasions when he became extremely inebriated and I had to call a taxi to get him home, virtually half carrying and dragging him out of the pub to get him into it.

It was the norm for the cast to congregate in the local pub after work. Bill Kerr recalls his days on the radio series. 'We all enjoyed getting together and having a bevvy. After the show was recorded we'd go to the nearest boozer; there would be wives, friends, girlfriends there as well—Tony, Kenneth and I even brought our mothers along occasionally. It was all about letting your hair down after the show.'

Kerr enjoyed working on the programme. 'I couldn't wait to arrive at the theatre for the first read-through of the script; we'd often fall about hysterically ourselves. Tony was a great reader—he could read the telephone book and make you laugh. He was brilliant. The pressure only came when we did the actual take.' Inevitably, the cast made mistakes and there is one particular moment Bill will never forget. 'I had to say something like, "Look at Tony having a stunt on a punt" but unfortunately it didn't come out as "punt"! There was the most ghastly silence you've ever heard in a studio—shocked silence. Everyone was muttering: "What did he say?" I turned beetroot. Then a friend of mine, sitting in the front row, started laughing and within a couple of seconds the whole audience was rocking with laughter. Dennis Main Wilson, in his best BBC voice, said: "Now, children. Bill, would you like to say those words again?" I did it three times and on each occasion made the same mistake. By then, we were nervous wrecks with laughter. It was my most funny and terrifying moment in show business.'

The BBC's Audience Research Department carried out their regular survey, only to find that just like the nameless husband and wife (played by Harold Goodwin and Margaret Flint) in the episode's opening scene, a significant number of people within the sample had reservations about the show. The reaction index of 60 meant the programme had fallen short of the average (66) for all Light Entertainment programmes televised during the first quarter of 1956. A number of fans of Hancock's radio series were disappointed with the first televised adventure, with one viewer stating: 'I seldom miss hearing Hancock on radio, but Tony on TV—never again!'[1] Sid James and Irene Handl, who played a nurse, were praised, but reaction to the programme itself was divided. A grocer commented: 'Adult mentality is surely above this sort of rubbish. Senseless bilge from beginning to end.' Other people were prepared to give the series time to settle and just over half the sample enjoyed the first edition on television: they voted it as entertaining and unusual in its format, and had nothing but praise for Hancock himself, particularly remarking on his 'delicious sense of timing', 'dry humour' and 'expressive face'.

The visual medium of television brought additional pressure and strain for actors, and being the leading man in a television series as highly rated as *Hancock's Half Hour* was no sinecure; Hancock, never the best scholar when it came to scripts, battled hard each week to learn his lines. But the medium also opened up opportunities for performers, writers and directors to exploit. In Hancock's case, he was able to develop his rich talent for reaction comedy, utilising one of his biggest assets. While Galton and Simpson provided the words, Hancock would provide the punctuation with a little grin, flick of the head and a myriad of subtle techniques. His character could be saturnine or ebullient and his expressive face alone was enough to convey this. Tony Hancock's face was ideal for comedy, with its ability to portray countless emotions, from bemusement and puzzlement to sadness and distress; often you didn't even need dialogue to move the story along.

As Alan Simpson recalls, though, Hancock's reactions and expressions were evident even in the radio series. 'We used to get lots of laughs on radio even though obviously no one listening could see the facial reactions. The medium of television was made for him, and he used to get laughs because of the visual reactions.' Simpson also feels lucky that Hancock 'looked the way he sounded'. 'You'd be amazed at the number of comedians in those days who'd made their name on radio, then moved on to television and people couldn't relate to them. The public had built up an image of what the person looked like and when they finally saw the artist, they were disappointed. Hancock was always a visual comic, to a point, playing to his visual strengths; without being grotesque, he looked funny. But the way he performed didn't vary much from radio to television.'

On television, of course, Hancock's array of facial expressions came to the fore, and it was something director Duncan Wood was desperate to harness: 'None of us had learnt how to use Hancock as a visual person,' Wood said. He began to realise that Hancock's strength lay in reaction rather than initiation. 'If you could give the plot carrying and the initiation to someone like Sid, or some of the other characters, and leave Tony to react then you were doubling his appeal.'[2]

Hancock quickly became aware of the power of television, and enamoured of the mechanics of the medium. Before long, he was suggesting various shots that would use his facial expression to convey meaning. While Hancock, the director and writers were novices in the screen world, Sid James was always willing to share his experience with Hancock and the rest of the team. Ray Galton noticed Sid sidling up to Hancock during rehearsals. 'He used to spend all the time watching the monitors, then would go up to Hancock and say: "Ask Duncan to use a close-up of you halfway through that scene." Tony wouldn't have thought of it, so Sid helped a lot, showing him how to work on camera. He was very influential with Tony when it came to camera angles.'

The evolution of *Hancock's Half Hour* saw the televised version rely increasingly on realism and continuity of storylines, instead of the *Comic Cuts* tendencies prevalent in many of the radio shows. Sid's character was mellowing (although in the final radio season, which was broadcast in 1959, some three years later, Sid was still breaking the law) and the small-screen version showed him turning his back on criminality and settling into his role as Hancock's manager and agent. Hancock's occupation as a failing actor remained implicit during the series, whereas in the radio version he regularly switched careers.

The mundanities, frustrations and shortfalls in Hancock's life were signified by the bleak appearance of 23 Railway Cuttings. Although one could never be certain if he lived in a flat or a terraced house, and whether it was council-owned or private, the abode's melancholy image was befitting to a man down on his luck and heading nowhere. The visual medium afforded viewers the chance to enter the private life of Anthony Aloysius Hancock, to share his misfortunes and challenges and to scorn his pugnacity, arrogance and rudeness. Yet in this overcoat-donning man from East Cheam, people found someone with whom they could empathise and were able to relate to one of life's eternal losers. Alan Simpson says: 'I always used to think that Tony's character summed up everything that people thought their next-door neighbour was like—they never saw themselves like it, though.' Hancock, the character, was burdened with all of man's known weaknesses, including cowardice, pomposity and pretentiousness, but Simpson points out that he had some saving graces, too, being a character with a host of vices and virtues wrapped up into one. 'He could be generous at times, and was occasionally sensitive to other people's needs. But success isn't as funny as failure so his funniest traits are the weaknesses. American shows in those days were all about lots of money, lovely apartments, beautiful women, whereas in this country it was all about tat and being unsuccessful. We found, and still do, much more humour in poverty, failure and unsuccessful people.'

Freddie Hancock saw a lot of Tony Hancock, the man, in the screen character. 'The hesitancy, the insecurity and the pomposity which covers that insecurity. The attitude towards other people is very much Tony, the man, and it's sometimes very difficult to see the difference. He occasionally recognised things he'd said in total honesty and sincerity—perhaps where he'd taken an attitude about something—coming back at him on a page in the script; he'd turn to the writers and say: "You cheeky buggers!" They'd used it out of context in another field. You can't help but inject some of your own personality into a character you play— even down to the timing of how you say something.'

A week later, on 13 July, the cast assembled to rehearse the second episode, 'The Artist', in which Hancock tries his hand at painting. When he runs out of canvases, he decides to save some money by reusing old canvases picked up at a nearby junk shop; unbeknown to Hancock, one of them is an original Rembrandt, which Sid, while being chased by police, had dumped at the shop after stealing it from the Tate Gallery. Playing an art dealer in the episode was Warren Mitchell, who was later hired for a handful of radio episodes before going on to make his name as Alf Garnett, the loud-mouthed bigot in *Till Death Us Do Part*. Mitchell feels he owes much to Tony Hancock and Sid James. 'When I turned up for the audition, Sid, who knew me, came up and said: "I'll mark your card. Go in there and do your funny foreigner and you'll get the job." So I went in, did my funny accent and was offered a part.'

During the episode, Mitchell was able to rescue Hancock when he suddenly forgot his next line. 'Hancock dried stone dead. He just laughed. So I said, "Master Hancock, a word in your ear." He came over to me and I whispered the line to him. He said: "Oh yes, thank you." He went on to do a

141

fabulous show.' Hancock was so grateful to Mitchell that he arranged for him to appear in several more episodes during the series, as well as arranging his first piece of publicity, as Mitchell recalls. 'I didn't find out that Tony had organised it until some time after. If people do you a good turn, often they like to let you know about it, but Tony never did. I suddenly found myself in the *Daily Mirror* with a half-page article about television's new bearded comedian. It wasn't until months later that someone at the BBC said, "That was nice of Tony, wasn't it?" When I asked what he meant, the guy told me that Hancock had come down to the office and said it was about time that I got a bit of publicity because I was doing so well in the show. It was very sweet of him.'

Four of the six episodes in the first television series were watched by over six million people, the two exceptions being instalments 2, 'The Artist', and 3, 'The Dancer', with an audience of 5.6 million each. 'The Dancer' saw Hancock being groomed as Britain's answer to Gene Kelly. When the country's biggest film producer, Mr Fancy, of British Star Films, asks Sid if he's got anyone on his books suitable for a small role in his next picture, Sid volunteers Hancock, even though the suitable applicant has to be able to dance. Sid enters Hancock for a ballroom dancing competition at the Hammersmith Palais, but when he can't find a partner for Hancock, he has no choice but to partner him himself—in drag.

In preparation for the dancing scenes, Duncan Wood completed a Wardrobe, Hair and Make-up Requirements form and distributed copies to all relevant members of his production team, detailing his exact requirements for what he classed as 'full cod drag'.[3] He wanted a blond wig, earrings, an impressive evening gown with shoulder straps, stockings and other accessories. It was an experience Sid James didn't enjoy. 'He hated every minute of it because he didn't like dressing up—he was afraid people would think he was a poof,' says Alan Simpson. While Sid was embarrassed, Hancock wasn't particularly keen himself, but for a different reason. 'He used to think it was a cheap way of getting laughs,' says Alan. 'Hancock would never swear, do *risqué* material, or touch sexual innuendoes. If he ever got a line that was that way inclined he would joke it away. At the end of the day, he'd do it if the part called for it, but was never comfortable with Julian Clary-type material.'

Two episodes in the series, 'The Bequest' and the final show 'The Chef That Died of Shame', were adaptations of radio scripts, transmitted in November and May 1955 respectively. When the idea of transferring the programme to television was first mooted, the hierarchy in BBC Radio were keen to prevent the writers simply adapting all their radio stories. Galton and Simpson are unsure why 'The Bequest' was used so early on in the run. Ray Galton suggests: 'For the first time in our career we were writing to strict deadlines to allow time for such things as scenery to be built, so we may well have been running behind and decided to redo the radio scripts. We tried to avoid doing that—it was only ever a last resort.' As for 'The Chef . . .' episode, circumstances forced the adaptation. Before holidaying in Spain, Galton and Simpson had penned what they thought would be the closing episode of the first series, titled 'The

143

Diplomat', which saw Hancock as a window cleaner—whose round included various embassies and ministerial buildings—passing on inaccurate information. His acts culminate in the British Government believing the country will be invaded and calling the armed forces to battle stations. Such references to military action, together with mention of the Suez Canal and library footage of battle scenes, meant the script was deemed inappropriate at that time: since the writers had completed the script, the Suez Crisis had reared its ugly head. The pace of events was quickening, with Egypt's Colonel Nasser rejecting US plans for international control of the Canal, and classing Anthony Eden's plan for a Suez Users' Association as provocative. With the writers away enjoying the Mediterranean sunshine, Johnny Speight, another client of Associated London Scripts, was asked to look through the archives and identify a radio script which could easily be adapted for television as a replacement. He picked 'The Chef That Died of Shame'.

It's unfortunate that the final script had to be changed at the eleventh hour because the replacement was criticised by a significant portion of the sample audience. It attracted a reaction index of 59, the lowest in the entire series, with many viewers considering it the weakest in the run and lacking in 'punch and timing'[4]. But half the sample praised the artists, writers and the show, with a student describing it as 'real English comedy, with that unexpectedness that is conspicuously lacking in the American slapstick we get dished up to us so frequently'.

Although it wasn't until the fifth series that the

144

programme broke through the 10 million barrier in terms of viewers, the decision-makers at the BBC were sufficiently impressed with the show's reception to begin discussions of a joint Sound and Television contract for Hancock, Galton and Simpson. The intention was to secure the services of the artist and writers long term and it would also ensure that BBC Radio and Television would work more closely, preventing a repeat of the difficulties encountered in scheduling and acceptance when the show first transferred to the small screen. Discussions took place between Pat Hillyard, Head of Variety, and Ronald Waldman, Head of Light Entertainment (Television). Waldman was aware that Hancock had six further ITV appearances to make before he was free of his commitments to Jack Hylton. After talking to Hancock and the writers once the first episode had been transmitted, he informed Hillyard that they had 'expressed themselves anxious' to know if the BBC would consider a combined Sound and Vision contract for any future series.[5] Waldman was in favour of the idea, especially as the trio was willing to make a second series for television in April 1957, a few weeks after the fourth radio series was due to finish.

After first considering the proposal with colleagues, on 3 August Pat Hillyard replied to Waldman's memo, laying out the arrangements favoured by the Light Programme. They wanted any contract to last two years, with an option for a third, with basic fees of 75 guineas for Hancock and 105 guineas for Galton and Simpson jointly per programme. Hillyard acknowledged that the writers' current contract didn't expire until

30 June 1957, but by the time the forthcoming radio series finished in February 1957, he felt, they would have 'earned their guarantee'[6]. He wanted Waldman to start the process formally. On 6 September, just before the first television series came to an end, Tom Sloan, then Assistant Head of Light Entertainment (Television), replied to Hillyard's memo of August detailing BBC Television's views on the proposal. They were interested in the proposal for a joint contract, but felt the option should be for a further two years, not one as suggested by Hillyard. However, they were unhappy about running a 12-episode second series from April 1957, preferring two seasons of six shows scheduled to avoid the summer months, when audience figures were traditionally lower, particularly as they were expecting to pay Hancock £500 an episode. A meeting was arranged to discuss concerns about any overlaps between the sound and television series, which everyone wanted to avoid. Hancock had also suggested making a weekly, rather than fortnightly series—something Sloan wasn't sure could be organised for 1957.

Hillyard wasn't totally agreeable to Sloan's suggestions. He didn't think Sloan's idea of splitting the television series into two series of six episodes, transmitted fortnightly, would work because the final season beginning in the autumn of 1957 would clash with the radio series Sound had wanted to schedule. As Hillyard explained, one of the successful features of the Sound series had been its topicality; he was reluctant to ask the writers to prepare their script earlier than planned in order to accommodate Television's predicament. As it transpired, Television won the battle and the fifth radio series was delayed until the end of January 1958.

It would be over six months before another series of *Hancock's Half Hour* appeared on the screen, by which time a further radio series had been aired and Hancock had completed the second, and final, series for Jack Hylton. But before the fourth radio series was broadcast, producer Dennis Main Wilson faced a battle over the use of incidental music, something that he regarded as integral to the show's success.

Chapter 9

With Dennis Main Wilson at the helm of the show, writers, actors and everyone associated with the programme knew they had an inimitable individual who would fight incessantly for what he thought was right and didn't mind whose feathers he ruffled along the way. One area he felt could be improved was the publicity given to the radio programme by the Beeb's own magazine, *Radio Times*. With the first episode of the Fourth radio series due to be broadcast on 14 October 1956, Main Wilson dropped a line to the editor reminding him of the new series. He hoped that, with the help of the magazine, *Hancock's Half Hour* would become the top comedy show for 1956–57. Main Wilson wanted the show to have front page treatment and plenty of coverage inside, feeling that over the last year or so the attention had been 'pitifully poor to say the least'.[1]

With a budget allocation of £285 per programme for the upcoming series, anything which threatened additional expense concerned Main Wilson. One such worry was a dispute with the Musicians' Union; earlier in the year, an issue over general conditions and payments had sparked a total strike. With relations still fragile, everyone at the BBC was keen to avoid a similar disaster, so when the Union raised the matter of 'all rights' use of incidental music the issue was given due attention. In use for three series, the original recordings of musical links and background music, as well as the signature tune, for which the musicians were paid an 'all rights' fee, had become a valuable part of *Hancock's Half Hour*. Now the Union became concerned that the musicians involved weren't benefiting from the repeated use of the music. Main Wilson didn't want to be stopped from using the recordings in any subsequent series and was so outraged when it was suggested he supplanted the existing music with material from other sources that he fired off a five-page memo to the Head of Variety.

Main Wilson believed that the BBC was legally entitled to use the music and decided to tell the Head of Variety what they would lose if it was decided to discard the fifty-plus individual compositions, lasting from a few seconds to two minutes, which had been 'hand-tailored to fit the script, and the script written to fit the music down to the last crotchet'[2]. Most of the music wasn't used for comedy links but as background music to inspire Hancock's performance. As far as the director was concerned, taking away the incidental music would rip a substantial chunk out of the show's character. To try and replace Wally Stott's music with extracts from the Corporation's catalogue of mood music in the Gramophone Library was, as far as Main Wilson was concerned, a non-starter.

Reluctantly, he proffered a second suggestion, which entailed replacing the recorded incidental music with a live orchestra on the programme. This was a route he was anxious to avoid, though, due to his experiences of working on *All-Star Bill*. As he explained, 'at an equivalent of one bar before the end of a scene, the conductor picks up his baton to cue in the orchestra and takes the attention of the audience away from the cast who are trying to get a big end-of-scene laugh.'[3] Further, Main Wilson said that the studio manager who has all the music on discs can direct his attention to the comedy unfolding in front of him instead of organising a multitude of microphones for the orchestra.

Main Wilson was firm in his resolve to oppose the use of an orchestra, claiming the programme's quality would suffer and that the Light Programme could ill afford the costs involved in hiring a 30-piece orchestra each week. He added: 'One might just as well suggest sacking Kenneth Williams, Sidney James and Bill Kerr and booking BBC Drama Rep. artists in order to save money. The result to the listening public's ear would be the same because the music is as much part of the show as the cast.'

Another factor Main Wilson presented was the potential reaction of Hancock if the incidental music was altered. He reminded the Head of Variety that he was trying to secure the artist's signature on a two-year contract, and warned that any changes to the music could antagonise Hancock and jeopardise the chance of him signing a new deal. Main Wilson felt it was 'madness to mess around' with what he classed as one of the most successful shows in postwar years. However, believing he was being presented with a *fait accompli*, he suggested some ideas as a compromise and met with Wally Stott on 25 September, just under three weeks before the start of the new series, to explore the options. After the meeting, Main Wilson reported back to the Assistant Head of Variety with, in his view, the most economical suggestion. The plan was to re-record the incidental music using a smaller orchestra (ten musicians were to be dropped from an orchestra of 35 members); Stott felt the re-scoring would be negligible. For the work, the musicians would be paid a standard fee for the original recording, plus a 50 per cent fee for each subsequent programme, including repeats. To help save money, Main Wilson discarded eleven items so that all the incidental music could be recorded in one session. His costings showed an initial fee of approximately £110, with £55 being paid out for each subsequent episode; to recoup the lion's share of the initial fee, Main Wilson said he'd instruct the writers not to use any guest stars or character performers in the first three scripts; he also mentioned that with Hattie Jacques (who was to play Hancock's new secretary) not joining the series until later in the run, an overall saving of £90 would be realised after the first three episodes. This could be offset against the cost of re-recording the incidental music. Main Wilson's tenacity paid dividends and his plan was given the go-ahead, with the signature tune and links being re-recorded on 3 October 1956 at an actual cost of £136 5 sh., including just over £10 for Stott's conducting fee. While other shows caught up in the dispute reverted to using mood music from the BBC's own library, *Hancock's Half Hour* remained relatively unscathed.

The fourth radio series opened with 'Back from Holiday'; in this episode Hancock and Bill's holiday to France is ruined when they spend most of their money on car repairs and return home early, only to find Sid has rented out their house in the meantime, causing all kinds of mayhem. Sid has even rented out the local police station: Unlike the television series, the new radio series still relied on unrealistic situations. Alan Simpson says: 'Radio allows you to be a little more fantastic. A lot of the storylines were more cartoony but, of course, when you get on television you can't do that, not that we particularly wanted to. You have to remember, when you're writing a 20-week radio series you're grateful to come up with any ideas, so if they turn out a bit over the top then so be it, you haven't got time to worry about that.'

However, several significant changes also took place during the season. The first was the departure of Andrée Melly. Although Galton and Simpson had used the girlfriend character since the series began it hadn't worked particularly well. The characterisation of Hancock didn't lend itself to having an admirer and the girlfriend, who resembled more of a friend, was often superfluous to the storyline. Melly is the first to admit the character wasn't a success. 'I don't think it worked for Hancock to have a girlfriend,' she says. 'He was more at ease with his mates because he rarely went on about girls and wasn't particularly romantic—it didn't fit in with his persona.' Andrée soon saw that there was little future for her character. 'There wasn't really anything she could develop into; I knew how to feed a comedian, but there was no relationship development.'

The arrival of Hattie Jacques in the fifth episode provided an additional boost to the series. Arriving on Hancock's doorstep in response to his advert for a secretary, she forces him into recruiting her with a veiled threat of violence, despite turning out to be more inefficient at keeping the paperwork under control than he is. The dominating and fearless secretary, Grizelda Pugh, provided Hancock with someone to bounce off, increasing the sources of humour. As far as Galton and Simpson were concerned, she was a welcome addition to the cast. 'She was a lovely, funny lady,' enthuses Ray Galton. 'She was purely his secretary who used to look down her nose at him—there was never any question of sex or a relationship forming between them.'

Unlike their previous experiences of writing for women, Galton and Simpson found it easier penning lines for Hattie, as Alan explains. 'We obviously needed a woman in the show but Hattie was almost like a fella in terms of playing comedy; you didn't write for her thinking she's a woman so we've got to write the feminine point of view. That made it easier for us.'

Hattie enjoyed working on the show. She once said: 'Tony's technique and way of working were so brilliant that sometimes I was even late on my entrances because I was so enthralled with watching him.'[4]

When it comes to deciding the origins of the name, Grizelda Pugh, Ray recalls a man called Pugh who was a patient at the tuberculosis sanatorium during their days of recuperation, while Alan states Grizelda was adopted for a cheap laugh, with the name sounding like grizzly. Both point out the advantages of having Jacques in the show. 'Whatever we wanted she would do it—and be funny at it,' explains Ray. 'She was a good actress, a great comedienne with a wonderful presence and perfect timing. It was a great stroke

153

of luck to get Hattie, she was good value for money.' Jacques was hired for 16 programmes at a fee of 22 guineas (£23 2 sh.) per programme and soon became the butt of jokes exploiting her ample proportions. 'We wouldn't get away with it today,' says Ray, 'but it was par for the course for Hattie in those days. She was a very good-looking lady. Yes, we made jokes about her size but no one seemed to mind—least of all her.'

Galton and Simpson didn't waste any time before using such quips, the first of many appearing in the script for 'The New Secretary', which marked her début in the series. When Miss Pugh turns up for an interview, Hancock is far from impressed.

HANCOCK: I'm sure there's plenty of other places that need staff—they'll give you a job.

MISS PUGH: Not to a girl of my size. They all make nasty cracks about lack of office space and lifts only carrying six people. I usually finish up by resorting to violence—I clout them with my umbrella.

In addition to being a fine actress, Hattie Jacques was to make a career out of her size. Although Alan Simpson happily created jokes exploiting her ample frame, Ray Galton was rather more reluctant. 'Being the sensitive soul that I am,' he smiles, 'I did worry about it; but at the same time, some of the jokes were very funny, such as her telling Hancock she's knitting a new jumper and Hancock replying that he wondered why a lorry full up with wool had pulled up outside.' She was far from being an overweight stooge. 'It certainly wasn't all one-way traffic in the show: she used to

154

insult Hancock.'

Despite the fourth radio series averaging 4.19 million listeners, over two million less than had tuned in to the previous season, some memorable episodes were broadcast during this 20-episode run. The cast were performing well together, providing more depth to their characterisations; they were at ease with the show, as shown by a scene in the 14th episode, 'Almost a Gentleman'. Hancock receives tuition from Sid, no less, on how he can become a gentleman and, therefore, improve his chances of being recognised in the next New Year's Honours List. During the episode, a relaxed-sounding Hancock interacts with the audience.

BILL: Ah, stop moaning, it's your pride, that's all. It's been nagging away at you ever since you found out I was an OBE.
HANCOCK: OBE?
BILL: Yeah, Order of the British Empire.
HANCOCK: Bill, you were ordered out of the British Empire!
(*Audience laugh loud, clap and cheer*)
HANCOCK: (*turns to the audience*) Don't go mad, we've got 25 minutes to go yet—save it.

In the programme's evolution two other changes affected the fourth series. Although they didn't become a consistent element in the show's make-up until later on, Bill Kerr and Sid James' characters underwent personality transplants. In the early series of *Hancock's Half Hour*, Kerr was a wise-cracking bright spark, a young blade about town who was always filled with *joie de vivre* and knew how to resolve Hancock's many dilemmas.

From this series he went through a metamorphosis and came out the other side as a dullard, a simpleton. Alan Simpson explains why they altered his personality. 'It was funnier for him to be thick—or thicker than Hancock—as opposed to the cheery Jack the Lad. It became more of a Laurel and Hardy relationship, with Hancock painstakingly trying to explain things to him.' As Simpson explains, Kerr was influential in creating a jovial working atmosphere. 'He was good to have around and was full of laughter. He had a feel-good manner which used to permeate rehearsals—everybody liked him.'

Although Bill's character changed gradually, there are some interesting episodes during the fourth series, including 'Agricultural 'Ancock', when Hancock, Miss Pugh and Bill discuss the reasons behind Hancock's decision to move from his house. His current property attracts a low rent for agricultural labourers but when it's discovered he doesn't work in the industry he faces an increase. Unable to pay, it seems he has little choice but to find alternative accommodation. In the early scenes there are examples of Kerr's more innocent nature. When Miss Pugh believes Hancock is misleading Bill and herself about his reasons for leaving, she turns to Bill and says, 'Don't listen to him, William.' He later expresses his sadness regarding having to move in an almost childlike manner. Yet it's Bill who dreams up the idea of Hancock trying his hand at agriculture, thereby entitling him to the lower rent. It wouldn't be long before he'd completed the transition.

During the fourth series, Sid James' role began to mirror his television persona to a degree. The

156

importance of this development was highlighted by the fact that James had claimed second spot in the cast list from Kerr for the first time in the show's history. 'Bill started as a Jack the Lad, inviting Tony to parties and suchlike, but in the end Sid's character took over that,' explains Alan Simpson. 'He ceased being a crook and became more Tony's mate. Bill was then the dim friend who made Hancock seem intelligent.'

'Bill seldom motivated the show,' adds Ray Galton. 'I don't think the early character worked out, for us or Bill. He wasn't very interesting, just like the roles we created for Moira and Andrée.' As soon as they altered the character, though, Galton and Simpson found it easier and more productive writing for him. 'We were able to get a lot more laughs from him,' says Ray. 'Sid was different. He was always trying to get money from Hancock, or get him involved in something for his own benefit. Many of the plots revolved around Sid until such time as Sid moved in with Hancock— even sharing the same bedroom for one or two episodes—and he became more of a friend, a sidekick of Hancock's, instead of running a completely separate life with Sidney James Enterprises.'

Radio scripts were often completed within days of the broadcast, allowing the writers the chance to be topical. An example popped up in the shape of 'Anna and the King of Siam', which was based on the recently released Yul Brynner film, *The King and I*. The episode, aired on 18 November 1956, found Hancock and his chums presenting their own version of the movie, and was well received by listeners. The Audience Research Department reported an appreciation index of 69, which compared favourably with the average for other comedy team shows of 58. Most people praised every aspect, and the script was classed as 'ingenious, imaginative and fresh'[5]. Tony Hancock's individual performance was also regularly complimented, with one listener stating: 'It's not always what he says, but the way he says it, and his good sense of timing, that makes him so funny.' The recent arrival of Hattie Jacques was a subject many people remarked upon: although some thought her character 'too loud and exaggerated' to settle naturally into the existing cast, others welcomed her to the fold and felt the programme was even better for her presence. For Dennis Main Wilson, comments from listeners stating how they enjoyed the musical effects were regarded as a vindication of his campaign to prevent the loss of his specially recorded incidental music.

Other memorable episodes include 'The Diary', which was influenced by the 1947 movie *The Secret Life of Walter Mitty* and contains, arguably, the most famous sketch in the series' entire history with Hancock dreaming of being a test pilot. 'The Wild Man of the Woods' is another episode which would feature in many fans' Top 5. The script contains a certain pathos in its theme of a man wanting to free himself from the trappings of life to return to a more simplistic way of living. Renouncing civilisation, he heads for the woods to live as a recluse, but his back-to-basics existence is ruined when Sid's idea of running coach trips to try and spot Hancock results in hundreds of people following Hancock into the woods.

Early in the run of the fourth radio series, Hancock appeared in the second television series of *The Tony Hancock Show* for Jack Hylton and Associated-Rediffusion, which Hancock undertook in return for Hylton releasing him from his exclusive contract. The first episode was transmitted on 16 November 1956, but a month later a problem forced Stanley Dale, a representative of Associated London Scripts, to write to Jim Davidson at the BBC. With Galton and Simpson under exclusive contract to the BBC and unable to write the scripts, the intention had been for Eric Sykes to write the first series and other writers at Associated London Scripts to pen the rest. In the end, Sykes also began the second series, but after two 'reasonable' episodes Dale explained to Davidson that the show planned for 14 December had had to be withdrawn and replaced by a variety-based instalment. Again, Dale asked if Galton and Simpson could take over the remaining three episodes and 'help the organisation out of an embarrassing situation'.[6]

Galton and Simpson were keen to help and told the BBC that refusing was short-sighted. 'If the series on ITV wasn't very good, it might not bode well for ours,' explains Alan Simpson. The fact that commercial television was paying almost double what they were receiving from the BBC was also a motivating factor. Meetings within the Corporation took place. Dennis Main Wilson spoke to Hancock personally and informed Davidson that it was probable that Galton and Simpson had already been approached for constructive criticism or advice on previous scripts; he also felt that it was important to help keep Hancock on an 'even nervous keel'.7 With the proviso that the writers would only be called upon to help and not to write entire scripts, and that any involvement didn't affect the quality or delivery of their work for *Hancock's Half Hour*, Main Wilson was happy to offer their services. By the time Davidson officially agreed to Dale's plea for help, there were only two programmes left in the series.

Before the end of 1956, the unresolved subject of a joint radio and screen contract for Hancock and the writers was raised again. William Streeton, Head of Programme Contracts, wrote to Pat Hillyard, Head of Variety, when the Variety Booking Manager was asked to negotiate a new sound series of 20 episodes to start in September 1957, only to discover Hancock had already committed himself to two further television series, the first scheduled for April 1957. Although Streeton questioned the practicality of pursuing a joint contract, he felt the matter needed resolving to avoid any future confusion between BBC Radio and Television. The original plan to try and secure Hancock's services hit the buffers when, during a conversation with Hillyard, Hancock stressed he didn't want to be tied up with any long-running contract, and as he had no intention of working for commercial television again, he didn't see the point in pursuing the matter further.

Hillyard was equally surprised to learn Hancock had already been contracted for a television series during the period when Radio hoped he would be free to record another radio season. The Controller of the Light Programme, like Hillyard, was upset that, for the first time in three years, they were unable to boast a series of *Hancock's Half*

160

Hour during the autumn and winter of 1957. Hillyard expressed his disappointment, once again, in a board report he completed for his superiors in December 1957. Reflecting on the final quarter of the year, he explained that his colleagues in Television frequently adopted programme formats and the artists who have become a success on the radio airwaves, resulting in difficulties in satisfying the requirements of both listeners and viewers. Feeling the flow was one-sided, he vented his disappointment about the forced postponement of *Hancock's Half Hour* and *Take it From Here*, a comedy series starring Jimmy Edwards, from the autumn schedules, resulting in the final quarter containing too many new programmes, which take time to establish themselves. But it wasn't the actions of BBC Television that delayed the transmission of the fifth radio series. Hancock had told Ronald Waldman, early in 1957, that he didn't want to commit himself to radio for 'some time'[8] after the fourth series closed on 24 February 1957; he wanted to rest the radio series for a year in order to concentrate on the television version of the show.

The final episode in the fourth radio series, 'The Last of the McHancocks' was transmitted on Sunday, 24 February 1957. In it, Hancock discovers he has Scottish blood running through his veins. He learns that he's to become the new laird of Glen Sporran, which also means taking possession of Castle Sporran; not everything runs smoothly, however, and the sworn enemies of the McHancocks, the McNastys, represented in the cast by the bearlike character actor, James Robertson Justice, are out to stop Hancock taking over the title and castle. To resolve the dispute, Hancock finds himself competing in some Highland Games, along with McNasty and Sid James, who suddenly arrives claiming ownership of the dwelling.

The episode was well received by the public, with the programme's appreciation index totalling 74, much higher than other comedy team shows reporting in the second half of 1956. Listeners enthused about the final episode and a series which was now well into its stride and although audience figures had dropped since its transfer to television, the responses from the millions for whom listening to Hancock on the radio was part of their staple diet revealed a show of growing popularity. Many people felt it outshone all other comedy programmes and eagerly awaited the next series. One listener stated: 'This series has provided first-class entertainment. Tony Hancock and his excellent team have dealt with the topical events of our times with unsurpassed wit and humour.'[9] A former nurse and chemist's assistant found it 'Extremely enjoyable. Did not bother to listen at first because of the awful ITV Tony Hancock Shows, but with the help of an excellent series of scripts, and first-class supporting actors (particularly Kenneth Williams) I now rate it the funniest programme either on TV or radio—even funnier than the Goons.' Other listeners singled out Kenneth Williams for praise, including some people who were critical of James Robertson Justice's inclusion in the episode because it helped to contribute to the 'almost total exclusion of a favourite character—the "little man"' of Kenneth Williams, or, as someone else described him, 'the

162

lovable little character that usually appears 5 minutes before the end'.

Kenneth Williams was equally dismayed at the lack of air time afforded his character in the final episode, remarking in his diaries: 'Rushed from rehearsing [for *The Wit To Woo* at the Arts Theatre] to BBC for Hancock show, and found I'd hardly any part at all. James Robertson Justice in as Guest Artist! Couldn't bloody care less.'[10] Williams would be hired for the next radio series, the fifth, which was just under a year away, to play his normal range of characters but with one exception: Snide was to be dropped from the show. It was to be Williams' final radio series.

Chapter 10

It was nearly a year before *Hancock's Half Hour* returned to the radio, by which time two further television series had been shown. The second televised season, comprising six instalments transmitted fortnightly, was due to kick off on 1 April 1957.

Preparations got under way well in advance, with director Duncan Wood sending Tony Hancock, who would receive £550 per episode, confirmation of the recording dates at the Riverside Studios. Filming commitments had at one point threatened to stop Sid James appearing in the series. He was away in Cortina, Italy, filming Rank's *Campbell's Kingdom* with Dirk Bogarde and Barbara Murray, but fortunately his absence was kept to just the opening two shows. Wood also required some new incidental music links so a studio at Maida Vale was booked for Tuesday, 26 March, and Bob Sharples and his orchestra hired to complete the work.

Tony Hancock was away but to keep him informed of progress as the date of the first show approached, Wood wrote on 21 March, reassuring him that everything was going to plan. He also kept him abreast of his casting decisions for the opening episode, 'The Alpine Holiday', including the bespectacled character actor Richard Wattis playing the hotel clerk, Kenneth Williams as Snide, June Whitfield as the attractive Miss Duboir and Peggy Ann Clifford as the air hostess, with Wood informing Hancock that 'she's the same size or bigger than Hattie.'[1] Wood was determined to keep Hancock updated on every aspect of the production, stating in his final paragraph that he hoped 'all this is as you would like it'.

The entire cast gave sterling performances in 'The Alpine Holiday'. While Peggy Ann Clifford provided one of her dependable characterisations as the air hostess who has to put up with a nervous Hancock, dressed in Swiss garb, as he flies to the Alps to enjoy some winter sports, Kenneth Williams also caused plenty of laughs as Snide. A yodelling champion from East Dulwich, who is visiting Switzerland for a tournament, he ends up sharing a hotel bedroom with Hancock. Watched by 8.7 million people—it was to have the largest audience of the series—Hancock was in sparkling form. While some viewers preferred his radio outings, finding it easier to imagine his adventures than to actually see them, most regarded him as a natural for television, citing, once again, his facial expressions and timing as particular qualities. Duncan Wood agreed with the viewers' opinions. In an interview for a television documentary, he said: 'I thought Tony Hancock's natural timing was the greatest that I had the pleasure to work with. I don't think the man could mistime a line if he tried.'[2] On the actor's facial reactions, he commented: 'In the scripts the stage directions about the face were very basic: "simulates sorrow", nothing much more than that, the rest of it was down to Tony. He used to invent new faces by the week.' There is no finer example of his adeptness in this aspect of comedy than his performance in a later episode from the sixth series, 'The Missing

Page', in which an entire scene in the local library is played out in mime, with Hancock trying to describe to Sid James a book's content through facial expressions and actions.

When Sid James returned to the fold in 'The Russian Prince' it was like returning to the radio series, for the cast also contained Hattie Jacques and Kenneth Williams; all of Williams' small-screen appearances were made in this series, while Jacques popped up two years later in 'The Cruise'. Williams' final appearance was in the closing episode, 'The Auction', which finds Hancock, short of cash, auctioning his house to pay for himself and Sid to fly to Monte Carlo to try and win money on the roulette tables. Williams was cast as an old man but it was a show he didn't enjoy, primarily because he thought (rightly, as it turned out) that he wasn't going to feature in any future television series of the sitcom. He felt he'd been treated poorly during the series and surmised from chatting to Tony Hancock that Hancock didn't want him in the set-up. In his diary entry for Monday, 10 June 1957, he records that Tony felt 'set characters make a rut in story routine'.[3] Although Williams was present for the next radio series, and the first two of the sixth season, in which he played several roles, the reason why Snide was never heard again was the result of Hancock's desire to rid the show of comic characters. When the writers later included dialogue for Snide in the radio script 'The Insurance Policy', transmitted in February 1958, Hancock reacted. Williams wrote 'he was angry about it, and that it should go. He really believes that it is "cartoon" and etc. etc . . . Every time he asks me if I mind, I have to say *no* because after all

166

this fuss I'd feel *awful* doing the damned voice!'[4]

It was the beginning of the end for Williams in the programme, but also marked a juncture in the show's life. Tony Hancock's influence was increasing and he began to analyse the sitcom's merits, as well as individuals' contributions to the final product. He'd started showing disquiet towards the end of the fourth radio series, earlier in 1957, when he chatted with Dennis Main Wilson. Recalling the conversation, Main Wilson later said:

Tony started to get a bit unhappy and said to me: 'Last week we ended up down the labour exchange, the week before we were in the nick . . . it's getting a bit down, down—I want to be up. Alan and Ray must write me up, I don't want to be dragged down because the higher up I am, the further there is to fall which, comedically, is useful. If the boys [Galton and Simpson] can't do it, I want to get Eric Sykes, he knows how to write me up.' That never happened, but the message went to Alan and Ray and they tried.[5]

Galton and Simpson recall Hancock beginning to question the continual use of funny voices, by which time they were inserting a small sketch into the scripts simply to accommodate the Snide character. 'Tony thought that, artistically, it was wrong,' says Alan Simpson. 'He was right, of course, but the voice had became very popular and was a godsend when, perhaps, we were stuck for a scene or two of dialogue. In the final radio series, though, we made a conscious effort to get away from Snide and the other funny characters of

167

Ken's.' Alan never detected any evidence of jealousy in Hancock's assessments. 'His suggestions weren't just aimed at Ken; he also started questioning the continual portrayal of Sid as a crook, believing it was getting too stereotyped. He was never a jealous performer; he didn't care who got the laughs, and his only concern about Kenneth Williams' roles were that they were becoming unnatural.'

Freddie Hancock says of her late husband: 'He was all about improving, improving, improving. The thing that drove him most was that if he was bored with something, the audience would become bored with it and so you should get rid of it now.' Freddie also recalls that he felt the strain of the show: 'He enjoyed the challenge each week. He wasn't aware of the pressures at first, but he was as the series progressed.' On the day he was completing a recording, the occasional smoker would become a chain-smoker. 'He used to play an active role in the editing process,' recalls Freddie. 'Again, he'd take to smoking, although always someone else's. I'd put packets of cigarettes in all his pockets but they'd still be intact when he got home.'

Hancock's desire to involve himself in the editing process, as well as other aspects of the production, was noted by Duncan Wood. 'It wasn't that he didn't trust people, but I think he wanted to do everybody else's job,' he once said. 'He wanted to be behind the camera, he wanted to do the lighting, he wanted to do everything including make the tea!'[6]

Meanwhile, the constant pressure of learning lines never abated, and was exacerbated by some substantial passages of dialogue, such as in 'The Auction'. The following sequence highlights the challenge facing the actor.

SID: Are you interested or not?

HANCOCK: Well, of course I'm interested. But you said yourself, we've got fourpence halfpenny between us.

SID: Ah, in currency yes. But we have other assets.

TONY: Have we?

SID: Of course we have.

TONY: What?

SID: Your home. (*Indicating the room*) Auction off all this lot.

TONY: This *lot*? This lot as you flippantly call it, is my home. These are my worldly goods, matey. Every article collected and tended with loving care; this isn't just a table, these aren't just chairs, everything you see in here reflects me; my personality has been injected into every bit of it over the years, they're as much a part of me as my arms and legs. And now, heathen that you are, you suggest I should put it under the hammer.

SID: Well why not? It's only a lot of rubbish.

TONY: Rubbish? Rubbish? Have a care sir, you're going too far. You're casting reflections on the taste of generations of Hancocks. Family heirlooms, this lot . . . handed down from one dynasty to another, in trust I may add . . . trust . . . that I will hand them on to my sons. Look at this. (*He picks up a big china dog*) Intrinsic sentimental value, this. It was my mother's, Clacton Fairgrounds 1926. She stuck three darts in the six of diamonds without batting an eyelid . . . and drunk, I may add. A feat unequalled by

169

the rest of the coach outing. And this . . . (*He picks up a standard lamp*) My father nearly killed himself to get this.

SID: How?

TONY: In 1936 he smoked ten thousand of the worst fags on the market so he could get the vouchers. In hospital for ten weeks he was, had a tongue like a piece of emery cloth. I couldn't allow it to be auctioned after all he went through to get it.

SID: What about this then? (*He picks up a tin box*)

TONY: Put that down, put that down. That's the only one of its kind in Cheam. An unopened tin of chocolate biscuits handed to my great-grandfather by Queen Victoria as he got off the troopship for South Africa.

SID: Got off.

TONY: Well he should have gone but his leg went bad just before they pulled the gangplank up. I can't get rid of any of this stuff, Sid, it means more to me than money. All priceless family history here, Sid. I couldn't part with it.

SID: Well there must be something in here we can flog. We could get rid of that horrible bird. (*Tony rushes across and stands next to Polly. Puts his hand round it.*)

TONY: How dare you. Go and wash your mouth out. You'll not touch Polly. How could you stand there and speak like that about her. A noble beast, a king among birds. Friends for years we were. Many's the autumn we've spent together in the Highlands, stag hunting. There I was standing in the burn with me kilt flapping in the breeze, and Polly perched on me wrist. Six foot spread, those wings. Many's the time she had me off the floor.

Halfway up to her eyrie sometimes before she'd let me go. What a combination we made. A legend we were up there in the hunting season. The natives still talk of Polly and Hancock up round Loch Rannoch. What a hunter. A flock of stags would fly over, I'd let go with both barrels, and she'd pick 'em up by their antlers before they hit the ground. It was a tragic loss when she went, Sid. A noble end though, in keeping with the way she lived. It was a summer's day, 1944. She was gliding home just above here, when a Spitfire flew alongside her and tipped her over with his wing tip—he thought she was a doodlebug. Ended her flying days of course. Come home from hospital and moped around the house for a few days. Pacing up and down the front room with her wings behind her back, I knew it was only a matter of time. She took to her cage on the Thursday and never came out again. Tragic. So I had her stuffed and mounted on the stick here. And I like to think that she would have done the same for me. (*He wipes his eye with a handkerchief*)

SID: I'm sorry, Hancock.

TONY: No, it's all right, I'll be all right. I go like that, it sends me off a bit when I talk about her. No Sid, I'm sorry, I couldn't part with Polly for all the money in the world.

SID: But Hancock, think of it. A hundred thousand nicker. Monte Carlo, yachts, big cars, beautiful girls, holidays in the sun, hot Mediterranean nights, glamorous starlets fawning round you.

(*Tony takes a label and sticks it on Polly's head*)

TONY: Lot one.

With a television script containing approximately

171

54 pages of dialogue, it was a weekly headache for Hancock. To help prevent any forgotten lines, he was provided with a safety net, something he could turn to if the need ever arose. If it was expected that a particular passage of dialogue might cause difficulties, the lines were scribbled on to card or pieces of paper and dotted all over the set. One member of the production team allocated the task of writing out the prompt cards was Gerry Mill, who worked on *Hancock's Half Hour* in various capacities before progressing to become a director/producer. Mill, who is currently responsible for Yorkshire Television's popular drama series, *Heartbeat*, says: 'There was a kind of pattern. He'd do two or three shows and would be word perfect; then, perhaps the third or fourth show, he would say: "Can you give me a cue card for that line?" Then a couple of days later he'd ask: "Would you do that other line?" Then I ended putting the lot on cue cards.' The live broadcast was a frenetic time for Gerry. 'I had to rush around and find the right card and hold it up for him.' Catering for the regular Galton and Simpson monologues was a hazardous time. 'I'd be holding up the cards and, sometimes, when Tony was halfway through he'd realise he knew the rest and would look away from the card. The trouble was, I didn't know the lines so I wouldn't know what card to reach for next. That nearly gave me a heart attack. Something else which worried me to death was that someone would move a particular cue card which I'd tucked behind the scenery.'

'They were there as a safeguard,' says Alan Simpson, who doesn't think Hancock used them very often. 'If, in particular, he had long speeches he'd have them written down and posted on a table, a wall or the side of a cabinet, just to give him some confidence that if he did dry up, he knew the words were there.'

As the cast worked through the rehearsal period towards the broadcast, Mill noticed Hancock losing his self-confidence, with more cue cards being requested. This was also noted by Hugh Lloyd, who appeared in 25 episodes. 'By the time we attended the read-through on the Monday, Hancock, who'd been working on the script the previous weekend, could practically do it without looking at the script. By Tuesday, he was word perfect, and was the only person I've ever seen in my career get applauded three times in the rehearsal room. When he arrived on Wednesday he'd have a slight doubt about a particular scene, then by Thursday he seemed to have doubts about everything. He had this terrible fear of not being able to remember the lines.'

Gerry Mill regards his days working with Tony Hancock as some of the happiest of his professional career. 'People said Tony was jealous of other actors but I never saw it. In fact, he would often ask Duncan Wood to use people again, especially the likes of Johnny Vyvyan and Arthur Mullard. He'd say: "They're hysterical, bring them back." ' So, at Tony's behest, some actors were used repeatedly.

Gerry also remembers the rehearsal period. 'Hancock was a perfectionist and, sometimes, until he was comfortable with his performance, he'd rehearse on his own. Anyone watching would fall about with laughter, but when he actually got to the studio, he always had something extra for the camera—perhaps certain expressions. As far as I was concerned, the man was a genius.'

The second series finished with 'The Auction', which was watched by 4.9 million people, the lowest audience figure in the series but from the sample who expressed their opinions to the BBC's Audience Research Department, it was clear the majority classed *Hancock's Half Hour* as one of television's best comedy shows, with Hancock and James being regarded as the perfect comedy partnership—something which ultimately led to Hancock severing his professional ties with James.

By the time the series ended, Galton and Simpson's three-year exclusive contract with the BBC had expired. Discussions were already under way regarding fees for the next radio series, which was due to begin by the end of January 1958. Their agent felt that the new fee should not be lower than 150 guineas per programme, which Main Wilson described, in a memo to the Assistant Head of Variety, as 'absolutely outrageous'. He explained that it was almost certain each show would be repeated within seven days, there would be a subsequent repeat on the Home Service and a strong possibility that the BBC's Transcription Services would accept the programme, increasing Galton and Simpson's fee to 600 guineas. Compared with the 325 guineas paid for the recently completed television series, which was transmitted fortnightly, Main Wilson felt a fairer offer would be in the region of 105 to 110 guineas per programme but realised the BBC found themselves in a ticklish situation because any refusal to pay Galton and Simpson what they were asking could result in Hancock refusing to make the series.

While BBC Sound mulled over their next step in securing writers and artists alike for their next season, Duncan Wood set the wheels in motion for the third television series, due to begin at the end of September 1957. An offer letter, for £750 per programme, was issued to Hancock on 23 July, while Wood arranged with Wally Stott to record incidental music every Friday from the Piccadilly Studios with a 20-member orchestra. But not everything was running to plan.

Duncan Wood and Ronald Waldman, the Head of Light Entertainment (Television), had become vexed about having to use the more cramped Studio G at Lime Grove for *Hancock's Half Hour*. Believing it was appropriate for single-set programmes but not multi-set shows like *Hancock's Half Hour*, Waldman—who preferred to use the more spacious Studio 1 at BBC's Riverside—raised the matter with the Controller of Programming. Waldman had visited various American studios in 1953 and been impressed by the effect of constructing sets side by side and placing the studio audience along the opposite wall of the studio. He believed it provided the maximum impact when producing a situation comedy. There was sufficient floor space in Riverside 1 to accommodate this layout but the studio at Lime Grove was too small: while the sets could be constructed, the audience numbers were restricted to under 100. Waldman felt concerned that such limitations would 'damage the show'.[7]

After Waldman's concerns had been considered, schedules were reorganised to allow 11 episodes to be made at the Riverside Studios. However, for the third episode, 'The Amusement Arcade', they had

175

to settle for Lime Grove's Studio G, much to the chagrin of Duncan Wood, who fired off a memo to Waldman detailing the alterations that would have to be made to the show, and the effects that might be apparent on the screen. Reflecting on using the studio for the first series of *Hancock's Half Hour*, Wood explained that lack of space meant there was no room for an orchestra if he chose to use one, the writers had to limit the number of sets required and couldn't write scenes that involved back projection, while the audience of only ninety sat in a long line, meaning half of them had to watch the action via a monitor, eliciting an insufficient reaction from the audience for many scenes. Wood said: 'Whichever way you look at it, it is a thoroughly retrograde step and one which everyone concerned with the show, especially Tony Hancock himself, views with not a little misgiving.'[8]

After expressing his views, Duncan Wood concentrated on the first episode, 'The Continental Holiday'. Just as the clocks crept past eight on the evening of 30 September, the much-loved signature tune was followed by Hancock entertaining Sid with tales of his recent holiday adventures. The episode was watched by just under seven million viewers, and the sample audience enthused about the return of the series, giving it a reaction index of 71, a healthy rise from 63, the average for the previous series. Hancock, once again, attracted many plaudits, with one viewer advising the BBC to 'hold on to this chap Hancock at all costs.'[9] All aspects of the programme, from the script to the film inserts showing far-off destinations, were praised, making this a promising start to the new series. Four weeks later, 'Air Steward Hancock' topped the previous episodes, all warmly received by viewers, with a reaction index of 75. As well as praise being bestowed upon Hancock and James, whom many regarded as a fine comic actor in his own right, Galton and Simpson were also patted on the back, with one person claiming the scriptwriters 'understand and make full use of the medium—and are furthermore scriptwriters with original ideas in dialogue and comedy situations'.[10]

In the fourth episode, 'A Holiday in Scotland', Hancock travels north of the border. When his doctor recommends that he gets fit, he heads for a hunting holiday with a reluctant Sid; while Hancock intends to live off the land, Sid plays safe and carries a mountain of tins and processed food. As expected, Hancock's plans backfire and he spends hours out hunting and fishing, with little to show for his efforts.

SID: Blimey, ten o'clock. He's been gone nearly eleven hours. Where's he got to?
(*Effects: Two rifle shots*)
Well he's getting nearer anyway.
(*The door opens and Tony appears, panting and exhausted. He leans up against the door*)
SID: About time too. Well, what did you get?
(*Tony holds up a string with a tiny three inch long fish on the end. Sid looks at it. Then at Tony. Milk this as long as possible.*)
SID: That's it, is it? That's the bountiful supply of riches from Mother Nature's larder, is it?
(*Tony just glares at him*)
SID: Shall I stoke the fire up or are you going to eat it raw?
(*Tony still just glares at him*)

177

SID: I'll hold a match under it if you like. (*Sid laughs*)

TONY: Har, har, har, har. Where's the frying pan?

(*He goes towards the stove. As he passes Sid, Sid stops him*)

SID: Show us that fish.

(*Sidney looks at the fish*)

SID: You had this when you went out. It was your bait.

TONY: I know it was. Obviously the salmon round here don't fancy English sprats.

SID: You're not having any of mine.

TONY: I wouldn't touch tinned food if I was starving.

(*He goes over to the stove, unties the fish, lays it out on the table. Takes a knife and delicately cuts off the head and the tail. Splits it down the middle and pulls the bone out. Holds it up and throws it in the bin.*)

TONY: I think I'll have it boiled.

(*Tony dangles it in a great big iron saucepan by the tail. Pulls it out again.*)

TONY: I think that's done enough.

(*He lays it out on a plate and takes it over to the table. Meanwhile Sid has laid his food out on the table. There are about six plates piled up with stuff. Tony puts a napkin on. Salts and peppers his fish. Eats it in one bite. Takes the napkin off, folds it up. Folds his arms and watches Sid tucking in. Ravenously. Tony trying hard not to appear envious.*)

SID: Sensational.

(*Tony unfolds his arms and refolds them. Fidgets about a bit.*)

SID: Hungry?

178

TONY: (*Casually*) No, no. That was quite enough for me. Does you good to go without. Gives the stomach a rest.

SID: Yeah. Good idea. (*Stuffs more food in his mouth*)

TONY: That little fish was the only thing I've had to eat in twenty-four hours, but I'm not hungry. I can honestly say I'm not hungry. Quite full up in fact. Amazing the nutrition in those little fish (*pause*) Er . . . I don't mind doing the washing up.

SID: It won't do you any good. I'm not leaving any.

In charge of props for this live broadcast was Cecil Korer. Now a producer and director, back then he worked on numerous episodes of the show as part of the scene crew. With just a few hours before the live show he was tasked with finding something to represent Hancock's little fish. He recalls:

Many years earlier I had worked in pantomime with Frank Randle. He had a routine where he walked on stage where there was a goldfish bowl and Frank used to dip his hand in and eat the fish. How this worked was that the goldfish were actually carved out of carrot and just before curtain up we used to stir the water, giving the appearance that the fish were swimming round the bowl. Frank's appearance and eating of what appeared to be live fish always brought gasps from the children in the audience.

'That's it,' I thought. I got a carrot from the canteen, carved it into the shape of a fish and coloured it in HP sauce and it looked pretty realistic. No time to rehearse, so "On Air" we went. Tony, who had only mimed the eating in rehearsal, popped the fish into his mouth, and couldn't speak. I had forgotten that Frank Randle's fish were boiled first to soften them. Tony was stuck with a mouthful of raw carrot, which he couldn't swallow. After the show, Duncan Wood told me that Tony wanted to see me. I thought I was in for a real rocket. Instead, he gave me a drink and thanked me; he and Sid were roaring with laughter.

A couple of years later, when I was based at BBC Manchester as an O.B. stage manager, I was walking along Oxford Road when I heard a voice from across the road shout, 'Lofty, you and your bloody fish!' It was, of course, Tony.

The instalment originally scheduled for 18 November, 'The Elocution Teacher', in which leading film actor Jack Hawkins made a guest appearance, had to be postponed when Hancock contracted flu. A repeat of 'The Alpine Holiday', which fortunately had been telerecorded for internal purposes only, was hurriedly slotted in and a special introduction penned for Sid James, who was paid his full fee of 100 guineas for this brief appearance informing viewers about the change of programme. The short introduction read:

SIDNEY: Ladies and gentlemen, I am here tonight to bring to your notice a dead liberty. In case you don't know, Mr Tony Hancock, my protégée, is incapaci . . . indis . . . inde . . . he's in bed with a touch of the old Asian. I thought he was looking one degree under the other day so I gave him two bottles of aspirins to take, but it didn't do any good because just after he took them he felt dickey and went to bed. So instead of the advertised show tonight, they're putting on a telerecording of one of the old ones. So I thought 'Hallo, this is all right,' I thought. 'Sid boy you're in . . . because they pay you, you see, for repeats. I thought this is money for old rope, I can do a bit of work on the side tonight as well.' But this is where the dead liberty comes in. The one they're showing you tonight, I'm not in it. I'm not *in* it. It's the one they did on April the first, and I'm the mug. Not a penny do I get for tonight's show. And on top of that they had the nerve to offer me thirty bob so here you are . . . a telerecording of the *Hancock's Half Hour*, first shown on April the first . . . without me. And if you're watching, Hancock, you'd better be out of bed before next Monday, because I'm not having any more of this mate. (*Looks off*) Right go on, show it . . . Cor . . . (*Reaction*)

'The Elocution Teacher' was rescheduled for 25 November, a postponement which nearly meant Jack Hawkins was unable to appear due to a prior promotional engagement in America for a forthcoming film. Galton and Simpson have happy memories of working with the esteemed actor. 'He was charming,' says Alan. 'We put him through a lot, having him dress up as a Teddy boy, with an Elvis Presley style wig, playing it as a rock 'n' roll star because Tony had persuaded him he wouldn't get anywhere as an actor, not with a name like Hawkins, which he thought sounded more like a rag-and-bone man.'

181

Other guest stars included leading actor John Gregson and veteran character performer Cecil Parker. 'People couldn't wait to get on the show,' adds Ray. 'Don't forget, it was the biggest comedy show on.'

The series finished on 23 December with an extended episode titled 'The East Cheam Repertory Company', a special show from the Television Theatre, regarded by many viewers as a disappointing end to a first-rate series, particularly as the episode returned to a variety-style format. It may not have been as memorable as other episodes in the series but at least it wasn't as problematic as the penultimate show, 'There's an Airfield at the Bottom of my Garden', which almost ended in disaster when the set started falling apart during the live transmission. The episode, which was influenced partly by the fact that Tony Hancock's brother, Roger, owned a house at the end of the main runway at Heathrow for thirty-seven years, begins with Hancock entertaining members of the East Cheam Musical Appreciation Society by playing the cello at his newly purchased country cottage in Little Codswallop. It's no surprise that Hancock encounters problems, bearing in mind he bought the property from Sid James. Before long he discovers it's located next to an aerodrome and whenever a plane lands it sends violent tremors throughout the house. When Sid won't refund the money, Hancock attempts to sell it himself, but just when he thinks he's secured a buyer, a plane flies overhead.

A set was specially prepared to fall apart at a given point within the programme but unfortunately it happened too soon, leaving the actors no option but to try and stop the items collapsing around them. Alan Simpson acknowledges that live television was frightening. 'The fireplace, furniture and walls were supposed to collapse at certain times but it all happened too early, leaving Dick Emery—who was in the scene—holding the fireplace up while Tony grabbed the table. Hancock was supposed to be showing these people around the house but instead of moving about the set, they were all standing around holding up the scenery. Finally this plane took off and they all stood back and the house collapsed. Tony looked at the camera and said: "Surprise, surprise."'

Despite this one-off disaster, Hancock as a character and comedy actor, as well as the show itself, had grown in stature during the year. In April, journalist David Lewin applauded the return of the series in the *Daily Express*, stating: 'It had wit. It had bite. It was a success.'[11] He expected Hancock to go on to become the 'star funny man' of 1957.

Ronald Waldman, Head of Light Entertainment, was also sufficiently impressed with the two series transmitted during the year to write to Ray Galton, Alan Simpson and Tony Hancock the day after the final episode was screened, stating he was proud to have been associated with the show, and hoping they would soon be discussing another series.

The pressures of making the show having eased, Duncan Wood decided it was an opportune moment to conduct a critical review of the third season and to record some matters that had become clear to him during the previous three months. Writing to Ronald Waldman on New

183

Year's Eve, he described the closing episode, 'The East Cheam Repertory Company', as a 'mistake'[12] and the worst in the series. Wood wasn't happy with Hancock's performance and wanted to retract opinions he'd given during an earlier discussion regarding whether to ask Hancock to perform in a 60-minute theatre show the following February. Wood admitted: 'Personally, I believe that this type of show will do him more harm than good with the viewers. Situation is the only medium for Hancock and without it he becomes a mediocre performer.' Wood was happy with the rest of the series, though, believing the episodes maintained high levels of writing and admirable performances from Hancock. However, Wood regarded Hancock as a 'highly nervous and, to a degree, temperamental artist' and felt that 13 weekly shows pushed him to his limits. In hindsight, Hancock's enforced absence, earlier in the series, due to flu had, as far as Wood was concerned, been advantageous because without the break he thought the final episodes would have suffered in terms of performance. Wood closed his memo by suggesting that if another television series was arranged (the fourth season began on Boxing Day 1958) it would be beneficial to telerecord four episodes in advance and insert them during the series, creating a week's break after every three shows. As it turned out, the first four episodes of the following series were telerecorded in advance, but circumstances forced them to be transmitted consecutively at the start of the series.

Chapter 11

Soon after welcoming in the New Year, Hancock and the rest of the radio cast were reunited for the fifth radio series. But one significant absentee was producer Dennis Main Wilson, who had switched media to work in television. Like a dynamo on full charge, he was responsible for steering the series from the very first episode, back in November 1954, and had played a fundamental role in creating one of the BBC's most successful programmes. Working behind the scenes meant Main Wilson didn't always receive the credit he deserved from those who sat back and wallowed in the delights offered by the cast each week on the Light Programme, but everyone working on the show, from the writers to the studio managers, knew the impact he'd had on shaping the relatively new genre of situation comedy this side of the Atlantic. His replacement for the remaining two series, apart from the first episode of series five and the 1958 Christmas Special, was Tom Ronald, a veteran producer who knew the industry inside out.

However, it was initally intended that Charles Maxwell, another senior producer at the BBC, would take over the helm, a decision communicated to Hancock in a letter from Jim Davidson, Assistant Head of Variety, the previous October. Hancock resented the fact that he hadn't been consulted over the matter, and although he wasn't against Maxwell personally, he pursued the issue out of principle. In his stinging reply, Hancock said he regarded it as 'extraordinary that any such decision could be contemplated, without any consultation whatsoever with the principal artiste concerned, and I must tell you now that I cannot accept it.'[1] Although it's unclear why Ronald took over the hot seat instead of Maxwell, it was clear that Hancock didn't take kindly to such a crucial decision being taken without his input.

Before Tom Ronald became the incumbent, Pat Dixon stepped in to produce the opening episode, appropriately titled 'The New Radio Series'. When the show, which had been recorded two days earlier, was broadcast on Tuesday, 21 January 1958, 5.29 million listeners tuned in to hear an upbeat Hancock, still patting himself on the back after his successful television series, considering retirement—that is until the BBC accept his decision and line up a replacement programme, *Kerr's Half Hour*. The show met with a mixed reaction, with some people believing it lacked its normal vitality, and others still missing Williams' Snide character. Some listeners, although pleased to have the team back on the airwaves, stated they needed a little time to 'reacquire the Hancock habit and mood',[2] perhaps an indication that with the previous radio series finishing nearly a year ago, it had been off the air for too long. However, the lion's share of viewers welcomed the programme's return and felt the episode reached the usual high standards in terms of script and acting, with the excellence of the teamwork being particularly noted.

Contrary to the world of television, Galton and Simpson were able to leave the writing of the radio scripts until the final moments. Such immediacy allowed the writers to latch on to current events, such as petrol rationing (the focus of a previous episode) or the release of a new film. Later in the series, 'The Foreign Legion', which was transmitted on 15 April, coincided with Hancock completing a three-week tour entertaining the troops. The episode saw Hancock hoping to entertain the military at Malta but ending up, thanks again to Sid, joining the Foreign Legion. In reality, Hancock began the Mediterranean tour on Monday, 24 March and didn't complete his schedule until Tuesday, 15 April. To accommodate his time away from the show, several programmes had to be pre-recorded, with Hancock flying back to London specially to record them.

By now, Bill Kerr's character had fully evolved into an intellectually challenged individual, consistently struggling to come to terms with the big, wide world around him. Examples of the change are heard in 'The Insurance Policy' and 'The Publicity Photograph', broadcast on 11 February and 18 February respectively. In the first, Bill is talking to Hancock, who is preoccupied, about a new pinball machine that has been installed in the local café.

BILL: I meant to tell you, they've just had a new pinball machine put in. You've only got to get 78,000 and you get a cheesecake.
HANCOCK: Why don't you go down to the garage and watch the buses going past.
BILL: No, I sat there all day yesterday.

In 'The Publicity Photograph', Bill is discussing

Hancock's publicity photograph with Hancock and Miss Pugh.

BILL: I had my photo taken once.

HANCOCK: I bet they had to put words under that.

BILL: Yeah, they did: 'Wanted. £5 reward. Answers to the name of Billy or Rat Bag. Will the finder please return to Mrs Kerr, The Sheds, Wagga Wagga.'

MISS PUGH: Ah . . . poor little boy, he got lost. How old were you?

BILL: Twenty-seven.

HANCOCK: I bet you had an exciting childhood. You ought to have done, it's lasted long enough. Now go and sit down and be quiet and I'll give you a chocolate biscuit.

While Bill Kerr remained with the cast for the final radio series, which would run during the autumn of 1959, it was Hattie Jacques' and Kenneth Williams' last full season. Other than four special remakes of 'The 13th of the Series', 'The New Secretary', 'The Bolshoi Ballet' and 'The Election Candidate' for the BBC's Transcription Services, Jacques' final performance was in the 1958 Christmas Special, 'Bill and Father Christmas', while Williams, in addition to the remakes for Transcription Services, would be heard in the first two episodes of the sixth series. Snide had already been dropped, but now the remainder of comic voices, executed successfully by Williams over the years, would be phased out. 'Ray and I decided to go back to our original thoughts and use actors for the final series,' explains Alan Simpson. 'The Snide character had become intrusive; we became aware that it seemed like the entire storyline had to stop to bring him in, so it was a relief not to have to worry about that. The last series became more natural than comic cuts.'

'I know it's been said many times that Tony was jealous of Kenneth Williams and the laughs he got, but I don't think he was—he wasn't a jealous performer,' says Ray Galton. 'But sometimes Tony would feel we were getting into a bit of a rut, or he thought we should move on in terms of the show's development, not that he would have the vaguest idea how to achieve that. So Alan and I had to sit down and think how to move on. I remember once he said: "That's not my role in life. I'm the performer, you're the writers: you write, I'll perform."'

By this time in Williams' career, he was utilising his funny voices to great effect on popular shows such as *Around the Home* and *Beyond Our Ken* and as the fifth series of *Hancock's Half Hour* progressed he became increasingly unhappy with every aspect of the show. In his diaries, he records that he felt the scripts were deteriorating. By the time he turned up at the Piccadilly on Sunday, 23 November to record the remakes of 'The 13th of the Series' and 'The New Secretary', he was clearly not enjoying his involvement with the show. He wrote: 'It was a general disaster. Really terrible. This team is so dreary to me now!—how different to the jolly warmth of BOK [*Beyond Our Ken*].'[3]

When it comes to injecting realism into their scripts, Simpson and Galton couldn't have done a better job than 'Sunday Afternoon at Home'. It's Sunday, the rain is pouring down outside 23 Railway Cuttings and its occupants are fed up.

Sid, Bill and Miss Pugh are better at whiling away the hours than Hancock, who grows increasingly bored. The opening scene sets the mood.

HANCOCK: (*Yawns*) Oh dear, oh dear, oh dear; oh, dear me. (*Sighs*) Stone me, what a life. What's the time?

BILL: Two o'clock.

HANCOCK: Is that all. (*Sighs*) Oh dear, oh dear. Oh dear me. I dunno (*Yawns*). Oh I'm fed up.

SID: Oi!

HANCOCK: What?

SID: Why don't you shut up moaning and let me get on with the paper.

HANCOCK: Well, I'm fed up.

SID: So you just said.

HANCOCK: Well, so I am.

SID: Look, so am I fed up, and so is Bill fed up. We're all fed up, so shut up moaning and make the best of it.

HANCOCK: (*Sighs*) You sure it's only two o'clock?

SID: No, it's . . . one minute past two now.

HANCOCK: One minute past two. Doesn't the time drag? Ooh, I do hate Sundays.

In this episode, heard by 4.54 million people, the writers play with silence, once regarded as a deadly sin in the medium of radio. 'That episode was a bit of a landmark,' says Ray Galton, 'We just wrote "pause" in the script and left it to the actors to experiment with how long it could be maintained. In those days, there was nowhere to go, nothing to do on wet Sunday afternoons; once you'd read the papers you were stuck: the pubs were shut and the pictures didn't open until about 5 p.m.' Ray and

Alan agree that the episode led to one of Hancock's finest performances. 'He was wonderful. It was a nice little gem for him to work at and he really got hold of the script—they all did.'

The episode, hailed as a classic within the Galton and Simpson canon, drew letters of protest regarding what some listeners saw as the guying of 'Sunday Observance'. Jim Davidson, Assistant Head of Light Entertainment, wrote to Tom Ronald on 1 May asking for his opinion on whether such complaints should be taken seriously; he also suggested they watched 'Messrs. Galton and Simpson's future plot treatments.'[4] Ronald took little time firing back a memo, exonerating the writers and dismissing the complaints, including one sent to the Director-General.

The series was well received by much of senior management. Pat Hillyard singled out the show in his quarterly board reports in March and June 1958, for helping boost listener appreciation of light entertainment; he believed it represented the 'highest level of our present comedy offering'.[5] In his next quarterly report he referred specially to 'Sunday Afternoon at Home', considering it 'the funniest script since Itma'.[6] But Galton and Simpson couldn't please everyone. The Assistant Director of Sound Broadcasting wrote to the Head of Light Entertainment admitting that he thought the *Hancock* shows had been 'rather falling off', with some episodes 'singularly unfunny'.[7] Believing Hancock's comedic techniques were as strong as ever, he thought the scriptwriting must be to blame. As for fans of *Hancock's Half Hour*, the majority were still enjoying the adventures of Hancock, James et al., even though four of the closing five episodes saw audiences drop below four million; this gradual decline reflected the growing trend towards television. The final sound series, still over a year away, would have audience figures averaging 3.36 million per episode, a drop of just over a million from series five, with one episode, 'Sid's Mystery Tours', suffering the ignominy of being the radio episode with the lowest audience figure—just 2.72 million.

In recent years, the British public have begun to appreciate once again the attractions of this vision-less medium, with the BBC releasing the surviving radio episodes on CD and audio cassette. Some of the best radio scripts originated in the latter years, such as 'The Americans Hit Town', in which Miss Pugh is ecstatic because the Americans are coming to Cheam. Hancock isn't so happy, because it will squash any chance he had of attracting a local girl. His depression is short-lived, though: soon he grasps the opportunity to earn a packet renting out rooms to the Americans for extortionate prices. 'The Grappling Game', meanwhile, finds Sid presenting a wrestling tournament and employs Kenneth Williams in six separate roles, including as a wrestler, an old cleaner at the Cheam baths, a snooty member of the audience and a commentator at the Albert Hall. The penultimate episode, 'The Threatening Letters', contained a degree of gravitas with Hancock the receiver of threatening correspondence stating the world would be a better place without him. The series ended with the transmission of 'The Sleepless Night' on 3 June 1958.

Before 1958 drew to a close, the radio cast would record a Christmas Special, 'Bill and Father

Christmas', remake four episodes for the BBC's Transcription Service for the foreign market, and Tony Hancock and Sid James would be preparing for the fourth television series, which kicked off on Boxing Day. Other than the festive episode, for which Hancock was paid 100 guineas, it would be over a year before he was heard in another radio series, much to the disappointment of everyone in Sound; attempts to persuade Hancock to commit to a further series before the end of 1958 had failed.

Fans were treated to a double dose of Messrs Hancock and James over the festive period. On Christmas Day, 'Bill and Father Christmas' was broadcast at 4.30 p.m. while the Boxing Day treat, the opening episode of the fourth television series, 'Ericson the Viking', battled against *Take Your Pick* and *The Army Game* on independent television for the Christmas audience. The show saw Hancock and James using Sid's company, Splendide Films, to make his latest television series, selling it on to the BBC in an attempt to make more money. Inevitably, it soon turns into a fiasco, with the Beeb pulling the plug on the show before the first instalment has even finished airing. The episode, which included an intriguing discussion between James and Hancock contemplating the merits of *Hancock's Half Hour*, wasn't one of Galton and Simpson's favourites. 'It was so amateurish and it looked it,' admits Alan. 'It was completely below par for us.' When the BBC decided to run an extended series of repeats a few years back, the writers asked them to exclude 'Ericson the Viking', much to the dismay of many fans. 'Members of the Tony Hancock Appreciation Society were very disappointed.'

'It was a funny idea: Sid James trying to make a cheap film,' says Ray. 'We had written a special intro based on the opening scene of *Robin Hood*: instead of "Robin Hood, Robin Hood" we had "Ericson the Brave", doing exactly as they did on the television series but taking the mickey. It was all done on the cheap.' Many viewers disliked the episode, claiming the script was weak, in parts 'ridiculous'[8], and that it provided little of substance for Hancock and the rest of the cast.

Hancock was being paid £750 for each episode while the writers received a joint £500 for each script—substantial amounts in the late 1950s, but Tom Sloan, the Assistant Head of Light Entertainment for television, believed Independent Television was trying to entice Hancock to switch channels with an offer in the region of £1250: Not wanting to lose one of the BBC's top artists, Sloan suggested a guaranteed amount over two years which, together with repeat fees, he hoped would secure the artist and writers' services for the foreseeable future. With the current television series running until the end of March, repeats in April and June and another new series in the autumn of 1959, it would guarantee a total income of £24,375 for Hancock and £18,250 for the writers. Sloan suggested submitting the offer immediately after Christmas. There was feedback from other parties, including William Streeton, Head of Programme Contracts. He didn't want any proposal to guarantee the number of repeats, but did offer a suggestion which might help convince Hancock to put pen to paper. Knowing BBC Radio was keen to recruit him for another radio series, although he'd initially backed away from the idea, Streeton described Hancock as someone who's 'well-known for changing his mind with some frequency'[9] so wondered whether the offer of a new radio series at an increased fee would act as an extra inducement.

While discussions continued amongst BBC management, the series, which was described by Peter Dickinson in *Punch* as 'easily the best of the domestic series'[10] progressed, with one script, 'The Italian Maid', causing Hancock to ask for alterations to be made. Hancock hires an attractive Italian maid who melts the heart of both Hancock and Sid; when they can't bring themselves to ask her to do the housework, Hancock ends up doing it himself. During rehearsals, Hancock turned to producer Duncan Wood and complained that the way the script began could be viewed by the public as having overtones of homosexuality. 'We had to tone it down,' admits Alan Simpson. 'The original script started with Hancock saying to Sid something like: "Here I am, working my fingers to the bone scrubbing and cooking, and you come in and use this place as a convenience." It was the sort of scene you'd get in *The Odd Couple*. Tony took the hump and wanted it changed.'

Over the course of the television series, there were several occasions when Hancock asked for major script changes, as well as rejecting a handful of scripts in their entirety; it was further evidence that he was having a greater influence on the direction the show took; he was also becoming increasingly concerned and careful about his own standing not just in his own eyes but in those of his public. As Ray Galton admits, he took the rejection of a script very hard:

Often it was the way Duncan Wood presented a script to Tony that led to the rejection. If Duncan thought the script was not up to scratch, he'd post it to Tony with a note saying something like: 'What do you think about this?' As soon as he did that, Hancock knew that Duncan was worried. So he'd read it but lose confidence straight away; then we'd be asked to rewrite it. I'd always think: 'What does Hancock know about it?' Looking at some of them, no—I don't blame him for turning them down. But we always knew that if we didn't hear from Duncan on the day he received the script, there was something wrong. I'd sulk and wouldn't speak to Duncan or Tony—it took me a long time to come out of it; then I'd finally get down to it and rewrite a new script while discarding the other one. Alan and I generally found it easier to write a new one. People like Eric Sykes and Johnny Speight, with whom we were sharing offices, thought we were mad if we gave in and started writing a new script. They said things like: 'Tell them to get stuffed and get on with it.' As much as we felt like saying it, we never did.

Meanwhile, Tom Sloan was still progressing plans for a two-year Sound and Television contract for Hancock, Galton and Simpson, effective from 1 August 1959, which would guarantee Hancock a salary of over £25,000 per annum, and a total of 33 programmes (radio and television) each year. Sloan felt it was unrealistic to expect Galton and Simpson to write 33 scripts each year, but nevertheless wanted to present the complete Sound and TV offers simultaneously to Stanley Dale of Associated London Scripts to gauge his reaction. After much deliberation with the Beeb, an informal meeting was arranged with Dale, to discuss matters regarding future shows, although William Streeton was keen to leave financial matters off the agenda for the time being. On 10 February 1959, the meeting took place in Streeton's office at Rothwell House, New Cavendish Road, just behind Broadcasting House. Dale confirmed that Hancock still didn't want to undertake radio but pointed out that this situation might change; however, he was emphatic in stating that Hancock had no intention to work for ITV. Sloan, in summarising for his boss the outcome of the meeting, explained that 'it was agreed that Hancock should be pressed to make up his mind once and for all as far as radio is concerned'[11] and a second meeting was suggested with, hopefully, Hancock and the writers invited to discuss the amount and type of work they wished to undertake for the BBC. Once again, attempts to pursue a joint contract collapsed, leaving Sound and Television to contend for the services of Hancock: the result was a radio and a television series overlapping for the first time in the history of the programme. To alleviate the problem Galton and Simpson wrote radio episodes in advance for the first time with, excepting the annual festive instalment, 'The Christmas Club', all 13 episodes being recorded within a three-week period during June 1959.

At this time, attempts were made to interest American television stations in *Hancock's Half Hour*. Initial interest was expressed by CBS and sample telerecordings dispatched to BBC representatives in New York who arranged a meeting with executives at CBS; but thier interest waned when they viewed the recordings because, as Ronald Waldman explained to Stanley Dale, 'everybody says they can't understand Tony!'[12]. It was frustrating for Waldman, for he felt Hancock's accent was a key element of his characterisation. Executives at NBC were now pondering the idea of a television series based on *Hancock's Half Hour* but had also suggested a one-off play as a vehicle for getting Hancock known by the American television audience. Meanwhile, contracts were issued this side of the Atlantic to writers and artists alike for the final radio series, even though Galton, Simpson, Hancock and James were still preoccupied with the closing episodes of the fourth television series.

Concern, once again, was shown about the cost of using incidental music for the radio series. Jim Davidson wanted to ensure the budgets were cleared with the Light Programme well in advance of the show moving into production. The cost per episode for the previous series had averaged £415, and the 1958 Christmas Special totalled £417, a sum which incorporated Hancock's rise in fee from 75 guineas to 100 guineas. Davidson was keen that costs should not exceed £435–445 for the new series; they later agreed on just over £463. However, he told Tom Ronald that the Light Programme was worried about the weekly costs of the incidental music and asked the producer to investigate cheaper alternatives. But, like his predecessor, Dennis Main Wilson, Ronald believed the show would suffer if Wally Stott's recorded music was dropped. Ronald informed Davidson that mood music was considered by Galton and Simpson when writing their scripts. He reminded him that Hancock was a 'valuable asset to the BBC', and said he felt the artist and scriptwriters would be upset if the BBC reverted to commercial recordings.

Despite the scare, Stott's musical links were maintained for what turned out to be the final radio series. 'To be honest, we had done so many radio shows that the ideas were drying up,' admits Alan Simpson. 'The television show became more important for Tony and ourselves so we decided to concentrate on that. I think Tony thought he was working hard enough.'

The last radio series was transmitted on Tuesdays at 8 p.m., with the 14 episodes running from 29 September to 29 December. It contained one of Galton and Simpson's favourite episodes, 'The Poetry Society', with Hancock and his new intellectual friends rebelling against the conformities of modern day society. Hancock, now an active member of the East Cheam Cultural Progressive Society, is hosting a poetry reading at his house; unexpectedly, Bill, who seems as asinine as ever, impresses everyone with his poetry and is invited to take over the leadership of the Society, much to Hancock's chagrin. 'It was a funny show,' says Ray Galton, who acknowledges that the lines they penned for Kerr have been classed as a great example of modern poetry. 'To us it was all gibberish, but people have asked us if they can reproduce it, they think it's so good.'

As the year drew to a close, the curtain came down on the radio version of *Hancock's Half Hour*.

Over fifty hours of scripts had been broadcast during the five-year run. The final show recorded was the penultimate episode, 'The Christmas Club', by which time Bill Kerr had returned to Australia. But the final episode, in terms of transmission, was 'The Impersonator', in which Hancock sues an impersonator whose voice has been used to promote a breakfast cereal. Actor Peter Goodwright was given the role of impersonating Hancock, and remembers arriving at the Playhouse Theatre in London's Charing Cross to record the episode.

I was very pleased to hear that those brilliant scriptwriters Ray Galton and Alan Simpson had conceived a plot which involved an impersonator—no one else at the time could re-create Hancock's voice with any accuracy—and I had recently done it to great acclaim on the television programme *Sunday Night at the London Palladium*.

I arrived at the Playhouse Theatre and was greeted enthusiastically by the scriptwriters, who took great care to see that I was happy with every line that they had written for Arthur Plowright, the part that I was to play. I made a few suggestions to include a recognisable phrase or two which Hancock used when annoyed, and these suggestions were immediately accepted by these two 'on the ball' writers.

The rehearsal in the afternoon had me worried. Although the cast were happy and outgoing in their welcome to me as an occasional artiste in their series of programmes,

Tony, whilst very polite and friendly, appeared withdrawn and hesitant in accepting a newcomer to the team.

During the run-through all the other artistes gave a performance for the producer. Tony did not. He just said the words on the script, and noted his position at the mike for their delivery. His voice was low, toneless and un-Hancock-like, and consequently I did not sound in the least like him.

I confided my concern to my new-found chums, Galton and Simpson. 'Oh don't worry about that,' they said. 'Come the show, he'll light up like a lamp and you won't recognise him!' They were surely right. When the audience were in place, and the show had begun, Hancock did indeed 'light up like a lamp'. His voice lifted and his comic timing was impeccable. It may sound trite, but he held the audience in the palm of his hand. His control was unmistakable and powerful. He was able to say something—or nothing—and the audience loved every moment.

Our face-to-face encounters brought loud laughter and afterwards he was full of compliments and kind words about my performance. 'We must have you on again!' he said—but sadly, this promise was never fulfilled.

Within these final scripts the writers had reached the levels of realism akin to their television series—gone were the fantastic storylines. But this move towards a more natural plot didn't satisfy everybody. Three of the shows selected for analysis by the BBC were regarded as 'pedestrian' by listeners.[13] In response to the final episode, one listener commented that 'instead of the erstwhile lively action, emphasis was now being laid on mental processes and "what might be called the psychological approach"'.[14] The pace of the episodes had slowed down, which wasn't to everyone's liking, but the vast majority still regarded *Hancock's Half Hour* as the best product on BBC Radio.

Chapter 12

Although *Hancock's Half Hour* had established itself as one of BBC Television's most popular comedy shows, and Tony Hancock was such hot property that his services were regularly being courted by executives in commercial television, the show wasn't excluded from occasional criticism within the Beeb. Days after the fourth series had finished, earlier in 1959, Cecil McGivern, the Deputy Director of Television Broadcasting, met with the Controller of Programmes and Head of Light Entertainment. Although contracts for Hancock and Galton and Simpson were the original reason for the meeting, McGivern had other points he wanted to raise. He felt *Hancock's Half Hour* had become an expensive programme to finance and wanted to ensure the maximum was obtained in terms of programme content, positioning within the television schedules, and size of audience. McGivern regarded the production process as too pedestrian. In a memo, dated 1 April 1959, he said:

I know the producer Duncan Wood would retort with the inevitable slowness of television as opposed to film, the changing of clothes and set, the necessity to hang on to captions, bridging shots and all the rest of it. Nevertheless, despite that, this production must be quickened up and the writers should be told this. Live television need not be so far behind the speed of Bilko.[1]

As for scheduling, McGivern recommended that *Hancock's Half Hour*, together with another (unnamed) comedy programme, could be used to bolster what he saw as a noticeably weak early Sunday evening in terms of television viewing. McGivern didn't get his wish and the next series went out on Friday evenings.

While McGivern's comments filtered down to appropriate parties involved in the show's production, Galton and Simpson were commissioned to write a further ten television programmes, divided equally between autumn 1959 and the following spring, for a fee of £600 per script. Four scripts were required by the end of August in preparation for the new series starting in September.

The emergence of telerecording as a feasible alternative to live broadcasting was something Duncan Wood championed in his drive to improve the overall presentation of *Hancock's Half Hour* and to address some of the concerns expressed by the Deputy Director of Television Broadcasting. In Wood's view, the primary reason for using telerecording was to eliminate long bridging shots and caption shots between scenes, which necessitated costume changes for either Hancock or James. Wood tacitly acknowledged McGivern's concern about the slowness of the production, pointing out that 'we have bent over backwards to put the show on live with the maximum continuity by faking costumes, re-writing the top and tail of scenes, etc., but still it is necessary to insert some kind of holding shot between scenes to effect costume changes.'[2] He accepted that this made the pace of the production slower, but thought that telerecording in approximately six separate takes, coincident with difficult costume or scene changes, would sharpen the overall pace.

There was an additional benefit in recording the episodes: Hancock was already an established name in parts of the Commonwealth, including Canada and Australia, via sales of his radio series, but the Corporation's Transcription Service was eager to exploit the television series; now seemed the opportune moment to telerecord the shows in a format suitable for television services around the globe.

Although the editing process was still rudimentary, it relieved some of the pressures of live broadcasting and helped to prevent another disaster à la 'There's an Airfield at the Bottom of My Garden'. 'It was still quite basic, though,' explains Alan Simpson. It was impossible to edit within a scene so if anything went awry, the entire scene had to be shot again. 'But it gave the actors a certain amount of reassurance that if something really went wrong, we could just re-shoot that scene.' The decision on whether to re-shoot was down to producer Duncan Wood who, like any producer working during the infancy of telerecording, was reluctant to halt proceedings unless absolutely necessary. During one scene in 'The Two Murderers', the second episode in series five, Sid and Hancock are sitting at the table at 23 Railway Cuttings, chatting; when Sid muddles up his words they make a joke about it and just carry on.

Fortunately there were no mishaps during the recording of the first episode, 'The Economy Drive', which was transmitted on 25 September 1959 and watched by 9.5 million, a figure that would peak at 11.2 million later in the series with 'The Big Night' and 'The Tycoon'. Viewers welcomed Hancock back with open arms and were extremely complimentary when the BBC conducted their regular survey; every aspect of the programme was showered with praise, from the supporting actors (Patricia Hayes and Peggy Ann Clifford in particular) and the swish presentation to the first-rate scripts and the inimitable Tony Hancock himself. The popularity of *Hancock's Half Hour* remained as buoyant as ever.

Patricia Hayes was hired for the second episode, 'The Two Murderers', to play a semi-regular character: Hancock's charlady, Mrs Cravatte, who had previously only been referred to during conversations. 'She was very bolshy, outspoken and rude,' says Alan Simpson. 'As far as I can remember, Tony came up with the name: where he got it from, I don't know—it could well have been the name of a landlady he came across once.'

Playing the moaning housekeeper, who is employed one hour a day by Hancock, Patricia Hayes enjoyed her time on the show. She once said: 'When I first started working with Tony Hancock . . . he was such a big star and I was more or less a nobody—and I was enormously in awe of him, but I had some rather nice bits to do.' Hayes had been playing the occasional character part when Wood approached her, one day, with some good news. 'He said to me: "A great honour is going to be bestowed upon you, Miss Hayes; you are going to play Mrs Cravatte. Now she's only ever been mentioned before, nobody has ever set eyes on her so you will create this person." And I did.' Hayes' scenes were recorded with Hancock yet she received little feedback or encouragement from the artist. 'In a sense, you just felt that the fact he went along with your performance was a compliment because anything he didn't like he'd say: "I don't think we want that." But if you were left in, occasionally you'd get a smile out of him.'

By the time 'The Train Journey' was transmitted on 23 October, with Hancock annoying a compartment of passengers during a long trip, the series was regularly attracting over ten million viewers. In response to this episode, the majority of viewers believed the script provided Hancock with 'just the type of larger than life situation in which he excelled.'[3] Hancock's performances and the scripts were of the highest quality, and the BBC was desperate for more in the future. In response to a meeting between Eric Maschwitz, the Head of Light Entertainment, and Lou Berlin, representing Hancock, at Associated London Scripts, on the afternoon of 24 November, Maschwitz updated the Assistant Head in a memo, stressing: 'We must not at any cost let Hancock go.'

The BBC was determined to retain Hancock and when the series finished he was showered with telephone calls and congratulatory letters, including one from Kenneth Adam, the Controller of Programmes, who enthused: 'We all think that this was without any doubt the finest you have done, and though we know the standard you are setting is very high indeed, we are confident that the next one will be even better.'[4] For Hancock, the

207

end of the series had been marred by the tragic death of his stepfather, Robert Walker, who had committed suicide at his Bournemouth flat just days before the actor arrived at the Riverside Studios on 23 November to record the final episode, 'Football Pools'.

By the time plans were afoot for the sixth series, which was transmitted in the spring of 1960, Hancock was earning £1,000 per episode, a phenomenal amount for a television artist at that time. However, an idea he formulated concerning the recording of the next series looked, for a time, as if it would test the relations between Hancock and his employer. Influenced, perhaps, by the working practices of the American television industry, Hancock decided he wanted to record each of the ten episodes in the forthcoming series over a period of eight hours using short takes. Through his agent, he made enquiries with the actors' union, Equity, to ensure he would not be breaching any regulations if such an idea was pursued. Although Hancock provided no explanation to the BBC as to why he wanted to follow this route for the next series, an increasing insecurity and his continual worry about remembering his lines may have been a key motivation. Harold Snoad, who worked on the sixth series in a junior capacity before climbing the ladder to become a producer–director, says: 'If an episode was made without the audience present it would mean that if he forgot his lines there would be no "public" witnesses to this which he would obviously have found embarrassing.' Assessing the benefits of employing this method, Snoad says:

As the *Hancock* shows generally didn't involve lots of different sets or that many costume changes it seems Tony's request for an eight-hour session was purely so that he didn't have the stress of having to remember long scenes. He would obviously have made some initial attempt at learning the whole episode but doing it this way would make life much easier for him. He would be able to split the various scenes into short sections and, if necessary, have several goes at each segment.

As Hancock awaited answers from Equity he holidayed in Paris, while the BBC, who were treading new ground, asked Duncan Wood to explore the practicalities of adopting Hancock's suggestion. Wood completed an initial report for Tom Sloan on 16 December: he felt that if Equity gave the green light, Hancock would push the BBC to take advantage of his suggestion; he also felt the matter could become an important contractual issue in future negotiations so thought it imperative that the BBC had its answers ready for any formal approach by Hancock. As well as a minimum of one recording and editing machine being tied up for a complete day, the chance of recording in front of a live audience would be lost; if Hancock's suggestion was adopted, the BBC would need to show the programmes to an audience at a later date and dub their reactions on to the tape—a complex job, considering the BBC's tape machines at that time. By 16 December, Tom Sloan was indicating that it looked unlikely that the BBC could meet Hancock's requirements; but, not wanting to dismiss the idea without having researched the matter thoroughly, Duncan Wood suggested visiting a television studio in the United States, a trip that had originally been planned before the start of the fifth series. He wanted to watch an American show, such as *Bilko*, being recorded because the system Hancock was suggesting was similar to that used on this popular Phil Silvers comedy. Wood knew that American film recording was far superior to the BBC's current system in relation to dubbing and editing, the main areas of concern facing the Corporation.

Although it's unclear from the various production files and records retained in the BBC's archives whether Wood's trip took place, it looks as if it became unnecessary when Dennis Scuse, a senior planning assistant, reported his views on 28 December. Scuse advised the Head of Programme Planning that the BBC would not have the necessary facilities for some time, but it could be possible if 35mm film was used, even though he believed the organisation could not afford to tie up the telerecording facilities for such a period of time. Another negative, as far as Scuse was concerned, was that the editing process would probably take longer than one day, with wastage of tape or film reaching an unacceptable level. Scuse concluded that it would be 'ill-advised to open the flood gates by accepting productions planned in this way.'[5]

The BBC decided it couldn't accommodate Hancock's suggestion and Tom Sloan met the artist in early January 1960 to inform him of the decision. Sloan classed the meeting as 'most cordial'[6] and although Hancock still wanted negotiations with Equity to continue, he accepted the decision

210

regarding his next series. Sloan also took the opportunity to raise the perpetual topic of long-term contracts, but Hancock remained noncommittal, preferring to see how his next series panned out before considering this; he did, however, assure Sloan that he had no intention of working elsewhere.

The advent of commercial television in Britain had caused a drop in audience share for the BBC, with viewers' curiosity in the immediate period after its introduction making them switch channels to find out what goodies were on offer; although such competition meant the Corporation never again enjoyed domination of the television world, audiences, with their newly found freedom of choice, returned to give the BBC the biggest slice of the viewing public. Throughout the sixth series, the majority of episodes attracted audiences above ten million, including the opening instalment, 'The Cold'. Hancock's return was welcomed wholeheartedly: he could do little wrong in the eyes of the viewers. Although some felt the storyline didn't lend itself to a host of opportunities for comic exploitation, the majority congratulated the writers on their script, with one interviewee classing it as a 'brilliantly observed, larger than life, slice of life.'[7]

The press welcomed the return of Hancock, too. In the *Listener*, Irving Wardle wrote: 'Hancock is back and the streets lie deserted on Friday evenings.' Of 'The Missing Page', the second episode, he added: 'I hope that Galton and Simpson will give more scope to Hancock's hitherto unexploited powers as a mime, revealed last week in his silent recital of the whole plot for

"Who done it?".[8] When Hancock causes a disruption in the local library he is asked to leave, but first re-enacts a vital scene from a book through mime to the attentive Sid James.

Other memorable episodes from the series include 'The Reunion Party', 'Sid in Love', 'The Babysitters' and 'The Ladies' Man', which finds Hancock enrolling at the Mayfair Charm School for Men to improve his chances with the opposite sex. The matter came to a head after yet another failed encounter with a girl, this time as part of a double-date. While Sid is getting on splendidly with his girl, Hancock is not so lucky.

HANCOCK: Well, stone me, woman; if you felt like that, why did you bother to go out with me in the first place?

MURIEL: I wouldn't have done if I'd known I was going to be lumbered with you.

HANCOCK: Lumbered?

MURIEL: I said to my friend when I met you: 'I bet I get lumbered with the fat one.'

As part of the course, Hancock learns to dance and is seen in a dream sequence dressed in Fred Astaire garb with top hat and cane. In the scene he dances with Barbara Evans, who was chosen by choreographer Eleanor Fazan. The sequence was filmed behind closed doors, as Barbara explains: 'Tony was very nervous. Sid, who I also danced with in the sequence, had no fears about dancing but Tony couldn't put one foot in front of the other so he didn't want a lot of people watching.' Although it wasn't her job to give Hancock lessons, Barbara inevitably helped her partner. 'Being a

212

professional dancer it was difficult dancing with someone who couldn't lift you, so you tried to make it look as easy as possible and therefore helped him along.'

To celebrate the final recording of the series on Friday, 29 April 1960, and in the hope that it might help persuade Hancock to enter into another contract, Eric Maschwitz, Head of Light Entertainment, arranged a cocktail party for thirty-five people in the dubbing theatre at the Riverside Studios, straight after the recording of 'The Poison Pen Letters'. The occasion would involve both Hancock and James being presented with inscribed bronze ash buckets, affectionately described as 'Oscars' by Maschwitz.[9] Still, Hancock wasn't prepared to discuss signing a long-term contract, as he wanted to focus all his attention on the feature film, *The Rebel*, which he was undertaking during the summer. The screenplay, depicting a bored city clerk who travels to Paris to become a successful artist, was written by Galton and Simpson, and Hancock hoped the film would bring the international stardom he craved.

As for the future of Anthony Aloysius Hancock, Tony Hancock broke the news to Galton and Simpson and Duncan Wood that he wanted wholesale changes to the structure of the show if he was to appear in any further episodes. For a while, Hancock had been feeling restless about the format of the show, fuelled partly by his longer-term career objective. As far back as December 1954, just after the first radio series had started, Hancock had told the BBC that he was keen to make his name in films. Now he had reached the point where he was analysing each show in depth,

213

dissecting every line, scene and script in his mind, trying to understand what made it tick and how it could have been improved. Duncan Wood felt such an approach was detrimental.

The trouble was afterwards you could say, 'That was marvellous' and he started to analyse it in depth as to how it could be better. It's an admirable trait of someone's character, but I wish he could have had a couple of large Scotches and said, 'Yes it was, wasn't it', and leave it at that. No one was really in the mood to take it apart; sometimes taking it apart is counter-productive but he couldn't stop fiddling with it. Taking it apart, word by word, there's no magic any more.[10]

Despite the show's obvious success, Hancock felt it was stagnating and needed a new impetus or it would begin to lose its polish, the sharpness which had been fundamental to its longevity. It was time the screen character evolved to move away from the world in which he existed—and that meant the setting of 23 Railway Cuttings in East Cheam, his friend Sid James and even the trademark homburg hat and astrakhan-collared overcoat. He felt it was best for the show's future and best for his own future, too. To Hancock, being associated professionally with Sid James was starting to become restrictive. As Alan Simpson explains, 'He would walk down the street and people would call out: "Where's our Sid?" Whereas Sid had a career of his own doing films, Tony was largely thought of in terms of *Hancock's Half Hour*. He felt he had to get away from the concept of a double-act because

214

it was becoming like Laurel and Hardy, the implication being that Tony didn't work without Sid—and Ray and I agreed.'

Although the character remained the same, he'd be placed in an entirely new world, and Galton and Simpson set out to formulate plans for the final series. It was to be titled simply *Hancock*, as the show was to be reduced to 25 minutes' duration to help sell the series to foreign stations which needed to insert commercials in the half hour. Hancock never spoke to James about his decision to work on his own in the final series, so Duncan Wood was left to break the news. James was, understandably, distraught when he was informed. Appearing in *Hancock's Half Hour* meant a lot to him, something he expressed in correspondence to Tom Sloan in January 1958. He stated: 'I think I'd rather *die* than not be in it! Nobody knows better than I do that *Hancock's Half Hour* has done me the world of good. All that remains then is to sort out the dates and the dough (formal letter this!) and we're away.'[11]

Valerie James, his widow, recalls: '*Hancock's Half Hour* was the highlight of his life—he loved working with Tony and was never happier. He was devastated when it all came to an end. He never wanted to be a star, saying he'd rather have the cameo parts and then steal all the notices; when he began working with Tony everything just took off and lots of things happened from then on.' As Valerie reveals, Sid was disappointed he hadn't heard the news directly from Hancock. 'It was very hurtful the way he did it: he couldn't face up to Sid personally and Sid ended up hearing through someone else.' It must have been difficult for

215

James to expunge the memories of his unexpected departure from the sitcom, but his high standards of professionalism saw him through.

Sid had become an integral part of the show and was much loved by the viewers; when the Audience Research Department conducted its regular surveys, Sid James' performance was frequently extolled. After watching 'The Emigrant', viewers made comments such as 'Sidney James was, as usual, the perfect foil' and 'Tony Hancock would not be the success he is without him', while one interviewee saw James as the natural partner for Tony Hancock.[12] This summed up what Hancock had been fearing: that the public were beginning to perceive the actors as a team. By the time the final episode of the sixth series, 'The Poison Pen Letters', had been transmitted on Friday, 6 May, news of the break-up had reached the public domain, leading one viewer to comment that Sid was as essential to the success of the show as Hancock himself. It was a view echoed by many, who regarded his plans to work alone as fatuous. Hancock was to prove them wrong when he returned in 1961 for his final series for the BBC.

To help soften the blow for James, Galton and Simpson agreed to write a new series for him, reuniting him with Bill Kerr and Liz Fraser, both of whom he'd worked with on *Hancock's Half Hour*. It was titled *Citizen James*, and the writers—who wrote only the first of the three series—were paid £600 for each of the six scripts. In this entertaining vehicle James adopted the persona he'd exploited so proficiently in *Hancock's Half Hour*; the first series ran between 24 November and 29 December 1960. Galton and Simpson were so determined to write a series for James that they agreed to forgo negotiations for a potential wage increase. When their agent Beryl Vertue wrote to the BBC regarding the fee on offer for the scriptwriting, she pointed out that it had been their intention to 'ask for an increase in their present fee, but in view of your remarks that the series depended upon their acceptance of the fee of £600 offered, they felt they must put Sid James' interests before their own.'[13] Vertue warned the BBC, though, that they would be looking for an increase when they started negotiating the next series for Tony Hancock.

Discussing, in *TV Times* in 1963, the dropping of James, Hancock said: 'People remarked on my breaking up with Sid James but it is quite simple: you work in a show with somebody, there is never any question of a hard and fast team and I liked having Sid in my shows very much. And then you move on to something else.'

If Sid James had worried about future job opportunities he needn't haven't concerned himself because, as he told a reporter in May 1960, he'd been besieged with offers. Regarding Hancock, he said: 'The Hancock show was a pleasure, it breaks my heart that we are not together any more, but he wants to go on his own.'[14] James felt they could have continued with the show for years, and said that at the end of each series, other television companies offered him roles but he turned them down because 'the only TV I wanted to do was Hancock. I put that first always, although I was paid less for doing it. I used to turn down films which would probably have brought me in twice the money because I thought: "No, this is better for me." Naturally I feel upset that a series like that should be thrown away, but Tony and I are still good friends.'

In an attempt to encourage discourse between the BBC and Hancock, in August 1960 Eric Maschwitz wrote to Hancock, who was busy working on *The Rebel*, inviting him to lunch once he was free from his film commitments. After the success of *The Best of Hancock*, a season of episode repeats, he was keen to discuss Hancock's return to television and, aware of Hancock's desire to develop a film career, he advised Hancock not to lose touch with his enormous fan base in the medium of television, saying that it should be possible to fit in a limited number of episodes around any filming. So keen was Maschwitz not to lose Hancock that after penning the letter to him, he rushed out a five-line memo to one of his colleagues, asking him to keep in touch with Hancock 'continuously' until he agreed to meet for lunch to discuss a possible reappearance for the BBC. Maschwitz closed with the statement: 'It is very important, repeat *very* important that we should see him before he disappears.'[15]

The lunch date wasn't organised until 21 November 1960; at it Hancock confirmed his interest in making another series for the BBC, early in 1961. He also expressed an interest in making a longer series during the autumn of that year, once he had finished his second film which was due to be shot between July and September. Tom Sloan wanted to secure Hancock's and Galton and Simpson's services by offering them £1,750 and £1,100 respectively. When other colleagues involved in the process started protracting proceedings, Sloan appealed to the Controller of

Programmes to help sort the matter out, explaining that with 'Hancock we are dealing with the most sought after piece of Light Entertainment in this country'.[16] Before breaking for Christmas, Tom Sloan was given the green light and sent contracts to Hancock and Galton and Simpson via Beryl Vertue. These covered six episodes during April or May, with an option for a further 13 episodes to be exercised by the end of June. The fees on offer were those Sloan had proposed earlier. Vertue replied to Tom Sloan in early January confirming her clients' acceptance of the offers save for the option of an autumn series, which she wanted removed from the contracts on Hancock's behalf, although she didn't dismiss the possibility of such a series going ahead. The first two scripts were required by 1 April, the next two arriving two weeks later, leaving the final two to be delivered as soon as possible thereafter.

Duncan Wood was concerned about whether Galton and Simpson could deliver the scripts in time and enlightened Sloan on the difficulties they were experiencing penning a suitable script for Hancock's next film. Contracted to Associated British Pictures to write a film script for Hancock each year, they were expected to deliver the next project on 31 March; with little over a month to go, they hadn't even agreed on a title. The main problem, however, was that Hancock had just rejected 59 pages of script, representing seven weeks' worth of work, leaving them no option but to start afresh. In a memo to Sloan, Wood said Galton and Simpson were 'in the writing doldrums at the moment, and we can only leave them to fight their way out of it'.[17] As the film represented a

219

prior commitment that had to be completed before work could begin on the television scripts, Wood was worried about when the writers would be free to turn their attention to the television series. His fears were alleviated when Beryl Vertue confirmed in the middle of March that Hancock's second film had been postponed until the autumn, due to the inability of formulating a mutually acceptable storyline. Galton and Simpson were now free to concentrate on the television scripts. The downside to the film's postponement was that it meant Hancock would be unavailable to film an autumn series, if he so wished. Vertue agreed to talk to Hancock about the possibility of another series to start in January 1962.

The arrival of spring found Galton and Simpson busy in their office at Cumberland House on Kensington High Street. Now that Railway Cuttings in East Cheam was defunct, one of the first issues they had to address was where the new series would be set. They opted for Earls Court, regarding it as the complete antithesis to East Cheam. 'In those days, Earls Court was very cosmopolitan and having a bedsit in that part of London was almost a cliché,' says Alan.

'It was full of youngsters, from all parts of the world, especially Australians—it became known as Kangaroo Valley,' recalls Ray. 'Hancock, as a character, was always trying to be young, hip and educated—up with what was going on in the world.' While his surroundings altered and he continued his life without the regular faces to whom he'd become accustomed, the man himself remained unchanged, full of the same beliefs, attitudes and philosophies.

For the opening script, which carried a working title of 'Hancock Alone' but became known as 'The Bedsitter', Galton and Simpson wrote an episode involving just Hancock. 'Alan and I mischievously wrote the first script where he was completely on his own; we thought: right, if you want to be on your own, you *will* be on your own. There was no one else in it. We had to use our ingenuity to do it without it becoming boring; we decided you could have people ringing up on the phone and could hear people outside his bedsit and gradually the story evolved.' When they'd completed a draft of the script, the writers needed to gauge the reaction of Hancock himself, so headed to Shrewsbury, where he was appearing on stage in his own show. Hancock read the script in silence. 'We didn't know how he'd react,' admits Ray, 'but he realised the challenge and couldn't wait to do it. He was potty about it.'

The script spotlighting Hancock in isolation was also the writers and actors taking a stand against the reaction and doubts shown in some quarters of the press about the feasibility of Hancock going it alone. As one journalist wrote: 'This solo performance for 30 minutes is a pretty challenging and interesting experiment. It could be a tour de force . . . or a tour de farce. The danger is monotony. We shall see.'[18] As it transpired, Hancock provided some powerful performances in the *Hancock* series; although the final two instalments were affected by Hancock's reliance on autocue, the performance and quality of the scripts reached a high standard. 'If anyone ever says to us that Hancock wasn't the same after he dropped Sid James, we remind them of "The Blood Donor",

"The Radio Ham", "The Bowmans"—episodes which all came from that final series. Hancock proved his point: he could work without Sid James,' states Ray.

By now, Hancock's influence on the mechanics of the programme had reached such a level that he was being consulted on every aspect, from preparation of the camera script to the overall production and direction of the shows. Before taking a short break in Paris, he spent two hours of Monday, 24 April 1961 in Lime Grove's Studio P filming the opening titles. Before long, everything was in place for what would be his final series with the BBC, the last stand before his career and life began its tragic downward spiral.

Chapter 13

The recording of 'The Bedsitter', the first episode of the seventh series Hancock had made for the Beeb, took place at Studio 4 in BBC's Television Centre on Friday, 5 May 1961, just over a year after the site in White City first opened its doors. The first page of Galton and Simpson's script set the scene for Hancock's new life in bedsit-land with a detailed description of his Earls Court abode:

Dissolve into Tony's room. It is a typical bedsitter. The kitchen is in one corner of the room partitioned off by a curtain. A single bed is up against one wall. There are a few pin-ups on the wall. These are coloured photos of sumptuous feasts from American magazines. Odd bits of furniture are scattered about the room. A table in the middle. There is a gas fire with a meter by the side of it. There is a wardrobe with a full length mirror in the door. There is a television set on a table in one corner with a record player on top of it and a small radio on top of that. Some books are opened face downwards on the table. We see the titles. 'Das Kapital', 'The Outsider', 'Look Back in Anger', 'The Decline of Western Civilisation', 'The Intellectual in a Decadent Society', 'Glam' (with a pin-up on the front), 'The Prisoner'. We discover Tony lying full length on the bed, which is made. He is fully dressed, staring up at the ceiling, smoking a cigarette. Up against the wall is a pole with a nuclear disarmament sign on the top of it. As he is lying there he starts trying to blow smoke rings ...

The episode was transmitted on Friday, 26 May 1961 at 8 p.m. and watched by 14.4 million, the largest audience the show achieved throughout its six-year run. As well as the millions of diehard Hancock fans tuning in to welcome back the artiste, the episode attracted additional interest from viewers simply curious to see how Tony Hancock could carry a series on his own without the able support of Sid James. With scriptwriting of the highest order and a performance straight out of the top drawer, the opening episode was 25 minutes of sheer quality. Not everybody felt this. James had been a hugely popular member of the show and many viewers were to mourn his loss throughout the life of this seventh series, missing those timely caustic comments which always managed to bring Hancock's flights of self-delusion back to terra firma with a bang. The BBC's audience research report, compiled soon after the transmission of 'The Bedsitter', focused on a large proportion of comments referring to the absence of James. While one interviewee saw Hancock without James as like 'tea without milk', and another remarked that he seemed lost on his own, one viewer provided a more in-depth analysis: 'Much of the best Hancock has truly dramatic quality; dramatic quality needs reaction from co-players.'[1]

A journalist in *Stage and Television Today* didn't agree, saying: 'If anyone needs lessons in the art of television comedy, he should consult Tony Hancock and his script writers, Alan Simpson and Ray Galton.' He classed the return of the series as a 'resounding triumph for all three'.[2] It may be that, like a good wine, comedy matures with age and it's not until much later that one appreciates its finer, more subtle qualities. The secret of the unqualified success lay deep down in the roots of the comedy show: here was a man who portrayed the fears, weaknesses and prejudices that live in most of us, hilariously ridiculing them in every breath and every step he takes in life; but there was much more depth to this comedic characterisation because beneath the veneer of laughter one discovers a layer of sadness, loneliness and frustration: this was a man who never progressed in life—a life he lived without the support, friendship or the love of a partner. This multi-layered character mirrors the emotional make-up of many of us at some point in our lives; as well as sympathising with Hancock, many people were able to empathise with him, too.

Regardless of whether the series was a success, Hancock was adamant he wouldn't return to the old East Cheam format with Sid James. No good could be gained by going back; as far as Hancock was concerned the present and future were all important. As the series progressed, Hancock's drive for perfectionism became more acute and he was increasingly conscious of the supporting performers around him. For this final series, more established character actors were employed alongside some of the regular artists, adding depth to the cast list. Performers such as John Le Mesurier, Colin Gordon, Brian Oulton and Jack

225

Watling were highly respected names in the industry. Playing two key roles, as the Producer in 'The Bowmans' and the Doctor in 'The Blood Donor', was Patrick Cargill, who recalled Hancock showing his approval of the calibre of actor now being recruited. 'When I got to know him I remember he told me that it was fascinating to work with real actors. He said: "I've been working with comics who put on the doctor's white coat or the postman's uniform, but underneath they're still a comic; working with actors you are the doctor, you are the postman. I'm able to rebound so much more because I've got real people there.'3"

Hancock wanted to ensure every scene was exploited for its full comedic potential; now that he was working alone, he knew the burden of responsibility weighed heavy on his shoulders, and his alone. He would still have preferred it if the episodes had been filmed rather than telerecorded because it would have given him the chance to perform a piece continuously until he was entirely satisfied. An increasingly tense performer wasn't helped by having to record the second episode in the series, 'The Bowmans', in front of an inappropriate audience, angering not only Hancock and his management but director Duncan Wood, too. So incensed was the director that he fired off a frank memo to the Head of Light Entertainment explaining that everyone's hard work and efforts were 'decimated by the composition of the studio audience',4 which included approximately seventy children around the age of eight. As they didn't understand a line of dialogue they reacted with complete silence, which was profoundly frustrating for all concerned, especially as they occupied such a large section of the seating. The situation impacted on the show, with retakes being required due to artists being 'completely thrown by the audience reaction or lack of it', said Wood.

The episode, nevertheless, is now regarded as one of the classics from the series. Hancock had played Joshua in the radio series, *The Bowmans*, for five years but when his character is killed off by falling into a threshing machine, hundreds of fans jam the BBC's switchboard, complaining about his demise. Such a response causes the Beeb to reconsider and he's reemployed as Ben Merryweather, Joshua's twin brother.

Although 'The Bowmans' was transmitted as the second episode in the series, it wasn't recorded until 26 May, by which time 'The Radio Ham' and 'The Lift' were already complete. They were subsequently aired as the third and fourth episodes. Next in the schedule was 'The Blood Donor', arguably the most well known of all the television episodes, and the penultimate in the series. But before rehearsals had begun, Hancock was involved in a car accident which would have a lasting effect on his performances in the medium of television. After the arduous recording of 'The Bowmans', Hancock was picked up from the studio by his wife, Cicely. The accident occurred as she drove him back to MacConkey's, their home in Blindley Heath, near Lingfield. As the Mercedes headed into Surrey, Cicely was forced to brake hard in order to miss some roadworks; the car ended up in a pit, and although both were fortunate to escape serious injury, Hancock smashed his head through the windscreen.

Next day, Duncan Wood raced to the hospital to

227

visit Hancock and described the patient as looking like 'a panda because he had two of the biggest black eyes I'd seen in my life'.[5] The fact that the severe bruising wasn't spotted by eagle-eyed viewers at home when 'The Blood Donor' was transmitted was a credit to make-up designer Elizabeth Armstrong, who had spent over an hour making up Hancock before the recording. More worryingly for Wood was the mild concussion suffered by Hancock, which prevented him learning his lines. Hancock, however, didn't want the show to be cancelled and so, deciding to go along with the actor, Wood called upon the services of Autocue to help Hancock through the episode. In hindsight, Wood wished he'd cancelled the recording, later commenting: 'It offended me professionally because although we did the best we could, if you look at the show now, the eyelines are totally wrong; it was a disgrace but his technique overcame a lot of that.'[6]

Alan Simpson regards 'The Blood Donor' script as probably the best he and Galton wrote and believes that if Hancock had recorded it at his peak, it could truly be regarded as a classic. Alan says: 'One classic line people always remember in the episode is "A pint, that's very nearly an armful." Well, we took about quarter of an hour over whether it would be "that's just about an armful" or what we finally decided on, "that's very nearly an armful." And the reason that's better is because it's even more precise. Little things like that are the difference between a big laugh, a little laugh or no laugh at all.'

On observing the episode today, with the knowledge that Autocue was used by Hancock, it's clear that his line of vision is always to the side of the person with whom he's conversing, but the majority of viewers at the time, oblivious to the problems Hancock had endured, didn't notice. Using Autocue heaped additional pressure on the supporting actors, like Frank Thornton, who later made his name playing Captain Peacock in David Croft and Jeremy Lloyd's department store sitcom, *Are You Being Served?* 'Considering it was the first time he'd used Autocue he did remarkably well,' says Frank. 'Knowing that he couldn't go wrong, though, put an extra strain on everybody else. June Whitfield, Patrick Cargill and I had to be spot-on: if we got a line slightly wrong and ad-libbed it a bit, giving Tony the wrong line, then he couldn't read it off the Autocue.'

Appearing in *Hancock* was an enjoyable experience for Frank, who had first met Hancock in the RAF. 'At the end of the war I was redundant aircrew doing various jobs, waiting to be demobbed, and I ended up in the Air Ministry Entertainment Unit which ran the RAF gang shows. I had to go round and watch all the shows, meeting all the participants. I remember seeing this one show and a man walked on playing this dismal character; he did this number which ended "I've 'ad it" and I thought: "This man is good, he's going somewhere."' Later on, as demobilisation began in earnest, the shows were rejigged and various performers spent time working in Thornton's office; at one time, his office staff consisted of Sergeant Tony Hancock and Corporal Peter Sellers. Later, when Thornton had returned to civvy street, he heard Hancock was appearing at the Shepherd's Bush Empire so took his friend, the actor Peter Jones, along to the venue

229

to show him this budding performer. 'Hancock came on in a white dinner jacket and did a different kind of act and I thought: "He's got it wrong." This wasn't the comedian I'd seen. Later on, he ended up on the radio in *Hancock's Half Hour* and he'd returned to the character I'd seen, all those years before: the pompous failure.' When the script arrived for his part in 'The Blood Donor', Frank was excited about appearing with his old friend. 'I thought it was a wonderful script that any competent actor could do well with, but with Hancock and his particular talent, he made it a great show, despite the use of Autocue.'

The series was brought to a close with the episode 'The Succession—Son and Heir', but Hancock insisted on retaining the Autocue, despite having recovered from the after-effects of the car accident. For Hancock, learning lines was the bane of his professional life, and now he'd been presented with an alternative which could alleviate all the hard work and fears of forgetting lines, it was too good to give up. Despite losing spontaneity and the facility to exploit those wonderful facial expressions which had become one of Hancock's trademarks, he insisted on keeping Autocue. Each of the cameras positioned around the set had a teleprompter underneath, but in concentrating on reading lines the extensive collection of facial reactions was rarely used. 'He never learnt another line as long as he worked,' says Alan Simpson. 'That killed him as a performer. His face became a rigid mask, all the reactions went. He ended up looking like a waxwork.'

Despite this, 'The Succession—Son and Heir' was a poignant episode with Hancock, at 35, reflecting on his uneventful, underachieving life and realising that if he had a son to carry on the Hancock dynasty, he'd ensure his boy didn't make the same mistakes. To get a son, though, means he needs to find a wife so he embarks on a quest to secure a bride.

The early scenes in the episode are dominated by Hancock's doleful soliloquy in which he reflects on his wasted life. It's a forlorn character who is seen pacing around his sombre Earls Court bedsit; the dismal weather mirrors the mood inside the property. He slumps on his bed and begins his appraisal of life before sinking deeper into a mood of melancholic introspection. He steps across to the mirror hanging on the wall but sees more than his simple reflection:

HANCOCK: Look at you: 35, over the hump. What have you achieved? What *have* you achieved? Two abandoned plays, three lay downs in Whitehall, two marches and a punch-up with the Empire loyalists. This is your life—a slim volume indeed. What happened to you? What went wrong? What went wrong? What happened to all your dreams when you were 16? . . . No, you lost your chance, me old son, you've contributed nothing to this life. A waste of time you being here at all. No plaque for you in Westminster Abbey. The best you can expect is a few daffodils in a jamjar, a rough hewn headstone with the inscription: 'He came and he went and in between—nothing.' No one will even notice that you're not here; after about a year afterwards somebody might say down the pub, ' 'Ere, where's old Hancock? I haven't seen him around

231

lately.' 'Oh he's dead, you know. Right, 301, then George, off we go.' (*Pretends to throw a dart*) A right *raison d'être* that is. No one will ever know I existed.

The show, which was Hancock's swan song with the BBC, was watched by just under eleven million people and was well received; a large proportion of the people providing feedback to the BBC, many of whom had had serious misgivings at the beginning of the series about whether Hancock was making a big mistake venturing into a new series without Sid James, were now staunch supporters. One man said: 'Take back what I said earlier of Hancock. He does not now require James as a stooge—he progresses unattached by leaps and bounds.'[7] Many people questioned whether Hancock would be a displaced comic without the support of James, but in his exacting performances he evinced qualities only seen in the industry's elite, and with top-notch scripts to match, the series became a surefire winner. Just before 8.30 p.m. on Friday, 30 June 1961, the closing credits rolled and the curtain came down on the BBC's flagship show.

BBC executives tried in vain to entice Hancock back to the small screen although he had already confirmed his future was in the movie industry. During the summer of 1961 Duncan Wood chatted to Tony Hancock's brother, Roger, who was now the actor's representative, and was told that Hancock was beginning his second film for Associated British in the autumn. Immediately after this project was complete, which was expected to be January 1962, the plan was for Hancock and Galton and Simpson to enter the preparatory stages for film number three, which contractually was to be completed by September that year. Wood saw little chance of Hancock working for the Corporation, save for the occasional Special. Tom Sloan, Assistant Head of Light Entertainment, in two separate letters, dated December 1961 and the following April, closed his correspondence with an open invitation for Hancock to return to the small screen. The letters were never acknowledged. Freddie Hancock explains that Tony had tired of the small-screen character he'd created with Galton and Simpson. She says: 'In the end he didn't like the character because it made him stay in one situation. That created a limitation, a prison of his own making, and no one wants to live the same day after day. He would feel that the end justified the means and there was no point in being sentimental. The moment something is over, it's over. He wanted to stay with Galton and Simpson but, perhaps, they were unmovable about moving out of the situation. I feel they were anxious to stay with what was familiar to them.'

The BBC's Tom Sloan, who had already been informed by Hancock and his representatives that the film world was where his interests now lay, was told that Hancock would approach the BBC if and when he wanted to return to television. Sloan, writing to the Controller of Programmes on 13 April 1962, had finally realised that Hancock wasn't returning to the BBC. Although he regretted the loss, he said: 'I am satisfied that we did everything possible to keep him within the fold but unless we were prepared to resign our production control and underwrite the project with something like £150,000 for 13 programmes *and* film them rather than telerecord them, we could not do business.'[8] Hancock never made another television series for the BBC.

Chapter 14

In early June 1961, Ray Galton and Alan Simpson finally placed their pens on the table, gave their trusty old typewriter a well-earned break and waved goodbye to Anthony Aloysius Hancock—a productive seven-year friendship which had spawned over 160 episodes.

It's time I put my pen down, too, because this is where my brief ends. As mentioned at the beginning of the book, this is not a biography of Tony Hancock, it's a journey charting the life of a ground-breaking comedy show that helped to shape a new dawn in the genre of situation comedy, first on radio and then on television. Hancock's later forays into television with the 1963 series *Hancock* for Associated Television, the 1967 series, *Hancock's*, for ABC and, a year later, the incomplete 1968 series for Australian television during which he tragically took his own life occurred long after he'd said goodbye to Anthony Aloysius Hancock and do not fall within my remit; besides, the trauma behind these programmes and the subsequent tragic events down under are well documented in other books and publications.

This volume is a history of six radio and seven television series, hours of entertainment that have enthralled millions of people, from all corners of the globe, for five decades. At any one moment, somewhere in the world, the chances are the booming tones of Hancock are being heard as broadcasting stations continue to repeat the shows.

While the man himself didn't survive to see what he had achieved, the legend lives on. In terms of comedic values, Hancock never realised just how deep-rooted his talents were, and, in later years, the endless effort to try and examine and understand why a simple look, a faint expression or the utterance of a single word could be enough to send his fans into sudden paroxysms of laughter mystified him more and more. This introspection—the questioning of his talents, the intensive analysis of his work—became something of an obsession with Hancock as he got caught up in a downward spiral.

During the life cycle of *Hancock's Half Hour*, Tony Hancock had moved through various phases, including the transition from radio to television and deciding to go it alone without the help of Sid James, both of which he mastered with aplomb. But parting with the writers who were fundamental to his success was arguably his biggest mistake, precipitating his eventual downfall. The severing of their working relationship occurred when Galton and Simpson had endured several rebuffs while trying to write the script for Hancock's second film with ABPC. Hancock wanted to become an international star in the film world, particularly in America, and it was down to Galton and Simpson to provide the scripts that would help him achieve his goal. After several abandoned attempts to find a vehicle that Hancock considered acceptable, Galton and Simpson finally completed a script but, again, it was turned down by Hancock, who regarded it as too parochial. 'Then he had an idea for doing a film about a Punch and Judy man on the south coast of England—very international!'

recalls Ray Galton. 'We discussed the idea with him and came up with three different ideas but he turned them all down. In the end, we told Tony that we couldn't go on like this because we had to make a living. Tony suggested we go and earn some money on television and he'd spend some time developing the idea of the Punch and Judy man. Then when we were all ready we'd get together again and work on it.' That never happened.

Galton and Simpson were given the chance to write their own series of *Comedy Playhouse*, from which *Steptoe and Son* emerged. Hancock teamed up with friend and writer Philip Oakes and penned the script for *The Punch and Judy Man*, his first venture without his long-term scriptwriters. Television series, as previously mentioned, followed. 'Hancock was convinced he could do it without us, that he didn't depend on the scripts Ray and I wrote,' says Alan Simpson. 'He thought he could achieve such success with other writers because he was the star and, therefore, would make it work. But that wasn't possible. Ray and I couldn't have written for Morecambe and Wise in the same way that Eddie Braben did. He took years to perfect that skill. So why would you expect someone else to be able to write the Hancock character? A lot of the people who tried missed the point, they made him belligerent for no reason. In his first ITV series after we'd finished working with him he came across as unpleasant for no reason, which means you lose all sympathy for the character. Of course, a character can be unpleasant but there has to be a reason.'

When asked if they would change anything about the premise of the show and the attitudes of their character if they were writing *Hancock's Half Hour* today, Ray Galton says: 'There are still Hancocks around but maybe the terms of reference would be different. The Hancock character is universal, for all generations and all periods. There are even Hancock characters in Dickens' work. But I don't think we would have made him so naïve if we were writing the show today—nowadays people aren't so gullible. But we'd definitely keep the same basic idea.'

'It's as relevant today as it's ever been,' adds Alan. 'Even young people who hear it, usually through their parents, think it's extremely funny. People see Hancock's mannerisms in their own friends. I'm convinced it will still be around in a hundred years' time, like Charlie Chaplin—a man for all seasons.'

Of their years spent in the company of Tony Hancock, Galton and Simpson agree that he was one of the greatest performers they've ever written for. Alan says: 'We were very fortunate to all come together at such an early time in our respective careers.'

Episode Guide: Radio

All scripts written by Ray Galton and Alan Simpson. Theme tune and incidental music composed by Wally Stott and recorded by the BBC Revue Orchestra for the first three series. Wally Stott and his Orchestra recorded the music for series four, five and six.

The first four series were produced by Dennis Main Wilson. Series five, six, 'Bill and Father Christmas' and the special remakes for the Transcription Services were produced by Tom Ronald, except series five, episode one, which saw Pat Dixon at the helm.

RADIO EPISODES AT A GLANCE

Series 1
The First Night Party
The Diamond Ring
The Idol
The Boxing Champion
The Hancock Festival
The New Car
The Department Store Santa
Christmas at Aldershot
The Christmas Eve Party
Cinderella Hancock
A Trip to France
The Monte Carlo Rally
A House on the Cliff
The Sheikh

The Marriage Bureau
The End of the Series

Series 2
A Holiday in France
The Crown Jewels
The Racehorse
A Visit to Swansea
The Holiday Camp
The Chef That Died of Shame
Prime Minister Hancock
The Rail Strike
The Television Set
The Three Sons
The Marrow Contest
The Matador

Series 3
The Pet Dog
The Jewel Robbery
The Bequest
The New Neighbour
The Winter Holiday
The Blackboard Jungle
The Red Planet
The Diet
A Visit to Russia
The Trial of Father Christmas
Cinderella Hancock (a new production of the
  episode from series one)
The New Year Resolutions
Hancock's Hair
The Student Prince
The Breakfast Cereal
How Hancock Won the War
240

The Newspaper
The Greyhound Track
The Conjurer
The Test Match

Series 4

Back from Holiday
The Bolshoi Ballet
Sid James's Dad
The Income Tax Demand
The New Secretary
Michelangelo 'Ancock
Anna and the King of Siam
Cyrano de Hancock
The Stolen Petrol
The Expresso Bar
Hancock's Happy Christmas
The Diary
The 13th of the Series
Almost a Gentleman
The Old School Reunion
The Wild Man of the Woods
Agricultural 'Ancock
Hancock in the Police
The Emigrant
The Last of the McHancocks

Series 5

The New Radio Series
The Scandal Magazine
The Male Suffragettes
The Insurance Policy
The Publicity Photograph
The Unexploded Bomb
Hancock's School

Around the World in Eighty Days
The Americans Hit Town
The Election Candidate
Hancock's Car
The East Cheam Drama Festival
The Foreign Legion
Sunday Afternoon at Home
The Grappling Game
The Junk Man
Hancock's War
The Prize Money
The Threatening Letters
The Sleepless Night

Christmas Special

Bill and Father Christmas

Special Recordings for London Transcription Service

The 13th of the Month (remake of 'The 13th of the Series')
The New Secretary
The Ballet Visit (remake of 'The Bolshoi Ballet')
The Election Candidate

Series 6

The Smugglers
The Childhood Sweetheart
The Last Bus Home
The Picnic
The Gourmet
The Elopement
Fred's Pie Stall

During a seven-year relationship, Alan Simpson (left) and Ray Galton (right) wrote over 160 radio and television episodes for Tony Hancock.

Bill Kerr (left) and Kenneth Williams (right) provided a valuable contribution to the success of the radio series.

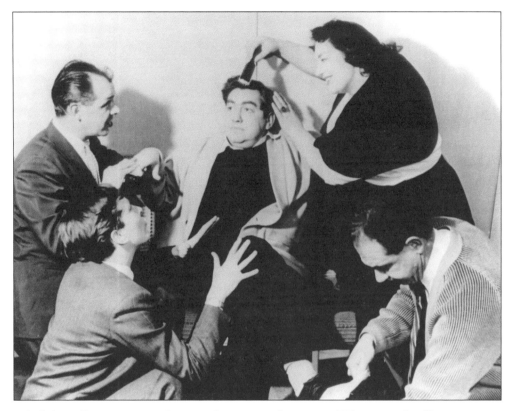

A bit of teamwork works wonders as Hancock discovers
when he's pampered by Hattie Jacques, Sid James,
Kenneth Williams and Bill Kerr during the radio show.

Railway Cuttings was brought to life in July 1956 with the launch of the first television series.

Johnny Vyvyan (left) and Hugh Lloyd (right) were two of the television show's regular faces.

As the series developed, Sid's character became increasingly important, but his working relationship with Hancock came to an end when Tony decided it was time to venture out on his own.

Looking back on a successful show, Hancock and James' acting styles were complementary.

HUGH LLOYD

JOHN VERE

DENNIS CHINNERY

Some members of the Duncan Wood Repertory Company.

IVOR RAYMONDE

EVELYN LUND

ALEC BREGONZI

ANNE MARRYOTT

PATRICK MILNER

Throwing a real spanner in the works, Hancock didn't possess a mechanical mind.

A tightening of the purse strings was called for when Hancock and Sid returned from their holiday to a mountain of bills in 'The Economy Drive'.

In 'Twelve Angry Men', Hancock tries to convince the jury that the accused is innocent.

Feeling under the weather in 'The Cold'.

When nearly every other country in the world doesn't want him, Hancock settles for a passage to Baffin Land.

His last television series in 1961 saw him out in the big wide world on his own, living in rented accommodation near Earl's Court.

With a touch of Archers flavour, Hancock played Old Joshua in 'The Bowmans', annoying everyone, including the producer (right, played by Patrick Cargill).

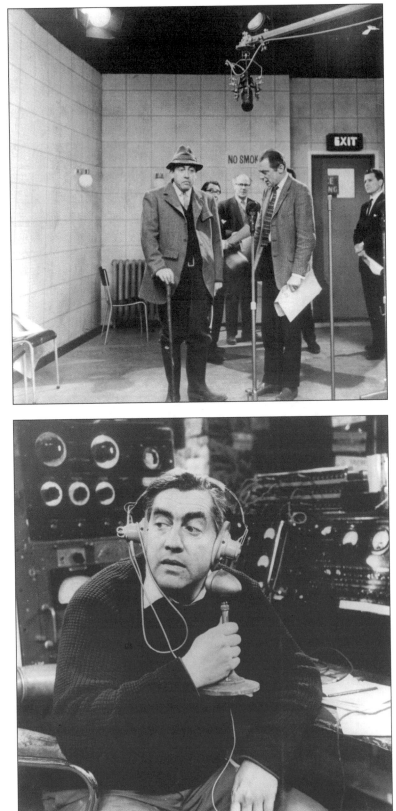

Hancock attempts to save a life during his days as a radio ham anorak.

A smartly dressed Air Marshall (John Le Mesurier, centre) found himself in the unfortunate position of being locked in a lift with Hancock.

Giving blood turned into an ordeal for Hancock.

Andrée Melly joined the radio team in 1955,
replacing Moira Lister.

Moira Lister was the original female in the radio series.

Hancock never imagined it would be so difficult winning the heart of a woman.

The writers in Ray Galton's (right) Surrey home in 2002.

The Waxwork
Sid's Mystery Tours
The Fête
The Poetry Society
Hancock in Hospital
The Christmas Club
The Impersonator

SERIES 1

Featuring: Tony Hancock, Bill Kerr, Moira Lister, Sidney James and Alan Simpson (except episode six).

1. The First Night Party

Recorded: Sat. 30/10/54
Transmitted: Tues. 2/11/54
First Repeat: Sat. 6/11/54
Audience figure: 4.51 million

(with Gerald Campion and Kenneth Williams)

It's the first night of Tony's radio series and to celebrate, he's throwing a cocktail and dinner party. Bill and Tony make all the arrangements from their West End pad, with leading critics and top BBC executives on the invitation list in an attempt to elevate Tony's status within the profession. Tony's keen to impress, although Bill's crazily typed invites will do little to help his cause, nor will the patched-up crockery. When Moira arrives, she states it will be an insult to hold the do in their decrepit flat, so Bill suggests acquiring the services of his old friend, Sid, who's just opened an estate agent's office.

Sid agrees to help them find a posh pad for the weekend, suggesting an apartment at 223 Park Lane, where all the food is supplied and free access to the wine cellar. Tony snaps it up for fifty quid, with Sid and his colleague—Coatsleeve Charlie—employed as butlers. The prestigious guests arrive, but one face Tony didn't expect to see was that of Lord Bayswater, the flat owner, who turns up unannounced to find his flat in ruins.

2. The Diamond Ring

Recorded:	Sat. 6/11/54
Transmitted:	Tues. 9/11/54
First Repeat:	Sat. 13/11/54
Audience figure:	4.89 million

(with Kenneth Williams)

No recording of this episode is available in the BBC archives

Short of money, Hancock and Bill go begging for a few pennies with Bill sitting in an old pram disguised as a Guy. When they're forced to move on by a policeman, they return home only to discover a diamond ring in their collection hat: there is a £500 reward for its safe return.

While they're discussing what to do, Moira enters the room and jumps to conclusions, believing it's an engagement ring from Tony. Claiming it's dirty, they manage to retrieve the ring and rush off to Sid James to arrange for a copy to be made, which they intend giving to Moira while they claim the reward. Sid, however, has other plans: he makes two copies and keeps the original.

After much confusion, Hancock and Bill find

themselves in court facing charges of attempted fraud. They're found guilty and given two choices: four years in jail or a £10,000 fine; they opt for the latter and end up begging with Bill as the Guy for next year's Bonfire Night to help pay the fine.

3. The Idol

Recorded: Sat. 13/11/54
Transmitted: Tues: 16/11/54
First Repeat: Sat. 20/11/54
Audience figure: 4.89 million

The Lad has received a letter from an ecstatic fan proclaiming he's 'the most handsome comedian on radio today'. Well, she obviously has taste as far as Hancock is concerned so he takes her comment to heart and allows himself to be drenched in fan adoration. All done up in a new outfit, his ego rises, his head expands and he's even taken the liberty of getting himself immortalised in oils to mark the occasion.

In order to cure his insufferable bigheadedness, Bill and Moira arrange for 200 girls from the local pickle factory to come round and mob him. All the girls ask in return is payment in cigarettes.

The girls arrive and Hancock is a picture of frozen fear, so much so that he takes refuge in a 'Stout & Bitter' barrel from the Dog and Duck Public House, much to Moira's amusement. Hancock tries every trick in the book to leave the house—wigs, glasses, masks—but all to no avail.

There's only one thing for it, bodyguards, and Sidney James's new protection service is just the ticket. He arrives with three burly bruisers, Maurice 'the Mangler', 'Shoulders' McGirk and

'Steamroller' Fred, all ready to escort Hancock from the house. Bill hasn't paid the girls for their service, though, leaving Hancock, Moira and Bill to make a great escape and tunnel out from the house. Sid's boys get scared and do a runner, leaving by an underground train, and Hancock and clan surface to find themselves in the middle of the pickle factory, with yet another escape on their hands, this time in pickle barrels.

4. The Boxing Champion

Recorded: Sat. 20/11/54
Transmitted: Tues. 23/11/54
First Repeat: Sat. 27/11/54
Audience figure: 6.02 million

(with Kenneth Williams and Paul Carpenter)

Hancock's doctor advises him to lose weight or suffer the consequences—a raw carrot and prune diet. Reluctantly, Hancock decides to visit a gymnasium to work off some of the excess pounds, only to find the establishment run by Sid James. Whilst more likely to lose pounds from his pocket than his waistline, Hancock gets involved in a boxing bout with Sid's main championship contender, Punchy, the Heavyweight Champion of Shepherd's Bush.

He defeats Sid's champion accidentally and, never one to miss a financial opportunity, Sid takes charge of his new boxing protégé, Two Ton Tony Hancock, and arranges a full-scale championship bout for him. But with Sid backing his new star in a fixed bout, Hancock may lose more pounds than he bargained for.

262

5. The Hancock Festival

Recorded: Sat. 27/11/54
Transmitted: Tues. 30/11/54
First Repeat: Sat. 4/12/54
Audience figure: 4.51 million

No copy of this episode is available in the BBC archives

Thinking he can replicate the success enjoyed by Somerset Maugham, who has just had three of his plays broadcast on the radio, Hancock submits three of his own scripts: the first about artist Paul Goggin and his adventures with a paintbrush in the South Seas, the second spotlighting a rich young man who heads to Monte Carlo to gamble away all his money, while the third is set on the North West Frontier, with Tony playing a tough British officer facing the prospect of being overrun by the advancing Afghans.

6. The New Car

Recorded: Sat. 4/12/54
Transmitted: Tues. 7/12/54
First Repeat: Sat. 11/12/54
Audience figure: 5.64 million

(with Kenneth Williams)

It's not easy being a comedy star, keeping up appearances, being seen at the right clubs with the right birds and the right car. After all, status is everything in this business and if Hancock wants to be seen alongside the likes of Terry-Thomas then he needs to swap his pushbike for some new wheels—four, to be precise.

Who better then to furnish him with a new motor than Sidney James who just happens to run Sid's Cars in a junkyard. As he needs something to set him apart from the others, Sid offers him an ex-police car minus the badges and flashing light.

He's soon spotted by the police and a chase ensues until the policemen are diverted to look for an escaped convict who's in the vicinity. As Hancock, Bill and Moira pull over to escape the police chase, they're approached by Butcher, the prisoner at large. Hancock never imagined buying a car would cause so much stress so he decides to return to Sid's Cars, with Butcher, only to find they're reuniting the criminal with his old boss.

Hancock finally gets a replacement vehicle from Sid but it turns out to be equally conspicuous, especially as it's red and has ladders, a fire bell and a water hose.

7. The Department Store Santa

Recorded:	Sat. 11/12/54
Transmitted:	Tues. 14/12/54
First Repeat:	Sat. 18/12/54
Audience figure:	4.89 million

(with Kenneth Williams)

No copy of this episode is available in the BBC archives

The Ministry of Labour demands that Tony secure a job, which upsets him because it will mean he won't be able to attend the Unemployed Working Men's Club any more. Reluctant to take just any job, he's keen on a Christmas job at a local department store because as it's seasonal, he'll soon be back at the Club.

The store manager is Sid James, who offers Bill a job as a floorwalker; although reluctant to employ Hancock in the same position, he decides to give him a chance but soon regrets the decision when Hancock rollerskates into a pile of records and crockery, causing over £3,000 worth of damage.

Hancock is so desperate to keep his seasonal job that he's forced to become the store's Santa, a job he endures despite taunts from the children. But he soon finds himself back at the Labour Exchange after being sacked for hitting the store's night-watchman.

8. Christmas at Aldershot

Recorded: Sat. 18/12/54
Transmitted: Tues. 21/12/54
First Repeat: Sat. 25/12/54
Audience figure: 4.89 million

(with Kenneth Williams)

No copy of this episode is available in the BBC archives

The feeling of goodwill is short-lived in Hancock's house when he and Bill receive their National Service call-up papers. Their mood worsens when they discover Sid James is their sergeant; equally shocked, Sid allocates them responsibility for cooking Christmas dinner for 4,000 troops. When half of the soldiers end up in hospital, surprisingly Sid gives Hancock and Bill a final chance by allowing them to cook the supper. The remaining soldiers, though, have had enough and attack them in the cookhouse.

A desperate Hancock and Bill go AWOL and return to Moira, only to learn that her parents, who hate Tony, are due to visit. Deciding life in uniform is better than a visit from Moira's parents, they return to barracks pronto.

9. The Christmas Eve Party

Recorded: Sat. 18/12/54
Transmitted: Tues. 28/12/54
First Repeat: Sat. 1/1/55
Audience figure: 4.89 million

(with Kenneth Williams)

No copy of this episode is available in the BBC archives

Hancock receives a summons requested by the residents of the entire borough, who are fed up with the noise caused by his Christmas Eve party, which started on 27 November. One complainant, Mrs Bloggs, explains that she couldn't hear her husband hit her because of the noise made by revellers in Hancock's house, but Hancock's version of events is completely different.

As the jury is undecided, the judge suggests the events of the evening are reconstructed in Hancock's flat, but before long everyone is up before another judge for causing a disturbance during the reconstruction.

10. Cinderella Hancock

Recorded: Mon. 3/1/55
Transmitted: Tues. 4/1/55
First Repeat: Sat. 8/1/55

Audience figure: 6.39 million

(with Dora Bryan, Kenneth Williams and Paul Carpenter)

No copy of this episode is available in the BBC archives

Hancock's in buoyant mood around town, but not for long. He's lodging at Bill's, but in order to live rent-free Tony is required to do all the housework and just about anything else.

Sid arrives with tickets for the National Film Ball and Hancock, tied to the apron strings, is left to fantasise about the big stars in attendance while Sid and Bill swan off in their best get-up to charm the starlets.

Determined to join the luminaries, Hancock rents a costume, the Sheik Aly Aga Khancock, though he wasn't banking on it being such a hit with an over-amorous lady, Dora Bryan. In true pantomime fashion, the costume is due back by midnight and in an effort to escape he leaves a tell-tale sign.

11. A Trip to France

Recorded: Mon. 10/1/55
Transmitted: Tues. 11/1/55
First Repeat: Sat. 15/1/55
Audience figure: 5.64 million

(with Kenneth Williams)

After playing battleships in the bath each day, Hancock decides he wants to have his own boat to explore the oceans of the world. As Sid is now in the boat business, Hancock, Moira and Bill set off to see him in Southampton. They arrive to hear Sid on the phone to France: he's looking for a crew to sail to France that night on a suspicious looking job and in Hancock he's found the ideal mug.

Nearing the French coast it becomes apparent that Sid is smuggling contraband—300 bottles of brandy. Customs and Excise officials become suspicious of Sid's vessel and search it. It's not long before they find what they're looking for. But discovering the officials are partial to a drop of brandy, Sid returns with a bigger boat to ensure there's enough for everyone.

12. The Monte Carlo Rally

Recorded:	Mon. 17/1/55
Transmitted:	Tues. 18/1/55
First Repeat:	Sat. 22/1/55
Audience figure:	6.02 million

(with Brian Johnston, Raymond Baxter and Kenneth Williams)

Captain Anthony 'Wheels' Hancock takes part in the Monte Carlo Rally, driving his 59-year-old car, but no sooner have he and his crew left London than his vehicle breaks down and there's little option but to push. Three hours late, they finally arrive at the starting point. Delayed further by Hancock's inability to start the car, they jump on the train to Dover, leaving their car in the guard's van.

Despite bad weather, resulting in the car being snowed in during the final stage of the rally, Hancock and his team go on to win, earning a cheque for 200,000 francs. But Hancock returns to reality with a bump when he wakes up from his dream to find he's been issued a parking ticket for being stuck on the starting line for four days.

13. A House on the Cliff

Recorded: Mon. 24/1/55
Transmitted: Tues. 25/1/55
First Repeat: Sat. 29/1/55
Audience figure: 6.02 million

It's time for a shake-up in the Hancock household. Tony wants to build a house to replace his ramshackle dwelling. So bad is the repair job he's done to the roof, there's enough work to keep thirty full-time labourers in employment.

It would all be plain sailing if a certain estate agent—none other than Sid James—kept away. He cons Hancock into buying two houses: one at the bottom of a cliff, the other at the top, on the basis that when the lower one floods because of the tide, Hancock can use the second house. Hancock, though, ends up building another house but his luck isn't in and it begins to sink.

14. The Sheikh

Recorded: Mon. 31/1/55
Transmitted: Tues. 1/2/55
First Repeat: Sat. 5/2/55
Audience figure: 6.02 million

(with Kenneth Williams)

Hancock's leisure time is valuable and there's no better way to spend it than a trip to the cinema, even more so if Moira's in tow. He becomes obsessed with the idea of a career in films and signs up as a dramatic actor at producer Sid James' deluxe film studios.

Even though his limited finances result in him only producing low-budget pictures, Sid wants to make a magnificent epic despite having a cast of only three. Sultan Hancock is not deterred, though, and begins preparing for movie stardom even though his screen career amounts to just three minutes of film on an ancient box camera.

15. The Marriage Bureau

Recorded: Mon. 7/2/55
Transmitted: Tues. 8/2/55
First Repeat: Sat. 12/2/55
Audience figure: 6.77 million

(with Peter Sellers, replacing Kenneth Williams)

No copy of this episode is available in the BBC archives

Behind with the rent, Hancock needs a job quickly; he's offered a post as a caretaker but with one proviso: he must be married. He proposes to Moira, who's quick to accept, but when he realises life with her will be too expensive, especially as she's planning a luxurious sightseeing tour of Europe, he heads for Sid's Lonely Hearts Matrimonial Bureau.

Sid's expecting a visit from the taxman any day so he lets Hancock run the bureau for a while, but before long the business is in a complete mess, thanks to Hancock sending out pictures of Stewart Granger to all the female clients and Ava Gardner to all the male clients, marrying everyone off before they know what's happened.

With all his clients demanding their money back, Sid fires Hancock, who ends up taking the post of caretaker, with Granny Higgins, whom the marriage bureau has had trouble satisfying, acting as his wife.

16. The End of the Series

Recorded: Mon. 14/2/55
Transmitted: Tues. 15/2/55
First Repeat: Sat. 19/2/55
Audience figure: 6.39 million

(with Kenneth Williams)

It's the end of the series and as the credits roll Hancock and Co. reflect on how they all first met. Hancock used to flog cough remedies down on the docks whilst Bill was making his way over from Oz. He ended up swimming part of the way after he was discovered stowed away in a lifeboat. As he came ashore he bumped into Hancock doing a runner from the police. They teamed up as a double-act selling the remedies, only to find Sid James doing likewise.

Giving up the medication game, they pick up jobs in a restaurant whereupon Hancock ends up serving Moira. Undeterred by his broken French, Moira is charmed by Tony and even though she has tickets to the opera she'd sooner stay and enjoy some idle chatter.

Now a foursome, they embark on a theatrical adventure staging *Romeo and Juliet* and before they know it end up at the end of a radio series together.

SERIES 2

Featuring: Tony Hancock (except episodes 1–3), Bill Kerr, Sidney James, Andrée Melly, Kenneth Williams and Alan Simpson (except episode ten).

1. A Holiday in France

Recorded: Sun. 17/4/55
Transmitted: Tues. 19/4/55
First Repeat: Wed. 20/4/55
Audience figure: 4.14 million

(with Harry Secombe)

No copy of this episode is available in the BBC archives

In the absence of Tony Hancock, Harry Secombe steps in, only to find himself heading to France with Bill instead of their intended destination, Southend. Upon arriving in Paris they realise they don't have enough money to pay for their train tickets and are sent to prison, but they make such a racket the other prisoners club together to pay their fine.

Relieved to be free, they end up at a fancy dress ball where a French girl, Andrée, steps on Harry's toes. Smitten with each other, they spend the evening enjoying themselves, but when Andrée says she'd love to visit England, he tells her that sadly he can't afford the fare. Back at Dover, Harry discovers Andrée hidden in his luggage, for which he knows he'll be fined; aware that he won't be able to pay, he resigns himself to another spell behind bars.

2. The Crown Jewels

Recorded: Sun. 24/4/55
Transmitted: Tues. 26/4/55
First Repeat: Wed. 27/4/55
Audience figure: 4.89 million

(with Harry Secombe)

No copy of this episode is available in the BBC archives

While showing Andrée the sights of London, Harry and Bill meet Sid, who is working as a Beefeater at the Tower of London. He tricks Harry into thinking a criminal is out to steal the Crown Jewels and they have permission to move them to his house—an excuse he also uses to collect treasures at the Tate Gallery and the British Museum.

When a news report provides a detailed description of the suspects, Sid decides to let Harry and Bill carry the can; Harry and Bill, meanwhile, finally realise that they're regarded as accomplices and try replacing the Jewels, but when a mix-up sees Harry leaving his bowler hat and walking out of the Tower wearing the Coronation Crown, it's not long before he feels the strong arm of the law.

3. The Racehorse

Recorded: Sun. 1/5/55
Transmitted: Tues. 3/5/55
First Repeat: Wed. 4/5/55
Audience figure: 4.14 million

(with Harry Secombe)

No copy of this episode is available in the BBC archives

Harry sends Bill out to buy some food, but he returns having spent it all on a three-legged horse, called Sabrina, and food for the animal. To make matters worse, one of its three legs is wooden.

Bill has arranged for Sid to train the horse, but when Sabrina takes hours to complete ten yards it's obvious the flat isn't her forte. Sid turns his attention instead to the jumps and enters the horse for the Britannia Steeplechase, with Harry as rider. With odds of 800,000 to one, Sid realises he could make a fortune if he nobbled the other horses, but when Harry resorts to carrying the horse over the early fences, it seems as if Sid's luck is out. As the horses race towards the finish line, it looks as if it will be a photo-finish until Harry unscrews Sabrina's wooden leg and holds it out to claim first place.

4. A Visit to Swansea

Recorded: Sun. 8/5/55
Transmitted: Tues. 10/5/55
First Repeat: Wed. 11/5/55
Audience figure: 5.26 million

(with Harry Secombe)

No copy of this episode is available in the BBC archives

Hancock returns to his flat to find Bill and Andrée, to whom he's immediately attracted, hanging around. They're eager to know where he disappeared to but all Hancock will say is that he had a heavy cold. Bill explains how successful

Harry, who's returned to his coal-mining job, has been in Hancock's absence and persuades Hancock to visit him in Wales to thank him personally.

Despite being hindered by Snide and his brother at the railway station, they finally board a Swansea-bound train. When they arrive at their destination Harry is busy working down the mine. Much to Hancock's irritation, everyone lauds Harry's performances in the show, but it doesn't stop him donning a miner's suit and searching for the Welshman. Eventually they meet and Hancock thanks Harry for his help and assures him he won't miss another show, but when his back suddenly plays up, just hours before the next show, it looks as if Harry might be deputising again.

5. The Holiday Camp

Recorded:	Sun. 15/5/55
Transmitted:	Tues. 17/5/55
First Repeat:	Wed. 18/5/55
Audience figure:	5.26million

(with Dennis Wilson on piano)

Hancock, Bill and Andrée arrive at Sid's while a board meeting is in progress with the local councillors. Sid tells Hancock and his companions that he wants them to run a new holiday camp he's just bought on the South Coast.

He's promoting his new purchase with the slogan, 'Come to Hancock's Holiday Camp, see the English Riviera, the Cannes of the Dorset Coast'. The truth is, it's a converted army camp on an artillery practice range he's bought on the cheap. The chalets come complete with slip trenches and overhead shells.

With a shortage of beds, a drunk chef who only cooks porridge and an evening cabaret that leaves much to be desired, some would say there is not much to lose when more shells fall, virtually destroying the camp.

Not everyone is out of pocket, though. Sid's quite happy, he's cleaned up on an insurance scam which nets him a cool £40,000, which he intends to reinvest in a camp Stateside.

6. The Chef that Died of Shame

Recorded: Mon. 23/5/55
Transmitted: Tues. 24/5/55
First Repeat: Wed. 25/5/55
Audience figure: 4.51 million

Grant Faversham tells the story of Percois Egance, a culinary legend, whom he knew before his days of fame as Percy Higgins of Higgins' Premiere Pie Stall, c/o The Horse Trough, Covent Garden.

He recalls their first meeting, one cold November night in 1948, when Higgins' food left much to be desired, and his ambition was to swap the stall for a little restaurant. Faversham took pity on Higgins and decided to take him to Paris to study cooking under one of the greatest chefs in the world. Higgins excelled, married, secured a job at London's Hotel Rubenstein and became the talk of the town.

Fame soon went to Higgins' head, though, and he started playing around with other women and drinking heavily. Soon he had hit rock bottom, but was given a second chance at the hotel when catering was needed for an important United

Nations banquet. When all the diners finished up collapsing after tasting the food, it's obvious the great chef had lost his touch for good.

7. Prime Minister Hancock

Recorded: Mon. 30/5/55
Transmitted: Tues. 31/5/55
First Repeat: Wed. 1/6/55
Audience figure: 5.26 million

No copy of this episode is available in the BBC archives

Hancock agrees to stand for Parliament when Sid promises to rig the result because the votes are being counted by his uncle, Edwardian Fred. When Hancock catches measles and spends the rest of his election campaign ill in bed, he dreams that he becomes the Prime Minister, quickly abolishing all taxes and converting the House of Commons into a dance hall.

Eventually he wakes to learn he's lost the election, thanks to Edwardian Fred's actions rendering all the papers invalid; he gets so upset he'd rather return to his dreams because he'd just promised Bessie Braddock, a Labour MP, the next dance.

8. The Rail Strike

Recorded: Mon. 6/6/55
Transmitted: Tues. 7/6/55
First Repeat: Wed. 8/6/55
Audience figure: 5.26 million

With no trains running because of a national rail strike, Sid, Hancock and Bill decide to run their own service. When Stephenson's famous train, the Rocket, disappears from the Science Museum it's obvious who's to blame. All they need now are carriages, a guard's van and a dining car which they resolve in the shape of prams, a night-watchman's hut and Charlie's pie stall from town.

Amongst the passengers on the maiden trip is Andrée, who's in a hurry to get to Brighton, and a ladies' man who takes quite a shine to her, much to her and Hancock's annoyance. It's costing the passengers a fortune, but Hancock would argue that they're travelling on a luxury slow train with food, board and a laundry service.

As they head along the coast, a violent storm derails the train but it keeps running on the road in the hope of rejoining the track further along its route. Even though Hancock thinks he knows where he's going, they end up riding the big dipper at the Battersea Park fun fair with the police on their tail.

9. The Television Set

Recorded:	Mon. 13/6/55
Transmitted:	Tues. 14/6/55
First Repeat:	Wed. 15/6/55
Audience figure:	5.64 million

Some might say that spending every evening with Andrée is enough entertainment for anyone, but not Hancock. He wants a television set. Fed up with being the only person in his street not to own one, it's time to hack down the wooden aerial and get fitted out with the latest high tech gadgetry from his local radio shop.

Sid's on hand to make the financial outlay a little

easier and if he hasn't got what Hancock wants he'll certainly find someone who has. Hancock has only got £15 to spend and with the cheapest set in the radio shop costing 60 guineas, Sid's intervention is welcomed for once. A 'What the Butler Saw' pier machine is not what he had in mind, or indeed a set with a starting handle, but he thinks the DIY set for a tenner is a bargain.

A 5,000-piece set of sheer DIY luxury is so large it necessitates the removal of a household wall and means it can only be viewed when sitting on the doorstep. But before long the screen blows up and the fire brigade is summoned to put out the flames.

10. The Three Sons

Recorded: Mon. 20/6/55
Transmitted: Tues. 21/6/55
First Repeat: Wed. 22/6/55
Audience figure: 5.26 million

No copy of this episode is available in the BBC archives

Old Ebadiah Hancock is close to death, although it doesn't stop him having amorous thoughts about his nurse; and he wants to see his three sons before he passes away so his butler, Meadows, is tasked with finding the men.

He returns with some grim news: they're all dead. Rodney, a captain in the navy, was blown up after landing on a mine while attempting to abandon ship; Gideon Hancock became a gangster and was trying to flee a gangland fight in Chicago when hit by a motorbike ridden by Meadows while out searching for him. His other son, Anthony

279

Hancock, meanwhile, became a doctor but died taking his own medicine.

Upon hearing the news, Ebadiah closes his eyes and prepares to meet his sons in Heaven, but as a result of harbouring naughty thoughts concerning his nurse, he ends up in Hell.

11. The Marrow Contest

Recorded:	Mon. 27/6/55
Transmitted:	Tues. 28/6/55
First Repeat:	Wed. 29/6/55
Audience figure:	5.26 million

Vegetable growing is a serious business, especially for Hancock, whose marrow has received nothing but tender loving care. And this has paid off because it's a giant. Hancock's plans to enter it in the local vegetable competition are threatened when the plot where it grows is threatened by Mayor James' road-widening scheme.

However, Hancock's initial worry is not the six yards he'll lose from his garden but the man next door sabotaging his marrow in order to prevent Hancock winning the £50 prize in the competition. As Mayor James will not change his plans for the road, Hancock takes his fight to his MP, Fred Churchill, at the Houses of Parliament. With shovels at the ready and diplomatic immunity claimed for the marrow, the whole matter is to be resolved in court.

Deciding that both parties are in the right, the judge requests the road be built but the marrow should not be destroyed. There's only one solution: to build a bridge over the marrow.

12. The Matador

Recorded: Sat. 2/7/55
Transmitted: Tues. 5/7/55
First Repeat: Thurs. 7/7/55
Audience figure: 4.89 million

No copy of this episode is available in the BBC archives

Hancock doesn't feel well but a visit to the doctor finds him being classed as a malingerer. When the doctor tells him to go away, Hancock thinks he's telling him to take a break, but with little money to his name, the choices are limited.

Bill and Andrée suggest he asks Sid because he's got lots of contacts in Europe and can secure cheap flights. Sid is on the phone when Hancock arrives at the office. He's just informed a client he can't supply the British bullfighter he'd promised because he was gouged while practising his act at home, but when Hancock walks in the door, Sid realises he's found the perfect mug to take his place.

Hancock can't believe his luck when Sid agrees to pay all his expenses on his trip to Spain, and it's not until he's donning a matador's uniform and being chased around the arena by a raging bull that he realises what he's let himself in for.

SERIES 3

Featuring: Tony Hancock, Bill Kerr, Sidney James, Kenneth Williams, Andrée Melly and Alan Simpson.

1. The Pet Dog

Recorded:	Sun. 16/10/55
Transmitted:	Wed. 19/10/55
First Repeat:	Sun. 23/10/55
Audience figure:	6.02 million

After three months off air, Hancock has managed to avoid the cast and, more importantly to his pocket, three of the cast members' birthdays. His scheming has come up short, though: he's forgotten it's Andrée's 21st birthday tomorrow.

Hancock decides Andrée can choose her own present this year, but he never expected she'd want a pet crocodile or an ostrich. To find a more suitable animal they visit the local pet shop where she spots a baby gorilla, which embarrassingly turns out to be Sidney James, the owner. She eventually opts for a puppy called Harry.

After a kennel has been built for it, the puppy grows and grows until it's six feet long with paws like globe artichokes. Not only that, Harry's buried the next-door neighbour and is now living in the house whilst Hancock and the others are in the garage. Even more trouble is on the horizon when it's discovered that Harry is, in fact, a bitch and she's about to deliver fifteen puppies.

2. The Jewel Robbery

Recorded:	Sun. 23/10/55
Transmitted:	Wed. 26/10/55
First Repeat:	Sun. 30/10/55
Audience figure:	4.89 million

Hancock has not paid his road tax for his car, Genevieve. With the tax costing more than the car,

282

Hancock decides it's time to update it for a classier model, such as a Rolls-Royce. At the showroom, the salesman is impressed by Tony's stories of grandeur but not by what's in his wallet. He finally opts for a 1923 Town Carriage Rolls-Royce for £250. All he needs now is a chauffeur to collect it, a job that is offered to Sid. With a jeweller's next door to the showroom, Sid is more than happy to help. Using the Rolls as a getaway vehicle, a smash and grab raid on the jeweller's is on the cards.

3. The Bequest

Recorded:	Sun. 30/10/55
Transmitted:	Wed. 2/11/55
First Repeat:	Sun. 6/11/55
Audience figure:	6.39 million

An unknown uncle leaves Tony £40,000 in his will, but there's a catch: he has to find a bride. Desperate to claim his inheritance, he contacts all his old flames but is met with rejection wherever he goes: Andrée, Gladys, Mabel and Deirdre—no one is interested in walking down the aisle with him. Accepting Bill's advice, he reluctantly agrees to visit the local Palais but doesn't feel at ease chewing gum and tousling his hair.

With Andrée his only hope, he tries to persuade her with soft music, cigarette holder and a Noël Coward-style smoking jacket, but she sees through the soft-soaping. In the end, a visit from a representative at the solicitor's dealing with the estate brings news of an updated version of the will.

4. The New Neighbour

Recorded:	Sun. 30/10/55
Transmitted:	Wed. 9/11/55
First Repeat:	Sun. 13/11/55
Audience figure:	5.64 million

(Adapted for television and shown as episode four of the second series.)

No copy of this episode is available in the BBC archives

Hancock is suspicious of his new neighbour so Bill hides in the bushes and records everything being taken into the house, including a collection of guns, knives and an acid bath. When the neighbour is seen leaving the house at midnight with a body over his shoulder and burying something in the garden the next day, Hancock and Bill are convinced he's a mass murderer. They head to the estate agency, owned by none other than Sid, who sold him the house, to find out as much as they can about the man from number 25.

Sid refuses to disclose anything, even though he discovers the man melts down waxwork models and makes new ones for Madame Tussaud's. Hancock eventually convinces the police to investigate, but when they all clamber over the garden fence and land in a bath full of wax, they're soon shifted to be exhibits in the Chamber of Horrors.

5. The Winter Holiday

Recorded:	Sun. 13/11/55
Transmitted:	Wed. 16/11/55
First Repeat:	Sun. 20/11/55
Audience figure:	6.39 million

No copy of this episode is available in the BBC archives

Hancock has been working as a lift attendant for years without having a holiday, so when his manager finally persuades him to take a break, he heads for Brighton with Bill and Andrée in tow. On the train they bump into Sid, who cheats Hancock out of his holiday money in a game of cards, and they end up spending the night under Brighton Pier, despite it being November.

After a freezing cold night, Bill and Andrée persuade a reluctant Hancock to return home, but when the sunshine finally breaks through the clouds, he decides on a paddle. The cold water brings on cramp, and when he begins struggling in the water, he cries out for help. Bill rushes to the lifeguard, who turns out to be Snide, but initially he's reluctant to help because he's only the paddling pool attendant and can't even swim. Eventually he tries to help but gets into trouble himself, leaving no alternative but to call the lifeboat.

Back at work, Hancock receives some good news when he's promoted and sent to work at head office, but when he learns he'll have to re-locate to Brighton, he hands in his notice.

6. The Blackboard Jungle

Recorded:	Sun. 20/11/55
Transmitted:	Wed. 23/11/55
First Repeat:	Sun. 27/11/55
Audience figure:	6.02 million

No copy of this episode is available in the BBC archives

Hancock joins the teaching staff of a grammar school and wants to reform the old-fashioned establishment, where behaviour is appalling. He meets with resistance from Sid, an older teacher, who only secured his job because his son, Bill, is the school bully; he fears he'll soon follow his son out of the school gates and devises a plan to try and get Hancock the sack.

Knowing a school governor is visiting the classrooms, Bill asks Hancock to correct the spellings of some rude words he has included in a letter, but just as Hancock writes them on the board, the governor walks in and is disgusted. Hancock is able to convince him that Bill is the culprit and the boy is expelled, leaving the school to become a centre of excellence.

A decade later, Hancock's own son is ready for his first day at school, but he's turned into a bully himself. Hancock realises that, in hindsight, it might not have been a good idea employing Bill as a babysitter.

7. The Red Planet

Recorded:	Sun. 27/11/55
Transmitted:	Wed. 30/11/55
First Repeat:	Sun. 4/12/55
Audience figure:	5.64 million

No copy of this episode is available in the BBC archives

Tony becomes interested in astronomy and makes his own telescope to view the stars. Sid decides to play a trick on his friend and paints a red spot on the lens, which he makes bigger each day; Hancock is convinced he's spotted a large planet that's on a collision course with Earth and reports his findings to the relevant authorities but no one takes any notice.

Deciding that Earth is doomed, Hancock decides to head for Mars and persuades Bill and Andrée to come along. Sid agrees to make their spaceship, for a large fee, out of dustbins and fireworks, and agrees to light the fuse. Surprisingly, the rocket roars up into the sky, but without a bottom leaves its passengers behind.

8. The Diet

Recorded:	Sun. 4/12/55
Transmitted:	Wed. 7/12/55
First Repeat:	Sun. 11/12/55
Audience figure:	6.39 million

No copy of this episode is available in the BBC archives

Hancock's been offered the romantic lead in a new film. There's only one problem, though: American producer, Mr Stroud, doesn't want the leading man carrying so much weight.

In the meantime, Stroud is also interested in a Mr Kerr. He's been told he's a slim, good-looking lad, but Hancock isn't so impressed. Undeterred by the producer's demands, he continues eating while Andrée informs him he'll have to diet, and quick. Meanwhile, Bill has been provisionally offered the role in Mr Stroud's film unless Hancock can shed the pounds.

After Hancock has endured three weeks of strained cabbage water, Andrée arranges a visit to a dietician, Mr James, who has guaranteed to take pounds off him. But just when he eventually reaches the desired weight, and is lean enough for the role, the producer changes his mind: he's now making a comedy and is looking for a fat man. Bill, who has suddenly put on weight thanks to some pills supplied by Sid, is offered the lead.

9. A Visit to Russia

Recorded:	Sun. 11/12/55
Transmitted:	Wed. 14/12/55
First Repeat:	Sun. 18/12/55
Audience figure:	6.39 million

No copy of this episode is available in the BBC archives

In the interests of East-West relations, Hancock decides to take his show to Moscow as a gesture of goodwill. After resolving some issues involving passports, they fly out to the Russian capital; their first stop is the British Embassy, where they find Snide employed as the Ambassador.

They share a few drinks with him and end up drunk, but by the time they record the show at the theatre they're so inebriated that they start making insulting remarks and jokes at the expense of their hosts. Such behaviour is rewarded with an enforced trip to a salt mine, where they're ordered to fill 3,000 bags of salt before they can be released.

10. The Trial of Father Christmas

Recorded:	Sun. 18/12/55
Transmitted:	Wed. 21/12/55
First Repeat:	Sun. 25/12/55
Audience figure:	6.77 million

(with Graham Stark and Ray Galton)

No copy of this episode is available in the BBC archives

While flying across the sky dressed as Father Christmas, Hancock spots the police waiting for him, intent on arresting him for neglect of duty and making children unhappy on Christmas morning. Hancock is taken to court where he decides to defend himself; the prosecution claims that as Father Christmas he hates children and that he plays around with married women, secretly gaining access via their chimneys. Witnesses are called to prove his claims. Father Christmas is found guilty and banished from Earth for ever.

Then Hancock wakes up and realises he's been dreaming. When he learns that it's Christmas Eve he feels he's still got time to save Santa, but in doing so ends up being arrested for shoplifting and G.B.H.

11. Cinderella Hancock

Recorded:	Sun. 18/12/55
Transmitted:	Wed. 28/12/55
First Repeat:	Sun. 1/1/56
Audience figure:	6.39 million

(with Dora Bryan)

(Remake of series one, episode ten, except that the

289

Hancock/Simpson interlude is deleted, and the soldier who arrives at the end of the show to take Hancock away is now Snide.)

12. The New Year Resolutions

Recorded: Sun. 1/1/56
Transmitted: Wed. 4/1/56
First Repeat: Sun. 8/1/56
Audience figure: 5.64 million

No copy of this episode is available in the BBC archives

Tony makes a series of resolutions: not to lie, cheat, borrow, lend or gamble, and tells Bill he'll give him £5 every time he lapses—and that's not long. *En route* to a meeting at Sid's office, Hancock sits next to a small girl on the bus who is crying because she's lost her fare; he takes pity and lends her the money, only to ask for it back when Bill reminds him he'll require a fiver. More tears, but when the girl claims she'll be sent to bed early and will miss her favourite programme, *Hancock's Half Hour*, Hancock furtively hands over the money, but Bill spots him and demands another fiver.

Hancock, again, requests the money back, but this time the girl attracts a lot of attention from the other passengers, who accuse Hancock of being a capitalist, forcing him to forsake the money. When the conductor collects the fares, Hancock finds he's now short of cash and is kicked off the bus.

After walking the rest of the way to Sid's office, they learn he wants Hancock to run his nightclub, the Three Red Flamingos. What he forgets to tell them is that he's expecting a police raid any minute. At first, Hancock is uninterested because he assumes gambling takes place there and that's against one of his resolutions. But he's taken in by Sid's claim that it's really a monastery, and finds himself arrested and owing Bill a packet thanks to the broken resolutions.

13. Hancock's Hair

Recorded: Sun. 8/1/56
Transmitted: Wed. 11/1/56
First Repeat: Sun. 15/1/56
Audience figure: 6.77 million

Hancock's in turmoil: he's been finding his hair all over the place and is convinced he's going bald. He's so paranoid he's even taken to keeping a diary of the fall-out. He remembers he gave Andrée a lock of his hair during a romantic evening but there's no time for romance now, he needs it back, and quick, or else he'll never be offered a romantic lead again.

Bill and Andrée aren't concerned: he's got more hair than Bill for a start, but it's no good, a trip to the barber's is required. Hancock wants his hair back desperately, so Sid, who's taken up hairdressing, concocts an elaborate plan involving applying beer to the scalp, as well as rubbing in several ingredients, including a boss-eyed rat and the back tooth from a crocodile.

When Hancock's hair turns green, he rushes to the barber's again, by which time it's gone purple, but the application of a specially prepared shampoo formula makes his hair fall out completely.

14. The Student Prince

Recorded: Sun. 15/1/56
Transmitted: Wed. 18/1/56
First Repeat: Sun. 22/1/5
Audience figure: 6.39 million

A baron from the European principality of Morovia is in town to visit Sidney James. He's heard that Sid is the man to see if he wants a job done without questions being asked. There is twenty grand up for grabs if Sid can find a replacement look-alike for the Crown Prince of Moravia; it's his coronation in a few days and there's talk that he's going to be assassinated.

As there is an uncanny similarity between the Prince and Hancock, Sid strikes a deal but is aware that the explanation he gives Hancock will have to be good to get him to travel to Moravia. And it is. Sid makes out that there is an outdoor presentation of *The Student Prince* that requires a lead actor and he's cast Hancock to appear in the production.

On arriving, Hancock is told to get his costume on before climbing into the open-top car. He's amazed to receive such a greeting from the locals, but it's not long before the first attempt on the Prince's stooge's life occurs. It's all good theatrical fun to the unaware British actor until he steps out on the balcony of the baron's palace and it collapses.

Fortunately he's unscathed but when he goes back inside the palace it becomes clear that the Prince's wife is the would-be assassin and she's prepared for them to die together, but then Sid arrives at an inopportune moment.

15. The Breakfast Cereal

Recorded: Sun. 22/1/56
Transmitted: Wed. 25/1/56
First Repeat: Sun. 29/1/56
Audience figure: 6.02 million

No copy of this episode is available in the BBC archives

Hancock is captivated by television adverts. Succumbing to marketing spiels, he rushes out and spends a fortune, particularly on a breakfast cereal that claims it will make him a new man and boost his earning potential to £15,000 per annum.

Feeling in a rut at work, where he's found himself stuck in the same lowly position for years, Hancock believes Crunchy Flakes are the answer to his prayers and eats them endlessly. But when he's sacked as a door attendant for falling asleep just as he was opening the door for the company chairman, he decides to complain to the firm which makes the breakfast cereal. It transpires that Sid owns the company and disagrees that the adverts are misleading, but when Hancock discovers that Sid had simply bought a bulk order of soap flakes and coated them with sugar to sell as a breakfast cereal, he sues him.

In court, the judge decides that he and the jury will try the cereal themselves, but when they end up in hospital, he orders Sid to pay Hancock £15,000 a year; when he can't pay, he passes the company to Hancock as compensation. But when more complainants force another court case, Hancock shifts the company on to Bill.

16. How Hancock Won the War

Recorded: Sun. 29/1/56
Transmitted: Wed. 1/2/56
First Repeat: Sun. 5/2/56
Audience figure: 7.14 million

No copy of this episode is available in the BBC archives

While Hancock is taking a makeshift shower, Andrée spots a scar on his chest. He makes out he's not one to talk about his wartime heroics, yet Andrée can't shut him up as he describes his seven years spent on the front line, even though the war only lasted five.

Hancock regales her with an array of tall stories, including the time he joined the commandos and rose through the ranks at a meteoric pace, winning countless medals in the process. During this time he encountered Sid and Bill and together they fought many a battle: for example, the three of them once overran 250,000 enemy troops. Andrée is overawed by his bravery—that is until Sid and Bill arrive and the actual truth concerning Hancock's war years emerges.

17. The Newspaper

Recorded: Sun. 5/2/56
Transmitted: Wed. 8/2/56
First Repeat: Sun. 12/2/56
Audience figure: 6.02 million

No copy of this episode is available in the BBC archives

Tony agrees to take over the running of his great-uncle's newspaper, *The Sentinel*, but visiting the premises in Fleet Street with Andrée is an eye-opener: in the basement of a disused barber's shop, Palmerston Hancock used antiquated equipment to hand-print the fifteen copies sold each day.

Determined to increase circulation and modernise the firm, Hancock invests in new state-of-the-art equipment and hires Sid as a crime reporter, who becomes an overnight sensation; his accurate and comprehensive reporting of crimes sees the circulation soar, and the police stop investigating cases and buy the paper instead. But his reporting on crimes before they've even occurred raises the police's suspicions and they arrest Sid. When he blames Hancock, both end up serving time in Dartmoor Prison, where they're responsible for the prison newspaper.

18. The Greyhound Track

Recorded:	Sun. 12/2/56
Transmitted:	Wed. 15/2/56
First Repeat:	Sun. 19/2/56
Audience figure:	7.14 million

Hancock is in the process of renovating his tranquil twelfth-century cottage. It's more than a home to Tony; it's a retreat with all the peace and quiet that the countryside offers.

That is, of course, until the cottage becomes imperilled when Mayor Sid James decides to build a dog track on the site. In an attempt to evict Hancock, Sid discovers that a public footpath runs right through the house. He exploits this by sending various callers to the house to walk the path, including the local East Cheam Cycling Club.

With Sid's dog track now under construction, Hancock gives in, moves out and takes the first available flat, which turns out to be right next door to the dogs.

19. The Conjurer

Recorded: Sun. 19/2/56
Transmitted: Wed. 22/2/56
First Repeat: Sun. 26/2/56
Audience figure: 7.14 million

Andrée and Bill suggest Tony updates his act. Fearing he's becoming unbookable, he accepts their advice and takes up conjuring again—even though the last time he did it was at his Aunt Alice's musical evenings. He advertises in the trade press but the phone is quiet until he's asked to perform for the staff and inmates at Dartmoor Prison.

The engagement is arranged by Sid, in his capacity as president of the Prisoners' Aid Society. Unbeknown to Tony, Sid is concocting an escape plan for half the prisoners with Tony as key to the plot.

20. The Test Match

Recorded: Sun. 26/2/56
Transmitted: Wed. 29/2/56
First Repeat: Sun. 4/3/56
Audience figure: 6.39 million

(with John Arlott, Godfrey Evans, Colin Cowdrey and Frank Tyson)

With Sid James, now chairman of the MCC, having

bet heavily on England losing to Australia, he makes Hancock captain. Fighting off barbed remarks from his fellow players, Godfrey Evans, Frank Tyson and Colin Cowdrey, Hancock is convinced he still has what it takes. Hancock's bowling figures are pathetic, however and he gives away 731 runs in just one over.

England are on 835 when they lose their ninth wicket; needing two runs to win, Hancock is required to see them home to victory. With the first ball glancing off Hancock's ear and running away for four, England win and Hancock is hailed a cricket hero. With the glory and adulation about to swamp him, he wakes from several hours of unconsciousness and learns that becoming a cricketing legend was just a dream.

SERIES 4

Featuring: Tony Hancock, Sidney James, Bill Kerr, Kenneth Williams and Hattie Jacques (episode five onwards).

1. Back From Holiday

Recorded:	Sun. 7/10/56
Transmitted:	Sun. 14/10/56
First Repeat:	Tues. 16/10/56
Audience figure:	3.01 million

(with Alan Simpson and Ray Galton)

Hancock and Bill were supposed to be spending two weeks travelling around France in their car, but after just three days they're short of money and are forced to head back to Blighty.

Hancock is baffled that his door key doesn't fit

297

any more and the bedroom light is on. They can't believe it when they discover a new tenant lying in Hancock's bed who claims he lives there. The estate agent who arranged the accommodation is good old Sidney James, so the boys pay him a visit. Sid's latest scam is to offer out people's homes while they're on holiday; he's even let the local police station out and is raking in a small fortune.

Much to Hancock's displeasure, Sid rehouses him and Bill at the local dosshouse. It's not long before Hancock and Bill get caught up in a house fire and experience other troubles.

2. The Bolshoi Ballet

Recorded:	Sun. 14/10/56
Transmitted:	Sun. 21/10/56
First Repeat:	Tues. 23/10/56
Audience figure:	3.01 million

(with Alan Simpson and Ray Galton)

The Bolshoi Ballet is performing in Covent Garden, much to Hancock's delight. He's already re-enacting *Swan Lake* all over the house after seeing their arrival on the newsreel.

Much to Bill's amazement, Hancock is insistent that he secure tickets to see this wonderful spectacle, but with all the publicity the tickets have sold like hot cakes. Sid then appears in the queue proclaiming he's got black market tickets, but fails to say for what. Cold and desperate, Hancock and Bill agree to buy two but soon find out they're not for the Bolshoi but for Coventry City Football Club.

3. Sid James's Dad

Recorded: Sun. 21/10/56
Transmitted: Sun. 28/10/56
First Repeat: Tues. 30/10/56
Audience figure: 4.14 million

(with Alan Simpson)

No copy of this episode is available in the BBC archives

It's a quiet afternoon in for Hancock and Bill playing Monopoly. Peace is short-lived, though, as Sid arrives needing some help. He's at his wits' end: his dad is coming to spend a short break with him. The only problem is, he hasn't fully explained to his dad what his job entails; he's told his father he's a judge. And, as much as his dad loves him, Sid is afraid his dad could turn him in if he found out the truth.

Hancock decides to cover for Sid and throws a party, which isn't good news for Bill because it means he'll be sleeping out in the kennel again; and if that's not bad enough, he'll have to share it with Sid's dad's pets.

While celebrating his birthday, Sid's dad is keen to catch up on lost time because it's been 25 years since he last saw his son. What he doesn't know is that Sid has spent 23 of the 25 years at Her Majesty's pleasure.

With more robberies taking place in the vicinity, the police arrive at Hancock's suspecting just one person: Sid James. But it's Sid's father who stops Hancock spilling the beans when he hides Sid under the floorboards.

A reward is offered for information about the

robberies and before long Sid's father is counting a stash of money and leaving with more than he arrived with.

4. The Income Tax Demand

Recorded:	Sun. 28/10/56
Transmitted:	Sun. 4/11/56
First Repeat:	Tues. 6/11/56
Audience figure:	3.38 million

(with Alan Simpson and Ray Galton)

Hancock's day gets off to a bad start. A letter he mistakes for an invite to some swanky do turns out to be a tax bill. The Inland Revenue has finally caught up with Hancock and he has ten years' worth of tax to pay.

Hancock is advised to get representation from a chartered accountant, who turns out to be Sid James, who's not prepared to pay the taxman a penny, preferring instead to fight it out. In an attempt to help, Sid decides to use an old set of accounts from a previous entertainer he represented but the plan backfires and Hancock is lumbered with an even higher bill.

Sid tries to create a whole new life for Hancock during the years in question, but even this idea fails dismally when Hancock ends up with tax bills for £170,000 and accountant's fees which are now higher than the initial demand.

After the fourth set of fraudulent accounts is submitted in court, Hancock has no choice but to claim insanity and blame Sid. The only problem is that Sid also does the judge's books, leaving Hancock wishing he'd settled the bill a long, long time ago.

5. The New Secretary

Recorded:	Sun. 4/11/56
Transmitted:	Sun. 11/11/56
First Repeat:	Tues. 13/11/56
Audience figure:	3.76 million

(with Alan Simpson)

No copy of this episode is available in the BBC archives

Miss Pugh is acting belligerently, in Hancock's opinion, and he curses the day he hired her. He reflects on that fateful day, a time when his office was a shambles and he couldn't find anything, leaving him no option but to take up Bill's suggestion of hiring a secretary.

He placed an advert, stating: 'Secretary wanted. Blonde, 19, 37–22–36 or nearest offer. Live in. £5 a week, more if can type', in a local tobacconist's window, and received only one response. But that sounded hopeful, especially when the sender claimed she was often mistaken for a famous beauty queen. But she's far from what Hancock was expecting.

Initially he turns her down, but when she tells Hancock nobody will give a job to a girl of her size and she always ends up having to resort to violence, Hancock thinks twice and reluctantly offers her the job, caving in to all her contractual demands.

Miss Pugh proves to be more disorganised than Hancock, but he can't find a way of sacking her, even when she ruins his chances of career advancement in the acting profession by mixing up

301

two letters.

6. Michelangelo 'Ancock

Recorded: Sun. 11/11/56
Transmitted: Sun. 18/11/56
First Repeat: Tues. 20/11/56
Audience figure: 3.38 million

(with Alan Simpson and Ray Galton)

As well as the usual stories of rock 'n' roll riots in the local paper, one headline catches Hancock's eye: a grand competition is being organised by the town council to find the best design for a new statue to be erected in the local park, with a prize of £250 for the winning entrant. Now at last Hancock has a chance to put the skills he acquired at Plasticine moulding classes to good use.

Miss Pugh helps carry the boulders and undertakes general labouring duties. Hancock's first attempt is a statue of an Olympic runner balancing perilously on his big toe, too perilously, in fact, because it falls and smashes. Two more tons of solid rock arrive courtesy of the quarry and Hancock creates a statue of a heavyweight boxer, but it's so heavy that it collapses into a pile of rubble.

When the quarry runs out of rock, Hancock has to do business with Sid, who promises he can find Hancock the best slabs at the best prices from the best landmarks in London. As slabs begin to disappear from famous landmarks around the city, Hancock works on his final masterpiece, the Descending Angel, which is none other than Miss Pugh winched up in the air by a thick cable. But

302

when the height needs to be altered, Sid provides a 125-foot pedestal: another landmark, namely Nelson's Column.

Hancock is finally announced as the winner of the competition but there are questions over the statue's decency so Hancock supplies the council with another statue, with Sid providing the stones. But before long they're both arrested when it's announced that the stones from Stonehenge are missing.

7. Anna and the King of Siam

Recorded: Sun. 18/11/56
Transmitted: Sun. 25/11/56
First Repeat: Tues. 27/11/56
Audience figure: 4.14 million

(with Alan Simpson, Ray Galton, and Max Harris on piano)

Hancock has just finished reading *Anna and the King of Siam* and after seeing Yul Brynner in the title role of the film, *The King and I*, fancies himself as the romantic lead, King Monkut, in his own play. He's even removed his hair for the part.

An operatic Miss Pugh takes the role of Anna, sent by the King to introduce education and moral values to his children and society. The only snag is, Miss Pugh keeps getting the story wrong and continually bursts into the incorrect song; even a Noël Coward number crops up.

It's not long before Anna finds out that the King is in fact barbaric and as childish as his numerous children. And when her personality leaves the King in an argumentative mood, it sounds like a normal day at the office for Hancock and Griselda. King Monkut didn't realise just how much influence Anna would eventually have on his country, but if it's anything like her influence as a secretary Hancock knows he's in for a rough ride.

8. Cyrano de Hancock

Recorded: Sun. 25/11/56
Transmitted: Sun. 2/12/56
First Repeat: Tues. 4/2/56
Audience figure: 4.51 million

Hancock becomes suspicious when Bill claims that Sid is a changed man, a view he's based on several factors: Sid bought him a drink, he couldn't care less when a man in a bar dropped half a crown and he slipped a violinist outside the hostelry a couple of bob to play 'My September Love'.

When Sid pops round for a man-to-man chat with Hancock, it transpires he's in love. Hancock is even more shocked when he discovers the object of his desires is, in fact, Miss Pugh. Not knowing whether the feeling is reciprocated, Sid has turned to Hancock for help. Regarding Hancock as a man of the world, he wants to know how he should propose.

After his first attempt fails dismally, Hancock shows Sid how it should be done, only for Miss Pugh to walk into the room at the opportune moment. Believing Hancock wants to propose, she accepts swiftly, claiming it's the happiest day of her life. While Hancock thinks how he can explain the misunderstanding, Miss Pugh races off and arranges the wedding. Finally, on the big day itself, a mix-up with the ring sees Hancock tying the knot with someone other than his secretary.

9. The Stolen Petrol

Recorded:	Sun. 2/12/56
Transmitted:	Sun. 9/12/56
First Repeat:	Tues. 11/12/56
Audience figure:	3.76 million

(with Alan Simpson and Ray Galton)

Sidney James has organised a celebration to welcome the return of petrol rationing. He sees the national crisis as another way of making a few quid, and, armed with siphons and hoses, starts draining all the vehicles in sight.

Hancock is fooled into thinking he's helping society by opening a garage. Little does he know that he's selling siphoned petrol and that some of the cars returning to his business have been victims of Sid's siphoning gang themselves. But, as usual it's not long before the siphoning plan gets out of hand, especially when the so-called fuel starts giving off a distinct odour of light brown ale.

10. The Expresso Bar

Recorded:	Sun. 9/12/56
Transmitted:	Sun. 16/12/56
First Repeat:	Tues. 18/12/56
Audience figure:	3.76 million

(with Ray Galton)

Hancock is on the phone to his agent because he hasn't secured him a job for ages; it's been so long that even his agent has forgotten who he is. He may as well retire, at this rate. To make him feel even worse, Bill reminds him that many people think he already has.

A business venture is what's required, so Hancock decides to open an espresso bar, which he'll call El Mombasa, seeing it as a place for actors to relax, a home for intellectual bohemians and survivors of society. As Sid is now in the property game, Hancock and Bill pop over to see him. Sid feels he has the ideal property, and at £500 it's a true bargain. Trouble is, it has a sewer running through it, but that doesn't deter Hancock.

It's not long before business is booming and Hancock wants to expand, but with the prison next door it seems impossible. That is, until Edwardian Fred visits Sid and reminds him that four of his boys are banged up in prison just the other side of Hancock's bar.

Soon Hancock is in joyous mood as his extension plans begin in earnest when he knocks through the wall, only to see four men fleeing from the other side. It's not long before the head warder from the prison appears and arrests Hancock, Bill and Miss Pugh for breaking in. Hancock and Bill are fined £1,000 for being the ringleaders and now they're back where they started—skint.

11. Hancock's Happy Christmas

Recorded:	Sat. 15/12/56
Transmitted:	Sun. 23/12/56
First Repeat:	Mon. 24/12/56
Audience figure:	3.76 million

(with Michael Anderson, Dorothy Marks, Alan Simpson and Ray Galton)

Hancock, lacking festive spirit, announces that Christmas Day will be just like any other:

miserable—which he proves by foul-mouthing a bunch of carol singers.

When Sid, who's trying to earn a few coppers, arrives on the doorstep carol singing, he ends up spending Christmas with Hancock and the rest of the crowd. The next caller at Railway Cuttings is the vicar, who wants to thank Hancock for his generous offer to accommodate two 12-year-old orphans over the holiday period. Bemused by the conversation, Hancock discovers it was Miss Pugh who made the generous offer, but when he learns that the orphans will bring with them a pudding, turkey and £5 pocket money, he soon changes his mind.

12. The Diary

Recorded:	Sun. 23/12/56
Transmitted:	Sun. 30/12/56
First Repeat:	Tues. 1/1/57
Audience figure:	4.91 million

Another year has slipped by and Hancock turns back time by browsing through his 1956 diary and dreaming of what life could have been like, had he chosen a different path. The brief, infantile entry on 8 January describing the day Bill cut his finger causes Hancock to contemplate whether he could have followed a life in medicine, while other recollections lead him to dream about life as Mad Jack Hancock, a lion tamer, and a wing commander in the Royal Air Force who is testing a new jet when a mechanic knocks on the cockpit and causes mayhem until the brave-hearted man in blue saves the day.

13. The 13th Of The Series

Recorded: Sun. 30/12/56
Transmitted: Sun. 6/1/57
First Repeat: Tues. 8/1/57
Audience figure: 4.91 million

Hancock is in trouble with the BBC over his decision not to record the 13th episode of his radio show. They're threatening to cancel the series and sue for breach of contract unless he honours his commitments. The trouble is, he's become very superstitious and won't take chances while the omens are against him.

Nothing will persuade Hancock, who recently joined the East Cheam Mystics, to fulfil his commitments unless he's visited by the head druid, the only person with the power to dispel the omens.

With the Beeb getting heavy, Hancock has no choice but to visit the head druid himself, but with Sid adopting the role it's clear it is all a sham and Hancock is being taken for a ride. Initially reluctant to help, Sid soon changes his mind when Hancock suggests he won't be able to keep up his membership contributions if his series is cancelled.

14. Almost A Gentleman

Recorded: Sun. 6/1/57
Transmitted: Sun. 13/1/57
First Repeat: Tues. 15/1/57
Audience figure: 4.54 million

Yet again Hancock has been overlooked in the New Year's Honours List and he's livid. As founder of the Relief Fund for Destitute Comedians he feels he warrants inclusion, even if he's been the only artist to draw upon the fund.

Miss Pugh points out that a man who holds a knighthood should be a gentleman, with impeccable manners and a decent education, not some 'scruff bag' like Hancock. Believing all he needs is a little tuition in etiquette before he's ready to take his rightful place in society, he enrols with Sid James, who has become a teacher in social etiquette—or that's what he claims. Yet again it's another of his illegal scams, with Hancock's gullibility leading him to steal a diamond tiara from an aristocratic party in order to receive his diploma.

15. The Old School Reunion

Recorded:	Sun. 13/1/57
Transmitted:	Sun. 20/1/57
First Repeat:	Tues. 22/1/57
Audience figure:	5.29 million

Hancock receives a letter from Dr Clanger, his old schoolmaster at Greystones, the public school he claims he attended for seven years, inviting him to a school reunion.

Hancock is excited about once again meeting old acquaintances. When Sid hears him suggest that they probably want him to hand out some prizes, like the silver cups, Sid spots a business opportunity and gets his suitcase ready.

En route to Greystones, Hancock recalls his days at the school, two decades earlier, including his time fagging for Rodgers and his time dating Gladys, whom he wanted to marry.

But when Dr Clanger catches Hancock with Sid's

suitcases, full of silver trophies, he accuses him of being an accomplice in their theft, as well as revealing the truth about Hancock's time at the school: he was the porter, not a pupil.

16. The Wild Man of the Woods

Recorded: Sun. 20/1/57
Transmitted: Sun. 27/1/57
First Repeat: Tues. 29/1/57
Audience figure: 4.91 million

Hancock is fed up with the world and calls a press conference to proclaim his dissatisfaction with civilisation. But there's a low turn-out and only the local *East Cheam Advertiser*, together with Sid, Bill and Miss Pugh, turn up to hear Hancock announce his decision to become a recluse and live in the wood—well, Clapham Common.

Hancock's plans to leave society behind are ill-prepared and he soon finds himself in hospital, seven stone lighter. But he remains determined to take a stand and is fooled into trying a piece of woodland offered by Sid, not realising that his crafty chum has plans for coach trips into the woods for any mugs mad enough to pay for a glimpse of an unsuspecting Hancock.

Little does he know that he has been turned into a tourist attraction and is annoyed when he finds out. He also can't believe it when he discovers Jungle Jim, a man who's been living in the woods for five years.

Just when his chums think he's settling into his new environment for good, Hancock returns to civilisation because the woods are swarming with hermits and all the trees have been removed to accommodate them.

17. Agricultural 'Ancock

Recorded:	Sat. 26/1/57
Transmitted:	Sun. 3/2/57
First Repeat:	Tues. 5/2/57
Audience figure:	4.54 million

For years, Hancock has been telling the council he's an agricultural labourer and taking advantage of subsidised rents, but when officials catch on to his little game, a notification of rent increases is hurriedly issued.

The decision to move to a cheaper district upsets Bill, who claims it's the only home he's really known; he suggests to Hancock that he actually become a farm labourer, but when he talks about planting chickens, it's obvious farming isn't Hancock's forte. So Hancock decides to set up his own farm instead, although asking Sid to locate the property isn't such a good idea, especially when he tries selling Hancock a cricket pitch.

18. Hancock in the Police

Recorded:	Thurs. 7/2/57
Transmitted:	Sun. 10/2/57
First Repeat:	Tues. 12/2/57
Audience figure:	4.54 million

With demand for the double-act, Hancock and Kerr—the Whistling Hillbillies, at a low ebb, Hancock turns to 'situations vacant' and is instantly attracted by the promise of a £475 starting salary with the police, even though he's too old and too short.

311

Somehow, Hancock and Bill talk their way into the force and report to Superintendent Farnsworth for initial training. Hancock passes with flying colours, but soon causes traffic chaos and is caught for speeding, dangerous driving, and drinking and driving while in charge of a panda car.

He's given another chance, but while on the beat meets Sid and foolishly tells him how to immobilise a burglar alarm at a jeweller's. A burglary then takes place at the Bond Street shop, followed by a similar offence at a local bank, another place whose security arrangements were openly discussed between Sid and Hancock, who even opened the door.

When all the businesses on Hancock's beat, bar one, are robbed, a trap is rigged with Hancock as a decoy, dressed in a skirt and high heels, but the wrong man is arrested and is sentenced to twenty years.

19. The Emigrant

Recorded:	Thurs. 14/2/57
Transmitted:	Sun. 17/2/57
First Repeat:	Tues. 19/12/57
Audience figure:	4.54 million

Hancock is fed up with his life in Britain, so decides to emigrate to a land of fresh opportunities, where there's an incentive to prosper. The trouble is, deciding where to go. He's spoilt for choice but decides to try Australia first of all and heads for Australia House, where proceedings don't go as planned.

After a tortuous meeting with an official he decides that perhaps Canada is a better bet, but does his best to annoy the official there, too. After trying every embassy in London, a dejected Hancock returns to Railway Cuttings. Still determined to emigrate, he has little choice but to turn to Sid for help. Knowing he was involved in the illegal trafficking of people, he asks him to get him abroad, with Bill tagging along, too.

With the aid of a couple of false passports, they set off by plane to pastures new, but when the plane crashes it's not long before they find themselves arriving at the Pearly Gates.

20. The Last of the McHancocks

Recorded: Thurs. 21/2/57
Transmitted: Sun. 24/2/57
First Repeat: Tues. 26/2/57
Audience figure: 4.91 million

(with James Robertson Justice)

When Hancock learns he's got Scottish blood running through his veins, he takes a liking to everything north of the border, including the bagpipes. He receives good news when his solicitor informs him he's going to be installed as the new laird of Glen Sporran, but is warned that the sole surviving member of the McNasty clan, sworn enemies of the McHancocks, is desperate to get his hands on their rightful home, Castle Sporran.

When Hancock arrives in Scotland he's confronted by McNasty, who is determined to force him out, but then Sid appears claiming to be a descendant of Bonnie Prince Charlie and has come to claim not just Castle Sporran, but every other castle in Scotland. To resolve the matter, Hancock,

313

McNasty and James compete against each other in some Highland Games.

SERIES 5

Featuring: Tony Hancock, Sidney James, Bill Kerr, Hattie Jacques and Kenneth Williams.

1. The New Radio Series

Recorded: Sun. 19/1/58
Transmitted: Tues. 21/1/58
First Repeat: Thurs. 23/1/58
Audience figure: 5.29 million

Sid and Bill arrive at Hancock's house to be met by Miss Pugh, who insists they must have an appointment. When they explain he's asked them over to discuss the new radio show, they're allowed in but not before Miss Pugh tells them that success has gone to Hancock's head.

Hancock appears on the scene and tells them he now wants to be addressed as 'Mr Hancock' or 'Your Grace', and that he's reached the pinnacle of his career and intends to retire. Sid and Bill's request that he reconsider is dismissed; the only thing he's bothered about is how to tell the Beeb. He needn't have worried, though, because the BBC have been trying to work out how they can tell him they want to drop the show. When he hears that his programme is being replaced with a new one starring Bill Kerr, he has second thoughts about his decision, but it's too late.

Hancock eventually makes a comeback, albeit short-lived, when he's seen sleeping rough under London's railway arches and interviewed for a

314

documentary programme.

2. The Scandal Magazine

Recorded:	Sun. 26/1/58
Transmitted:	Tues. 28/1/58
First Repeat:	Thurs. 30/1/58
Audience figure:	4.91 million

(with John Vere)

The latest edition of *Blabbermouth*, a scandal mag, carries an exposé of Hancock's evening spent under the table with a cigarette girl at the Bag of Nuts. Determined to defend his name, he claims the story is untrue and demands an apology from the editor, none other than Sid, who's unwilling to retract his story; he's even planning on using more stories, leaving Hancock no option but to sue. After clearing his name and winning £10,000 damages, it soon becomes apparent that there's truth in the stories after all!

3. The Male Suffragettes

Recorded:	Sun. 2/2/58
Transmitted:	Tues. 4/2/58
First Repeat:	Thurs. 6/2/58
Audience figure:	4.54 million

Hancock establishes the Militant League of Male Suffragettes with the sole objective of reinstating man in his rightful place: as master in his own house. The inaugural meeting at the local pub establishes their first course of action: to visit every church where a wedding is taking place in an attempt to talk the groom out of it.

At the next meeting, Sid claims enthusiastically that fifty-nine men were saved, but it's now time for members to give up their freedom for the fight; Bill is an unwilling volunteer for the first act of power: to throw a brick at 10 Downing Street. Unfortunately for him, a minister opens a window just as he releases the stone, and it ends up hitting the Prime Minister on the head. Fortunately Bill escapes, only to find himself chained to railings outside the House of Commons for the League's next course of action.

4. The Insurance Policy

Recorded: Mon: 10/2/58
Transmitted: Tues. 11/2/58
First Repeat: Thurs. 13/2/58
Audience figure: 5.29 million

Hancock is determined not to pay tax and keeps dodging the Inland Revenue's demands, which are piling up alongside unpaid telephone, gas and electricity bills. Miss Pugh badgers Hancock into taking out an insurance policy, and arranges a visit from a salesman, who turns out to be Sid, representing the Sidney James Friendly Accident Society.

He tries selling Hancock a convoluted savings scheme, which isn't worth the paper it's written on, but with Miss Pugh cajoling him along, he scrawls his signature on the dotted line, even though he'll be left with pennies after paying the weekly premiums. The magnitude of his mistake hits home when he finds himself working 14-hour days just to pay the premium.

When a £1,500 final tax demand arrives, Hancock

316

tries every conceivable way to claim on his policy, including being attacked by a snake, but finds out just how useless Sid's policy really is.

5. The Publicity Photograph

Recorded: Sun. 16/2/58
Transmitted: Tues. 18/2/58
First Repeat: Thurs. 20/2/58
Audience figure: 4.91 million

Tony is persuaded to update his publicity photograph in an attempt to attract new offers of work. Sid, his agent, takes him along to his mate, claiming he's the best photographer in the business, who specialises in retouching photographs in an attempt to accentuate one's best points.

Tony is flattered with the results, even though the photos bear little resemblance to the man himself; so pleased is he with the shots that he authorises them to be sent to fans and film producers. Sid is the bearer of good news when producers are falling over themselves to cast Tony and turn him into the next screen heart-throb; the only trouble is, he has to turn himself into the man in the photo—no easy feat. But when the film producers change their mind and announce they're looking for comics, not pretty boys, Tony is distraught, especially as the image they're looking for was him prior to his alterations.

6. The Unexploded Bomb

Recorded: Sun. 23/2/58
Transmitted: Tues. 25/2/58

317

First Repeat: Thurs. 27/2/58
Audience figure: 4.54 million

(with Alan Simpson)

Hancock is entertaining the local vicar, who tells him about the number of unexploded bombs that were dropped in the area. When Hancock pops down to the cellar with Bill to collect some drink, he notices a strange object hanging precariously in the ceiling. It turns out to be an unexploded bomb.

The army's bomb disposal team arrive on the scene, but the lieutenant in charge doesn't fill Hancock with confidence, especially when he announces he's only been working in the division for a week after transferring from the catering department. Sid, however, has a smile on his face because if the house blows up, he could use the space as a used car lot.

In the end, Hancock's house is bulldozed to the ground, only for the bomb to be confirmed as a prop from the BBC TV's scenery department, something left behind by the previous resident, who was a television producer. Hancock is homeless and has no alternative but to sell the land to Sid, but all the cars are blown sky-high when a real bomb is, in fact, discovered on the site.

7. Hancock's School

Recorded: Sun. 2/3/58
Transmitted: Tues. 4/3/58
First Repeat: Thurs. 6/3/58
Audience figure: 4.54 million

An illiterate Bill, who's applying for a job with the bank, is receiving lessons from Hancock; when Sid arrives representing the Sidney James Educational Supply Company, he tells Hancock that everyone in the neighbourhood is talking about how well he's teaching the kid from down under. Before he leaves, he's persuaded Hancock to set up his own school at the house.

With Bill appointed assistant headmaster and in charge of French, Latin, advanced physics and maths, Miss Pugh as matron and gym mistress and Sid running citizenship, the school's future looks far from rosy, especially when it turns out the kids know more of the curriculum than the teachers.

Before long, an official from the Ministry of Education comes calling and informs Hancock that the police will soon be closing down the school and arresting him for fraud.

8. Around the World in Eighty Days

Recorded: Sun. 9/3/58
Transmitted: Tues. 11/3/58
First Repeat: Thurs. 13/3/58
Audience figure: 4.54 million

At the East Cheam Gentlemen's Club, Lord Cheam tells Sid and Hancock how impressed he was with the film he's just seen, *Around the World in 80 Days*. A blasé Hancock remarks that one can get around the world in less time than that, and accepts the lord's bet to beat 80 days.

On their day of departure it seems the elements have ganged up on them when fog forces the airport's closure; they decide to fly from Prestwick Airport, only to find they've forgotten their visas to enter America and need to head back for the Embassy in London, but snow has caused train cancellations.

Next they're heading for Russia but engine trouble forces Hancock, Sid and Bill to return to the airport, so it's just as well Bill had the foresight to book the three of them on a world cruise, due back in port just twenty-four hours before the Lord's 80-day deadline—or they would have been if they'd got on the right boat.

9. The Americans Hit Town

Recorded: Sun. 16/3/58
Transmitted: Tues. 18/3/58
First Repeat: Thurs. 20/3/58
Audience figure: 4.16 million

(with Jerry Stovin)

The Americans are coming to Cheam and Miss Pugh is ecstatic, seeing it as her last chance to find the man of her dreams. Hancock, meanwhile, isn't so happy, believing he won't stand a chance with the local girls. The only man who isn't sceptical is Sid, who's spotted all the business opportunities, including taxi firms, nightclubs and sightseeing tours.

Hancock soon becomes pro-America when he picks up on Sid's idea to rent out a room, at extortionate rates, to one of the new arrivals, who turns out to be a colonel from West Virginia. Before long, there are ten Americans crammed into the house and, for Hancock and Sid, the money is rolling in. Their days of affluence, however, are short-lived when the Ministry of Housing, believing people are exploiting the Yanks, sends an inspector to investigate.

Just when it looks as if Hancock, who pretends to

be one of the lodgers and praises the landlord, has got away with it, an American airman makes an emergency visit to the house, advising Hancock, who he believes to be an American airman, he's required urgently at the airbase—he has to fly a plane.

10. The Election Candidate

Recorded:	Sun. 23/3/58
Transmitted:	Tues. 25/3/58
First Repeat:	Thurs. 27/3/58
Audience figure:	4.16 million

(with Alan Simpson)

When Hancock's local MP resigns, a by-election is called, with the usual old candidates putting themselves forward for selection. Hancock hasn't got any time for politicians, but when a member of the East Cheam Independents comes calling and asks him to be their candidate, Hancock decides to give it a go.

After a round of speeches trying to convince the wary folk of East Cheam to put a cross against his name on the voting card, he's in for the biggest defeat of his life, bringing his political career to an abrupt end, when he receives only one vote—and that was his own.

11. Hancock's Car

Recorded:	Sun. 30/3/58
Transmitted:	Tues. 1/4/58
First Repeat:	Thurs. 3/4/58
Audience figure:	4.54 million

(with Alan Simpson)

Hancock's pride and joy, his car, has been parked outside his house for ten years without moving, because he can't drive. The road has been resurfaced eight times since the war, except for the patch underneath Hancock's car, which is eight inches lower than the rest of the road.

It's time for another resurfacing and Hancock has been ordered by the police to move the vehicle, or they'll do it for him. He refuses and ends up in court, where he's fined 55 shillings. Defiant, he still won't budge and even the police's attempt at towing the car away fails.

Eventually the parties reach an agreement: the car is moved up the road and returned once the resurfacing is complete, but now the car is higher off the road, it's in line for the stray pieces of coal that come flying from the nearby railway line every time a train rushes by. There is only one thing for it: the trains will have to be stopped.

12. The East Cheam Drama Festival

Recorded:	Sun. 23/3/58
Transmitted:	Tues. 8/4/58
First Repeat:	Thurs. 17/4/58
Audience figure:	3.40 million

(with Kathleen O'Hagan on piano)

To celebrate the East Cheam Festival of Arts' centenary, the BBC is broadcasting excerpts of this year's production from the stage of the Scout hall, Cheam. The programme consists of three short playlets presented by Hancock and his repertory company: *Jack's Return Home*, *Look Back in Hunger*, a modern psychological drama written by

John Eastbourne dealing with a young misfit, and the last piece, combining music and theatre, a dramatised version of the life and work of Ludovic Van Beethoven.

13. The Foreign Legion

Recorded: Sun. 6/4/58
Transmitted: Tues. 15/4/58
First Repeat: Thurs. 17/4/58
Audience figure: 4.54 million

Sid, Bill and Miss Pugh are busy sorting through the morning's mail. Surprisingly, they've all got more mail than Tony and, more annoyingly, it's fan mail. Hancock has received three letters and they all start the same, 'Dear Bighead . . .', but one of them is from Major 'Bloods & Guts' Farnsworth, Hancock's old CO in the army, who has been instructed to hire Tony for a tour of the Middle East.

A visit to the War Office to sign the necessary paperwork and Tony is all ready to jet off to Malta to start the tour. That's until Sid realises Tony and Bill have to make their own way to the Mediterranean island.

Sid is running his own employment bureau for overseas workers and he'd hate to see Tony waste his time trying to entertain the troops, so arranges for Tony and Bill to embark on another flight where his skills and army knowledge would be more beneficial in making Sid money.

Suspicions arise when all Hancock sees from the plane is a vast desert. They're greeted by a French legionnaire who advises Hancock of his wage and contract, in French. As long as he thinks there are

323

troops to be entertained, Hancock is happy to oblige.

Hancock's played some pretty rough venues in his time but he's never played to Arabs who want to kill him, not even at the Glasgow Empire. Unaware that he's joined the Foreign Legion, he can't understand when he's shot at by his supposed audience.

14. Sunday Afternoon at Home

Recorded: Sun. 20/4/58
Transmitted: Tues. 22/4/58
First Repeat: Thurs. 24/4/58
Audience figure: 4.54 million

It's Sunday, it's raining and Hancock is bored. While Sid, Bill and Miss Pugh find themselves in the same boat, they're handling the passing hours better. Hancock contemplates returning to bed, even though he's only been up an hour. He becomes so fed up, he begins to question the meaning of life, especially when you spend your entire week dreading Sunday. To make matters worse, Miss Pugh has eaten all his liquorice allsorts.

15. The Grappling Game

Recorded: Sun. 27/4/58
Transmitted: Tues. 29/4/58
First Repeat: Thurs. 1/5/58
Audience figure: 4.91 million

Sid's latest venture finds him presenting an all-star wrestling tournament at Cheam Baths, and Tony, Bill and a reluctant Miss Pugh are dressing up to the nines to attend the opening bouts.

Regarding it as a barbaric form of entertainment, Miss Pugh isn't enamoured of the idea of attending the contest, but ends up loving the primitiveness of it all and is one of the noisiest members of the audience. But when she becomes over-enthusiastic and squeezes the winner, Crusher, half to death, she's announced the overall champion.

Impressed by her strength, Tony and Sid dream up the name, 'Grizzly Bear—the female maneater', and arrange a competitive fight for her without asking her first. Such are their hopes, they see the contest as the prelude to a world championship bout at Madison Square Gardens when she's expected to massacre the reigning champ. But what Tony and Sid hadn't anticipated is that Miss Pugh would fall in love in the ring and allow her opponent to take the honours.

16. The Junk Man

Recorded:	Sun. 4/5/58
Transmitted:	Tues. 6/5/58
First Repeat:	Thurs. 8/5/58
Audience figure:	3.78 million

Hancock has accumulated so much junk it's time for a clear-out. Bill and Miss Pugh encourage him to bin the lot, including a 1936 wireless licence and a selection of stones from Bognor Regis, but all he's brave enough to get rid of is a thimble.

When Sid, who has fallen on hard times and set himself up as a rag-and-bone man, comes calling he offers to buy any rubbish Hancock has got, including all his furniture; Hancock won't part with anything, but when Miss Pugh persuades him to check the loft, she sells Sid the entire contents of an overloaded drawer and other items, ranging from his stuffed eagle to a potted palm.

Horrified at the thought of losing his most prized possessions, Hancock tries his utmost to retrieve them, even though it means forking out a fortune, which isn't surprising as Sid is involved in the plot.

17. Hancock's War

Recorded: Sun. 11/5/58
Transmitted: Tues. 13/5/58
First Repeat: Thurs. 15/5/58
Audience figure: 3.78 million

Hancock has invited the vicar for tea but when he decides to show him his photo albums, Bill and Sid flee, leaving the Reverend to suffer in silence. When the vicar notices there are no photos of Hancock in uniform, Hancock claims it's because he served in M15, then indulges his love for tall stories with tales of being placed in charged of a small group of agents who parachuted behind enemy lines, only to land in a prisoner-of-war camp and be sentenced to death.

After a failed attempt to escape, they find themselves facing a firing squad, but avoid death thanks to the cigarette cases in their jackets deflecting the bullets. Overcoming the soldiers, they finally find their way back to home shores.

The vicar is uplifted and proud of Hancock, but when the redcaps arrive to arrest him, he dashes off and the truth about his war service, including desertion to a cave in the Yorkshire Dales, finally emerges.

18. The Prize Money

Recorded: Sun. 18/5/58
Transmitted: Tues. 20/5/58
First Repeat: Thurs. 22/5/58
Audience figure: 4.16 million

(with Alan Simpson, Patricia Hayes and Christina Horniman)

Hancock wins four grand as a contestant on *Take Your Pick*, and when Miss Pugh, Bill and Sid all advise him how to spend his money, he tells them it's being kept for his old age. They put their heads together and devise a scheme whereby women, whom they'll hire, arrive on the scene, claiming Hancock had promised to marry them years ago and suing him for breach of promise, with the hope he'll settle out of court.

Next morning, two women arrive on the doorstep and in the ensuing chaos Hancock is only too relieved to accept Sid's suggestion that he pay them off with £2,000 each.

19. The Threatening Letters

Recorded: Sun. 25/5/58
Transmitted: Tues. 27/5/58
First Repeat: Thurs. 29/5/58
Audience figure: 3.78 million

(with Alan Simpson)

Everything is well in the world, as far as Hancock's concerned: it's a beautiful morning, the BBC want to double his salary and renew his contract and he's receiving fan mail. But dark clouds arrive on the horizon when a letter drops on his doormat.

327

Hancock can't believe what he's reading when it turns out to be a threatening letter, whose author claims the world would be a better place without him and states that Hancock is top of the hit list of people he wants eliminated.

Miss Pugh, Bill and Sid try to comfort him, suggesting it's from a crank, but Hancock feels sufficiently threatened to show the letter to the police. Constable Perkins, however, is far from interested, even when Hancock receives another letter stating the sender is in London and looking for him. Finally the police take the matter more seriously but end up arresting the wrong man—Bill; when a third letter arrives, Sid is taken into custody, too.

Fearing the anonymous letter writer is still at large, Hancock spends an evening alone and is frightened when he receives a strange phone call, then hears footsteps approaching the front door. The pressure becomes too great and Hancock attacks the caller, who turns out to be a vacuum cleaner salesman.

20. The Sleepless Night

Recorded:	Sun. 1/6/58
Transmitted:	Tues. 3/6/58
First Repeat:	Thurs. 5/6/58
Audience figure:	3.78 million

Hancock is starting a new job at the BBC, so he's determined to get a good night's sleep, but it's not easy with the likes of Sid, Bill and Miss Pugh around. Thanks to Bill's snoring and counting sheep aloud, Sid's loud singing and the ticking of his wristwatch, the hours slip by without a wink of sleep. Before the night is out, Hancock finds himself running up and down the stairs to answer the phone and investigating Miss Pugh's claims that she's heard burglars.

After a sleepless night, Hancock arrives at Broadcasting House to present his early morning show, *Keep Fit with Anthony*, but after yawning his way through the first exercise he falls asleep.

CHRISTMAS SPECIAL

Featuring: Tony Hancock, Sidney James, Bill Kerr, Hattie Jacques and Warren Mitchell.

Bill and Father Christmas

Recorded:	Sun. 7/12/58
Transmitted:	Thurs. 25/12/58
First Repeat:	Fri. 26/12/58
Audience figure:	Not available

Much to his disgust, Hancock has the job of dressing up as Santa again because Bill, despite being 34, still believes in the man with the white beard. He also writes a Christmas wish list and stuffs it up the chimney, but when he overhears Hancock, Sid and Miss Pugh discussing the fact that Santa doesn't exist, he becomes forlorn and feels his Yuletide has been ruined, and perhaps life isn't worth living.

When a doctor recommends they try to re-create the world of Bill's childhood to help him recover from his upset, Hancock, Sid and Miss Pugh adopt Aussie accents and go swimming in the park—even though it's a freezing cold day. But in an attempt to cure Bill, Hancock ends up in bed himself with flu.

SPECIAL RECORDING FOR LONDON TRANSCRIPTION SERVICE

Featuring: Tony Hancock, Sidney James, Bill Kerr, Hattie Jacques and Kenneth Williams

The 13th of the Month

(remake of 'The 13th of the Series')
Recorded: Sun. 23/11/58
Transmitted: Sun. 4/1/59

The New Secretary

Recorded: Sun. 23/11/58
Transmitted: Sun. 11/1/59

The Ballet Visit

(remake of 'The Bolshoi Ballet')
Recorded: Sun. 30/11/58
Transmitted: Sun. 18/1/59

The Election Candidate

Recorded: Sun. 30/11/58
Transmitted: Sun. 25/1/59

SERIES 6

Featuring: Tony Hancock, Sidney James and Bill Kerr (except episode thirteen).

1. The Smugglers

Recorded: Sun. 7/6/59

Transmitted:	Tues. 29/9/59
First Repeat:	Sun. 4/10/59
Audience figure:	3.25 million

(with Kenneth Williams, Patricia Hayes and Noel Dryden)

The lads are returning home from their holidays on the cross-Channel ferry from Calais to Dover. They've covered nineteen countries in six days yet Bill hasn't seen anything to rival his beloved Clacton.

While Hancock and Bill soak up the sea air, dreaming of returning home to chat up the girls with their broken French, Sid is propping up the bar with much on his mind. He's so nervous even his nose has started throbbing and his furtive movement gives Hancock and Bill reason to be suspicious.

Sid wants to smuggle some watches back into the country and inveigles Hancock and Bill into strapping the illegal cargo around their waists and proceeding through Customs on his behalf, but Bill forgets his new French persona should be kept for the girls in Clacton and ends up getting them both arrested.

2. The Childhood Sweetheart

Recorded:	Sun. 7/6/59
Transmitted:	Tues. 6/10/59
First Repeat:	Sun. 11/10/59
Audience figure:	3.11 million

(with Kenneth Williams and Patricia Hayes)

It's a special anniversary for Hancock because it's

twenty-five years since he made a pact with his childhood sweetheart—Olive Locksmith—to meet again, even though they were only nine at the time and Olive's parents moved in order to break up the relationship.

Sid and Bill don't think she'll turn up, but Hancock is confident, until he discovers the restaurant at which they intended to meet has been turned into a laundry. The manager, though, has some good news for Hancock: he hands over a letter from Olive, explaining she's waiting at the nearby coffee bar.

Unfortunately, when Hancock finally meets up with his sweetheart he feels she's gone a little sour and decides to scarper, leaving Bill to entertain her. It's not the end of the world, though, because Hancock has plenty of other anniversaries to celebrate this month.

3. The Last Bus Home

Recorded:	Sun. 14/6/59
Transmitted:	Tues. 13/10/59
First Repeat:	Sun. 18/10/59
Audience figure:	3.33 million

(with Warren Mitchell and Hugh Morton)

After spending an evening at the cinema, Hancock, Sid and Bill are unable to catch the last bus home because it's full. With the next one not due until six the following morning, they're in for a long, cold wait. To keep themselves dry and warm, they take refuge in a shop doorway but are moved on by the local police.

They keep walking and by 2.30 a.m. they find

themselves miles from anywhere. Suddenly Bill thinks he recognises an air raid shelter in which he used to woo his old flame, Phyllis, but he proves to be mistaken.

There is nothing for it but for Hancock to negotiate the sodden party back to Cheam with the aid of the stars. His navigational skills leave a lot to be desired and they end up back in the shop doorway. The whole sorry episode looks like being resolved by the arrival of the 6.30 a.m. bus—until the conductor notices the state they're in.

4. The Picnic

Recorded:	Wed. 10/6/59
Transmitted:	Tues. 20/10/59
First Repeat:	Sun. 25/10/59
Audience figure:	3.16 million

(with Wilfred Babbage, Patricia Hayes, Anne Lancaster and Liz Fraser)

It's 6 a.m., not a cloud in the sky and Hancock is full of joy, knowing he's to spend the day entertaining the three girls he chatted up with Sid and Bill last night at the Palais. What better way to impress them than a trip to Bluebell Woods for a picnic? Bill has been up most of the night making plum sandwiches, much to Hancock's disgust; he hates plum jam.

They pick up the girls in their car at 8 a.m. outside the town hall and head for the woods. Having splashed out on the trip, Hancock is keen to get something back in return, but the girls seem intent on sticking together.

Tony suggests a game of hide-and-seek to split

them up but, seeing through his flimsy guise, the girls insist there is to be no funny business and they need to be home by 9 p.m. Not even Hancock's mother's potato wine can loosen them up.

The girls decide that bluebell picking will be more entertaining. After suggesting that splitting up will be more efficient, Hancock finally gets Hermione on his own to drown her with his charm and diction. That is, until a Scout group invades the area.

The day turns into a damp squib when the girls decide to leave the boys and catch a train home. To make matters worse, the car has a puncture on the way home. With no repair kit in the boot, the jam sandwiches finally come in useful for plugging the hole in the tyre.

5. The Gourmet

Recorded:	Sun. 14/6/59
Transmitted:	Tues. 27/10/59
First Repeat:	Sun. 1/11/59
Audience figure:	3.52 million

(with Warren Mitchell, Hugh Morton and Raymond Glendenning)

As a self-confessed gourmet, Hancock always insists on quality before quantity at his local restaurant, Chez Claude's. The only trouble is he has to take those uncouth layabouts James and Kerr with him.

In Sid's eyes food is something you get down you when your trousers start to slip and Bill has no idea what he's ordering as he's without a menu. Sid knows his grub and orders jellied eels, chips and saveloys to be getting on with. Bill's order, on the other hand, is described as a mess by the waiter.

Whilst they've both finished and are looking forward to chatting up birds at the coffee bar, Hancock is still perusing the menu and contemplating his order. By the time he's ready to order, the cook has already left and the only choice is sandwiches.

A swift pint at the local sees Sid catching up with an old pal, Edwardian Fred. He's in town promoting his new protégé, Arnold Trubshaw, the 29-stone South-east England Eating Champion who's in training for the Great Britain all-comers final. It's easy money: all the food is paid for and there is a £1,000 prize for the winner. Sid has an idea: to enter Hancock as a challenger.

6. The Elopement

Recorded:	Thurs. 18/6/59
Transmitted:	Tues. 3/11/59
First Repeat:	Sun. 8/11/59
Audience figure:	3.67 million

(with Lillian Grasson, Wilfred Babbage, Fraser Kerr and Leigh Crutchley)

Bill is feeling depressed and Hancock's attempts to lift the cloud of gloom fail, but when the Aussie asks directions to Gretna Green, the reason for his sorrow is revealed. Bill is madly in love with 18-year-old Constance Fenton, whose father is against the relationship and will do everything within his power to break them up, so he sees no alternative but to elope with his intended.

When Sid and Tony hear that she'll soon be

335

inheriting over a million pounds, they're keen to help their friend, but their plan to make out he's a member of foreign royalty to try and convince Mr Fenton his daughter is marrying the right man, fail; they agree that eloping is the only answer.

Before the couple can tie the knot, though, Mr Fenton arrives on the scene and confirms he'll cut her off without a penny. Sid and Hancock are quick to swap sides and, for £750 each, agree to help Fenton prevent the lovers from getting hitched.

7. Fred's Pie Stall

Recorded:	Wed. 17/6/59
Transmitted:	Tues. 10/11/59
First Repeat:	Sun. 15/11/59
Audience figure:	3.74 million

(with Wilfred Babbage, Hugh Morton and Harry Towb)

Old Fred has been ordered by the local council to move his meat pie stall from Market Square in East Cheam, a decision which incenses Hancock, who feels it's yet another part of tradition being eaten away by the authority's drive to modernise the area.

Determined to reverse the decision, Hancock establishes the Friends of the Pie Stall and decides the only way to get the councillors to see sense is to invite them along to the stall for a free pie. The evening is a major success and Fred is granted a reprieve, but before long he's become so successful that he moves upmarket, forgetting his roots and his loyal customers, including Hancock.

336

8. The Waxwork

Recorded:	Sun. 21/6/59
Transmitted:	Tues. 17/11/59
First Repeat:	Sun. 22/11/59
Audience figure:	3.63 million

(with Warren Mitchell)

Hancock has finally arrived: Madame Tussaud's want an exhibit of him in the world of waxworks. Hancock, Sid and Bill meet Humphrey Williams, chief model maker, to sketch out some ideas. Tussaud's have already acquired 14 pounds of wax—and that's just for Hancock's head. It has been decided that he'll be placed alongside Jimmy Edwards in the Entertainment suite but Hancock's not happy. Neither is Sid, as he can't make any money from it.

They decide to create their own waxwork museum, Madame James', full of all the stars you've never heard of. They knock up a waxwork of Hancock with candles, a football, wicks as hair and marbles for eyes. It's more like a great, fat Guy Fawkes than Hancock himself. But Hancock's waxwork is soon sold to a cinema owner who wants to promote the movie *I Married a Monster from Outer Space*.

9. Sid's Mystery Tours

Recorded:	Sun. 21/6/59
Transmitted:	Tues. 24/11/59
First Repeat:	Sun. 29/11/59
Audience figure:	2.72 million

(with Warren Mitchell, Errol McKinnon and Mavis Villiers)

Bill and Hancock are keen to make the most of their weekend and are interested in an advert in the local rag for free tours of the local area. Further scrutiny reveals the trip is being organised by Sid, but Hancock goes along out of interest and finds, as usual, it's not as simple as it seems: the tours are on foot and there's no guide, but as Sid explains, a tour of the high street needs little explanation.

Before the afternoon is out, Hancock has been fooled into buying a controlling share of the business and a coach from Sid, only to find an executive from London Transport instructing the police to arrest Hancock because the newly acquired coach has been stolen from a museum.

10. The Fête

Recorded:	Wed. 24/6/59
Transmitted:	Tues. 1/12/59
First Repeat:	Sun. 6/12/59
Audience figure:	3.40 million

(with Wilfred Babbage, Jack Watson and Hugh Morton)

Hancock is at the East Cheam Round Table to discuss proceedings for the forthcoming carnival. However, after past experience of using Hancock, the committee are not interested in his views this year. That is until he mentions his contacts in the showbiz world who are bound to put Cheam's carnival in the spotlight.

Although he supplied an actor last year who managed to upset everyone leading to calls for Hancock's resignation, committee members are

338

most interested when Hancock tells them that this year Laurence Olivier is available. The committee agree that he's to open this year's fête. All Tony has to do is find him, with the assistance of Bill and Sid.

After a quick scout through the telephone directory they find his number and give him a call, only to find he's out of the country but due to arrive back at London Airport that evening. The plane is diverted to Gatwick, leaving Hancock, Sid and Bill with no chance to meet him.

There is little choice but to send Bill in Olivier's place, so they cover him in rolls of bandages, claiming he's in character for the role of the Invisible Man. But too much tampering with the costume leaves Bill exposed to all as a fake, and Hancock with his marching orders.

11. The Poetry Society

Recorded:	Thurs. 25/6/59
Transmitted:	Tues. 8/12/59
First Repeat:	Sun. 13/12/59
Audience figure:	3.29 million

(with Fenella Fielding, Fraser Kerr and Warren Mitchell)

Hancock and his newly found friends are rebelling against the conformities of everyday life, trying to better mankind via their East Cheam Cultural Progressive Society. They meet each night at a local coffee bar and indulge in philosophical analysis, but as it's Thursday evening, and the Society's poetry reading night, Hancock is entertaining them at his place.

339

Initially wanting Bill and Sid out of the house, he reluctantly lets them stay, and before the evening is out, Bill impresses everyone—save Hancock—with his poetry. So much so, that he's invited to take over the leadership of the Society.

12. Hancock in Hospital

Recorded:	Sun. 28/6/59
Transmitted:	Tues. 15/12/59
First Repeat:	Sun. 20/12/59
Audience figure:	3.74 million

(with Patricia Hayes and Joan Frank)

Hancock is in hospital recovering from a broken leg, and his misery is compounded by the fact he's received no visitors since his admission. Instead, he gets other patients' visitors, who feel sorry for him and offer biscuits and cakes in an attempt to cheer him up.

Things look up when Sid and Bill turn up, but Sid dents Hancock's self-confidence when he admits he isn't looking well. The visitors, lacking any news or conversation, do little to cheer up the patient, especially when Sid spots an old friend, Arthur Phillips, and ends up spending most of the time down the other end of the ward.

13. The Christmas Club

Recorded:	Sun. 6/12/59
Transmitted:	Tues. 22/12/59
First Repeat:	Sun. 27/12/59
Audience figure:	3.06 million

(with Hugh Morton, Wilfred Babbage and Frank

Partington)

Hancock can't wait until the annual handout of the local savings club at the Hand and Racquet. He's saved enough, or so he thinks, to ensure he has the necessary finance to provide Christmas fare befitting a gourmet of his capacity.

Expecting a pay-out in the region of £150, he's dumbfounded when Bert Stringer, the treasurer, presents just over £59, and part of that has been promised as a donation to the Police Benevolent Fund.

By mistake, Sid gives the money to the policeman who comes collecting the following evening, leaving the empty envelope meant for the donation to the police fund standing empty on the mantelpiece. Attempts to retrieve the money fail, so when the vicar calls asking if Hancock would like to donate food for a party organised by the church for the parish's needy, Hancock explains they haven't got a crumb themselves. But worse is to come when Hancock and Sid end up in hospital.

14. The Impersonator

Recorded:	Sun. 28/6/59
Transmitted:	Tues. 29/12/59
First Repeat:	Sun: 3/1/60
Audience figure:	3.44 million

(with Anne Lancaster, Peter Goodwright, Ronald Wilson, Jerry Stovin, Wilfred Babbage and Jack Watson)

After a busy week on the road in his stage play, Hancock returns to London for a weekend's rest only to spot an actor impersonating him on a

Harper's Corn Flakes TV commercial. Hancock is incensed, but worse is to follow: when he returns to the stage the following week at Scarborough, the play is brought to a halt when members of the audience keep shouting comments about the advert.

When he's paid off by fifteen different management companies, Hancock believes he's ruined, so he hires Sid and sets about suing the company who made the advert for damages of £100,000, even though his actual loss of earnings is a mere £73.

He's triumphant in the court case, but fails to win substantial damages. Realising his stage career is over, he's grateful he's still got his radio show, until Sid informs him that a member of the BBC was in court. Believing the impressionist, Arthur Plowright, sounded more like Hancock than the original article himself, he's fired Hancock and booked Plowright instead.

Episode Guide: Television

Tony Hancock appeared in every episode, while Sid James was seen in all but episodes one and two of series two and the final series, *Hancock*.

NOTE:

The majority of scripts weren't originally allocated episode titles, but on the few which contained working titles I've included these in brackets alongside the more familiar title which has been adopted over the years.

TV EPISODES AT A GLANCE

Series 1
The First TV Show
The Artist
The Dancer
The Bequest
The Radio Show
The Chef That Died of Shame

Series 2
The Alpine Holiday
Lady Chatterley's Revenge
The Russian Prince
The New Neighbour
The Pianist
The Auction

343

Series 3

The Continental Holiday
The Great Detective
The Amusement Arcade
A Holiday in Scotland
Air Steward Hancock—The Last of the Many
The Regimental Reunion
The Adopted Family
The Elocution Teacher
The Lawyer: The Crown v. James, S: Hancock QC
   Defending
How to Win Money and Influence People
There's an Airfield at the Bottom of My Garden
Hancock's 43 Minutes—The East Cheam
   Repertory Company

Series 4

Ericson the Viking (a.k.a. The Vikings)
The Set That Failed
Underpaid!, or, Grandad's SOS
The New Nose (a.k.a. The Nose)
The Flight of the Red Shadow (a.k.a. Desert Song)
The Horror Serial (a.k.a. Quatermass)
The Italian Maid
Matrimony—Almost (a.k.a. The Wedding)
The Beauty Contest (a.k.a. Mr East Cheam)
The Wrong Man
The Oak Tree (a.k.a. The Tree)
The Knighthood
The Servants (a.k.a. The Last Show)

Series 5

The Economy Drive
The Two Murderers

Lord Byron Lived Here
Twelve Angry Men
The Train Journey
The Cruise
The Big Night
The Tycoon
Spanish Interlude
Football Pools

Series 6

The Cold
The Missing Page
The Emigrant
The Reunion Party
Sid in Love
The Babysitters
The Ladies' Man
The Photographer
The East Cheam Centenary
The Poison Pen Letters

Series 7

The Bedsitter
The Bowmans
The Radio Ham
The Lift
The Blood Donor
The Succession—Son and Heir

SERIES 1

1. The First TV Show

Transmitted live, Fri. 6/7/56, 8.45 p.m., from Studio G, Lime Grove.
Audience figure: 6 million

CAST:

Harold Goodwin	Husband
Margaret Flint	Wife
Irene Handl	Nurse
Peter Haigh	Announcer
Ian MacNaughton	Hospital patient
Graham Leaman	Doctor
Chris Dreaper	Hospital patient
Kim Corcoran	
James Bulloch	Male nurses
Ivor Raymonde	
Frank Pemberton	Seamen
Patrick Milner	
Fraser White	Workmen

Talk about perfect timing: it's Hancock's first television show and he finds himself in hospital with his leg in plaster and a bandage around his head, resulting from a visit he made to a viewer who didn't like the look of him and who turned out to be a heavyweight wrestler.

Sid, though, is determined the show must go on, partly because he's invested a lot of money in Hancock over the years; he isn't prepared for a little hospitalisation to ruin it now he's made the break into television.

With only ten minutes of the first show

346

remaining, it's decided that the episode will end on a Nelson sketch from Hancock's bedside, with Hancock playing Nelson and his bed substituting for HMS *Victory*, thanks to a little help from the prop boys.

2. The Artist

Transmitted live, Fri. 20/7/56, 9.30 p.m., from Studio G, Lime Grove.
Audience figure: 5.6 million

CAST:

Valentine Dyall	Art connoisseur
Irene Handl	Model
Warren Mitchell	Art dealer
Desmond Rayner	
Ivor Raymonde	Gallery guides
James Bulloch	Policeman
Eleanor Fazan	
Leslie Cooper	Art students

Also: Pat Symons, Pat Horder, Esme Easterbrook, Barbara Grant, Anne Marryott, Daphne Johnson, Patrick Milner, Kim Corcoran, Chris Dreaper, Malcolm Watson, Arthur Hosking, Grant Duprez

Hancock has taken up painting but he's not selling many of his masterpieces and blames this on the fact that the public aren't ready for him. When he runs out of canvases, he heads for the local junk shop and buys some old ones to paint over, not realising that one is none other than a Rembrandt, which Sid had dumped there after being chased by police who spotted him stealing it from the Tate Gallery.

347

Sid had stolen it for a customer, and when they find out that Hancock has bought it, they rush over to his pad, but find he's already painted over it. There's no other option for Sid's 'fence' but to buy Hancock's entire set of canvases.

3. The Dancer

Transmitted live, Fri. 3/8/56, 9.35p.m., from Studio G, Lime Grove.
Audience figure: 5.6 million

CAST:

Warren Mitchell	Film producer
Hermione Baddeley	Dance instructress
Lorrae Desmond	Secretary
Frank Lonergan	American
Elizabeth Fraser	
Eleanor Fazan	
Jessica Dent	Teddy girls
Michael Boudot	
Philip Casson	
Roslyn Ellis	
Kay Rose	Dancers (jitterbug)
Alan Simpson	Floor manager
Harry Smith-Hampshire	
Doreen Casey	
Nina Hunt	
Melville E. Noelly	Professional ballroom dancers
Desmond Rayner	Master of Ceremonies, Indian, etc.

Also: Ivor Raymonde, Fraser White, Murray Kash, Patrick Milner, Kim Corcoran

One of the biggest film producers in the country, Mr Fancy of British Star Films, turns to Sid's theatrical agency after exhaustive attempts to find an actor for a small part in his next film fail.

He's making a musical and needs someone for a special dance sequence; he explains he's looking for England's answer to Gene Kelly, and Sid claims he's got just the man—Hancock.

The trouble is, Hancock can't dance, so he attends Madam Freda's ballroom dancing classes. Meanwhile, Sid enters him for a dancing competition at the Hammersmith Palais and invites the producer to see him, but as he's got no partner, Sid has no choice but to dress up in drag and help him out.

Suitably impressed with Hancock's efforts on the dance floor, the producer offers him the part, but Hancock didn't expect to be in a scene involving an Indian dance.

4. The Bequest

Transmitted live, Fri. 17/8/56, 9.30 p.m., from Studio G, Lime Grove.
Audience figure: 6.8 million

CAST:

Reginald Beckwith	Mr Witherspoon
Irene Handl	Miss Medworthy
Rose Howlett	Mrs Battleaxe
Claude Bonser	Uncle
Totti Truman Taylor	Aunt
Gordon Phillott	Grandad
Fraser White	Relative
Ivor Raymonde	Fred

Elizabeth Fraser   Linda

Also: Margaret Flint, Veronica Moon, Patricia Martin, Anne Lancaster, George Dudley, John Vyvyan, Diana Vernon, Alan Simpson, Esme Easterbrook, Paula Delaney, Mary Collins

(Children and Chaperon) Juleen Clow, Terry Scott and John Pike.

5. The Radio Show

Transmitted live, Fri. 31/8/56, 9.45 p.m., from Earls Court.
Audience figure: 6.4 million

CAST:

Warren Mitchell	Head of TV Variety
Eric Sykes	Army private
Manville Tarrant	Policeman
Alan Simpson	Corporal
Ray Galton	Lance-Corporal
Ian MacNaughton	Scottish private
George Crowther	Fat man
Roy Patrick	Thin man
Desmond Rayner	Corporal
John Vyvyan	Guardsman
Graham Stark	Sergeant (Welsh Guards)
Fraser White	
Kim Corcoran	
Mario Fabrizi	Privates
Frank Lonergan	
Peter Emms	Military policemen
Elizabeth Fraser	NAAFI girl
Terry Gilbert	
Leonard Martin	

350

Peter Brownlee
David Hyme   Dancers

Also: Fifteen members of the George Mitchell Choir and Spike Milligan

From the Earls Court Radio Show, Hancock presents a series of sketches which look back on how he came to be performing on the show, starting with a scene at his director's office when he was first asked to take part.

When he reflects on having to assemble a cast, he recalls the first time he met Sid, while for the finale Hancock tells the audience that the Red Army Choir has just finished a successful season at the Empress Hall, which prompted the British government to form their own group, the British Army Choir, who are making their first public performance today.

6. The Chef that Died of Shame

Transmitted live, Fri. 14/9/56, 9.30 p.m., from Studio G, Lime Grove.
Audience figure: 6.4 million

CAST:

Warren Mitchell	Grant Faversham, Gentleman from the opera
Constance Wake	Martine Dubois
Peter Haigh	Announcer
Raymond Rollett	Head chef
Dennis Chinnery	Rich man
John Vere	Rich man

Also: Claude Bonser, Leonard Sharp, Gordon Phillot, George Crowther, Ian MacNaughton,

Manville Tarrant, Desmond Rayner, Kim Corcoran, Ivor Raymonde, Patrick Milner, Hugh Warren, James Bulloch and George Clouston

[Margaret Flint was booked to appear, but the script was amended and she wasn't used.]

(Remake of the sixth radio episode from series two)

SERIES 2

1. The Alpine Holiday

Transmitted live, Mon. 1/4/57, 8p.m., from Studio 1, Riverside Studios.
Audience figure: 8.7 million

[Without Sidney James]

CAST

Richard Wattis	Hotel manager
Kenneth Williams	Yodeller of Dulwich
June Whitfield	Miss Dubois
Peggy Ann Clifford	Air hostess
John Vere	Passenger on aircraft
Dennis Chinnery	Air pilot
Patrick Milner	
Victor Bryant	Swiss gendarmes
Manville Tarrant	Porter
Rose Howlett	Hotel visitor
Elizabeth Fraser	Autograph hunter

Also: Fraser White, Alan Simpson, Jane Rieger, Charles Julian, Con Courtney, Harry Drew, Evelyn Lund and Dorothy Robson

Dressed in Swiss garb, Hancock jets off to the Swiss

Alps to enjoy the winter sports. Being an inexperienced flyer, he frets about everything and annoys all and sundry.

He arrives at the hotel to find that no room has been reserved for him and he'll have to share, but he's shocked when he thinks the attractive Miss Dubois, who has mistaken Hancock's room for hers, is his roommate. While Hancock is more than happy to put up with the inconvenience, Miss Dubois isn't and she is moved to a better room. Eventually Hancock's roommate turns up in the shape of the yodelling champion of East Dulwich, who is over for the yodelling championships.

After a disastrous time on the piste next day, Hancock, who has arranged to be moved to a nicer room, heads upstairs, but once again confusion reigns and Miss Dubois ends up in Hancock's new room; her screams bring the hotel manager who, believing Hancock is making a nuisance of himself, calls the police and Hancock ends up behind bars.

2. Lady Chatterley's Revenge

Transmitted live, Mon. 15/4/57, 8 p.m., from Studio 1, Riverside Studios.
Audience figure: 7.6 million

[Without Sidney James]

CAST:

Warren Mitchell	Lew Silver
John Vere	Humphrey Clanger
Paddy Edwards	Silver's typist
Kenneth Williams	Rep Company producer
Hattie Jacques	Actress (Gertrude and Lady

353

	Chatterley)
John Vyvyan	Call boy
Dennis Chinnery	Actor (Theodore)
Desmond Rayner	Actor (Roger)
Raymond Rollett	Actor (Stanley and Lord Chatterley)
Anne Lancaster	Actress (Cynthia)
Rose Howlett	
Evelyn Lund	
Anne Reid	Actresses
Alan Simpson	1st man
Charles Julian	2nd man
Manville Tarrant	3rd man
Claude Bonser	4th man
Lynne Cole	1st girl
Jane Rieger	2nd girl

Lew Silver, a director of the Ace Theatrical Agency, is auditioning various small-time performers, including Hancock, who want Silver to represent him. Hancock has been out of work for three months, but all Silver can offer is three weeks' work with the East Cheam Repertory Company, earning little more than four quid a week.

The Company is rehearsing *Moon Over Tahiti*. Hancock is unhappy to find he has only a few lines to learn and is shot in the first scene, but grudgingly takes the part.

On the opening night, news arrives in the theatre that the Lord Chamberlain has banned the play, which leaves the producer little option but to revert to the previous week's production, *Lady Chatterley's Revenge*, resulting in no part for Hancock. Unfortunately, no one tells him and he still makes his entrance.

3. The Russian Prince

Transmitted live, Mon. 29/4/57, 8 p.m., from Studio 1, Riverside Studios.
Audience figure: 6.8 million

CAST:

Tony Hancock	Prince Nicolai
Sidney James	General Sidski
Kenneth Williams	Another Prince Nicolai
Hattie Jacques	Countess Olga Romanoff
Bill Fraser	Fred
Michael Balfour	Charlie
Mario Fabrizi	Prince Paul Alexandrovitch
Leonard Sharp	Grand Duke Peter Ilievitch
Harry Lane	Prince Ivan Ivanovitch
Dennis Chinnery	
Raymond Rollett	
Janet Barrow	
Anne Lancaster	Russian Aristocrats
Ian MacNaughton	Footman
Roger Oatime	1st flunkey
Fraser White	2nd flunkey
Frank Pemberton	Baron Gregoffski
Gordon Phillott	Count Petroff Stravinski

Also: Claude Bonser, Eileen Delamere, Rene Roberts, Esme Easterbrook, Harry Drew, Ralph Covey, Rex Rashley and Con Courtney

As usual, money is tight in Hancock's house. Sid and Hancock start discussing a missing Russian princess called Anastasia and the unclaimed millions donated by a Tsar. Sid also reads that the

355

Princess' brother is thought to still be alive but suffering from amnesia, yet if he can prove his identity, he can claim half the fortune.

When Hancock bangs his head on a door and loses his memory, Sid comes up with an idea and gets Hancock to believe he's Prince Nicolai Romanoff, heir to the imperial throne of Russia. But just when everything is going to plan, someone else turns up claiming to be the missing prince.

4. The New Neighbour

Transmitted live, Mon. 13/5/57, 8 p.m., from Studio 1, Riverside Studios.
Audience figure: 6.4 million

CAST:

Hattie Jacques	Tony's secretary Grizelda Pugh
Kenneth Williams	Policeman
John Vere	Neighbour
Bill Fraser	Clerk (Estate Office)
Mario Fabrizi	Waxwork Museum guide

Also: Harry Drew, Manville Tarrant, Eileen Delamere, Claude Bonser, Esme Easterbrook, Evelyn Lund and Anne Reid

(Remake of the fourth radio episode from series three)

Hancock is suspicious of his new neighbour, Mr Thompkins, particularly as he's only seen at night. Miss Pugh spotted him carrying an old sack of bones, which he buried in the garden, an axe is thrown from his window and he disposes of clothes in an incinerator.

Hancock heads to the estate agency, which Sid James owns, to find out as much as he can about the man in number 25. Despite discovering that he makes waxwork models, Hancock, Miss Pugh and another neighbour, John, remain worried when they spot Thompkins bringing dead bodies into the house so decide to start their own investigations.

5. The Pianist

Transmitted live, Mon. 27/5/57, 8 p.m., from Studio 1, Riverside Studios.
Audience figure: 6.4 million

CAST:

Hattie Jacques	Baroness Helen
Kenneth Williams	Prince Paul
Mario Fabrizi	
Roger Oatime	Aides
Manville Tarrant	Policeman
Graham Leaman	City gent
John Vere	Bird lover
Ivor Raymonde	Pianist
Claude Bonser	
James Bulloch	Undertakers
Harry Drew	Ambulance man
Leonard Sharp	Waiter
Raymond Rollett	Consul
Dennis Chinnery	Assistant consul
Harry Lane	Aide
Angela Crow	Housemaid
Norman Grant	
Nicky Grant	Tap dancers

Also: Gwertl Hamer, Joanne Dainton and Eve Joyner

357

While sitting on a park bench Hancock suffers a bad turn and dreams he begins work as a pianist at the Scarlet Pimpernel Club in London's Park Lane, a club owned by Sid.

Billed as Thunderclap Hancock, he meets Baroness Helen de Cordova who takes a shine to him and invites him to play for her at her private apartment; it's not long before she's smitten with him and asks for his hand in marriage. But he's not the only one determined to wed the Baroness, and Hancock is challenged to a duel to the death in Hyde Park. Just as he thinks his life is slipping away, a policeman wakes him up in the park.

6. The Auction

Transmitted live, Mon. 10/6/57, 7.30 p.m., from Studio 1, Riverside Studios.
Audience figure: 4.9 million

CAST:

Kenneth Williams	Old man
Hattie Jacques	Mrs Witherspoon
Gordon Phillott	Junior partner
Manville Tarrant	Auction attendant
George Crowther	Man at auction
Mario Fabrizi	Casino croupier

Also: (at auction and as casino gamblers) Graham Leaman, Claude Bonser, Roger Oatime, Dennis Chinnery, Con Courtney, Rose Howlett, Peggy Ann Clifford and Evelyn Lund

Hancock's series is finishing and with four months until the new one, he must earn some much-needed cash. Once again, he's taken in by Sid, who tells him that for years he's been working on a foolproof system designed to break the roulette tables. He's prepared to give Hancock 50 per cent of his winnings, but there's only one snag: he'll have to auction his house to pay for the fares to Monte Carlo.

At the auction, his prized possession, a stuffed eagle, sells for little over six shillings, and even when the house is sold they're still short of their target. Then an old man comes calling from Crabbe, Crabbe, Scampi and Crabbe, a firm of solicitors, regarding the stuffed eagle Hancock bought from Harold Russell, a taxidermist, the previous year.

When they hear that it was stuffed with cash, they tell the man they can't help find it, but afterwards set off to try and retrieve it, knowing it will be the answer to all their problems.

SERIES 3

1. The Continental Holiday

Transmitted live, Mon. 30/9/57, 8.05 p.m., from Studio 1, Riverside Studios.
Audience figure: 6.8 million

CAST:

Anton Diffring	Mr X
Tutte Lemkow	Spanish dancer
Peter Allenby	Spanish waiter
George Elliott	Spanish guitar player
Mario Fabrizi	Beggar
Edouard Assaly	The Golden Scorpion
Peter Elliott	The Black Beetle

Alec Bregonzi	The Crimson Alligator
Anthony Shirvell	The Blue Hedgehog
Bruce Wightman	The Green Lizard
David Graham	Police Inspector
Arthur Bennett	Abdul the Nubian
Eugenie Sivyer	Spanish dancer
Leslie Smith	
Richard Statman	
Manville Tarrant	
Thomas Symonds	Arabs

Also: (Spaniards) Philip Carr, Pat O'Meara, Harry Robins, Len Felix and Harold Holness

Hancock returns from his holidays and entertains Sid with tales of his supposed adventures in every resort from Marseille to Cairo. The castanets he picks up lead him to tell the story of an adventure involving romance which started in Madrid.

  A chesspiece, meanwhile, reminds him of the Riviera where he found himself caught up in a web of international intrigue, all starting from the time he was invited to play chess with a friend at his Mediterranean villa.

2. The Great Detective

Transmitted live, Mon. 7/10/57, 8.05 p.m., from Studio 1, Riverside Studios.
Audience figure: 7.2 million

CAST:

John Vere	Rupert
Peggy Ann Clifford	Patricia
Cameron Hall	The Colonel
Evelyn Lund	Mrs Colonel

Graham Leaman	Robert
Terence Alexander	John
Paddy Edwards	Joselyn
Totti Truman Taylor	Cynthia
Pat Coombs	Matilda
Gordon Phillott	Lord Beaumont
Manville Tarrant	Police inspector
Anne Reid	Maid
James Bulloch	
Patrick Milner	
Peter Emms	
Basil Beale	Policemen
John Vyvyan	Body

Hancock, with his addiction to bedtime reading, has devoured 74 books in four weeks, and each time he feels his powers of deduction are better than the author's as he unravels the crimes; he's convinced that if he'd been the detective in the books there wouldn't have been any mistakes.

Hancock eventually falls asleep and dreams of being Sexton Hancock, the great detective, except on Thursdays when he is a chimney sweep; he is called upon by Lord Beaumont, a friend, to be in attendance when he tells his family that he's changing his will. He soon has a crime to solve when a murder is committed.

3. The Amusement Arcade

Transmitted live, Mon. 14/10/57, 8.05 p.m., from Studio G, Lime Grove.
Audience figure: 7.2 million

CAST:

Bill Fraser	Educated Albert
John Vere	Councillor Sproggs
Evelyn Lund	
Rose Howlett	
Elizabeth Gott	
Peggy Ann Clifford	Lady councillors
Claude Bonser	
Manville Tarrant	
Con Courtney	Councillors
Leslie Smith	
Patrick Milner	
Bruce Wightman	
Richard Statman	
Alan Simpson	Teddy boys
Alec Bregonzi	Listener
Dick Emery	Ballot teller
John Vyvyan	Voter
Thomas Symonds	
Anthony Shirvell	Ambulance men
Ray Grover	
Anthony Wiles	
Pat Wallen	
Iris Eve	Dancers

Certain factions in East Cheam would like to see Sid's amusement arcade closed. When his accountant, Educated Albert, reminds him that the council elections are being held that week and that there is one man, Hancock, who, if elected, will do everything he can to close them down, Sid takes steps to prevent his election. He starts off by getting a group of Teddy boys to disrupt Hancock's campaign speech at the local church hall.

It's all to no avail: Hancock is elected and is

362

congratulated by many when he wins his fight and forces the closure of Sid's arcade. But when Sid simply moves premises, occupying Hancock's lounge instead, the new councillor is forced to resign.

4. A Holiday in Scotland

Transmitted live, Mon. 21/10/57, 8.05 p.m., from Studio 1, Riverside Studios.
Audience figure: 7.9 million

CAST:

Raymond Huntley	Doctor
Ian MacNaughton	
Richard Statman	Weathermen
Anne Marryott	Nurse
Eileen Delamare	Mrs Brown
Manville Tarrant	
John Vyvyan	
George Crowther	
Charles Julian	Patients

Hancock is feeling unwell and is advised to take a holiday by his doctor. He persuades Sid to go with him and heads for the Scottish Highlands. While Hancock plans to live off the land, Sid has played safe and brought along a quantity of tinned food, much to Hancock's chagrin.

After eleven hours spent hunting in the cold for his dinner, all he's got to show for his efforts are three tiny fish—and they were used as his bait. While Sid tucks in to a six-course meal, Hancock has to be satisfied with his fish. Breakfast isn't much better, when all he can catch is a rabbit's tail; he becomes so desperate he buys Sid's entire rations for £439, only to find the tin opener is broken.

5. Air Steward Hancock—The Last of the Many

Transmitted live, Mon. 28/10/57, 8.05 p.m., from Studio 1, Riverside Studios.
Audience figure: 8.3 million

CAST:

Leslie Smith	1st pilot
Richard Statman	2nd pilot
Philip Carr	3rd pilot
Stuart Hillier	4th pilot
Anne Marryott	Tannoy girl
John Vere	Catering officer
Peter Allenby	Customs officer
John Vyvyan	Passenger
Basil Beale	Constable
Bill Fraser	Police inspector
James Bulloch	Security policeman
Manville Tarrant	Police sergeant
Dave Freeman	Police constable
Alec Bregonzi	Pilot

Also: (Passengers) Rose Howlett, Harry Drew, Cameron Hall, Evelyn Lund, Stella Kemball, Charles Julian, Con Courtney, George Crowther and Susan Cox

It's Hancock's first day as a qualified air steward, but when the chief catering superintendent tells him he's heading for Bermuda on his inaugural flight, Hancock is horrified because he didn't think he'd actually have to set foot inside a plane. His boss puts it all down to first flight nerves and sends him on his way.

Hancock feels even worse when he learns Sid James is on the flight, seemingly on the run, smuggling £750,000 out of the country. Just as Hancock tries to get him arrested, Sid tells him he'll be implicated because he's stuffed Hancock's suitcase full of notes as well. To make matters worse, plainclothes policemen are catching the same flight in pursuit of a criminal.

Amid all the confusion, the police attempt to arrest Hancock, who tries to escape their clutches by jumping out the plane—but his parachute isn't all it seems to be.

6. The Regimental Reunion

Transmitted live, Mon. 4/11/57, 8.05 p.m., from Studio 1, Riverside Studios.
Audience figure: 8.3 million

CAST:

Campbell Singer	Mr Spooner
Claude Bonser	1st clerk
Alec Bregonzi	2nd clerk
Con Courtney	3rd clerk
Bruce Wightman	4th clerk
Manville Tarrant	5th clerk
John Vyvyan	Office boy
Terence Alexander	Ex-Major
Graham Leaman	Ex-Colonel
Guy Middleton	Ex-Captain
Stuart Hillier	Ex-Major (No. 2)
Cameron Hall	Ex-Colonel (No. 2)
John Vere	Mr Filley
Raymond Rollett	Mr Gale

Peter Allenby	Inspector
George Crowther	1st millionaire
Arthur Mullard	2nd millionaire
Harry Robins	3rd millionaire
Harry Lane	Flunkey

Hancock has been working as a junior clerk at Gale and Filley Ltd, importers and exporters, for nineteen years. When he arrives late one morning, his boss tells him he's unimpressed with his performance and that Hancock needs to buck his ideas up.

Hancock, who served with the regiment of the Queen's Own East Cheam Light Horse, receives a letter from Major-General Chumley-Farquarson inviting him to a regimental reunion.

When his employers receive substantial orders totalling nearly £4 million from his ex-army chums, Hancock is promoted and remunerated handsomely, only for the orders later to be classed as fraudulent and for Sid to be identified as the culprit.

7. The Adopted Family

Transmitted live, Mon. 11/11/57, 8.05 p.m., from Studio 1, Riverside Studios.
Audience figure: 8.7 million

CAST:

Anne Marryott	Secretary
Ian Fleming	Housing officer
Pamela Manson	Bertha
John Vere	Judge
Patrick Milner	Usher

Anne Reid	Young wife
Stuart Hillier	Young husband
Hugh Lloyd	1st son
Mario Fabrizi	2nd son
John Vyvyan	3rd son
Manville Tarrant	4th son

When Hancock discovers that his landlady, Mrs Cravatte, is doubling the rent, he decides it's time to move. Sid reminds him that just after the war he placed his name on the waiting list for council houses, so Hancock thinks it's about time he was given an update.

Sid agrees to help Hancock secure a property in return for free lodgings, and heads off to the housing officer with a tale about Hancock's doctor advising him to swap his cold house for a council property or he won't last the winter.

When Hancock learns that he'll need to have a wife and five kids to promote himself to the top of the waiting list, Sid calls in his mates and helps secure the place. The trouble is, Hancock can't get rid of them afterwards and ends up becoming a slave to them all.

8. The Elocution Teacher

Transmitted live, Mon. 25/11/57, 8.05 p.m., from Studio 1, Riverside Studios.
Audience figure: 8.3 million

CAST:

Jack Hawkins	As himself
John Vere	Ponsonby Everest
Nora Nicholson	Mrs Fazakerly

Mary Reynolds	Miss Perkins
Stuart Hillier	Announcer
John Vyvyan	As himself

Rock 'n' roll musicians: Don Rendell (tenor sax), Bob Robert (bass), Mickie Greene (drums), Eric Cooke (piano) and Ronnie Hunt (trumpet)

Hancock is operating as a drama tutor, but with only five clients and Mrs Cravatte breathing down his neck for the rent, he's desperate to find a pupil with talent whom he can coach and Sid manage, splitting their earnings fifty–fifty.

Their prayers seem to be answered when Jack Hawkins comes calling, although Hancock has never heard of him; he's been offered a role in a Shakespeare play and wants to take a refresher course, but Sid talks him into paying 20 guineas for a more comprehensive course. Jack soon rues the day he ever met Hancock, though, when he's a failure at the rehearsals.

9. The Lawyer: The Crown V. James, S: Hancock QC Defending

Transmitted live, Mon. 2/12/57, 8.05 p.m., from Studio 1, Riverside Studios.
Audience figure: 8.3 million

CAST:

John Le Mesurier	Judge
Arthur Mullard	PC Trubshawe
Raymond Rollett	Barrister
John Vere	Prosecuting counsel
Hugh Lloyd	Clerk of court
Claude Bonser	Defendant

Bill Fraser	Police sergeant
John Vyvyan	Barrister's clerk
Anthony Shirvell	Foreman of the jury
Manville Tarrant	
Roger Oatime	
John Foster	Police constables
Anne Marryott	WPC
Patrick Milner	Usher
Alec Bregonzi	
Richard Sullivan	Court officials

Also: (Jury men and women) Nicholas Sandys, Alistair Audsley, Bart Allison, John Herrington, Mark Bennett, Collett O'Neill and Joyce Hemson

Hancock has graduated from evening classes with a second-class diploma and is working as a barrister, but his record is appalling and after he loses his tenth case in a row, he's summoned by his boss, Sir Jasper Worthington, QC. Initially intending to sack him, Worthington gives Hancock one last chance and he's asked to defend one of the practice's regular clients—Sid James. It looks a hopeless case, especially as James is facing 58 charges.

After a bit of bother over some motoring charges, which sees Hancock behind bars before being released on bail, Hancock finally represents Sid in court and plays the sympathy card, trying to persuade the jury that poor old Sid could never commit the crimes with which he's charged. His attempts pay off and James is acquitted, but Hancock ends up in Dartmoor.

10. How to Win Money and Influence People

Transmitted live, Mon. 9/12/57, 8.05 p.m., from Studio 1, Riverside Studios.
Audience figure: 9.1 million

CAST:

John Vyvyan	Newspaper boy
Dick Emery	Postman
Campbell Singer	Policeman
John Vere	Mr Pools
Bruce Wightman	1st assistant
Basil Beale	2nd assistant
Alec Bregonzi	2nd man
Philip Carr	3rd man
Leslie Smith	4th man
Anthony Shirvell	5th man
Mario Fabrizi	Waiter
Burt Kwouk	1st Japanese
Nelson Grostate	2nd Japanese
Jimmy Raphael	3rd Japanese
Manville Tarrant	Policeman
Hugh Lloyd	Last man

Hancock has ditched his road-sweeping job with the council to become a professional entrant in newspaper and magazine competitions; he's not enjoying much luck, though, and after six months has only won six bob. Having entered competitions by the barrowload, his luck finally changes when he wins, among other prizes, over £300,000 on the pools, two pubs in Bournemouth, a block of flats, a bunch of teacosies and some televisions.

Eager to get his hands on Hancock's newly acquired wealth, Sid conjures up some suspect plans and, like a fool, Hancock falls for them.

While Sid splashes out on expensive clothing, puffs oversized cigars and lunches at the Dorchester, Hancock lives like a pauper and looks forward to one consolation: the date he won with Jayne Mansfield; but when she can't turn up, it's Sid that's hired as a replacement.

11. There's An Airfield at the Bottom of My Garden

Transmitted live, Mon. 16/12/57, 8.05 p.m., from Studio 1, Riverside Studios.
Audience figure: 8.3 million

CAST:

John Vere	Vicar
Dick Emery	Surveyor
Esther MacPherson	Surveyor's wife
Cameron Hall	Colonel
Nancy Roberts	Emily
Gordon Phillott	Emily's husband
Paddy Edwards	
Leslie Smith	Young couple
Claude Bonser	Henry
Vera Elmore	Elderly lady
Anne Reid	Sid's secretary
Brenda Duncan	Mrs Farley
Elizabeth Gott	Woman guest
Alec Bregonzi	Violin player
Evelyn Lund	Viola player
John Vyvyan	Bass player

Also: Dorothy Robson, Philip Carr, Manville Tarrant, Eileen Delamere and Rose Howlett

Hancock is playing cello at the East Cheam

371

Musical Appreciation Society's musical evening, which is being held in the country cottage he bought from Sid, in Little Codswallop. The trouble is, he viewed it while it was foggy and didn't realise there was an aerodrome at the bottom of the garden, which means every time a plane lands it shakes the walls.

When several planes land during the evening, the guests can't stand the racket and head home. Fed up, Hancock demands a refund, but Sid refuses, leaving Hancock with no alternative but to try and sell the property himself. Just when he thinks he's secured a purchaser, a plane flies over.

12. Hancock's 43 Minutes—The East Cheam Repertory Company

Transmitted live, Mon. 23/12/57, 8.05 p.m., from Television Theatre Shepherds Bush.
Audience figure: 9.5 million

CAST:

John Gregson	Guest star
Max Geldray	Harmonica player
Alf Silvestri	Juggler
The Glamazons	Chorus dancers
The Keynotes	Vocal group

Also: Dido the Chimp, John Vere, John Vyvyan, Dennis Chinnery, Mario Fabrizi, Arthur Bennett, Tommy Eytle, John McRay, James Avon, Richard Wharton, Michael Ely and Ivor Raymonde

Hancock appears on stage dressed in a white tuxedo made specially by the BBC, making him believe that he's been recognised at long last. After telling the Beeb that he wanted an hour-long show or he was off, he was offered 43 minutes instead.

With Sid in charge of hiring performers, it was inevitable that problems would occur: he spent all the money and didn't secure any artists, except a group of overweight female dancers. In the absence of a proper act, Hancock tries in vain to entertain, including giving a rendition of *The Three Musketeers*.

SERIES 4

1. Ericson The Viking (a.k.a. The Vikings)

Recorded: Tues. 16/12/58, at Studio 1, Riverside Studios.
First transmission: Fri. 26/12/58, 8.20 p.m.
Audience figure: 8.7 million

CAST:

Laurie Webb	1st electrician
Ivor Raymonde	2nd electrician
John Vyvyan	1st Viking
Mario Fabrizi	2nd Viking
Arthur Mullard	3rd Viking
John Vere	Saxon king
Manville Tarrant	1st stagehand
Anthony Shirvell	2nd stagehand
Alec Bregonzi	Cameraman
Louis Adam	Clapper boy
Pat Coombs	Saxon princess
Herbert Nelson	1st Saxon
Pat O'Meara	2nd Saxon

Rufus Cruickshank	3rd Saxon
George Crowther	4th Saxon
Richard Statman	Sound assistant

It's Boxing Day and tonight sees the first episode of a new-style Hancock television show: *Ericson, King of the Vikings*. While Sid gorges himself on the festive fare, Hancock frets because he's convinced his latest televisual venture will be a flop, especially as he took up Sid's suggestion that they make the production themselves, allowing them the chance to make more cash selling the show to the BBC.

The commissioning of an entire series depends on tonight's instalment, and during a flashback to the recording at Sid's Splendide Film Studios, we discover the reason behind Hancock's lack of confidence. Inadequate equipment, an uninspiring cast, Sid's rudimentary editing style and Mrs Cravatte responsible for costumes do not bode well for the future, so no one's surprised when the Beeb pulls the plug halfway through the show.

2. The Set That Failed

Recorded: Tues. 18/11/58, at Studio 1, Riverside Studios.
First transmission: Fri. 2/1/59, 8.15 p.m.
Audience figure: 7.2 million

CAST:

Hugh Lloyd	1st TV repair man
John Vyvyan	2nd TV repair man
John Vere	Mr Biggs
Rose Howlett	Mrs Biggs

Claude Bonser	1st Biggs' visitor
Evelyn Lund	2nd Biggs' visitor
Sidney Vivian	Uncle Fred
Patricia Hayes	Aunt Edie
Robert Dorning	Mr Smith
Margaret Flint	Mrs Smith
Harry Robins	1st Smith's visitor
Stella Kemball	2nd Smith's visitor
Mario Fabrizi	Albert
Anne Marryott	Barbara
Ivor Raymonde	Herbert
Leslie Smith	Tommy
Anthony Shirvell	Jack

Hancock's television is on the blink and he frets because he'll be without it for an entire evening, claiming this is enough to break the strongest of men. He tries convincing himself it will give him time for more intellectual pursuits, such as making jigsaws, but ends up impersonating Long John Silver sitting in front of the box.

Eventually the agony becomes unbearable. Needing his small-screen fix, he finds all the excuses under the sun to visit other people in order to catch a glimpse of television, including returning half a loaf of bread to his neighbours below, even though he borrowed it a year ago, visiting his long-forgotten auntie and uncle and even pretending to be part of a nearby family.

Finally, the television is repaired and life can return to normality, or so Hancock thinks.

3. Underpaid! Or, Grandad's SOS

Recorded: Tues. 2/12/58, at Studio 1, Riverside

Studios.
First Transmission: Fri. 9/1/59, 8.15 p.m.
Audience figure: 7.2 million

CAST:

Mario Fabrizi	
John Vyvyan	Street musicians
Harry Drew	Arthur Biggs
George Crowther	Frederick Higgins
Arthur Mullard	Share-buyer
James Bulloch	City gent
Con Courtney	1st man in pub
Claude Bonser	2nd man in pub
Anthony Shirvell	3rd man in pub
Rolf Harris	Australian barmen
Len David	
Evelyn Lund	Phyllis
Voices on radio:	
Andrew Faulds	'D'Arcy Villiers'
Warren Mitchell	'Grimaldo'
Richard Statman	'Nick'
Philip Carr	Announcer
Tony Hancock	Tony's grandfather
Sidney James	Sid's grandfather

Also: Bob Marshall, Arnold Lock, James McCloughlin, Herbert Nelson, Manville Tarrant, Patrick Milner and Stella Kemball

While Hancock is listening to the radio, an SOS is broadcast, asking Anthony Hancock, last known at Rowton House, Hammersmith, to go to his grandfather, Kitchener Hancock, because he's dangerously ill.

Sid tries convincing him it could wait until the morning, but when he discovers that the last time

376

Hancock saw his grandfather he'd struck gold and was a multimillionaire, he's keen to reunite them as soon as possible—the problem is, the old man is living in Australia now.

Needing to raise £300 for the air fares, Sid and Hancock pose as ex-servicemen collecting in the high street, but when they fail to raise even a pound, Sid suggests an accumulator on the dogs. Sadly, their luck isn't in.

Desperate to get Hancock down under, Sid suggests selling shares in his grandad's will for a pound. The sale goes well, with up-to-the-minute progress reports on his grandfather's failing health helping boost sales. With £500 they've got enough, but when Sid learns that Hancock's grandfather hasn't seen him for twenty-five years, he knocks him out and takes his place, only to discover it's all a lie and his grandfather wanted him over there to scrounge some cash for himself.

Before he can return home, another SOS is heard on the radio, this time for Sid, whose grandfather is ill in prison. As Sid can't get back, Hancock decides to seek revenge and take Sid's place.

4. The New Nose (a.k.a. The Nose)

Recorded: Tues. 23/12/58, at Studio 1, Riverside Studios.
First transmission: Fri. 16/1/59, 7.30 p.m.
Audience figure: 7.6 million

CAST:

Barbara Archer	1st girl at Tony's
Mario Fabrizi	Milkman
Roger Avon	Counter hand

Anne Marryott	Nurse
John Le Mesurier	Dr Worthington
Annabelle Lee	2nd girl at Tony's
Elizabeth Fraser	1st girl in milk bar
Pamela Manson	2nd girl in milk bar
Alec Bregonzi	1st man at bus stop
Ivor Raymonde	2nd man at bus stop

Also: Arthur Mullard, Herman Miller, Bill Matthews, Tom Payne, Joseph Levine and John Scott Martin

When a girlfriend falls into hysterics about the shape of Hancock's nose, he gets a complex and sends her packing; but when Sid confirms he *has* got a hideous hooter, a depressed Hancock heads to the local milk bar for a drink.

He overhears two girls discussing someone's boyfriend and believes they're making fun of him, and when he thinks the same about two men standing at the bus stop, he decides to become a recluse and won't even open the door to the milkman.

When Sid hears that Arthur, the proprietor of the local milk bar, had plastic surgery on his nose, giving him a confidence boost, he persuades Hancock to do the same. After browsing through the pattern book in Dr Worthington's surgery, he decides on the required shape and goes under the knife. Although he ends up with a hooter twice the size of his original, Hancock is pleased with his new look, believing it will do wonders for his chances with the girls. But he hadn't anticipated his next girlfriend bursting into fits of laughter over his jug-shaped ears.

5. The Flight of the Red Shadow (a.k.a. Desert Song)

Recorded at Studio 1, Riverside Studios, no date specified.
First transmission: Fri. 23/1/59, 7.30 p.m.
Audience figure: 7.9 million

CAST:

Louise Howard	Singer
Mario Fabrizi	
George Crowther	
Louis Adam	Arabs
Alan Simpson	Warder/barracker
Ray Galton	Barracker
Robert Dorning	Manager
Alec Bregonzi	Balloon seller
Ivor Raymonde	Toy seller
Rolf Harris	Sailor
Arthur Mullard	Policeman
Con Courtney	Civic dignitary
John Vere	Vicar
Bert Simms	Mayor
Evelyn Lund	Mayoress
Harry Drew	Colonel
Guy Mills	Maharaja
James Bulloch	Prison governor
Ben Bowers	Maharaja's attendant
Patrick Milner	
Herbert Nelson	
Stanley Segal	Foreign legionnaires
Stanley Ayres	Strong man
Frank Littlewood	
Anna Churcher	
Ann Jay	Civic dignitaries

379

The East Cheam Repertory Company is performing *The Desert Song*, with Hancock cast as a sheikh, but his performance is so rotten that the audience throw coins on to the stage. The audience's reaction forces the theatre manager to cancel the show, leaving Sid and Hancock in a predicament because the cast are up in arms as they haven't been paid.

Sid and Hancock run away from the theatre with the cast, dressed in Arab costumes, in pursuit. They finally shake them off, but Sid doesn't think it will be for long, with Hancock dressed as a sheikh. As they have no clothes, save for a few other costumes, Sid persuades him to change into his maharaja's outfit: he has an idea.

Before long, Hancock is mistaken for the Maharaja of Renjipur and uses diplomatic immunity to get himself out of a scrape. He then finds himself guest speaker for the Friendship Society of Coalport, talking about education in the Far East, while Sid collects from the audience. All is going well until the real maharaja turns up, followed by the rest of the repertory company.

6. The Horror Serial (a.k.a. Quatermass)

Recorded at Studio 1, Riverside Studios, no date specified.
First transmission: Fri. 30/1/59, 7.30 p.m.
Audience figure: 6.8 million

CAST:

Dennis Chinnery	Lieutenant
John Le Mesurier	Colonel
Alec Bregonzi	1st soldier

John Vyvyan	2nd soldier
Laurie Webb	3rd soldier
Hugh Lloyd	Sergeant
Arthur Mullard	Mr Biggs
Phyllis Norwood	Mrs Biggs
Anne Marryott	Nurse

After frightening himself out of his skin watching the last episode of *Quatermass and the Pit* at Sid's mother's house, Hancock jumps at every sound and is convinced he'll soon be seeing aliens on Earth.

Next day, Sid hits a metallic object while digging the garden and Tony is horrified, believing it to be an alien spacecraft; even Sid is concerned when they unearth a bone nearby. When they spot what could be a fuse, Sid calls in the military, who believe it to be an unexploded bomb, despite Hancock's attempts to convince them it's a spaceship from Mars.

Tony gets so uptight about the object that he decides to detonate it, and in doing so blows up the house and puts Sid in hospital.

7. The Italian Maid

Recorded at Studio 1, Riverside Studios, no date specified.
First transmission: Fri. 6/2/59, 7.30 p.m.
Audience figure: 7.9 million

CAST:

John Vere	Domestic agent
Harry Lane	Italian father
Michael Stainton	1st man
James Bulloch	2nd man

Marla Landi	Silvano
Elizabeth Gott	Lady Plunkett
Jeanette Edwards	Secretary
Betty Lloyd-Davies	Italian mother
Frederick Schiller	Swiss man
John Vyvyan	Telegraph boy

Also: (Italian daughters and sons) Mary Abbott, Anita Loghade, Virginia Mollett, Sandra Robb, Jenny Jones, Biddy Lennon, Harry Wright, Louis Adam, Anthony Wiles, Ronnie Robinson, Dennis Mallard and Francis Lennon

Hancock feels he needs some sunshine in his life. Too much time is spent cleaning his house, which is causing havoc with his hands. He agrees with Sid's opinion that he needs a maid, leaving him time to enjoy his pastimes, so heads for the employment office.

While Hancock suggests a woman with stamina who won't shy away from hard work, Sid was hoping for some flighty French girl. The manager offers an Italian girl.

Back at home, Hancock lets the work pile up, but when a beautiful Italian girl called Silvano arrives, Hancock and Sid fall over themselves to help; their attentions are too much and the girl threatens to leave if they don't ease up.

In their attempts to woo her, neither lets her carry out her household chores, treating her, instead, to chocolates and breakfast in bed. While Hancock ends up doing all the work, Sid develops his relationship with Silvano, and agrees that her family, who are visiting from Italy, can stay, causing even more work for Hancock.

With no option but to recruit another maid,

Hancock fills in an application at the employment exchange. Unknown to him, he completes the form incorrectly and ends up being employed as a maid himself in a Swiss chalet.

8. Matrimony—Almost (a.k.a. The Wedding)

Recorded at Studio 1, Riverside Studios, no date specified.
First transmission: Fri. 13/2/59, 7.30 p.m.
Audience figure: 8.3 million

CAST:

Terence Alexander	Reggie/guest
Vivienne Martin	Elizabeth
Cardew Robinson	Percy/guest
Cameron Hall	Mr Wetherby
John Vere	Vicar
Philip Carr	Nigel/guest
Alec Bregonzi	Freddie/guest
Mario Fabrizi	Bandleader/guest
Ivor Raymonde	1st broker's man
Arthur Mullard	2nd broker's man
Edith Stevenson	Mrs Wetherby
Elizabeth Fraser	Maid
Frank Littlewood	Mr Wetherby's friend
Michael Greenwood	guardsman/guest
Lionel Wheeler	1st musician
Louis Adam	2nd musician
Patrick Milner	3rd musician/PC
Philip Howard	4th musician/PC
James Bulloch	Butler/sergeant
Evelyn Lund	Harmonium player

Also: Gwenda Ewan, Anne Marryott, Paddy

383

Edwards, Patricia Veasey, Deirdre Bellar, Judy Nash, Con Courtney, Harry Drew, Shirley Patterson, Edna Stevens, Alan Simpson, John Caesar and Bill Matthews

An unhappy bride-to-be tells her mother she's only marrying her man for his money because her father's business has collapsed. Once they've tied the knot, she takes some satisfaction in knowing that at least she won't have to laugh at his silly jokes.

The intended husband is Hancock, who is having doubts himself. Unsure whether he really loves her, he confides in Sid, who reminds him that her family is very rich—or so they think—and for the first time in their lives they will be able to enjoy the comforts of high-class living.

After all these years of feeling undesirable, Hancock is suspicious of his future wife, Elizabeth Wetherby, who is set to marry him after only two weeks. He then discovers Sid has been telling Elizabeth that Hancock has several thousand in the bank.

During the wedding service, the Wetherbys' furniture starts to be reclaimed on behalf of finance companies, but Mr Wetherby buys more time by pointing out his daughter is marrying into money. Sid gets wise to what's happening and saves Hancock in the nick of time.

9. The Beauty Contest (a.k.a. Mr East Cheam)

Recorded at Studio 1, Riverside Studios, no date specified.
First transmission: Fri. 20/2/59, 7.30 p.m.

Audience figure: 8.3 million

CAST:

CAST:

John Vere	The Mayor
Robert Dorning	Alderman Biggs
James Bulloch	Alderman Jones
Frank Littlewood	3rd Alderman
Harry Lane	4th Alderman
Charles Julian	5th Alderman
Bert Simms	6th Alderman
Roger Avon	Gym instructor

Entrants in competition:

John Vyvyan	Jim Banstead
Mario Fabrizi	Percy Whyteleafe
Arthur Mullard	Arnold Nonsuch
George Crowther	Harry Mortlake
Herbert Nelson	
Richard Statman	
Con Courtney	Bath attendants
John Blyth	Master of Ceremonies
Alan Simpson	
Patrick Milner	Dance hall attendants
Ann Smith	
Phillipa Steward	Glamour girls
Joe Robinson	Competition winner

The East Cheam Borough Council's Carnival Committee decide they can't hold a Miss East Cheam beauty contest because there are no beauties to parade. Deciding it's time for a change, Councillor Biggs suggests a Mr East Cheam instead, with £50 and a film test the prize for the winning man.

Sid announces his intentions to enter the competition, but at first Hancock isn't interested, regarding himself as too good-looking for such events; however, he soon changes his mind and bets Sid £100 that he'll win.

Even though the councillors feel the standard of applicants is worse than the women, it's too late to cancel the competition, which will be judged on physique, looks, charm and intelligence. Hancock and Sid attempt to get in shape, but it's all in vain because a late entrant, Reg Morris, steals the show, and they find themselves tying for last place.

10. The Wrong Man

Recorded at Studio 1, Riverside Studios, no date specified.
First transmission: Fri. 6/3/59, 7.30 p.m.
Audience figure: 8.3 million

CAST:

Roger Avon	Constable
James Bulloch	Sergeant
Campbell Singer	Inspector
Harry Locke	Detective Soames
Nancy Roberts	Mrs Haggett
Gordon Phillott	Mr Hardacre
Alec Bregonzi	3rd witness
Pamela Manson	Cinema cashier

Men in identity parade:

Arthur Mullard	Bruiser
John Vyvyan	Little man

Also: Alan Simpson, Laurie Webb, Herbert Nelson, Con Courtney, Don Matthews and Anthony Gould

When a tobacconist's in the high street is burgled,

Sid and Hancock are asked to take part in an identity parade at the local police station. Mrs Haggett, sales assistant at the shop, is adamant she'll recognise the villain and strolls down the line. To everyone's surprise, she identifies Hancock as the culprit.

When two other witnesses confirm Hancock is the man, he has no alternative but to appoint Sid as his legal representative. Hancock's alibi that he was at the pictures doesn't convince the police, however, because no one can corroborate his story.

When Hancock is released on bail he sets out to clear his name by reconstructing the crime at the tobacconist's, only to be caught in the act by a passing policeman, who marches him off to the station again. When he arrives, it looks as if his troubles are behind him when they find the real criminal, but soon he's in hot water again.

11. The Oak Tree (a.k.a. The Tree)

Recorded at Studio 1, Riverside Studios, no date specified.
First transmission: Fri. 13/3/59, 7.30 p.m.
Audience figure: 8.3 million

CAST:

John Vere	Man from Ministry
Reginald Beckwith	Clerk of Works
Hugh Lloyd	Trees inspector
Robert Dorning	Timber merchant
Arthur Mullard	1st workman
Laurie Webb	2nd workman
Mario Fabrizi	
John Vyvyan	Marchers

387

Graham Leaman	Police inspector
Gwenda Ewan	Secretary
Mary Fletcher	
Joyce Hemson	
Margerie Mason	
Sonia Peters	
Edwin Morton	
Albert Grant	Passers by
James Langley	Small boy
John Caesar	
Norman Taylor	
Robert Pitt	
Bill Matthews	
Victor Charrington	
Anthony Jennett	Policemen

Hancock is proud of the ancient oak tree which dominates his garden, especially as it's the only specimen in Railway Cuttings. When a council official arrives to inform him it's classed as a hazard to passing buses and must be felled, an irate Hancock decides to fight for the tree's rights.

Visiting the Clerk of Works in the council's Tree Department gets him nowhere, so he decides the only answer is to arrange a march to Downing Street. At the local market he takes to his soapbox and tries to summon up support without success, so when a couple of professional marchers offer their services, he accepts. But their protestations are futile, largely because they get lost *en route* and end up miles from Downing Street.

As a last ditch attempt to save the tree, Hancock, Sid and the marchers form a human chain around the trunk, but discover that a protection order has been slapped on the tree, securing its future; that is, until a local timber merchant offers Hancock £100!

12. The Knighthood

Recorded at Studio 1, Riverside Studios, no date specified.
First transmission: Fri. 20/3/59, 7.30 p.m.
Audience figure: 7.9 million

CAST:

Richard Wattis	Old Vic manager
Robert Dorning	Cheam Rep manager
Mario Fabrizi	Master of Ceremonies
Lynne Cole	Dancer
Ivor Raymonde	Pianist
Andrew Faulds	Richard III
John Vyvyan	
Jack Leonard	Pub customers
James Bulloch	Barman

Also: (pub customers) Con Courtney, Doris Littel, Doris Hall, John Cabot and Michael Middleton

While reading *Burke's Peerage*, Hancock imagines what it would be like being the first Duke of Cheam. When the morning mail fails to bring news of his knighthood, he complains to Sid that he deserves to be recognised for, among other things, his twelve years on stage and three years in the Home Guard. Sid states that the only way he'll get noticed on the stage is if he turns to serious theatre.

Hancock visits the managing director of the Old Vic Trust at the famous theatre but takes umbrage when he's told to gain some first-hand experience

389

at a repertory company—not even the East Cheam Repertory Company is interested in his services until he's established a proven track record.

Sid manages to secure Hancock two weeks at Stratford, which more than satisfies Hancock, until he finds out it's at the Stratford Arms, a pub. An impression of Long John Silver and his own interpretation of Shakespeare fail to excite the crowd and his act is cut short when he's thrown off the stage. But a few white lies later and the manager of the East Cheam Rep is signing him up, which leads to employment at the Old Vic—even if it is as a prompter.

13. The Servants (a.k.a. The Last Show)

Recorded at Studio 1, Riverside Studios, no date specified.
First transmission: Fri. 27/3/59, 7.30 p.m.
Audience figure: 7.9 million

CAST:

John Le Mesurier	Colonel Winthrop
Mary Hinton	Mrs Winthrop
Alec Bregonzi	Male secretary
Hugh Lloyd	1st old man
Nancy Roberts	1st old woman
Charles Julian	2nd old man
Evelyn Lund	2nd old woman
Gordon Phillott	3rd old man
Patricia Hayes	3rd old woman
James Bulloch	1st city man
Con Courtney	2nd city man
John Vyvyan	3rd city man

It's the last episode in Hancock's show and with the new series not starting until September, Hancock is scouring the situations vacant for work. One advert in particular catches his eye: old couple required to work as a gardener and housekeeper at Colonel Winthrop's country mansion, with good wages, clothes and accommodation provided.

Convinced he could play an old man, Hancock persuades Sid to play his wife, dressed in an ankle-length dress and shawl. After scaring off other people attending interviews by claiming the Colonel and his wife work their employees like slaves, Hancock and Sid are offered the posts.

They get off to a poor start by oversleeping on their first morning, but it's not long before the Colonel gets suspicious and they're back reading the situations vacant.

SERIES 5

1. The Economy Drive

Recorded at Studio 1, Riverside Studios, Fri. 4/9/59.
First transmission: Fri. 25/9/59, 8.30 p.m.
Audience figure: 9.5 million

CAST:

Arthur Mullard	1st man
Frank Pemberton	2nd man
Laurie Webb	3rd man
Herbert Nelson	4th man
Alec Bregonzi	5th man
Patricia Hayes	Cashier

Totti Truman Taylor	Woman in queue
Peggy Ann Clifford	Lady almoner
Pamela Manson	1st counter girl
Elizabeth Fraser	2nd counter girl
Anne Marryott	Tea girl
Mario Fabrizi	Tray snatcher
Beatrice Ormonde	1st waitress
Joanna Douglas	2nd waitress
Jeanette Edwards	Nurse/café customer
Michael Ward	Man at lunch

Also: (customers in self-service canteen) Margaret Jordan, Tracy Vernon, Anne Reddin, Judith Pearson, Barbara Adams, Barbara Ball, Alan Darling, Bill Matthews, Dick Downes, Michael Oaley, Robin Kildair, Stephen Fawcett.

After holidaying abroad for three months, Hancock and Sid return home to find hundreds of milk bottles cluttering the doorstep. Sid forgot to cancel the delivery, but that's not all he forgot. Inside, the lights have been left on, the papers weren't stopped, the television is talking to itself and every other electrical appliance in the house is switched on.

Horrified at the thought of his electricity bill, Hancock decides on an economy drive, living on the absolute minimum until he's solvent again. But eating at self-service restaurants and burning just one lump of coal per hour isn't easy, nor is climbing the stairs without the lights switched on, which results in Hancock and Sid falling down and ending up in hospital. Four weeks in hospital, with free food, turns out to be just what the doctor ordered, or so Hancock thinks, until he's asked to foot the bill. Worse is to come because when he arrives home he finds, once again, that he hadn't cancelled his deliveries.

2. The Two Murderers

Recorded at Studio 1, Riverside Studios, Fri. 18/9/59.
First transmission: Fri. 2/10/59, 8.30 p.m.
Audience figure: 9.9 million

CAST:

Robert Dorning	Bank manager
Hugh Lloyd	Librarian
Patricia Hayes	Mrs Cravatte
Mark Singleton	Tony's doctor
Ralph Nossek	Sid's doctor
Arthur Mullard	1st bruiser
Tom Clegg	2nd bruiser
Albert Grant	
Betty Miller	
John Vyvyan	
Louise Stafford	Members of the public

Sid's finally investing in a legitimate business: Mabel's fish and chip parlour in the high street. He needs some extra cash and tries persuading Hancock to become a partner, but to no avail, so Sid has to find the money by other means. When the bank agrees to an overdraft, Sid borrows some books on running a business from the library; the librarian, knowing Sid would be interested, gives him another book to take home: *Perfect Murders of the 20th Century*.

Hancock can't understand how Sid has secured the extra funding he needed and becomes suspicious. When he discovers he's reading a book about murders, he panics and thinks Sid has it in for him; but when Sid overhears Hancock reading from the same book he's convinced his days are numbered, too.

3. Lord Byron Lived Here

Recorded at Studio 1, Riverside Studios, Fri. 25/9/59.
First transmission: Fri. 9/10/59, 8.45 p.m.
Audience figure: 9.1 million

CAST:

John Le Mesurier	National Trust officer
Hugh Lloyd	The Disbeliever
Robert Dorning	The American
William Mervyn	The man from the council
Stan Simmons	
Raymond Grahame	National Trust attendants
Judy Rogers	
John Vyvyan	
Marylyn Thomas	
Frances St Barbe-West	
Dorothy Watson	
Susan Hunter	
Robert Bryan	
Michael Wyatt	Members of the public

His house is in such a dilapidated state, Hancock racks his brains to think of someone he can persuade to help with repairs. When Sid mentions that the National Trust is only interested in houses which are architecturally significant or where a famous person once lived, Hancock is sure that someone famous must have stayed there. After all,

394

the property used to be a boarding-house.

When it's discovered that East Cheam was one of Lord Byron's favourite weekend retreats, they opt for the poet and begin searching for evidence. After scribbling some lines of so-called poetry on the wall, Sid convinces Hancock that Byron did reside at Railway Cuttings.

When the National Trust shows no interest in their claim, Sid and Hancock decide to go it alone, opening Lord Byron Cottage to the public, as well as earning extra pounds selling off items they claim to be Byron's personal property. They are stopped in their tracks, though, when a council official calls and declares they'll be prosecuted and the house condemned unless they decorate the place and stop pretending it was the poet's home.

4. Twelve Angry Men

Recorded at Studio 1, Riverside Studios, Fri. 2/10/59.
First transmission: Fri. 16/10/59, 8.30 p.m.
Audience figure: 8.9 million

CAST:

Ralph Nossek	Mr Spooner, Prosecuting counsel
Robert Dorning	Police inspector
Leonard Sachs	Defending counsel
Austin Trevor	The Judge
Hugh Lloyd	Usher
Herbert Nelson	The Prisoner
William Kendall	Military juror
Leslie Perrins	Company director juror
Philip Ray	Farmer juror

Kenneth Kove	Old man juror
Betty Cardno	1st woman juror
Lala Lloyd	2nd woman juror
Alec Bregonzi	Young man juror
James Bulloch	Bank clerk juror
Mario Fabrizi	12th juror
Marie Lightfoot	Old lady juror
David Grain	
James Cliston	
Keith Ashley	
John Vyvyan	Junior counsel
Robert Pitt	
Gilbert McIntyre	
Christopher Dyer	
Kenneth Cowan	Police constables
Alex Wright	
John Tucker	Solicitors

John Peabody is on trial for theft and Hancock, as foreman of the jury, is making a mockery of court proceedings; he even gets a ring, which is part of the evidence, stuck on his finger and asks the judge for some butter.

After taking an instant dislike to Mr Spooner, the prosecuting counsel, Hancock takes the rest of the jurors off to consider their verdict. Although everyone wants a guilty verdict, Hancock sides with the defence and won't budge. When Sid, who's also on the jury, learns that he's earning 30 shillings a day, more than he earns outside, he's determined to delay proceedings as much as possible.

Hancock tries persuading the others to see his point of view, but does his case no good by admitting that he feels the accused isn't guilty because he has a 'nice face'. Deadlocked, Sid and

Hancock resort to emotional blackmail and gradually get their way, but just when it looks as if they're ready to announce their verdict, Hancock decides that perhaps Peabody is guilty after all.

5. The Train Journey

Recorded at Studio 1, Riverside Studios, Fri. 11/9/59.
First transmission: Fri. 23/10/59, 8.30 p.m.
Audience figure: 9.3 million

CAST:

Raymond Huntley	The Doctor
Cameron Hall	The Colonel
Henry Longhurst	The Vicar
Totti Truman Taylor	Woman
Eve Patrick	The Girl
Robert Dorning	Railway guard
Hugh Lloyd	Railway ticket clerk
Philip Carr	Radio announcer

Also: (passengers) Judy Roger, Pauline Walker, Jean Mockford, Anthony Ray, Michael Harrison, Charles Gilbert, David Graham and Eileen McCleland

Hancock has been offered a week's work at the Giggleswick Drama Festival, playing Henry V, which seems too good an opportunity to miss. But when the ticket office at the railway station hasn't heard of the destination, Hancock starts wondering if it's just another dead-end booking courtesy of his so-called agent, Sid James.

During the long train journey, Hancock annoys all the other passengers so much with his singing, incessant talking, whistling and tapping, that everyone's relieved when the train arrives at Leeds, where Hancock and Sid catch a connecting train, knowing they won't set eyes on the two of them again—or so they believe. After a disappointing week on stage, watched by just twenty-seven people, Hancock and Sid head home by bus, only to be joined by some familiar faces.

6. The Cruise

Recorded at Studio 1, Riverside Studios, Fri. 23/10/59.
First transmission: Fri. 30/10/59, 8.30 p.m.
Audience figure: 9.9 million

CAST:

Gwenda Ewan	1st girl
Philip Carr	1st man
Ivor Raymonde	2nd man
Patrick Milner	1st Steward
Hattie Jacques	Amorous lady
Harry Brunning	Old man
Evelyn Lund	Old lady
Dennis Chinnery	First officer
John Le Mesurier	The Captain
Brian Oulton	Ship's doctor
Paddy Edwards	2nd girl
Richard Statman	Radio operator
Frank Littlewood	Man in crowd
Herbert Nelson	Sailor at wheel
Brian Tyler	1st junior officer
Astor Sklair	2nd junior officer
Ricky Felgate	3rd junior officer
Mario Fabrizi	Ship's bandleader

Patricia Shakesby	3rd girl
Una Trimming	4th girl
Laura Thurlow	5th girl
James Bulloch	1st air line steward
Lionel Wheeler	Second air line steward
Hugh Lloyd	
Laurie Webb	Stewards

Also: (ship's passengers) Ivor Kimmell, Lee Richardson, Howard Charlton, Robert Weeden, Anne Clunes, Viera Shelley, Nancy Adams, Olga Regan and Elizabeth Bergen; (flight passengers) Ruby Archer, Tracy Vernon, Terry Howard, Barbara Muir, Rex Roland, William White and Alec Wallace

Hancock and Sid are cruising the Mediterranean on the RMS *Moravia*, but while Sid's enjoying the warmth of the October sun, Hancock is bored stiff. Inappropriately dressed in his overcoat and hat, he feels conned because Sid promised him girls would be swooning all over them, which is far from the truth.

With nothing to do, Hancock decides to immerse himself in his book, *Great Sea Mysteries*, and reads about the sinking of the *Mauretania*. When he misinterprets a steward's instruction to another crew member to go down and check the leeks, he panics and believes the ship is sinking after being struck by an iceberg, even though they're sailing the Mediterranean. Before long, he has all the passengers believing they're going down, until the Captain restrains Hancock, prescribes medication and has him locked in his cabin.

With Sid's help he escapes in time for a fancy dress party, but before they know it, Hancock and

Sid are ordered off the boat at the next port of call and are flying home.

7. The Big Night

Recorded at Studio 1, Riverside Studios, Fri. 30/10/59.
First transmission: Fri. 6/11/59, 8.30 p.m.
Audience figure: 11.2 million

CAST:

Patricia Hayes	Mrs Cravatte
Hugh Lloyd	Launderette attendant
Robert Dorning	Launderette manager
Anne Lancaster	Receptionist
Sam Kydd	
Mario Fabrizi	Men in launderette
Michael Balfour	Cinema manager
Tom Clegg	Commissionaire
Paddy Edwards	1st girl
Annabelle Lee	2nd girl
Ivor Raymonde	Man in cinema
Joanna Douglas	1st cinema girl
Beatrice Ormonde	2nd cinema girl
Laura Thurlow	
Patricia Shakesby	Policewomen
James Bulloch	Police constable
Leonard Kingston	Policeman

Also: Dorothy Watson, Ann Jay, Rosamund Tattersall, Susan Kay, Vivien Weldon, Mary Chirgwin, Felicity Peel, Dick Downes, Bill Matthews and Peter Badger

Hancock and Sid are excited because it's Saturday and tonight they're having a night out on the town.

400

Sid has arranged a blind date for Hancock and if they play their cards right it will be their best evening for years.

After collecting their suits from the dry cleaners, they discover that Mrs Cravatte, Hancock's housekeeper, hasn't washed their shirts. There is no alternative but to nip down the local launderette. Hancock hasn't a clue how to work the machines, which explains why his shirt comes out ripped to shreds.

With no shirt, Hancock suggests Sid goes out alone, but because it's a double date, it's imperative Hancock turns up, even if that means arriving at East Cheam's Classic cinema disguised as a 'bourgeois beatnik' covered in shaving plasters. Not surprisingly, his appearance frightens off every girl they try chatting up. But when they try their luck with a couple of WPCs, they end up being nicked.

8. The Tycoon

Recorded at Studio 1, Riverside Studios, Fri. 6/11/59.
First transmission: Fri. 13/11/59, 8.30 p.m.
Audience figure: 11.2 million

CAST:

William Kendall	Sir Thomas Edgington
Ralph Nossek	Company secretary
Mark Singleton	Businessman
Robert Dorning	Art gallery man
James Bulloch	Tony's dentist
Hugh Lloyd	Secretary
Alec Bregonzi	Tony's tailor
Ivor Raymonde	Tony's barber

John Vyvyan	Bootblack
Una Trimming	Tony's manicurist
Rosamund Lesley	1st secretary
Anne Marryott	2nd secretary
Anne Reid	3rd secretary
Bernice Swanson	4th secretary
Harold Kasket	Aristotle Thermopolae
Bob Marshall	
Leonard Graham	Aides

Also: Glyn Jones, Patrick Desmond, William E. Rayner, Robert Young, Edna Stevens, Shirley Patterson, Susan Kay, Ann Harper, Beatrix Carter, Brian Vaughan, Ryan Jelfe, Stanley Paige, Martin White, Eric Martin, Bernard Dudley, Robert Croudace, Rex Rashley, Charles Western, Charles Gilbert, Royston Tickner, John Caesar, Philip Howard and Frank Littlewood

Hancock is having a bad time on the stock market: his shares have hit rock bottom and he fears financial ruin; feeling suicidal, he's ready to end it all by leaping from his window, even though it's on the ground floor. He finally decides to attend the shareholders' meeting of the East Cheam Building Society, in which he only owns two shares, because it's the only investment performing well. During the meeting, Hancock nods off and dreams he's a successful entrepreneur who takes over the Society as well as half the world; but even in his dreams he can't escape Sid.

9. Spanish Interlude

Recorded at Studio 1, Riverside Studios, Sat. 14/11/59.

First transmission: Fri. 20/11/59, 8.30 p.m.
Audience figure: 10.5 million

CAST:

Annabelle Lee	1st girl
Paddy Edwards	2nd girl
Lynne Cole	3rd girl
David Lander	Spanish waiter
Brian Worth	Nightclub manager
John Vyvyan	A matador
Ronnie Brody	English bullfighter
Patrick Milner	
Herbert Nelson	Bullring attendants
Astor Sklair	
Pat O'Meara	
Lionel Wheeler	Matadors
Tom McCall	Pianist

Also: (nightclub patrons) Betty Mowles, Carole Brett, Judi Vague, Carmen Capaldi, Nancy Adams, Heather Russell, Astrid Anderson, Colin Dudley, Wilfred Greves, Jos Tregoningo, Alan Vicars, Norman Miller, Ray Marioni, Donald Walker and Roy Spence

Hancock is getting increasingly depressed by the dearth of decent acting jobs being offered; for the last engagement Sid promised him a leading role in a film, only for Hancock to end up standing around in the rain dressed as a raja advertising an Indian restaurant. When Hancock remarks that it might be time to look elsewhere for an agent, Sid tells him not to be hasty and promises a nice, juicy part next time; but his luck doesn't change and his next job is promoting a Chinese restaurant.

Hancock doesn't like to hear the truth when Sid

403

is frank and explains that no one is interested in hiring him any more; he suggests Hancock makes a new start abroad, beginning at the Las Flamenco nightclub in Madrid. Naïvely, neither Sid nor Hancock considered the language barrier, and an inability to speak the native tongue turns their show into a sham when they have to employ an interpreter. The manager gives them notice and they have to raise enough cash for the return journey, so when Sid is presented with the chance of earning £500, he's not prepared to throw it away by telling Hancock he's set him up to be a bullfighter.

10. Football Pools

Recorded at Studio 1, Riverside Studios, Mon. 23/11/59.
First transmission: Fri. 27/11/59, 8.30 p.m.
Audience figure: 10.1 million

CAST:

Robert Dorning	Rosette seller
Hugh Lloyd	Cashier
Sidney Vivian	1st spectator
Laurie Webb	2nd spectator
Richard Statman	Spectator
John Vyvyan	Footballer
Alec Bregonzi	1st football player
Lionel Wheeler	2nd football player
Patrick Milner	3rd football player
Herbert Nelson	4th football player
Philip Carr	5th football player and announcer
Tom Clegg	Goalkeeper

James Cliston
  Edward Willis
  Ryan Jelfe
  David Bell   Footballers

Also: (spectators) John Caesar, Philip Howard, Peter Jesson, Kenneth Alan Taylor, Ronald Mayer, Keith Goodman, Peter Burden, Edmund Dring, Brian Pollitt, Norman Coburn, Michael Lehrer, Leslie Wright, Laurence Archer, Jerry James, Robert Weedon, Charles Gilbert, Alan Darling, Robert Pitt, Roger Williams and Louis Hasler

Ever since Sid was refused a licence for a betting office, he has been opposed to all forms of gambling, and tells Hancock he's wasting his time completing the pools. But when Hancock marks off seven score draws, he become hysterical, though it's his final fixture, an evening kick-off, which will decide his fate.

Sid and Hancock decide to watch the deciding match, Chelsea versus East Cheam United, and find themselves supporting both teams, praying for a draw, much to the consternation of the home crowd surrounding them.

With Chelsea winning 3–1 at half-time, Sid and Hancock, desperate for the draw, take matters into their own hands. They visit the Chelsea dressing room, pretending to be club officials, and change the players' positions, leaving them in unfamiliar roles. The trouble is, the team loses 15–3, and it's a low pools payout for Hancock.

SERIES 6

1. The Cold

Recorded at Studio 1, Riverside Studios, Fri. 19/2/60.
First transmission: Fri. 4/3/60, 8.30 p.m.
Audience figure: 10.1 million

CAST:

John Le Mesurier	Doctor Callaghan
Hugh Lloyd	Patient
Patricia Hayes	Mrs Cravatte
Anne Marryott	Nurse
Richard Statman	Patient
Herbert Nelson	Boxer
Tom Clegg	Boxer's manager

Hancock is suffering from a heavy cold and is relying on 'Cough It Up Cold Capsules' and other dubious treatments to aid his recovery. Sid doesn't approve of such actions, regarding everything Hancock is taking as useless.

While Sid has avoided catching a cold this year, Hancock has endured six and he's feeling peeved and sorry for himself. In desperation, he asks Mrs Cravatte for help; when her suggestions of herbal remedies fail, he turns to Doctor Callaghan, but he's just as useless and is suffering from a cold himself. As a last resort, Hancock accepts Sid's offer of organising a keep fit routine for him; before long, although he has shifted the cold he is suffering more ailments than before, including blisters and sprains, which leaves him praying for the return of his cold.

2. The Missing Page

Recorded at Studio 1, Riverside Studios, Fri. 26/2/60.
First transmission: Fri. 11/3/60, 8.30 p.m.
Audience figure: 9.8 million

CAST:

Hugh Lloyd	Librarian
George Coulouris	Mr Proctor
Gordon Phillott	British Museum librarian
Totti Truman Taylor	Woman in library
Peggy Ann Clifford	2nd woman in library
Joanna Douglas	3rd woman in library
Kenneth Kove	
Gibb McLaughlin	
John Vyvyan	
Alec Bregonzi	
James Bulloch	
Frank Littlewood	
Ray Grover	Men in library

Hancock is engrossed in the murder mystery, *Lady Don't Fall Backwards* which he has borrowed from the library. Even Sid, a reluctant reader, is anxious to establish the identity of the murderer, so both are incensed when they discover that the final page is missing. Desperate to find out who committed the murder, they search for another copy of the book, but the hunt is equally frustrating.

3. The Emigrant

Recorded at Studio 1, Riverside Studios, Fri. 12/2/60.
First transmission: Fri. 18/3/60, 8.35 p.m.

Audience figure: 10.6 million

CAST:

Brian Oulton	Australia House clerk
Gordon Sterne	Canada House clerk
Joe Enrikie	India House clerk
Alec Bregonzi	Baffin Land clerk
David Lander	Tramp steamer captain
John Bramley	Eskimo

Also: Richard Statman, Hugh Lloyd, Edna Stevens, Louise Stafford, Anne Marryott, Joanna Douglas, Charles Julian, Philip Howard, John Scott Martin, Herbert Nelson, Samuel Manseray, John Vyvyan, Harry Robins and Johnnie Lee

The council has increased Hancock's rates by sixpence a week, infuriating him so much that he decides to emigrate to a land of fresh opportunities, where there's an incentive to prosper. The trouble is, deciding where to go. He fancies himself down under or even in Canada— he's spoilt for choice. He decides the way to pick is to close his eyes, plonk his finger down on to a map and see where it lands. He wasn't expecting Baffin Land, and finally settles for Australia.

Down at Australia House, proceedings don't go as planned. After a tortuous meeting with an official he decides that perhaps Canada is a better bet, but does his best to annoy the official there, too. After trying every embassy in London, a dejected Hancock returns to Railway Cuttings. Still determined to emigrate, he has little choice but to turn to Sid for help. Knowing Sid was involved in illegal people-trafficking, he asks if he'll get him abroad. Unfortunately Hancock doesn't know the whereabouts of his future home until it's too late and he ends up in Baffin Land.

4. The Reunion Party

Recorded at Studio 1, Riverside Studios, Fri. 4/3/60.
First transmission: Fri. 25/3/60, 8.30 p.m.
Audience figure: 10.3 million

CAST:

Sidney Vivian	Licensee
Hugh Lloyd	Smudger Smith
Eileen Way	Mavis Smith
Cardew Robinson	Chalky White
Laurie Webb	Man in off-licence
Clive Dunn	Ginger Johnson
Robert Dorning	Scrounger Harris

It's fifteen years since Hancock last saw his old army pals, so he decides to hold a reunion for his three best mates from the 3rd East Cheam Light Horse. Inseparable and adventurous, they were known as the Four Musketeers, and Hancock is looking forward to reliving old times with the help of a few pints and a bite to eat.

But Hancock should have realised you can't relive the past: Smudger turns up preferring tea to alcohol and has his overbearing wife, Mavis, in tow, while Ginger sports a bald pate, opts for a sherry and isn't hungry because he's just eaten. Hancock prays that the evening will be saved by the arrival of Chalky White, who always had his mates in stitches with his *risqué* stories, but he's become a man of the cloth.

With nothing in common any more, he bids farewell to his old friends, but before he can shut the door, an uninvited guest turns up.

5. Sid in Love

Recorded at Studio 1, Riverside Studios, Fri. 4/3/60.
First transmission: Fri. 1/4/60, 8.30 p.m.
Audience figure: 10.9 million

CAST:

Joan Heal	The clippie
Hugh Lloyd	Bert
Robert Dorning	Bus driver
James Bulloch	Policeman
John Vyvyan	
John Bramley	Men in fish shop
Vi Stevens	Fish shop proprietress
Peggy Ann Clifford	Woman in bus
Douglas Robinson	Mr Smallpiece
Denny Dayviss	Cynthia Smallpiece

Also: Drummond Marvin, Philip Decker, Guy Grahame, Alfred Hirst, John Clevedon, Norman Hartley, Leslie Wright, Louis Hasler, James Cliston, Martin White, Judy Roger, Rosamund Tattersall, Diana Walker, Beatrix Carter, Mary Power, Viera Shelley, Ann Jay, Lizanne Marshall, Alison McMurdo, Jeanette Edwards and Anne Marryott.

Sid is smitten with a clippie on the number 93 bus but can't pluck up the courage to exploit the situation. Hancock offers to help and catches the next bus with Sid, but his attempts at matchmaking

410

end in chaos, especially when the clippie's husband, who happens to be the driver, makes an appearance.

6. The Babysitters

Recorded at Studio 1, Riverside Studios, Fri. 25/3/60.
First transmission: Fri. 8/4/60, 8.30 p.m.
Audience figure: 12.8 million

CAST:

Terence Alexander	Mr Frobisher
Annabelle Lee	Mrs Frobisher
Herbert Nelson	1st burglar
Alec Bregonzi	2nd burglar
Robert Dorning	Police inspector
Patrick Milner	1st policeman
Michael Earl	2nd policeman

The squalid conditions of Railway Cuttings are starting to get Hancock and Sid down, so in an attempt to share the comfort and luxury enjoyed by those more fortunate, they sign up with a local babysitting agency. Their first assignment is looking after the Frobishers' baby boy, but far from caring for the toddler, they're more concerned with enjoying the grub, cigars and fancy TV. They make themselves so comfortable, they fall asleep, and are oblivious to the burglars who strip the place of all its goodies.

7. The Ladies' Man

Recorded at Studio 1, Riverside Studios, Fri.

1/4/60.
First transmission: Fri. 15/4/60, 8.35 p.m.
Audience figure: 12.7 million

CAST:

Brian Oulton	Gregory Chandler
Robert Dorning	Receptionist
Elizabeth Fraser	Muriel
Annabelle Lee	Edie
Laura Thurlow	Miss Pringle
Honor Shepherd	Woman
Laurie Webb	Bus conductor
Barbara Evans	Dancer
Gwenda Ewan	The Hon. Susan Plunket
Arthur Mullard	
George Crowther	
Herbert Nelson	
Harry Robins	
Stan Simmons	
John Vyvyan	Charm School pupils
Bert Waller	Pianist (not in vision)
Eleanor Fazan	Choreographer (not in vision)

Hancock is out on a double-date, but while Sid is striking up a relationship, Hancock is struggling with blonde-haired Muriel; ultimately, he ruins the evening for both of them and feels even worse when one of the girls tells Sid that Hancock is cramping Sid's style.

Determined to do something about it, he enrols at the Mayfair Charm School for Men to learn everything from ballroom dancing to articulation. Graduating with a diploma under his arm, with his newly acquired confidence he entertains Miss

Plunket, an heiress. Everything is running smoothly until Sid arrives home and steals his girl, resulting in Hancock ripping up his diploma in disgust.

8. The Photographer

Recorded at Studio 1, Riverside Studios, Fri. 15/4/60.
First transmission: Fri. 22/4/60, 8.30 p.m.
Audience figure: 10.8 million

CAST:

William Kendall	Businessman
Herbert Hare	Man in restaurant
Hugh Lloyd	Photographer's assistant
Robert Dorning	Manager of restaurant
Totti Truman Taylor	Woman in restaurant
Laura Thurlow	Secretary
Joanna Douglas	Waitress
Edward Malin	Mr Dimwitty
Murray Kash	1st tourist
Laurie Webb	2nd tourist
Anthony Shirvell	3rd tourist
Michael Earl	
Kenneth Firth	
Philip Howard	Waiters
John Vyvyan	Man in restaurant
Ann Bassett	Waitress

Also: Louise Stafford, May Hamilton, Jennifer Thorne, Una Trimming, Cynthia Marshall, Joy Leggat, Nicholas Hay, Jack Leonard, Keith Goodman, Albert Grant, Norman Kaye and Gavin Reed

Hancock has persuaded a reluctant Sid to pose for

a photo session. For fifteen years, he's prayed that his local camera club will accept one of his pictures for their Festival of Photography, but hasn't been successful, which Sid blames on his outdated equipment. When the camera blows up and nearly sets the house alight, Hancock has to buy a newer model.

Enamoured of his purchase, he becomes a nuisance at a restaurant, roaming around the tables taking unauthorised pictures of other diners; finally, one man, out on the town with his mistress, becomes furious and accuses Hancock of taking snaps to send to his wife. After this commotion, Hancock and Sid are thrown out.

With the first instalment of the hire purchase agreement imminent, Hancock has to earn some money if he's to keep his camera. Sid suggests staging a human interest story so he can sell the photos to the unsuspecting newspapers. It's a worried Hancock, though, who finds himself talked into standing on a high ledge threatening to jump. Sid, down below, is ready to catch the shot, but discovers that Hancock forgot to load the film. Other people have their cameras at the ready and rush off to cash in on their exclusive photos.

Then, Sid sees an advert in a paper offering a £1,000 prize for an underwater photo, so it's off to Brighton for Hancock to find a giant octopus. It's not long before the lifeboat is called out.

9. The East Cheam Centenary

Recorded at Studio 1, Riverside Studios, Fri. 22/4/60.
First transmission: Fri. 29/4/60, 8.30 p.m.

414

Audience figure: 10.8 million

CAST:

Robert Dorning	Mayor of East Cheam
Cameron Hall	1st councillor
Hugh Lloyd	2nd councillor
James Bulloch	3rd councillor
Eddie Malin	4th councillor
Lala Lloyd	1st woman councillor
Evelyn Lund	2nd woman councillor
Brian Oulton	BBC Outside Broadcast director
Leslie Perrins	Producer
Anne Marryott	Secretary
Sidney Vivian	Peanut man
John Snagge	As himself
Astor Sklair	Scotsman/Scoutmaster
Sylvia Osborn	Marcher/Britannia
Frank Littlewood	Councillor
George Crowther	Marcher/road sweeper
Herbert Nelson	Marcher/medieval soldier
John Bramley	Marcher/medieval soldier
John Vyvyan	Marcher/Father Time
Michael Earl	Cameraman
James Langley	
Michael Phillips	
John Bosch	Boy Scouts

After much deliberation, the East Cheam Centenary Committee decide to hold a carnival to celebrate the borough's centenary. Hancock is convinced his theatrical experience means he's the ideal candidate to organise events.

Sid and Hancock decide to try and make some money out of the procession by selling exclusive

415

rights to the BBC for 3,000 guineas; but when the Mayor demands the procession travels up Woodland Park Road, where he happens to live, Hancock becomes suspicious. His worst fears are confirmed when the Mayor takes a phone call from an independent television station—he's already sold the rights to the carnival, leaving Hancock no choice but to organise his own. It turns into a sham, with a handful of friends playing a multitude of characters; the BBC soon find out and Hancock and Sid face legal action.

10. The Poison Pen Letters

Recorded at Studio 1, Riverside Studios, Fri. 29/4/60.
First transmission: Fri. 6/5/60, 7.30 p.m.
Audience figure: 10.3 million

CAST:

Patricia Hayes	Mrs Cravatte
John Welsh	Police sergeant
Anna Churcher	A woman
Totti Truman Taylor	Eccentric spinster
Andrew Lieven	Police constable

In Hancock's morning post, hidden amongst an invitation to a local slide show and some fan mail, is a nasty poison pen letter. Its arrival upsets Hancock and when more arrive he admits to Sid that it's getting him down. He racks his brains to establish who would have a grudge against him.

Feeling he has no alternative, Hancock shows the letters to the police; after investigating, it's confirmed the letters were all posted in the box

416

right outside 23 Railway Cuttings, leading Hancock to accuse Sid of writing them.

The police agree to keep an eye on the post box, and for a while several people are suspects, including Mrs Cravatte, who is spotted posting a letter. But when it turns out to be nothing more than her footbal pools coupon, they're none the wiser. Finally, the culprit is caught when Hancock sleepwalks and scribbles a letter to himself. A complete rest is recommended, but just when Hancock is making his travel arrangements to get away for a while, a letter turns up for Sid.

SERIES 7

The seventh series was retitled *Hancock* and did not include Sid James.

1. The Bedsitter

Recorded at Studio 4, Television Centre, Fri. 5/5/61.
First transmission: Fri. 26/5/61, 8 p.m.
Audience figure: 14.4 million

CAST:

Michael Aspel   As himself

It may be a change of scenery for Hancock since his move to a bedsit in Earls Court, but life's just the same. He burns his lip with a cigarette and struggles to find suitable medication, then opts for alternative medicine with a dab of butter. But life looks rosier when Joyce calls. Although she wants Fred, the previous resident, Tony strikes up a conversation and gets invited to a party. After dusting off his medallion, jeans and black shirt, he applies an assortment of aftershaves only to receive a further call from Joyce announcing the party's off and she's traced Fred. So it's back to his books for poor old Hancock.

2. The Bowmans

Recorded at Studio 4, Television Centre, Fri. 26/5/61.
First transmission: Fri. 2/6/61, 8 p.m.
Audience figure: 11.3 million

CAST:

Brian Oulton	Dan Bowman
Constance Chapman	Gladys Bowman
Meadows White	George
Peter Glaze	The dog
Alec Bregonzi	Fred
Gwenda Ewan	Diane
Ralph Wilson	Doctor
Patrick Cargill	Producer
William Sherwood	Julian Court
Victor Platt	Postman
Hugh Lloyd	Florist
Bruno Barnabe	BBC official
Dennis Chinnery	Reporter

Also: Charles Young, James Fitzgerald, Bruce Wightman, Richard Carpenter, Bernard Hunter, Richard Simpson, Joan White, Charles Gilbert, Robert Manning, James Ure, Frank Littlewood, Laurence Hepworth, Andre Ducane, Carl Lacy, Arthur Lown, Peter Chault, Kevin Davies, David Franks, Simon Moore, Aubrey Danvers Walker, Stuart Anderson, Olwen Coates, Anne Kennedy,

Antonita Dias, Carmen Dias, Moira Flynn, Caroline Aylett, Sian Price, Norman Hartley and Donald Heath.

Hancock has been playing Joshua in *The Bowmans*, a successful radio series, for five years, causing mayhem for fellow cast members with his ad-libs and altering of dialogue. When he's given the script for the next programme, he's dismayed to find his character is being killed off by falling into a threshing machine. Hancock is shocked, believing his acting talents are a cut above the rest, but the director defends the decision by explaining there is a decline in the character's popularity.

After making a meal of his death scene, Hancock is asked to leave the studio. His confidence takes a further battering when he's rejected for a part in *Hamlet*, but when he lands work in commercials for Grimsby Pilchards, he carries the can for poor sales figures and is shown the door.

His luck changes for the best when the BBC receive thousands of complaints from angry listeners of *The Bowmans*, all upset at Joshua being killed off. Suddenly he's back in demand and the recipient of expensive cigars and cheesy grins from BBC executives desperate to reunite him with the show. When he returns as Ben Merryweather, Joshua's twin brother, he's the one who wields the power.

3. The Radio Ham

Recorded at Studio 4, Television Centre, Fri. 19/5/61.
First transmission: Fri. 9/6/61, 8 p.m.

Audience figure: 11.5 million

Bernard Peake
  Annie Leake   Neighbours
Edwin Richfield
  Bernard Hunter Policemen
Andrew Faulds   'Mayday'
John Bluthal
  Geoffrey Matthews
  Honor Shepherd
  Geoffrey Lewis   Other radio voices

Hancock has turned into a short wave radio fanatic ever since splashing out £500 on equipment enabling him to communicate with like-minded people around the globe. Yet although he's talking to acquaintances from as far afield as Brazil and Japan, he craves a little excitement in his life: his wish comes true when he picks up a distress call from a sailor, whose boat is sinking 300 miles off the African coast.

Vital minutes are lost when Hancock's pencil breaks, he loses the wavelength, has to assuage his neighbours' anger and deal with a power cut and a radio malfunction. When a replacement valve finally arrives, he discovers that the sinking sailor has been rescued, thanks to Hancock's mate in Tokyo, preventing Hancock from becoming the hero.

4. The Lift

Recorded at Studio 4, Television Centre, Fri. 12/5/61.

First transmission: Fri. 16/6/61, 8 p.m.
Audience figure: 11 million

CAST

Charles Lloyd Pack	Mr Humphries
Diana King	Girl
Jack Watling	Producer
John Le Mesurier	Air Marshal
Noel Howlett	Vicar
Colin Gordon	Doctor
Jose Reed	Mrs Humphries
Hugh Lloyd	Lift assistant
William Sherwood	Maintenance engineer
James Fitzgerald	
Ralph Wilson	Firemen

Hancock has been waiting ages to catch the lift at the BBC. Fed up, he opts for the stairs, but just at that moment it finally arrives at the eighth floor. He races back to the lift, by which time others have poured in, and Hancock is told by the lift attendant that there is no more room. After much arguing, he's allowed in but the attendant isn't accepting any responsibility because the lift is only supposed to carry eight people, not nine.

En route to the ground floor, the lift gets stuck and as it's gone midnight, the building is empty. Everyone prepares for a long ordeal, made worse by Hancock's incessant chatter. At the end of a terrible night, the doors are finally opened. But it's not the end of Hancock's time in the lift.

5. The Blood Donor

Recorded at Studio 4, Television Centre, Fri. 2/6/61.
First transmission: Fri. 23/6/61, 8 p.m.
Audience figure: 10.3 million

CAST:

June Whitfield	Nurse
Patrick Cargill	Doctor
Peggy Ann Clifford	
Frank Thornton	
Hugh Lloyd	Patients
Anne Marryott	2nd nurse
Jean Marlow	3rd nurse
James Ottoway	2nd doctor

Also: Kenneth Cowan, Frances St Barbe-West, Michael Earl and Albert Grant

Hancock attends a blood donation session at the South London General Hospital. It's the first time he's given any of his life fluid away, so it comes as a nasty shock when the doctor tells him he'll be donating a pint. Naïvely, Hancock worries that giving away so much will leave him with an empty arm and starts having second thoughts; but when he discovers his blood group is AB negative, one of the rarest around, he's full of self-importance and is prepared to help the nation. He also enjoys telling everyone within earshot about his worth to mankind.

6. The Succession—Son And Heir

Recorded at Studio 4, Television Centre, Fri.

9/6/61.
First transmission: Fri. 30/6/61, 8 p.m.
Audience figure: 10.6 million

CAST:

Myrtle Reed	Olive Hobbs
June Whitfield	Veronica Stillwell (the beatnik)
Gwenda Ewan	Pamela Ffortescue-Ffrench

Hancock is weighing up his lot in life: he's 35 and has achieved nothing; as far as he's concerned, his life story would make a very slim volume. He muses about how he'd make sure his son—if he had one—didn't make the same mistakes as him.

Deciding it's time he fathered a son in order to continue the Hancock dynasty, he has to find a wife, so he turns to his little black book and sifts through the entries until he's found three possibles: Olive Hobbs, Veronica Stillwell and Pamela Ffortescue-Ffrench.

He invites Olive to dinner at his house, but she fails the examination when it comes to intellectual chat, and after telling Hancock she'd call a son Elvis, he reaches for her coat and ushers her out of the door.

Thinking brains are more important than the dolly bird look, Hancock invites Veronica, a vicar's daughter, who sits reading a higher metaphysics textbook while her host cooks his frozen four-course meal. Being vegetarian she rejects the food, and shocks Hancock by telling him she loathes kids and only accepts them because they're essential for the continuation of mankind. When she admits she's against marriage and frightens Hancock with

423

her modern outlook on life, she's sent packing, too.

It looks like the aristocratic Pamela is the one for Hancock, especially when she adores his meal, his bedsit and agrees to get married. The trouble is, her diary is so jampacked there won't be time for children.

Hancock's troubles worsen when the other two girls turn up at his house stating they're prepared to change their views, marry and have the child Hancock craves. Realising that perhaps he doesn't want a kid that much after all, he lets the girls fight it out while he slips away for some peace and quiet.

Unheard Radio Script: 'The Counterfeiter'

Only one radio script was never broadcast, 'The Counterfeiter'. It's nearly fifty years since Alan Simpson typed the final words 'Play Out', signifying the episode had come to an end and that the closing theme should begin. When I asked Ray Galton and Alan Simpson for their permission to reproduce the unheard script in this book, they took the opportunity to read their long-forgotten piece of work, which in its early form still includes corrections, insertions and deletions. Although with the passage of time they're unsure why the work was rejected, Alan commented: 'The interesting thing is that it's the only script where Tony wasn't in it for long stretches; there are two or three scenes, lasting two or three pages, where he's not in it. Bill Kerr had a bigger part that week. Whether that had anything to do with it I don't know.'

TONY: I'm sorry, Andrée, I've had just about enough. He's got to go. I'm not putting up with it any longer.

ANDRÉE: You've been saying that for the last two years.

TONY: I know, but this time he's gone too far. I had the police around this morning.

ANDRÉE: What's he done now?

425

TONY: For the last six months he's been going round the Labour Exchange to collect dole money twice a week.

ANDRÉE: Well?

TONY: On Thursdays he's been giving *my* name. It's not good enough. A man in my position cannot afford to have people think he's out of work. It's probably gone all round the business. Hancock's on the dole. Ted Ray, Jimmy Edwards, all that lot having a good old laugh. You see, they'll be doing charity concerts for me at the Albert Hall.

ANDRÉE: Oh don't be silly, of course they won't.

TONY: They'd better, I've had the posters printed. And Kerr's not getting any of it. He's had enough of my money. I've kept that man for years. He'll do anything rather than go out to work.

ANDRÉE: Oh I don't know, Bill has done a bit of work this year.

TONY: Work. Three minutes in *The Dam Busters* and that was his lot. He was exhausted.

ANDRÉE: I didn't know Bill was in *The Dam Busters*.

TONY: Neither did anybody else. I turned round and asked somebody for a light and he'd been and gone.

ANDRÉE: What part did Bill play?

TONY: (*Disinterested*) I don't know, the bomb I think, I wasn't looking. And there's another thing. Look at the social circles he moves in. He gets a strange delight out of mixing with these people. Sidney James, Edwardian Fred, Briefcase Bertie, Light Fingered Louis. How he never got called as a witness in the Jack Spot case I'll never know.

ANDRÉE: (*Amused*) There's nothing wrong with

426

Bill. He just likes to enjoy life. He's young and irresponsible . . .

TONY: He's a layabout.

ANDRÉE: He isn't really. He just doesn't believe in taking life too seriously. He's just naturally gay and light hearted. He likes to get as much as he can out of things.

TONY: Especially me. He's got no sense of responsibility. Wine, women and song, that's all he thinks about.

ANDRÉE: The trouble with you is that you're an old plodder. A stick in the mud. An old fuddy duddy.

TONY: Fuddy duddy? It's true that I'm serious minded, but on the right occasions I can let my hair down with the best of them . . . as anyone who goes to the Potters Bar croquet club socials will tell you. You should have seen me on VJ Night. I had a paper hat on. Of course, a couple of draught bitters and I go berserk. But that sort of thing is all right in its place. The rest of the time one must be a respectable, sober minded member of the community. One has a debt to society . . . and Bill's is mounting up daily.

ANDRÉE: Well what do you propose to do about it?

TONY: Either he gets a job, or out he goes. He's been a non-paying guest here for five years now . . . and it's got to stop. I shall tell him straight. As soon as we've finished tea, I shall go straight upstairs and get him out of bed.

BILL: (*Off mike. Singing*) I'm wild again, beguiled again, a simpering, whimpering child again, bewitched, bothered and bewildered, am I . . .

TONY: Hallo, something happened, he's up. The bedclothes must have fallen off.

(*Door opens*)

BILL: (*Singing*) In an old Australian homestead . . . ah, good morning Tub.

TONY: Good evening William.

BILL: Oh . . . yeah, so it is. I must have been in bed for three days. I wonder what got me up?

TONY: Hunger?

BILL: Yeah that was it. I'm starving. Why didn't you bring me something up on a tray? I could have died up there.

TONY: No, you wouldn't. You haven't done a thing to help me since you've been here.

BILL: (*Yawns*) Oh boy, I'm tired. I think I'll grab some dinner and turn in again. Andrée, pop over the pub and fill my hot water bottle up will you?

TONY: Oi . . . Oi . . . Rip Van Winkle, a word in your ear.

BILL: Yeah?

TONY: You can take that bib off, the restaurant's closed.

BILL: Huh?

TONY: You're having no more free meals in this house. From now on, no pay . . . no eat.

BILL: Tub . . . you're joking?

TONY: Put that crust down.

BILL: Tub, what's got into you?

TONY: I'll tell you. I'm finished. I'm not keeping you in idleness a minute longer. It's hard enough keeping this house going. Rent, rates, food, running

(*line missing in original script*)

Not a very dainty dish to set before the Labour Exchange.

BILL: Yeah, I'd be more trouble than I'm worth. I'll just go back to bed and keep out of everybody's way, huh?

428

TONY: Sit down. Your boots are not going to touch those pillows again until you get a job. You will present yourself at the Labour Exchange first thing in the morning in a clean collar and fresh boots.

BILL: What's wrong with my usual gear?

TONY: Oh, please. Supposing you get a job in the City. How could you walk into the Corn Exchange in an Hawaiian shirt and jeans?

BILL: Well. I can see I'm going to have a tough day tomorrow. I'd better go back to bed and get some rest.

TONY: (*Calling*) Make the most of it. It'll be your last chance to lie in bed. And don't you dare come back tomorrow night without a job.

(*Door shuts*)

TONY: William.

(*Door opens*)

BILL: Yeah?

TONY: (*Patiently*) Put that crust back.

(*Orchestra link*)

(*Crowds at Labour Exchange*)

KENNETH: . . . and if you tell the manager the Labour Exchange sent you, I'm sure he'll be able to offer you suitable employment. Next.

BILL: Morning, Charlie.

KENNETH: Oh, hello, William. You're a bit early this morning. Just in time for some tea. I'll put the kettle on. Oh, by the way, we've got a little surprise for you. I'll just get my other assistants. (*Calls*) I say chaps, William's arrived. All together now . . .

OMNES: (*Sing*) Happy birthday to you, happy birthday to you, happy birthday dear William, happy birthday to you.

429

BILL: Say, what's all this in aid of?

KENNETH: You've been with us seven years today, congratulations. And here's a greetings telegram from Sir Walter Monckton.

BILL: Oh how nice. Thank you, fellows.

OMNES: Speech. Speech.

BILL: (*Embarrassed laugh*) Well . . . I'd just like to say thank you very much, and as your oldest customer, I'd like to take this opportunity of paying tribute to the wonderful treatment and kindness that has always been afforded me at this Labour Exchange.

OMNES: (*Embarrassed denials*)

BILL: No, no I mean it, fellows. I've patronised Labour Exchanges all over the world, but nowhere else have I known such service and hospitality. I would never have been able to stay out of work so long if it hadn't been for your help. Charlie there . . . dear kind-hearted old Charlie. Always sends me a postcard when you've run out of jobs and it's safe for me to come round. And Cyril . . . lovable old Cyril, always a kind word and a bowl of soup waiting for me on a cold day. And Percy . . . dear friend Percy always a couple of bob over the odds on the dole money whenever he could afford it. A man doesn't easily forget kindness like that . . . and believe me, fellows, I'm going to miss you all.

KENNETH: (*Worried*) Miss us? I don't understand you, William? You . . . you can't mean . . .

BILL: (*Grave*) Yes Charlie . . . even in the midst of laughter, there is tragedy. I've got to get a job.

OMNES: (*Horrified gasps and cries*)

KENNETH: Smelling salts, quickly, smelling salts. Poor Cyril. It's his heart, you know. Sudden shocks . . . He shouldn't be working . . . but you know William. This . . . this terrible thing. This, this job. You can't leave us now. Don't all the good times we've had together mean anything to you? You're joking . . . say you're joking.

BILL: No Charlie, it's true. I've got to get a job.

KENNETH: (*Hopefully*) It's only temporary. You'll come back to us after the Christmas rush.

BILL: No, Charlie, it's . . . it's for keeps.

(*Orchestra: sad music under*)

KENNETH: So it's come to this. I suppose I shouldn't be surprised really, it . . . it had to come . . . it couldn't last . . . we've been too happy. I suppose I . . . (*Sudden fear*) William . . . William, it's not . . . it's not . . . oh no, no, it couldn't be that.

BILL: What?

KENNETH: It's . . . it's not somebody else. It's not another Labour Exchange that's come between us?

BILL: No, Charlie, no of course not.

KENNETH: Oh thank heavens. I . . . I don't think I could have stood that. (*Eagerly*) It's the seven-year itch, that's what it is, isn't it. It happens every seven years . . . you get the sudden urge to go out to work . . . but it wears off. You'll come back. We can start all over again.

BILL: Charlie no . . . stop deceiving yourself. There's nothing I can do about it. I've got to go out to work . . . for good.

KENNETH: All right then. If you've made up your mind to go, I can't stop you. O cursed be the serpent that drags thee from thy family's bosom to serve a foreign master . . . Shelley.

BILL: Well . . . goodbye Charlie.

KENNETH: No. Not goodbye. Au revoir. Here, take this address. They'll look after you. They're a good firm. The least I can do is give you a job with which you'll be happy. And now, go quickly. Don't look back. Don't make it any harder. Goodbye William.

(*Door shuts*)

KENNETH: (*Calls plaintively*) Bill . . . Bill . . . (*Breaks down and sobs, then very brokenly*) . . . he's gone.

(*Orchestra: up to dramatic climax*)

TONY: Ah Andrée, is dinner ready? It's nearly one o'clock.

ANDRÉE: Just dishing it up, Tony.

TONY: Aha . . . today is an historic occasion, Andrée. Kerr's first day at work. The battle has been won. Oh er . . . this my dinner?

ANDRÉE: No . . . Bill's. I'm just taking it to him.

TONY: Where is he?

ANDRÉE: In bed.

TONY: In bed?

ANDRÉE: He doesn't start till three o'clock.

TONY: What time does he finish?

ANDRÉE: Five-thirty.

TONY: Five . . . what sort of job's that?

ANDRÉE: He washes glasses up at the King's Head.

TONY: I'm not having it. He's not lying in bed all day. That's just the thing I've been trying to stop. I'm not encouraging his laziness. He's going straight back to that Labour Exchange and get another job. One that starts at a respectable hour in the morning.

(*Orchestra: link*)

KENNETH: . . . well I'm sorry the glass washing wasn't satisfactory William, but here's something that should suit you. Just the sort of thing you're

432

looking for. Start tomorrow morning, nine o'clock.

BILL: Thanks a lot, Charlie. See you.

(*Orchestra: link*)

ANDRÉE: Dinner's ready Tony.

TONY: Ah, good, good. (*Hums*) Ah I'm in a good mood this week. Ha ha, I have enjoyed waking old Kerr up at half past seven every morning. He couldn't get over it. It's the first time he's ever seen the sun on that side of the sky.

ANDRÉE: And he doesn't finish until half past five at night.

TONY: Quite right too. A good hard day's work. He'll soon get used to it.

ANDRÉE: Oh he already has. I saw him hard at work this morning when I went shopping.

TONY: Oh? Where?

ANDRÉE: In the furniture shop.

TONY: What was he doing?

ANDRÉE: He was in bed.

TONY: In bed?

ANDRÉE: Yes. He's in the window, demonstrating mattresses. They're very pleased with him. No shirking. He sleeps all day long.

TONY: (*Angry*) And he comes here and crawls straight up to bed saying he's exhausted. And there's me feeling sorry for him, taking his tea up to him. Wait till he comes in, I'll give him his tea. Right down his throat . . . tray and all.

ANDRÉE: Well at least he's bringing some money in.

TONY: That's not the be-all and end-all. He can't go through life being lazy. If we don't get him out of his bad habits now we never will. He's going to turn his pyjamas in to the manager first thing in the morning and find another job.

433

ANDRÉE: Are you going to send him down to the Labour Exchange again?

TONY: No, he's too well in with them. The next job he'd get in the research department of a sleeping pill factory. No . . . *I'm* going to take him out and find him his next job. We'll make sure this time.

(*Orchestra: Link*)

(*Phone bell. Receiver up*)

KENNETH: Hallo. Sidney James Duplicating and Printing Services Ltd. Edwardian Fred speaking. Oh . . . just a minute. Sid.

SIDNEY: Hallo.

KENNETH: It's Carey Street Albert, the moneylender. He wants to know when the next lot of pound notes'll be ready.

SIDNEY: Give us the phone. Hallo Albert. How many do you want this time? Hundred thousand quid. By Tuesday? Do me a favour. We can't make 'em that quick. It's all handmade stuff here, you know . . . none of this shoddy mass production lark. Anyway, you had fifty thousand last Wednesday, what's the matter with you. You know what Mr Butler said, we've got to cut down on spending. Wait a minute, I'll just check up what we've got in stock. Let's see, there's fifteen hundred in fivers . . . hanging up on the clothes line in the garden. They should be dry by tomorrow. There's four thousand oncers in the oven. They're going to take a bit longer. We haven't got a shilling for the gas. And there's two hundred in ten bobs that Fred hasn't finished ironing yet. That's a grand total of five thousand seven hundred quids' worth. How much? Oooh, to you . . . thirty-five and a tanner including postage. In real money if you please. No, I'm sorry, that's all I've got. I'm short staffed. Too many lads getting thrown in the nick these days. And you can't get the youngsters to go into the business. Too dangerous. Still, I've got an advert in the window for a new printer . . . but until I can find some Charlie to do it, I can't let you have any more.

(*Door opens*)

TONY: Good afternoon.

SIDNEY: Albert, I'll post 'em first thing in the morning. Cheerio.

(*Puts receiver down*)

SIDNEY: Well, well, well, Hancock and Billy the Kerr. What brings you round here?

TONY: We've come in answer to your advert in the window. Smart lad wanted to learn printing trade. No experience necessary. Anything from fourteen days to six months holiday a year guaranteed.

SIDNEY: Yes that's right.

TONY: Well here's the smart lad.

SIDNEY: What Billy?

TONY: Yes. I want him to learn an honest trade.

SIDNEY: How right you are.

TONY: What's the money like?

SIDNEY: Perfect. It fools me sometimes.

TONY: Well . . . what about it, William?

BILL: I don't care what I do as long as I make a lot of money.

SIDNEY: You'll get the push if you don't.

TONY: That's what I like to hear. An employer who insists on his employees having a share in the fruits of his business.

SIDNEY: Certainly. They get some of it in their pay packets.

TONY: I can see you're going to be very happy here,

William. I shall leave you to your work. Oh and Sidney.

SIDNEY: Yeah?

TONY: See he doesn't slack or go to sleep. Keep his head away from anything soft. He'll have his head underneath a newspaper before the bell's stopped ringing.

SIDNEY: Don't worry, I'll watch him. See you.

(*Door shuts*)

BILL: Well now, what do I have to do?

SIDNEY: You're going to be a printer.

BILL: Don't I have to serve an apprenticeship?

SIDNEY: Oh er . . . yes all right then, if you want to. Here's a press. Put a bit of paper in.

BILL: Right.

SIDNEY: Turn the handle.

BILL: Right.

(*Clank of handle turning once*)

BILL: Right.

SIDNEY: Welcome to the printing trade.

BILL: Now wait a minute, I thought an apprenticeship lasted seven years.

SIDNEY: Well normally it does, but I don't think we'll stay open that long. Now . . . all you have to do is turn this handle.

BILL: I've got you.

(*Handle turning*)

SIDNEY: That's it. Now all them bits of green paper coming out, you bundle them up into hundreds and put 'em in the oven. Regulo one.

BILL: What are they?

SIDNEY: Er . . . dance tickets.

BILL: Oh. (*Pause, then suspiciously*) Hey . . . wait a minute.

(*Handle stops turning*)

436

BILL: These dance tickets look like pound notes.

SIDNEY: Never mind, you've only just started, you're bound to make a few mistakes.

BILL: I know what you're up to. You're a forger. You're making counterfeit notes.

SIDNEY: No, Billy, you've got it all wrong.

BILL: Then what are you doing?

SIDNEY: Well um . . . er . . . if I was to tell you they were fourpenny bus tickets for conductors with big ticket racks, you wouldn't believe me, would you?

BILL: No.

SIDNEY: Then I'll have to think of something else, won't I? No, you see what's really happening is we're printing them for another firm.

BILL: Who?

SIDNEY: The Bank of England.

BILL: Don't give me that, they print their own.

SIDNEY: Yes, but they've had a sudden rush. Wilfred Pickles cashed a cheque last week. So they've had to farm out the work. We've all been called in on it. Old Harry down the road . . . the bloke who owns the beer bottle top factory . . . he's doing tanners and bobs . . . and Rooftop Ronnie . . . the bloke who whips the lead from the churches, he's providing his own material and doing the pennies. We're just trying to do our little bit to help the old country.

BILL: Well I don't know, it seems a bit . . .

SIDNEY: Billy, you know me. I wouldn't do anything that was dishonest now, would I?

BILL: Well . . . no, Sid but . . .

SIDNEY: Well then. Just you do your job and stop poking your nose in. Now then . . . I've got some homework for you to do tonight.

BILL: Homework?

SIDNEY: Yeah. Five hundred oncers to be printed, dried and ready for circulation by tomorrow morning. Take a portable printing press home with you and do 'em tonight.

BILL: Right.

SIDNEY: Oh and you'd better give me your insurance cards before you go. I have to put the stamps on for you.

BILL: Yeah OK.

SIDNEY: And stop worrying, everything done here is strictly legal.

BILL: Yeah sure.

SIDNEY: What price stamps do you have on your insurance card?

BILL: Five and fourpence.

SIDNEY: Right. (*Calls*) Fred.

KENNETH: (*Off*) Hallo.

SIDNEY: Roll off another batch of five and fourpenny health stamps. There, now you're stamped up till February 1964. Gooday.

(*Orchestra: Link*)

(*Off mike as if coming from upstairs, clanking of printing press*)

ANDRÉE: (*Calls*) Tony, dinner's ready.

TONY: Eh?

ANDRÉE: (*Louder*) Dinner's ready.

TONY: Oh all right. Coming.

ANDRÉE: (*Calls*) In the front room.

TONY: Eh?

ANDRÉE: (*Louder*) In the front room.

TONY: Oh cor . . . that perishing printing press. You can't hear yourself eat. Every night for a week . . . he's been working in his bedroom up there. At least when he lay in bed all day we got a bit of peace and quiet.

ANDRÉE: It's your own fault. It was you who got this job for him.

TONY: Yes, but I didn't know he was going to work at home. (*Yells*) Ah shut up.

(*Printing press stops*)

TONY: (*Still yelling*) I can't stand any more of it, all this noise, it's driving me off me crust, me nerves are going . . . look at me eyes . . . they're red . . . sunken . . . I can't stand it.

ANDRÉE: (*Quietly*) Tony.

TONY: (*Yells*) What?

ANDRÉE: (*Quietly*) It's stopped.

TONY: (*Yelling*) How can you tell it's stopped with all this noise going on, I tell you . . . I can't stand it, I can't stand it, don't you understand, I can't stand it . . . (*Sobs*)

ANDRÉE: Tony, control yourself, it's stopped.

TONY: (*Shouting*) Well re-start it, you'll never hear acting like this again.

(*Door opens*)

BILL: Well, that's another day's work finished. Aha dinner . . . ah lovely. You're right about this working lark Tub, it's good for you. It gives you an appetite.

TONY: Put my dinner down. Scraping it on to your plate, what's the matter with you.

BILL: Oh I'm sorry, I thought you'd finished.

TONY: I haven't even started yet. That's the size dinners I've been getting since you started work. Andrée thinks you need feeding up. Why don't you go back to bed, you're more trouble than you're worth.

BILL: Ah no, Tub. I'm getting to like work. I wish I'd thought of it before. It makes a man fit . . . I

439

don't feel a bit tired. I think I'll grab a few hours' rest then get up at about two in the morning and do some more.

TONY: Blimey, another plateful of aspirins for breakfast. (*Groans*)

BILL: Ah . . . that was a great meal, Andrée.

ANDRÉE: Bit more pie?

BILL: Thanks.

ANDRÉE: You've had enough, Tony.

BILL: Hey Tub, have you finished already?

TONY: Of course I have. Don't bother about a plate next time, Andrée, just put it on the fork.

BILL: Well seeing you're finished you can nip upstairs and get my fags. I've left them on the printing press.

TONY: Perishing lackey now. Give us twopence and I'll dance for you. (*Mumbling to himself*) Can't even be master in your own home now, I don't know what it's coming to . . .

(*Door shuts, footsteps going upstairs under dialogue*)

TONY: (*Mumbling*) . . . thinks he owns the place just because he's earning a few bob. Me . . . I've had it, I have. Don't get no grub. (*Mimics*) Bit more pie, Bill. You've had enough, Tony. *She'll* have to watch her step as well. I've a good mind to go back to Mum. I might as well, I'm just a lodger here . . .

(*Footsteps stop. Door opens*)

TONY: Now, where's these perishing fags. Ah, here they are. Hallo, you can see he's working. Three and sevenpenny ones. Used to be ten one and fourpence halfpennies and roll up the dog ends. He's getting above himself I . . . hallo, money. A big bundle of pound notes. New ones too. That's not bad for a week's wages. There's more money

440

in this printing game than I thought. I'll have this lot. Back rent. He owes me hundreds . . . all I've done for him in the past. I'll spend this lot before he finds out I've got 'em. That'll teach him to leave money lying around. Ha ha . . . yes . . . I'll nip down the tailors first thing in the morning and get meself a few suits.

(*Orchestra: Link*)

(*Door opens and shuts*)

BILL: Hiya Andrée, dinner ready?

ANDRÉE: (*Unenthusiastically*) Yes, Bill . . . sit down and I'll dish it out.

BILL: Hey, only two places set? Where's Tub?

ANDRÉE: He's in prison.

BILL: He's in prison? I'd better get down there.

ANDRÉE: I wouldn't if I were you. The safest thing you can do is emigrate.

BILL: Why . . . what's it got to do with me?

ANDRÉE: I don't know. But when they dragged him out of the house, I blushed at the things he was calling you.

BILL: I don't understand, what's he done?

ANDRÉE: He bought three suits and a television set with dud pound notes.

BILL: Dud notes? But where did he get them from? I . . . Dud notes. Oh no . . . quick, Andrée, my hat and coat.

(*Orchestra: Link*)

(*Prison cell clanking open*)

ALAN: (*Echo*) Number 1857369.

TONY: Speaking.

ALAN: Number 1857369 . . .

TONY: Just a minute me good man. 1857369 Esquire if you please. I still have me dignity. This is only a temporary arrangement. I'll have you

441

know, I am in direct communication with the Governor.

ALAN: How?

TONY: I've been bashing me tin mug on the bars all night long. I'm expecting to hear of me reprieve on the hot water pipes any minute now.

ALAN: Well anyway, visitor to see you. You've got two minutes.

BILL: Er . . . (*embarrassed laugh*) Hiya, Tub. (*Laugh*)

TONY: (*Sour laugh with him*)

BILL: Er . . . I er I like the suit.

TONY: (*Sarcastically*) Naturally. One of those you bought. I always choose this pattern. Harris tweed arrows and round hat to match. Wait till I get out of this. This is all your fault. Other people go out to work all their lives without causing all this trouble. Making counterfeit notes. The shame of it. They'll take me name off the Windmill discovery board. How could you do it?

BILL: Look Tub, I'm sorry about this, I can explain . . .

TONY: Take this wire net away. Just for thirty seconds. One punch that's all I ask.

BILL: Tub please, don't get upset. Look on the *funny* side of it.

TONY: Har. Har. Right, I've looked. Now what are you going to do about it?

BILL: Believe me Tub, I had no idea those notes were duds. I was taken in.

TONY: So was I . . . four hefty great coppers. Now get me out of here.

BILL: Leave it to me Tub, I'll get this sorted out. You'll be a free man without a stain on your character within twelve hours . . . or my name's not Ned Kelly.

TONY: It's not.

BILL: I'm just covering myself.

(*Orchestra: Link*)

BILL: You've got to do something, Sid. You've got to get Tony out of prison . . . or I'll tell the police it's you who's behind this forgery racket.

SIDNEY: What forgery racket?

BILL: All these printing presses.

SIDNEY: I don't know what you're talking about. I'm printing margarine labels.

BILL: Since when?

SIDNEY: Since Hancock got picked up. We were in production thirty seconds after the cell door slammed.

BILL: But you can't just leave him there.

SIDNEY: Look Billy, stop worrying. I've never failed to help a friend yet. I'll get him the best lawyer in town. He's got nothing to worry about.

(*Orchestra: Link*)

ALAN: (*Echo*) Number 1857369, Esquire.

TONY: Hallo.

ALAN: Visitor to see you.

TONY: Who is it this time?

ALAN: Your lawyer.

TONY: Aha, now we'll see who's master. I'll show you you can't keep me locked up. You may pack my things, I shall be leaving immediately. Now . . . where is he?

KENNETH: (*Snide*) Good evening.

TONY: Oh cor blimey, it's him. What are you doing here?

KENNETH: I'm your lawyer.

TONY: Warder, can you direct me to the condemned cell.

KENNETH: Oh don't be like that. I'll get you off. I've never lost a case yet. You mark my words, after I've defended you, no court in the country will convict you.

(*Orchestra: Ominous slow link*)

(*Hollow court atmosphere. Rapping of gavel*)

KENNETH: (*Judge*) . . . with the powers invested in me I hereby sentence you Anthony Alouitious St John Hancock to a term of imprisonment not exceeding six months.

HANCOCK: Everything Kerr does lands me right in it. Six months. (*Mimics Snide*) You mark my words, after I've defended you, no court in the country will convict you.

KENNETH: (*Snide*) Well there's no need to get shirty, it wasn't my fault. It was just that the judge didn't like us.

TONY: Yes, but six months.

KENNETH: Well that's all right, I got nine months and I've got nothing to do with it. I'll appeal for you if you like.

TONY: No thanks. Six months is enough. Just wait till I get out. I'll see that Kerr doesn't cause me any more trouble . . . and there's only one way to do that.

(*Orchestra: Link*)

KENNETH: Six months later.

BILL: . . . yeah, it sure is nice to have you back, Tub. You know something?

TONY: What?

BILL: I'm going to go out and get another job.

TONY: No, don't trouble.

BILL: No, I insist. You were right about me being a layabout. The least I can do is bring in some money to help you keep things going.

444

TONY: No Bill, don't you bother yourself. You stay where you are.

BILL: But Tub, you've kept me strapped in this bed for three weeks now. I want to get up and go to work.

TONY: (*Clenched teeth*) You're staying where you are. You're not getting any more jobs. I've done enough time as it is. I'll send your food up. You're not setting foot outside this house. Shut up and go to sleep. (*Etc . . .*)

BILL: (*Tries to protest at end of every sentence*)

(*Orchestra: Play Out.*)

Unseen Television Script: 'The Diplomat'

After writing this script, which was originally intended for the first TV series in 1956, Ray Galton and Alan Simpson went on holiday; shortly after, the Suez crisis arose. Because the script was about war and contained library footage of battle scenes, it was deemed inappropriate for transmission and the programme was never made. As the writers were away, Johnny Speight, another client of Associated London Scripts, was asked to look through the archives and identify a radio script which could easily be adapted for television as a replacement. He picked 'Fred's Pie Stall', and 'The Diplomat' was assigned to the shelf to collect dust for nigh on fifty years—until now.

TONY'S FLAT

(*The breakfast table is laid. Mrs Biggs, Tony's help, is putting the finishing touches to it. She goes to the door. Calls up.*)

MRS B.: Hurry up, Mr Hancock, breakfast is ready.

TONY: (*Off stage*) Coming.

MRS B.: Porridge and kippers.

TONY: (*Off stage*) Cor. Give it to the cat.

(*Noise off. Cat meowing frantically and disappearing*)

MRS B.: (*Looks off at cat disappearing*) Well, that's the last we'll see of him for a fortnight. (*Calls up*

447

to Tony) Oh do hurry up, Mr Hancock, it's half past seven, you'll be late for work.

(*Tony comes in door, he is wearing striped morning trousers, black jacket, spats, wing collar and grey tie*)

TONY: (*As he comes in*) Porridge and kippers. What sort of meal is that for a man just back from a day trip to Boulogne.

(*Goes over and lifts up salver on plate*)

TONY: Look, dear . . . just tell me . . . has porridge got bone in it?

MRS B.: No.

TONY: Then this is the kipper. No, wait a minute, it's not, I . . . (*suddenly realising*) Why don't you use separate saucepans? I don't hold with his saving yourself on the washing up. Putting it all in the pressure cooker, it's not good enough. Take it away, I'll have some toast instead.

(*Mrs Biggs hands him toast rack. Tony takes a large black slice. Looks at her.*)

TONY: I know I paid the gas bill yesterday, but there's no need to go mad. Could well be a slate off next door's roof.

MRS B.: You can scrape it, can't you?

TONY: Scrape it? You've only been here a week and I've worn three knives down already.

(*He starts scraping the toast*)

MRS B.: This is a big day for you, isn't it?

TONY: Yes. Been promoted at last. Three years at the Foreign Office and now I've been transferred to Whitehall.

MRS B.: I'm so glad, you've worked so hard for it.

TONY: It had to come. Man of my calibre. They knew, they knew, they were no mugs. They know when they've got brains working for them. I'm

448

destined for bigger things. It's Whitehall now, it'll be Downing Street before I'm finished. They're grooming me you see, I'm earmarked. The bloke they've got there now can't go on forever.

MRS B.: I hope you do well, you're a natural for Downing Street.

TONY: Of course I am. I'll alter things a bit when I'm there. I'm not at all satisfied with the way things are being run, there'll have to be some changes made and . . .

(*He has finished scraping the toast and he looks at the finished result. The centre of the bread is missing leaving the outside crust intact.*)

TONY: Another three mornings we'll be able to set up our own hoop-la stall. In future I'll have tinned grapefruit and cold milk . . . even you won't be able to mess that up.

(*He has got up from the table. Takes out his gold hunter. Bangs it on the table. Then looks at it.*)

TONY: Better get a move on, I'll be late.

(*Puts it back in his pocket. Goes over to hallstand. Puts bowler on. Starts putting gloves on.*)

MRS B.: Where have you got to go today?

TONY: Oh, usual stuff. Russian Embassy, Foreign Office, Ministry of Defence, three conferences scheduled for today, mustn't miss them. Where's my brolly?

MRS B.: In your bedroom.

TONY: Oh yes, it was raining last night. Must get that ceiling fixed. I'll take yours.

(*Takes brolly out of horsestand. Picks up briefcase. Goes to door.*)

MRS B.: Will you be in for dinner?

TONY: Not if I can help it.

(*He goes out of door*)

FILMED EXCERPT

(*Tony coming down steps of Victorian type terraced house. 'Room to let' in window. He hails taxi.*)

TONY: Whitehall please, me man.

(*Gets in, drives off. Shot of taxi driving through traffic. Shot of taxi going past Cenotaph. Tony getting out of taxi. Paying fare. Walking up to front doors of Foreign Office—have plate on wall saying 'Foreign Office'—he is saluted by commissionaire on door.*)

(*Dissolve into him coming out. Now wearing overalls and carrying a ladder, bucket and chamois leather. Walks out of picture.*)

(*Tony walking back down steps of Foreign Office with the window cleaning gear. Commissionaire acknowledges him. Tony puts ladder up against wall few yards from commissionaire and starts climbing. Pan camera up the wall taking in the office windows.*)

(*End of film sequence*)

LIVE

(*Conference room in Foreign Office. Conference table with seven distinguished diplomats sitting round it. Usual paraphernalia. Papers in front of them, etc.*)

FOREIGN MINISTER: . . . well, gentlemen, the position is this. The Moravian Government have rejected our note of protest about the incident outside the Embassy last week.

1ST MINISTER: Disgusting. Chalking things like that on the wall.

2ND MINISTER: (*Old Man*): Send a gunboat.

3RD MINISTER: Action, sir, action.

4TH MINISTER: We can't be kicked around any longer, we must do something.

5TH MINISTER: Hear, hear. If we don't take action we shall lose face all over the Balkans.

2ND MINISTER: Send a gunboat.

FOREIGN MINISTER: My dear Farnsworth, Moravia is five hundred miles inland.

5TH MINISTER: I demand the Minister take firm action against this outrage.

3RD MINISTER: Freeze their assets in London.

FOREIGN MINISTER: They haven't got any.

4TH MINISTER: Can't we bring this up at UNO?

5TH MINISTER: What's that?

4TH MINISTER: It's that Organisation affair in New York . . . something or other . . . we've got a fella there, I believe, we've paid our subscription anyway.

1ST MINISTER: This sort of thing goes on too much. We must act. A show of force.

3RD MINISTER: A parade in Hyde Park.

OMNES: Excellent. Capital.

4TH MINISTER: That'll show them they can't twist the lion's tail.

2ND MINISTER: Send an aeroplane.

FOREIGN MINISTER: Then it's settled. The usual action.

OMNES: Agree.

FOREIGN MINISTER: Right (*To Male Secretary on his left*) Worthington, get the Minister of Supply to send out a wet cloth to wipe the wall down.

OMNES: (*Applaud.*) Well done, sir. Good show. Etc . . .

(*Tony appears at the window behind the Foreign Minister. Starts cleaning the windows.*)

FOREIGN MINISTER: And now gentlemen, to the

451

Boronian question. We have reason to believe that the Government of Boronia are thinking of breaking off diplomatic relations with us.

(*Tony lifts up a window*)

TONY: Rubbish.

FOREIGN MINISTER: (*Reacts*) I beg your pardon?

Tony: I said rubbish. They're doing no such thing. They're dead friendly. Harmless is more the word. I happen to know they're thinking of sending another football team over this year. There's international solidarity if you like.

3RD MINISTER: (*Spluttering*) I say . . . I . . . who the devil are you?

TONY: I'm the window cleaner, who do you think I am?

4TH MINISTER: How dare you listen in to secret sessions of Cabinet, what do you know about it anyway?

TONY: What do I know about it? Me, The Selwyn Lloyd of Amalgamated Greater London Cleaners Ltd. I've been cleaning Government office windows for nigh on the twelve month. There's nothing goes on in London that I don't know about. I know the internal secrets of every country that's got an Ambassador to the Court of St James.

5TH MINISTER: Ridiculous. Even we don't know that.

TONY: Well of course not. You're not window cleaners. Even me mate Harry, who holds the bottom of the ladder knows more about it than you lot do.

1ST MINISTER: Do I understand that you clean embassy windows as well?

TONY: Do all the embassies once a week . . . and

the conference rooms. Just keep your ears open as you're polishing you'd be surprised what you pick up. I know the contents of every diplomatic bag that's brought into the country. Watches, whisky, rolls of cloth, cameras, you don't know half of it.

2ND MINISTER: Send a gunboat.

3RD MINISTER: This is fantastic. No diplomatic secret is safe with men like this about. He should be dismissed.

TONY: I should be a bit more cagey if I were you, matey. There's a few things I could tell about you, me old soldier.

3RD MINISTER: Eh, eh, what what . . . lies . . . lies . . .

TONY: It's no use locking the door when your secretary's with you . . . not if you don't draw the curtains. I'm sure Her Ladyship would like to know you weren't working late on the Suez Canal Conference the other week.

FOREIGN MINISTER: (*Alarmed*) What do you know of the Suez Canal Conference?

TONY: Know it off by heart. They've got a lot of windows in that conference room, took me three days. Didn't miss a trick. Made a few suggestions meself.

4TH MINISTER: You?

TONY: Certainly. Always making suggestions. Well received by some ministers, I might add. You know Dulles' plan for the international control of the Canal?

FOREIGN MINISTER: Well.

TONY: Me. I would have whispered it to someone else, but well, he was nearest, and he hadn't been saying much, so I gave it to him. And then there

453

was the last Budget.

FOREIGN MINISTER: That was you too.

TONY: Every word of it. Well . . . poor old Butler was sitting there . . . worried sick, he was counting the money . . . so I lifted up the window and helped him out. Very grateful he was . . . gave me a premium bond to take home. I think I can safely say I've had a hand in all the major political decisions in the last year or so.

5TH MINISTER: I don't believe it. Ridiculous.

TONY: (*Indignant*) I'll have you know, it was me who put the restraining hand on the Government over the Diana Dors incident. The navy was halfway across the Atlantic when I poked my head in and told 'em off. Many a minister don't dare make a move without consulting me. Many's the time the windows go up along Whitehall, all looking for me . . . so's they can call me over to see what I reckon.

FOREIGN MINISTER: Most interesting. As a matter of fact we were just discussing the Moravian problem.

TONY: Ah yes, yes . . . very tricky, that one. I haven't quite made up me mind about them.

3RD MINISTER: The point is, if the worst came to the worst, I wonder what the War Office have available?

TONY: Hang on.

(*Tony climbs down the ladder. Disappears from view. Pause. He comes back up.*)

TONY: Three tanks, hundred men and a Naafi.

4TH MINISTER: Not enough.

2ND MINISTER: Send a gunboat.

FOREIGN MINISTER: Oh shut up . . . Your Lordship.

5TH MINISTER: (*To Tony*) Tell me, what are your

impressions of the situation?

TONY: Well, I had a good think about it on the Tube last night . . . and . . . (*Tony climbs into room*)

TONY: (*To Foreign Minister*) Move up a bit.

(*Foreign Minister gets up and moves along a seat. Tony sits in his seat, hands him the bucket*)

TONY: Hold this, matey. Don't spill any, it's almost clean. Now then . . . personally, I think the Moravians have got to be watched. I've been worried about them for some time now. Ever since I was cleaning at the Balkan Conference I didn't like their attitude at all—specially their Prime Minister General Pirelli. You know, little fellow with a beard . . . didn't take to him at all.

3RD MINISTER: What do you think they intend to do?

TONY: I don't know . . . I just don't know.

FOREIGN MINISTER: Then I suggest you find out. We must know. I suggest you go round there this afternoon and see what you can pick up.

TONY: No, I'm sorry. I don't do the Moravian Embassy. That's Charlie's area.

FOREIGN MINISTER: Then I suggest you change over with Charlie.

TONY: Ooooh, Charlie won't like that. He likes doing the Moravian Embassy. He's going it a bit heavy with the char there. They throw wet rags at each other. Laugh . . . cor . . .

4TH MINISTER: This is a National Emergency. We demand you clean the Moravian Embassy windows and report back here when you find out anything about their plans.

TONY: All right, I'll see what I can do.

(*Tony gets up*)

TONY: All the best lads. And don't do anything till I get back, cos I can't answer for the consequences. Give my regards to Clem when you see him.
(*He climbs out on to ladder and disappears down it*)
FOREIGN MINISTER: Remarkable fella.
2ND MINISTER: Send a gunboat.
(*They all throw their notepads at him. FADE.*)

FILMED SEQUENCE
(*Tony walking down street with window cleaning gear. Stops in front of large building. Looks up at it. Camera pans up the side of the building.*)
(*Corridor with two doors next to each other. One marked 'MORAVIAN EMBASSY' . . . The other marked 'GRIMSBY FISH AND CHIP SHOPS LTD.' The camera closes in on the Grimsby door.*)

INSIDE GRIMSBY FISH AND CHIP SHOPS LTD.
(*Board meeting. Sidney in chair, Warren on his left. Three or four other characters sitting round the table.*)
SIDNEY: Well gentlemen, we all know what we're here for today: to discuss a programme of expansion for our fish and chip shops. I think we're all agreed the idea is to establish a chain of shops all over England.
WARREN: Definitely, definitely . . . and we must incorporate a pease pudding and faggot department in every shop.
SIDNEY: Yeah, well that'll come later, Rodney. One thing at a time.
WARREN: I was just mentioning it, Sidney, because there is an increasing trade for pease pudding and faggots in this country . . . not forgetting

456

saveloys and those little meat puddings which are a big attraction, we would be foolish to deny it.

BOARD MEMBER: (*Distinguished type*): Well I don't know, I don't altogether hold with this contemporary style of shop. I feel we should concentrate on fish and chips as we have always done . . . it's so much more dignified.

WARREN: Ooooh no, Morrie, no, my own brother should be such a radical. I could not disagree more, Morrie . . . don't you see we have a responsibility to our public. Pease pudding and faggots was a dying culinary art, which I personally wish to see revived.

BOARD MEMBER: Fish and chips only.

WARREN: No, no, we must not restrict our outlook, we must broaden our mind and our vistas, we must not allow ourselves to be submerged by Conservatism, we must restore to this country of my adoption the former glories of pease pudding, faggots and saveloys . . . not to mention an idea for a kosher counter I have in mind.

BOARD MEMBER: Monstrous. Have you no respect for tradition?

WARREN: Progress is the keyword.

BOARD MEMBER: Tradition.

WARREN: Pease pudding.

BOARD MEMBER: Fish and chips.

SIDNEY: Oi . . . oi . . . oi, shut up arguing, gentlemen . . . the only reason we're in this business is to make money.

WARREN: Ah, the voice of sanity.

SIDNEY: We haven't been making as much as we ought to. Apart from opening new shops, we got to make more on fish.

WARREN: We can't cut down on the size any more.

SIDNEY: Yes we can, we'll use smaller bits, put twice as much batter round 'em and only one shovelful of chips for a tanner.

WARREN: Very wise, very wise.

SIDNEY: Water down the vinegar in the bottles on the counter.

WARREN: Hear, hear.

SIDNEY: Bung up every other hole in the salt cellars.

WARREN: Brilliant, such imagination already.

SIDNEY: But first we must expand. We've got to open shops all over the country. At the moment we've got two shops in Grimsby and one in Dover. Now this is what I propose. We open another one in Dover, then we slowly work our way up to London. Then we go for the Midlands trade. Half a dozen in Birmingham, and a few in Nottingham. By this time we should be ready for Manchester, then the whole of the North Country, and by next year we'll have to go to Scotland and Wales.

WARREN: And then the pease pudding and faggots.

SIDNEY: If there's a demand. I've got me agents looking out all over the country for likely premises.

WARREN: That's marvellous, I think I shall go to Madeira for my holidays next year.

(*A ladder appears at the window behind Sid. Then Tony appears with his chamois leather and starts cleaning the windows, taking careful stock of what is going on in the room. He lifts up the window. They all look round at him.*)

TONY: Window cleaner. Don't bother about me, just carry on. Affairs of state mustn't be held up . . . I understand . . . good health.

458

(*Starts singing and cleaning*)

SIDNEY: Hurry up, we're busy. Now gentlemen, I'll just run over the plans again.

(*Tony takes notice. Sidney gets up and goes over to the wall where there is a large map of England and Wales pinned up.*)

SIDNEY: This is the map of England. Now we make our initial attack here in Dover on January the first.

(*Sticks a pin in Dover*)

(*From now on Tony reacts at the appropriate places as he thinks they're talking about invasion plans. Cut to Tony's reactions at the salient points.*)

SIDNEY: We should have the whole of Dover taken care of in two weeks. Then a couple more coastal ports, so we can bring in our own supplies. Then we should be ready to move towards London.

(*Sidney points the move out with a pointer*)

SIDNEY: We surround London by establishing strong points here . . . here . . . here . . . here . . . here . . .

(*Puts pins in at five different places surrounding London*)

SIDNEY: Now we're ready to spread out northwards.

(*Indicates the directions with pointer*)

SIDNEY: We've got our agents in the Manchester area waiting for the word to start an all-out offensive. Manchester and the North'll be a pushover . . . we should have the whole of England under our control by March next year. Then we can start our Scottish campaign. Glasgow, Edinburgh, Aberdeen . . . (*Points them out on map*) There it is, gentlemen, by the end of next year our Empire will include the whole of the British Isles. No one can stop us.

OMNES: Applaud. Well done, etc.

WARREN: Gentlemen, gentlemen a vote of confidence in our President. This king among men here.

OMNES: Applaud.

(*Tony has been getting more and more horrified through all this and now he disappears down the ladder*)

SIDNEY: So there it is, gentlemen, we open our first fish and chip shop at Dover on January the first.

(*Fade*)

(*Fade in the foreign office conference room*)

(*All the ministers are there. Tony is standing at the end of the table in the Foreign Minister's place.*)

TONY: . . . and I tell you they're going to invade Dover on January the first. Their agents are everywhere . . . waiting for the signal. It'll be France all over again.

FOREIGN MINISTER: Are you sure about this?

TONY: Yes, I heard it all. They had the map out.

1ST MINISTER: Didn't they see you listening?

TONY: Course they did . . . they didn't take any notice, though. Thought I was an idiot. I heard it all, though. Every detail of their vile plans.

FOREIGN MINISTER: This is serious. What did you find out?

TONY: Everything. (*Goes over to map on wall*) They're invading Dover first . . . (*Points with pointer*) . . . Then they're taking control of some more coastal ports, so they can bring in reinforcements, ready for the offensive against London. Tanks, artillery, the lot, then their troops are going to surround London, here, here, here and here.

460

OMNES: (*Horrified reactions.*)

TONY: Then when they've captured London, they're going to spread out northwards . . . surround Manchester, occupy Blackpool, Birmingham, Scunthorpe . . . well that won't be too bad . . . but we can't let them get away with the others. They're going to start on Scotland next year. They reckon that by the end of 1957, they'll have the whole of the British Isles under their heel. Gentlemen, this is an emergency. We must act, and act now. (*Thumps desk*)

OMNES: He's right. Action. Hear, hear, etc.

TONY: We must mobilise, defend our shores against the invader, fight on the beaches, in the streets, let them come from the four corners of the earth, some chicken, some neck, this was our finest whatsit, blood sweat toil and tears, it won't be easy my friends, but we can do it.

(*Tony lights cigar as they all applaud. Foreign Minister picks up phone*)

FOREIGN MINISTER: Hall. Get me the War Office. Hallo, Monty? Scramble.

FILMED SEQUENCE

(*Accompanying music: 'There'll Always Be An England'*)

(*Soldiers running across the parade ground. Aeroplane being wheeled out of hangar. Sailors running up gangplank. Soldiers leaning out of train windows waving goodbye to their relatives. Hundreds of tanks going along a road. Loads of aeroplanes taking off. Several battleships ploughing through heavy seas. Picture of Tony on poster pointing. Caption: 'Your Country Needs You'. Blokes digging shelters in Hyde Park. VE Day*)

461

march-past. Thousands of cheering people. The British Army, Navy and Air Force marching past. Tanks. Armoured cars, the lot. While this is showing, have massed band and choir playing 'Goodbye Polly, I Must Leave You'.

Newspaper placards: 'Total Mobilisation', 'London Evacuated', 'Prime Minister Flies to UNO' and 'Australia All Out 140'.)

(*End of filming sequence*)

(*Shot of door marked 'Grimsby Fish and Chip Shops Ltd.' Dissolve into board room. The Board members and Warren are seated round the table waiting for Sidney to arrive.*)

BOARD MEMBER: He's late. He should have been here ten minutes ago.

2ND MEMBER: What did he call the meeting for? We only met last week. What's gone wrong?

1ST MEMBER: I've no idea. I got a message to come round right away, that's all I know.

(*Sidney comes in door. He is in battledress . . . tin hat and rifle.*)

SIDNEY: Gentlemen, there's been a change in plans.

BOARD MEMBER: What's happened?

SIDNEY: I've been called up.

WARREN: You, too.

SIDNEY: Why, have you?

WARREN: Oh no, no. I'm going to be interned. Regulation 18B. They're sending me to the Isle of Man.

SIDNEY: Our plans have been messed up rotten. The country's gone bonkers. As soon as this Moravian invasion scare started, I got me papers. I shouldn't be here now. I'm supposed to be on guard duty. I had to board up me sentry box so they wouldn't notice I'd gone.

462

BOARD MEMBER: Can't we still go ahead with our arrangements as planned?

SIDNEY: Gentlemen, please. We are patriotic men I hope. This is a national emergency, our country is on the brink of war, we must put aside all thought of personal gain . . . from now on all our labours must be concentrated on working for our country and not to exploit the situation to make money for our own ends.

SIDNEY & OMNES: Hear, hear.

WARREN: Which brings me to a little idea I have for mobile fish and chip shops to serve our brave boys, at prices considerably less than the NAAFI. Sidney is now in the army so he can operate the shops for us while he is off duty and . . . etc . . .

(*Fade*)

(*Fade in on mobile fish and chip shop*)

(*Sidney has his back to camera. He is testing the chips in the pan and sorting out the fish in the compartments above the frying tanks. A couple of squaddies are eating fish and chips out of some paper. They saunter off. Enter Tony in uniform*)

TONY: Gratitude for you. I'm the one who warns them . . . tells them of the danger. Cor . . . if I'd known they were going to call me up I wouldn't have let on. Private. I thought at least after all I've done . . . a General. It's that Monty bloke. Dead jealous. Can't stand competition. I'm being wasted here. Cleaning windows on ATS Nissen huts.

(*Bangs counter*)

TONY: Shop, shop. Come on, wake your ideas up, what's the matter with you?

(*Sidney doesn't turn round*)

SIDNEY: What do you want?

463

TONY: Ninepenny and threepennorth . . . with a bit
  of crackling.
SIDNEY: I've run out of paper.
TONY: Well put them in me hat.
(*Takes hat off. Sidney turns round with a shovelful of
  chips. Empties them into Tony's hat. Tony shakes
  salt and vinegar into the cap. Doesn't look at
  Sidney while talking*)
TONY: Looks like being a big do, doesn't it? Four
  million men called up. Factories all turned over
  to munitions. Fleet's sailed. Twenty million a day
  it's costing them. And do you know who's
  responsible? Me. It was me who found out about
  the Moravians invading us. I could well have
  saved this country. Churchill's already writing a
  new volume about me. I overheard the whole
  plan. I was cleaning the windows outside the
  Embassy. Nasty lot they were.
SIDNEY: Their office is right next to mine. I thought
  they were nice blokes. They were very puzzled
  when they were kicked out. Most sorry to leave.
TONY: (*Still not looking at Sid*) No . . . cut-throats
  the lot of them. I overheard them making their
  plans to invade . . . went straight round to the
  Foreign Office and told them . . . acted straight
  away on my advice. You should have seen this
  Moravian Ambassador. The one making all the
  plans.
SIDNEY: I've seen him. Little old boy with a white
  beard.
TONY: No, that's not him. He's an ugly looking
  bloke, dead vicious, big nose . . . lines on his face
  . . . bit of a spiv . . . flashy sort of . . . (*Turns and
  looks at Sid's face . . . does a slow take*) . . . dresser
  . . . little eyes . . . ears a bit . . . sort of wavy hair

and . . . like a boxer with . . . (*Pause looking at Sid*) Haven't I seen you somewhere before?

SIDNEY: Maybe . . . your face is familiar.

TONY: Yes. What were you in before you joined up?

SIDNEY: Fish and chips.

TONY: Oh. Nothing to do with politics?

SIDNEY: No. No. Big business. Grimsby Fish and Chip Shops Ltd. If this lot hadn't started I would have made a fortune. I was just going to take over the whole of England. Fish and chip shops everywhere. I was going to start at Dover . . . then some more coastal ports . . . bring me own supplies of fish in . . . move up on London . . . then the North . . . Manchester. Had all me agents looking out for new premises . . . then I would have Scotland by next year . . . cleaned up, I would.

TONY: (*Hesitant*) Dover . . . then surround London . . . and then capture the North. Take over Manchester . . . then Scotland . . . Where did you say your office was?

SIDNEY: Stratton Square. Next to the Moravian Embassy.

TONY: Next to the . . . ha ha ha. Cor dear. (*Thoughtful*) I wonder if they'll blindfold me.

(*Goes off, leaving his cap on the counter. Sid looks out after Tony . . . shrugs his shoulders. Fade on Sid eating chips out of Tony's cap.*)

THE FOREIGN OFFICE BOARDROOM

(*The Foreign Minister and his gang are seated round the table. A General, a Navy and an RAF officer are with them, poring over plans on the table.*)

GENERAL: . . . as I see it, they'll probably start the

invasion just there. If we move five divisions across here, and you, Bob bring a few of your battleships down the Channel here . . . and you, Frank can give us an aerial counterattack just here . . . and we'll have another ten divisions in reserve just about here . . .

FOREIGN MINISTER: Another ten divisions. That'll mean calling up another sixty thousand men.

GENERAL: Then call them up. After all, this is an emergency.

NAVY LAD: We'll probably need more naval reinforcements.

FOREIGN MINISTER: That's taken care of. If we give Australia to America I'm sure they'll let us have a few destroyers . . . pre-1914 of course . . . but it all helps.

RAF LAD: I must congratulate you on finding out about this impending danger in such good time. You may have saved the country. Now we're all prepared and ready for any eventuality. I don't know how you did it but . . . good show.

FOREIGN MINISTER: We have our methods . . . we have some good men working for us.

(*Knock on door.*)

FOREIGN MINISTER: Come in.

(*Tony enters.*)

FOREIGN MINISTER: Ah . . . the hero himself . . . The man we owe everything to.

TONY: Evening. Er . . . everything ready?

FOREIGN MINISTER: Yes. The country is fully mobilised. And tonight the Prime Minister will speak to the nation.

TONY: Yes, that's what I was afraid of.

FOREIGN MINISTER: What's wrong?

TONY: Well . . . I've got some rather interesting

news for you. You'll like this, you will . . . Very amusing really . . . if you've got a sense of humour . . . I . . .

(*Tony looks round. Assumes a helpless 'Not going to enjoy this' expression.*)

(*Fade on Tony's expression*)

GRIMSBY FISH AND CHIP SHOPS LTD. BOARDROOM

(*Sidney, Warren and the others round the table*)

SIDNEY: Well now, gentlemen, I'm glad to say that now the war scare has finished, we can go ahead with our plans to take over the fish and chip business in this country. The plans are the same as before. We start at Dover, and work our way up through the whole of the British Isles.

(*A ladder appears at the window. Tony climbs up it and sits on the windowsill to the left of the ladder and starts cleaning the windows.*)

TONY: Morning. Shan't be long.

SIDNEY: Well hurry up, we've got business to attend to.

TONY: I'll be as quick as I can. I've got a new helper with me this morning. Get it done in no time. (*Calls*) Harry, bring us up the chamois leather.

(*The Foreign Minister comes up the ladder dressed in overalls and hands Tony the chamois leather.*)

FOREIGN MINISTER: This is all your fault. Five thousand a year I was getting and now look at me.

TONY: Oh shut up. It's your own fault. You shouldn't listen to window cleaners. What do they know about it.

FOREIGN MINISTER: But you said you knew everything that went on.

467

TONY: We all make mistakes. Get on with your windows, I'm in charge now.

FOREIGN MINISTER: It's all very well for you . . . etc.

. . .

(*Tony and the Minister argue.*)

(*Fade out and closing credits.*)

Production Team: Television

All episodes were written by Ray Galton and Alan Simpson.

PRODUCER
Duncan Wood

PRODUCER'S ASSISTANT
Valerie Willis

PRODUCTION ASSISTANT
Philip Barker (series 1 and 3); Ronnie Marsh (series 2); no one acknowledged for series 4; John Rickword (series 5 and 6); Bob Gilbreath (series 7)

DESIGNER
Stewart Marshall (series 1); Roy Oxley (series 2, episodes 1–4 & 6; series 4, episodes 1–4); Malcolm Goulding (series 2, episode 5; series 7); George Djurkovic (series 3, episodes 1–5 & 9–12); Neil Parkinson (series 3, episodes 6–8); Lawrence Broadhouse (series 4, episodes 5–13; series 5; series 6)

ASSISTANT DESIGNER
James MacDougal (series 6, episodes 5–10)

FLOOR MANAGER
Philip Barker (series 1, episodes 1 & 2); no floor manager acknowledged for rest of series 1 or series

2; Patrick Dowling (series 3, episodes 1–5); no floor manager acknowledged for series 3, episodes 6–10; John Rickword (series 3, episodes 11–13; series 4); no floor manager acknowledged for series 5 or 6; Bob Gilbreath (series 7, episode 1); no floor manager acknowleged for rest of series 7

ASSISTANT FLOOR MANAGER
John Rickword (series 1; series 3, episodes 1–9); Ian Smith (series 2); Gerry Mill (series 3, episodes 10–12; series 4; series 5, episodes 1–2; series 6); Ronnie Sowton (series 5, episodes 3–10); Robin Kerr (series 7)

CALL BOY
Noel Ranken (series 1, episodes 1, 2 & 6); Roy Baker (series 1, episodes 3–5); Gerry Mill (series 2, episodes 1–2); Harold Snoad (series 2, episodes 3 & 4; series 6); Peter Dudley (series 2, episode 5); Terry Henzell (series 2, episode 6); Philip Dudley (series 3 and series 4, episodes 2 & 3); Roger Race (series 4, episodes 1, 4–13; series 5, episodes 1–6, 8–10); Gareth Davies (series 5, episode 7); William G. Stewart (series 7)

TECHNICAL OPERATIONS MANAGER
Basil Bultitude (series 1, episode 1); Frank Sellen (series 1, episode 2); Tommy Holmes (series 1, episodes 4, 5 & 6); Bill Bayliff (series 2, episodes 1, 2 & 3; series 3, episodes 1–7); Reg Callaghan (series 2, episodes 3, 5 & 6; series 3, episodes 8–12; series 4, episodes 7–13; series 5, episodes 1–4, 7, 8 & 10; series 6, episodes 1–4, 9 & 10; series 7); Sam Hutchings (series 4, episodes 1–3; series 5, episode 5); Norman Taylor (series 4, episodes 4–6; series 5,

episode 6; series 6, episodes 5–8); Graham Sothcott (series 5, episode 9)

LIGHTING SUPERVISOR
Tom Moncrieff (series 1, episodes 1 & 5); Jimmy Richardson (series 1, episodes 2 & 6; series 2, episodes 1, 2 & 4; series 3, episodes 1–7; series 4, episodes 4–7, 11 & 13; series 6, episode 3; series 7, episodes 1–4 & 6); Don Cowie (series 1, episodes 3 & 4); Sam Barclay (series 2, episode 3; series 3, episodes 8–13; series 4, episodes 8–10; series 5, episodes 1–4, 6–8 & 10; series 6, episodes 1, 2, 4–10; series 7, episode 6); Bryan Forgham (series 2, episodes 5 & 6); Derek Lightbody (series 4, episode 1; series 5, episode 5); Bob Simmons (series 4, episodes 2 & 3); Ken MacGregor (series 4, episode 12); Geoffrey Shaw (series 5, episode 9)

SOUND SUPERVISOR
Geoff White and John Eden-Eadon (series 1); Brian Forgham (series 2 and 3; series 4, episodes 4–13; series 5, episodes 1–4, 6–9 & 10; series 6); Norman Bennett (series 4, episodes 1–3; series 5, episode 5); Hugh Barker (series 5, episode 9); no one acknowledged on series 7

CHIEF CAMERAMAN
Sydney Lotterby (series 1, episodes 1, 3–6); Mark Levy (series 1, episode 2); Lawrie Duley (series 2 and 3; series 4, episodes 4–6, 8–13; series 5, episodes 1–4, 6–8, 10; series 6, episodes 1, 2, 4–10); Bernard Fox (series 4, episodes 1–3; series 5, episode 5); Ken Major (series 4, episode 7; series 6, episode 3); Peter Hills (series 5, episode 9); no one acknowledged for series 7

RACKS SUPERVISOR
Frank Rose (series 1, episode 1); Jack Shallcross (series 1, episode 2); no one acknowledged for rest of series 1; Jack Gill (series 2 and 3; series 4, episodes 4–13; series 5, episodes 1–4); Neil Campbell (series 4, episodes 1–3; series 5, episode 5); Jack Walsh (series 5, episodes 6–8 & 10); Jack Gray (series 5, episode 9); Peter Jarrett (series 6) no one acknowledged for series 7

VISION MIXER
Bob Gilbreath (series 1, episodes 1, 3–6); Phyllis Stein (series 1, episode 2; series 5, episodes 6–8 and 10; series 6); Nellie Southcott (series 2 and 3; series 4, episodes 4–13; series 5, episodes 1–4); Rachael Blayney (series 4, episodes 1–3; series 5, episode 5); Tony Bacon (series 5, episode 9); no one acknowledged for series 7

GRAMS OPERATOR
Gladys Davis (series 1, episodes 1 & 6); Dave Hawthorn (series 1, episodes 2–5); Chick Anthony (series 2 and 3; series 4, episodes 4–7; series 5, episodes 1–4 & 6); Jack Brumitt (series 4, episodes 1–3); Chris Holcombe (series 4, episodes 8–10); Peter Wineman (series 5, episode 5); Clive Stevens (series 5, episodes 8 & 10); Dennis O'Grady (series 5, episode 9; series 6, episodes 1–5, 8–10); John Holmes (series 6, episode 6); Denise Daveluy (series 6, episode 7); no one acknowledged for series 7

WARDROBE SUPERVISOR
Pam Glanville (series 1, episode 1); Helen Malcolm

(series 1, episodes 2–6; series 4, episodes 4–13; series 6); Annie Robb (series 2; series 3, episodes 1, 3–13); Elizabeth Agombar (series 3, episode 2); Maureen Copley (series 4, episodes 1–3); Maureen Muggeridge (series 5); Ena Nickalls (series 7)

MAKE-UP SUPERVISOR
Jill Summers (series 1, episodes 1–3 & 5–6; series 5; series 6); Toni Chapman (series 1, episode 4); Susan Pring (series 2); Jean Lord (series 3); Cherry Alston (series 4); Elizabeth Armstrong (series 7)

PRODUCTION SECRETARY
No one acknowledged for series 1 and 2; Elsa Bradley (series 3); Margaret Brabham (series 4); Valerie Simons (series 4, episode 10); Gillian Ford (series 5, episodes 1–6); Monica Mason (series 5, episodes 7–10); Pamela Berg (series 6, episodes 1–6); Sally Penn (series 6, episodes 7–10); Isabel Logan (series 7); Joyce Mortimer (series 7)

Hancock's Half Hour: **Merchandise**

BOOKS

(Books specifically about the programme, *Hancock's Half Hour*, as well as biographies/studies of Tony Hancock, which include detailed accounts of the programme, are listed below.)

Title: *Hancock—Scripts*
Authors: Ray Galton and Alan Simpson
ISBN: n/a
Format: hardback
Publisher: André Deutsch Ltd
Publication date: 1961
Notes: A paperback edition was published by Corgi Books in 1962.

Title: *Hancock*
Authors: Freddie Hancock and David Nathan
ISBN: 0718302915
Format: Hardback
Publisher: William Kimber Ltd.
Publication date: 1969
Notes: A paperback version (ISBN: 034020513X) was published by Coronet Books in 1975. A further edition was issued in paperback (ISBN: 0563204613) by the BBC in 1986, reprinted in 1996.

Title: *Hancock's Half Hour*

Authors: Ray Galton and Alan Simpson
ISBN: 0713000872
Format: Hardback
Publisher: Woburn Press
Publication date: 1974
Notes: A paperback edition (ISBN: 0860072460) was published by Futura Publications Ltd. in 1975.

Title: *The Entertainers—Tony Hancock*
Author: Philip Oakes
ISBN: 0713001437
Format: Hardback
Publisher: Woburn Press
Publication date: 1975
Notes: A paperback edition (ISBN: 0713001380) was published by Woburn in 1975.

Title: *Tony Hancock—Artiste*
Author: Roger Wilmut
ISBN: 0413386805
Format: Hardback
Publisher: Methuen
Publication date: 1978
Notes: A revised paperback edition (ISBN: 041350820X) was published by Methuen in 1983, while a revised hardback (ISBN: 0413151905) was issued by Bibliophile Books in 1986.

Title: *Illustrated Hancock*
Author: Roger Wilmut
ISBN: 0356123669
Format: Hardback

Publisher: MacDonald Press
Publication date: 1986
Notes: A paperback edition (ISBN: 0356147819) was published by MacDonald Press in 1987.

Title: *The Best of Hancock—Scripts*
Authors: Ray Galton and Alan Simpson
ISBN: 086051367X
Format: Hardback
Publisher: Robson Books
Publication date: 1986
Notes: Robson Books issued a paperback edition (ISBN: 0860518868) in 1993, while Penguin published it in paperback (ISBN: 0140097570) in 1987.

Title: *Hancock's Half Hour—The Classic Years*
Authors: Ray Galton, Alan Simpson and Chris Bumstead (editor)
ISBN: 0563206101
Format: Hardback
Publisher: BBC Books
Publication date: 1987

Title: *Hancock's Last Stand*
Author: Edward Joffe
ISBN: 1857763165
Format: Hardback
Publisher: The Book Guild
Publication date: 1998
Notes: A paperback (ISBN: 0413740404) was published by Methuen in 1999.

Title:	*When the Wind Changed—The Life and Death of Tony Hancock*
Author:	Cliff Goodwin
ISBN:	0712676155
Format:	Hardback
Publisher:	Century
Publication date:	1999
Notes:	A paperback (ISBN: 009960941X) was published by Arrow Books in 2000.

VIDEOS

Title:	*Hancock—Volume 1: The Blood Donor*
Release date:	April 1987
Catalogue no:	BBCV4037
Status:	Deleted 5/4/04
Episodes:	'The Blood Donor', 'The Missing Page' and 'Twelve Angry Men'

Title:	*Hancock—Volume 2: The Lift*
Release date:	April 1987
Catalogue no:	BBCV4038
Status:	Deleted Nov. '94
Episodes:	'The Lift', 'The Ladies' Man', 'Lord Byron Lived Here'

Title:	*Hancock—Volume 3: The Bowmans*
Release date:	July 1987
Catalogue no:	BBCV 4047
Status:	Deleted Oct. '94
Episodes:	'The Bowmans', 'The Two Murderers', 'The Crown v. James, S.'

Title: *Hancock—Volume 4: The Radio Ham*
Release date: July 1987
Catalogue no: BBCV4048
Status: Deleted Oct. '94
Episodes: 'The Radio Ham', 'The Economy Drive', 'The Cold'

Title: *Hancock—Volume 5: The Bedsitter*
Release date: Oct. 1987
Catalogue no: BBCV4049
Status: Deleted Nov. '94
Episodes: 'The Bedsitter', 'The Reunion Party', 'The New Nose'

Title: *The Very Best of Hancock*
Release date: May 1994
Catalogue no: BBCV5343
Status: Deleted Feb. '99
Episodes: 'The Bedsitter', 'The Bowmans', 'The Radio Ham', 'The Lift', 'The Blood Donor'

Title: *Hancock's Half Hour: The Competitions*
Release date: Sept. 1996
Catalogue no: BBCV5850
Status: Deleted Aug. '98
Episodes: 'How to Win Money and Influence People', 'Air Steward Hancock', 'The Alpine Holiday'

Title: *Hancock's Half Hour—The Cruise*
Release date: Jan. 1997

Catalogue no: BBCV5961
Status: Deleted Dec. '03
Episodes: 'The Cruise', 'The Tycoon', 'The Babysitters'

Title: *Hancock—Volume 6: The Poison Pen Letters*
Release date: April 1997
Catalogue no: BBCV6234
Status: Deleted April '03
Episodes: 'The Poison Pen Letters', 'The Emigrant', 'The Big Night'

Title: *Hancock—The Train Journey*
Release date: May 1999
Catalogue no: BBCV6782
Status: Still available
Episodes: 'The Train Journey', 'The Photographer', 'Sid in Love', 'The Ladies' Man'

Title: *Comedy Greats—Hancock*
Release date: June 1999
Catalogue no: BBCV6797
Status: Still available
Episodes: 'The Bedsitter', 'The Bowmans', 'The Radio Ham', 'The Lift', 'The Blood Donor'

AUDIO CASSETTES

Title: *Hancock's Half Hour—Volume 1*
Release date: Sept. 1988
Catalogue no: 0563225459
Status: Original product deleted Jan. 2000,

but re-issued (cat. no. 0563406275) in 1992 and still available

Episodes: 'The Americans Hit Town', The Unexploded Bomb', 'The Poetry Society', 'Sid's Mystery Tour'

Title: *Hancock's Half Hour—Volume 2*
Release date: Nov. 1988
Catalogue no: 0563225467
Status: Original product deleted Jan. 2000, but re-issued (cat. no. 0563406283) in 1992 and still available
Episodes: 'The Scandal Magazine', 'The Last of the McHancocks', 'The Sleepless Night', 'Fred's Pie Stall'

Title: *Hancock's Half Hour—Volume 3*
Release date: March 1989
Catalogue no: 056326366
Status: Original product deleted Jan. 2000, but re-issued (cat. no. 0563406291) in 1992 and still available.
Episodes: 'Hancock's War', 'The Christmas Club', 'The Lift', 'Twelve Angry Men'

Title: *Hancock's Half Hour—Volume 4*
Release date: Nov. 1990
Catalogue no: 0563410388
Status: Original product deleted Jan. 2000, but re-issued (cat. no. 0563406305) in 1992 and still available
Episodes: 'The Diary', 'The Old School Reunion', 'Hancock in the Police', 'The East Cheam Drama Festival'

480

Title: *Hancock's Half Hour—Volume 5*
Release date: Sept. 1992
Catalogue no: 0563410647
Status: Still available
Episodes: 'Cyrano de Hancock', 'The Threatening Letters', 'Visiting Day', 'The Impressionist'

Title: *Hancock's Half Hour—Volume 6*
Release date: Nov. 1994
Catalogue no: 0563395052
Status: Still available
Episodes: 'Almost a Gentleman', 'Sunday Afternoon at Home', 'Childhood Sweetheart', 'The Elopement'

Title: *Hancock's Half Hour—Volume 7*
Release date: Nov. 1995
Catalogue no: 0563391057
Status: Still available
Episodes: 'Hancock's Happy Christmas', 'The Emigrant', 'Hancock's School', 'Hancock's Car'

Title: *Hancock's Half Hour—Volume 8*
Release date: Nov. 1996
Catalogue no: 0563389044
Status: Still available
Episodes: 'The Bequest', 'The Conjurer', 'The Publicity Photograph', 'The Grappling Game'

Title: *Hancock's Half Hour—Volume 9*
Release date: Nov. 1997

Catalogue no: 0563381493
Status: Still available
Episodes: 'The 13th of the Series', 'The Wild Man of the Woods', 'The Junk Man', 'Bill and Father Christmas'

Title: *Hancock's Half Hour—Volume 10*
Release date: Nov. 1998
Catalogue no: 056355729X
Status: Still available
Episodes: 'Agricultural 'Ancock', 'The New Secretary', 'The Insurance Policy', 'The Election Candidate'

Title: *Hancock—A Celebration*
Release date: May 1999
Catalogue no: 056355844X
Status: Still available
Episodes: A celebration of Hancock's life, this cassette includes clips from various episodes as well as tributes from colleagues.

Title: *Hancock's Happy Christmas*
Release date: Oct. 1999
Catalogue no: 0563552581
Status: Still available
Episodes: 'The Christmas Club', 'Hancock's Happy Christmas', 'Bill and Father Christmas', 'The Diary'

Title: *Hancock—Four Original BBC TV Episodes*
Release date: Sept. 2003
Catalogue no: 0563495197

Status:	Still available
Episodes:	'The Radio Ham', 'The Blood Donor', 'The Bowmans', 'The Bedsitter' (original soundtracks)

Title:	*Hancock—A Comedy Genius*
Release date:	Oct. 2004
Catalogue no:	0563525401
Status:	New release (also available on CD)
Description:	This two-hour show traces Hancock's early career and charts his appearances on shows such as *Variety Bandbox* and *Happy-Go-Lucky*. Told from recordings, scripts and press cuttings, this is the story of Hancock's rise to fame.

Title:	*Hancock—TV Volume 2* (working title at date of writing)
Release date:	Oct. 2004
Catalogue no:	0563525509
Status:	New release (also available as CD)
Episodes:	Still to be confirmed at date of writing.

CDs

Title:	*Hancock's Half Hour—The Collectors' Edition: Series 1*
Release date:	Nov. 2000
Catalogue no:	0563477547
Status:	Still available
Episodes:	All of series one

Title:	*Hancock's Half Hour—The*

Collectors' Edition: Series 2
Release date: March 2001
Catalogue no: 0563478004
Status: Still available
Episodes: Five episodes from series two

Title: *Hancock's Happy Christmas*
Release date: Nov. 2001
Catalogue no: 056353513X
Status: Still available
Episodes: 'The Christmas Club', 'Hancock's Happy Christmas', 'Bill and Father Christmas', 'The Diary'

Title: *Hancock's Half Hour—The Collectors' Edition: Series 3*
Release date: Nov. 2001
Catalogue no: 0563478136
Status: Still available
Episodes: Eight episodes from series three

Title: *Hancock's Half Hour—The Collectors' Edition: Series 4*
Release date: March 2002
Catalogue no: 0563528079
Status: Still available
Episodes: Seventeen episodes from series four

Title: *Hancock's Half Hour—The Collectors' Edition: Series 5*
Release date: Nov. 2002
Catalogue no: 0563528923
Status: Still available
Episodes: All of series five

Title: *Hancock's Half Hour—The Collectors' Edition: Series 6*
Release date: Feb. 2003
Catalogue no: 0563529210
Status: Still available
Episodes: All episodes from series six, plus four episodes recorded for the BBC Transcription Service, the 1958 Christmas Special and 'The Stolen Petrol', both recently rediscovered episodes from series four

Title: *Hancock—Four Original BBC TV Episodes*
Release date: Sept. 2003
Catalogue no: 0563495200
Status: Still available
Episodes: 'The Radio Ham', 'The Blood Donor', 'The Bowmans', 'The Bedsitter' (four original BBC TV soundtracks, plus an interview with Galton and Simpson)

Title: *Hancock's Half Hour—The Radio Archive*
Release date: Oct. 2004
Catalogue no: 0563495774
Status: New release
Episodes: Complete box set, containing volumes one to six of *Hancock's Half Hour—The Collectors' Edition*

Title: *Hancock—A Comedy Genius*
Release date: Oct. 2004
Catalogue no: 0563525452

Status: Due for release 4/10/04 (also available on audio cassette)

Description: This two-hour show traces Hancock's early career and charts his appearances on shows such as *Variety Bandbox* and *Happy-Go-Lucky*. Told from recordings, scripts and press cuttings, this is the story of Hancock's rise to fame

Title: *Hancock—TV Volume 2* (working title at date of writing)

Release date: Oct. 2004

Catalogue no: 056352555X

Status: New release (also available as cassette)

Episodes: Still to be confirmed at date of writing

Title: *Hancock's Half Hour—The Radio Archive*

Release date: Nov. 2003

Catalogue no: 0563495774

Status: Still available

Episodes: Complete box set, containing volumes one to six of *Hancock's Half Hour—The Collectors' Edition*

DVDS

Title: *The Very Best of Hancock*

Release date: 1/10/01

Catalogue no: BBCDVD1061

Status: Still available

Episodes: 'The Bedsitter', 'The Bowmans',

'The Radio Ham', 'The Lift', 'The
Blood Donor'

Title: *Hancock's Half Hour—Volume 1*
Release date: 13/9/04
Catalogue no: BBCDVD1447
Status: New release
Episodes: 'The Alpine Holiday', 'Air Steward
                    Hancock—The Last of the Many',
                    'The Lawyer: The Crown v. James,
                    S.', 'How to Win Money and
                    Influence People', 'There's an
                    Airfield at the Bottom of My
                    Garden', 'Hancock's 43 Minutes:
                    The East Cheam Repertory
                    Company'

LPs/EPs

(Although there have been many more LPs and
EPs issued over the years, containing extracts from
various episodes, the following are regarded by
many as the principal releases.)

Title: *This is Hancock*
Release date: 1960
Label/catalogue no: Pye-Nixa (PLP1039)
Details: Mono. 'Sunday Afternoon at Home'
                        and 'Wild Man of the Woods'

Title: *Pieces of Hancock*
Release date: 1960
Label/catalogue no: Pye-Nixa (PLP1110)
Details: Mono. Various extracts with links
                        specially recorded by Hancock

Title: *Hancock*
Release date: 1961
Label/catalogue no: Pye-Nixa (PLP1092)
Details: Mono. Studio remakes of 'The Blood Donor' and 'The Radio Ham'

Title: *It's Hancock*
Release date: 1965
Label/catalogue no: Decca (LK4740)
Details: Mono. Studio remakes of 'The Missing Page' and 'The Reunion Party'

Title: *The Unique Hancock*
Release date: 1973
Label/catalogue no: BBC (REC150M)
Details: Mono. Extracts from the Transcription Service versions.

Title: *Hancock*
Release date: 1976
Label/catalogue no: BBC (REB260)
Details: Mono. Television soundtrack of 'Twelve Angry Men'

Title: *Hancock's Half Hour*
Release date: 1981
Label/catalogue no: BBC (REB394)
Details: Mono. Radio recordings of 'The Poetry Society' and 'Sid's Mystery Tours'

Title: *Hancock's Half Hour*
Release date: 1981

Label/catalogue no: BBC (REB423)
Details: Mono. Radio recordings of 'The Americans Hit Town' and 'The Unexploded Bomb'

Title: *Hancock's Half Hour*
Release date: 1982
Label/catalogue no: BBC (REB451)
Details: Mono. Radio recordings of 'The Scandal Magazine' and 'The Last of the McHancocks'

Title: *Hancock's Half Hour*
Release date: 1983
Label/catalogue no: BBC (REB485)
Details: Mono. Radio recordings of 'Fred's Pie Stall' and 'The Sleepless Night'

Title: *Hancock's Half Hour*
Release date: 1984
Label/catalogue no: BBC (REB526)
Details: Mono. Radio recordings of 'Hancock's War' and 'The Christmas Club'

Title: *The Wally Stott Signature Tune*
Release Date: 1976
Label/catalogue no: United Artists (UAG29739)
Details: Stereo. The signature tune, arranged by Paul Fenoulhet, included in a medley of comedy show themes.

Title: *Little Pieces of Hancock—Volume 1*
Release date: 1960

Label/catalogue no: Pye (Nep24146)
Details: Mono. Seven-inch EP. 'The Secret Life of Anthony Hancock' (the Test Pilot sequence) and extract from 'The Threatening Letters'

Title: *Little Pieces of Hancock—Volume 2*
Release date: 1960
Label/catalogue no: Pye (Nep24161)
Details: Mono. Seven-inch EP. 'The East Cheam Drama Festival' (Jack's Return Home and Look Back in Hunger sequences).

Title: *The Publicity Photograph*
Release date: 1960
Label/catalogue no: Pye (Nep24170)
Details: Mono. Seven-inch EP. Extracts from 'The Publicity Photograph'

Title: *Highlights from 'The Blood Donor'*
Release date: 1961
Label/catalogue no: Pye (Nep24175)
Details: Mono. Seven-inch EP. Highlights from 'The Blood Donor'

Notes

Apart from those listed below, all the quotes used throughout the book were taken from interviews carried out by the author.

WAC: BBC Written Archives Centre, Cavershan.

INTRODUCTION

1   Dennis Main Wilson interviewed on BBC's *Omnibus* programme, 'Hancock: from East Cheam to Earls Court', transmitted 26/4/85.
2   Bill Kerr interviewed on the above documentary.

CHAPTER 1

1   Bob Larbey, interview with the author, 1999.
2   BBC WAC: Gale Pedrick memo dated 26 June 1951 to Roy Speer, subject: 'Happy-Go-Lucky'.

CHAPTER 3

1   Interview on BBC's *Omnibus* programme, 'Hancock: from East Cheam to Earls Court', transmitted 26/4/85.
2   BBC WAC: BBC memo to Head of Variety from Peter Eton, dated 8/7/52, titled: 'Programme Suggestion'.
3   As above.
4   As above.
5   BBC WAC: Memo from Dennis Main Wilson, 1/5/53, which he read during an interview with

the Tony Hancock Appreciation Society, 1996.
6 Ibid. (BBC memo).
7 BBC WAC: Memo from M. Lipscomb, 20/11/53, titled: Tony Hancock Series (Working Title).
8 As above.
9 BBC WAC: Memo from Main Wilson, 12/2/54, titled: Tony Hancock Series—Starting in Week 43.
10 Interview with the Tony Hancock Appreciation Society, 1996.
11 *The Kenneth Williams Diaries*, p. 105.
12 Kenneth Williams, *Just Williams*, p. 60.

CHAPTER 4

1 Letter from Robin Boyle, June 1991, titled 'Memories of Tony Hancock'.
2 *The Kenneth Williams Diaries*, p. 105.
3 BBC WAC: Audience Research Report, 18/11/54.
4 *TV Times*, 1963.
5 BBC WAC: Minutes of Light Programme Variety Meeting, 3/11/54.
6 BBC WAC: Memo from Dennis Main Wilson to Assistant Head of Variety (Productions), 6/12/54.
7 Ibid.
8 BBC WAC: Audience Research Report, 2/2/55.
9 BBC WAC: Audience Research Report, February 1955.

CHAPTER 5

1 Tony Hancock Appreciation Society interview

with Dennis Main Wilson, 1997.

2 BBC WAC: Letter from Patrick Newman (BBC's Variety Booking Manager) to Jack Adams (Kavanagh Productions), 15/4/55.

3 Sir Harry Secombe, *Strawberries and Cheam*.

4 Tony Hancock Appreciation Society interview with Dennis Main Wilson, 1997.

5 Letter from Jimmy Grafton to Jim Davidson, dated 20/4/55.

6 As above.

7 BBC WAC: Handwritten note from Jim Davidson recorded on Jimmy Grafton's letter to Davidson, dated 20/4/55.

8 'Why A Star Cracked Up', by Anthony Carthew, in the *Daily Herald*, 7/5/55.

9 BBC WAC: Audience Research Report, 21/6/55.

10 Kenneth Williams, interviewed on the *Ed Doolan Show*, BBC West Midlands, c. 1985.

CHAPTER 6

1 BBC WAC: Audience Research Report, 29/12/55.

2 BBC WAC: Memo from Dennis Main Wilson to Head of Variety re 'Audience Reaction', 3/1/56.

3 Ibid.

4 Ibid.

5 BBC WAC: Memo from Dennis Main Wilson to Assistant Head of Variety, 30/12/55.

6 BBC WAC: Jack Adams letter to Jack Hylton, 19/8/55.

7 BBC WAC: Memo from Head of Copyright, 7/2/56.

8 BBC WAC: Handwritten (unsigned) record of Galton and Simpson's response when asked about writing radio and television episodes. Recorded 15/11/57.
9 BBC WAC: Memo from Pat Hillyard, dated 10/2/56, re Tony Hancock.
10 'Tony Hancock Team', in *The Times*, 2/3/59.

CHAPTER 7

1 Hugh Lloyd, *Thank God for a Funny Face*, p. 54.
2 Ibid.
3 John Le Mesurier, *A Jobbing Actor*, pp. 87–88.

CHAPTER 8

1 BBC WAC: Audience Research Report, 26/7/56.
2 BBC *Omnibus* programme, 'Hancock: from East Cheam to Earls Court', transmitted 26/4/85.
3 BBC WAC: Wardrobe, Hair and Make-up Requirements form, completed by Duncan Wood, 3/8/56.
4 BBC WAC: Audience Research Report, 27/9/56.
5 BBC WAC: Memo from Ronald Waldman to Head of Variety, 16/7/56.
6 BBC WAC: Memo from Pat Hillyard to Head of Light Entertainment (Television), 3/8/56.

CHAPTER 9

1 BBC WAC: Memo from Dennis Main Wilson

to editor of *Radio Times*, 21/9/56.

2   BBC WAC: Memo from Dennis Main Wilson to Head of Variety, 20/9/56.

3   Ibid.

4   Source of interview with Hattie Jacques unknown.

5   BBC WAC: Audience Research Report, 7/12/56.

6   BBC WAC: Letter from Stanley Dale, Associated London Scripts, to Jim Davidson, BBC, 18/12/56.

7   BBC WAC: Memo from Dennis Main Wilson to Assistant Head of Variety, 31/12/56.

8   BBC WAC: Undated memo (*c.* early 1957) from Ronald Waldman, recording the key points after a discussion with Tony Hancock.

9   BBC WAC: Audience Research Report, 20/3/57.

10 *The Kenneth Williams Diaries*, p. 130.

CHAPTER 10

1   BBC WAC: Letter from Duncan Wood to Tony Hancock, 21/3/57.

2   Duncan Wood, interviewed for BBC's *Omnibus* programme, 'Hancock: from East Cheam to Earls Court', transmitted 26/4/85.

3   *The Kenneth Williams Diaries*, entry for 10/6/57, p. 132.

4   Ibid.

5   Duncan Wood, interviewed for BBC's *Omnibus* programme, 'Hancock: from East Cheam to Earls Court'.

6   Ibid.

7   BBC WAC: Memo from Ronald Waldman to

Controller of Programmes, (C. P. Tel.) 23/8/57.
8 BBC WAC: Memo from Duncan Wood to Head of Light Entertainment (Television), 23/9/57.
9 BBC WAC: Audience Research Report, 18/10/57.
10 BBC WAC: Audience Research Report, 19/11/57.
11 David Lewin, in the *Daily Express*, April 1957.
12 BBC WAC: Memo from Duncan Wood to Ronald Waldman, 31/12/57.

CHAPTER 11

1 Letter from Tony Hancock to Jim Davidson, 3/11/57.
2 BBC WAC: Audience Research Report, 12/2/58.
3 *The Kenneth Williams Diaries*, entry for 23/11/58, p. 146.
4 BBC WAC: Memo from J. H. Davidson to Tom Ronald, 1/5/58.
5 BBC WAC: Report to the Board, compiled by Pat Hillyard, 10/3/58.
6 BBC WAC: Report to the Board, compiled by Pat Hillyard, 11/6/58.
7 BBC WAC: Memo from R. D'A. Marriott to Head of Light Entertainment, 7/5/58.
8 BBC WAC: Audience Research Report, 8/1/59.
9 BBC WAC: Memo from W. L. Streeton to C. P. Tel, 29/12/58.
10 Peter Dickinson, in *Punch*, 26/2/58.
11 BBC WAC: Memo from Tom Sloan to C. P. Tel., 10/2/59.
12 BBC WAC: Letter from Ronald Waldman to

Stanley Dale, 25/2/59.

13 BBC WAC: Audience Research Report, 20/11/59.

14 BBC WAC: Audience Research Report, 21/1/60.

Chapter 12

1 BBC WAC: Memo from Cecil McGivern to C.P. Tel. and Head of Light Entertainment (television), (H.L.E. Tel), 1/4/59.

2 BBC WAC: Memo from Duncan Wood to H.L.E. Tel, 8/6/59.

3 BBC WAC: Audience Research Report, 5/11/59.

4 BBC WAC: Letter from Kenneth Adam to Tony Hancock, 30/11/59.

5 BBC WAC: Memo from Dennis Scuse to Head of Programme Planning (H.P.P.), 28/12/59.

6 BBC WAC: Memo from Tom Sloan to C.P. Tel., 13/1/60.

7 BBC WAC: Audience Research Report, 29/3/60.

8 Irving Wardle, in the *Listener*, 17/3/60.

9 BBC WAC: Memo from Eric Maschwitz to Assistant Light Entertainment Organizer (A/L.E.O.Tel.), 19/4/60.

10 Interview with Duncan Wood on BBC's *Omnibus* programme, 'Hancock: from East Cheam to Earls Court', transmitted 26/4/85.

11 BBC WAC: Letter from Sid James to Tom Sloan, 15/1/58.

12 BBC WAC: Audience Research Report, 6/4/60.

13 BBC WAC: Letter from Beryl Vertue to the BBC, May 1960.

14 Article in the *Hull Daily Mail*, 13/5/60.
15 BBC WAC: Memo from Eric Maschwitz to Chief Assistant (Programmer) Light Entertainment (television), 18/10/60.
16 BBC WAC: Memo from Tom Sloan to C.P. Tel, 30/11/60.
17 BBC WAC: Memo from Duncan Wood to Tom Sloan, 20/2/61.
18 Article in the *Birmingham Evening Despatch*, 10/5/61.

CHAPTER 13

1 BBC WAC: Audience Research Report, June 1961.
2 Article in *Stage and Television Today*, 1/6/61.
3 Interview for BBC's *Omnibus* programme, 'Hancock: from East Cheam to Earls Court', transmitted 26/4/85.
4 BBC WAC: Memo from Duncan Wood to Head of Light Entertainment, 29/5/61.
5 Interview with Duncan Wood on BBC's *Omnibus* programme, 'Hancock: from East Cheam to Earls Court'.
7 BBC WAC: Audience Research Report, 17/7/61.
8 BBC WAC: Memo from Tom Sloan to C.P. Tel., 13/4/62.

Bibliography

Donovan, Paul, *The Radio Companion* (London: Grafton, 1992)

Goodwin, Cliff, *When the Wind Changed—The Life and Death of Tony Hancock* (London: Arrow, 2000)

Hancock, Freddie and David Nathan, *Hancock* (London: BBC, 1986)

Le Mesurier, John, *A Jobbing Actor* (London: Sphere, 1985)

Lister, Moira, *The Very Merry Moira* (London: Hodder and Stoughton, 1969)

Lloyd, Hugh, *Thank God for a Funny Face* (London: John Blake, 2002)

Secombe, Harry, *Strawberries and Cheam* (London: Robson Books, 1996)

Stark, Graham, *Stark Naked* (London: Sanctuary, 2003)

Tony Hancock Appreciation Society, The, *The Missing Page—The Quarterly Newsletter of the Tony Hancock Appreciation Society* (various editions)

Williams, Kenneth, *The Kenneth Williams Diaries*, ed. Russell Davies (London: HarperCollins, 1993)

Williams, Kenneth, *Just Williams* (London: J.M. Dent, 1985)

Wilmut, Roger, *Tony Hancock 'Artiste'* (London: Eyre Methuen, 1978)